Before They Wore Dodger Blue
Tommy Lasorda and the Greatest Draft Class in Baseball History

Eric Vickrey

August Publications

August Publications
215 10th Av. S., Unit 621
Minneapolis, MN 55415
augustpublications.com

Copyright © 2026 by Eric Vickrey. All rights reserved.

No part of this book may be reproduced in any form or by any electronic or mechanical means, including information storage and retrieval systems, without written permission from the author, except for the use of brief quotations in a book review.

All trademarks, logos and brand names are the property of their respective owners.

ISBN 978-1-938532-94-8 (Print)
ISBN 978-1-938532-95-5 (eBook)

9 8 7 6 5 4 3 2 1

Designer (cover): Natalie Nowytski. Cover photo courtesy Spokane Indians.

Praise for Before They Wore Dodger Blue

"In the early days of the MLB draft, and before the advent of free agency, the core of four pennant-winning teams came up together, along with their manager, through the Dodger farm system. The last chapter before big-league glory played out in Spokane, where Tommy Lasorda's squad of future Dodger stars won the Pacific Coast League championship. This is a significant piece of baseball history, and a story brimming with figures soon to become bold-face names."

— Bob Costas, longtime MLB broadcaster

"Eric Vickrey has captured the magic behind the Dodgers' legendary 1968 draft class—the greatest in baseball history. As the grandson of Al Campanis, the visionary scouting director who was mentored by Branch Rickey and who orchestrated that unprecedented haul of talent, I'm proud to see my grandfather's genius and the 'residue of design' he championed brought to life in these pages. This book is a must-read for any baseball fan who wants to understand how luck, skill, and sheer determination built a dynasty."

— Jim Campanis Jr., former professional baseball player and author of Born Into Baseball

"Unparalleled stories behind the Dodger stars of the '70s and 80's. A must-read for any baseball fan!"

— Jerry Reuss, former Los Angeles Dodgers pitcher

"Like many fans, I enjoy baseball books that examine a nexus point in the history of the sport. Think of Jim Bouton's *Ball Four* here, or Roger Kahn's *The Boys of Summer*, or Dan Epstein's *Big Hair and Plastic Grass*. Eric Vickrey's *Before They Wore Dodger Blue* opens with the well-covered heyday of the early 1960s Los Angeles Dodgers but then breaks new ground by examining how the first major-league amateur draft, instituted in 1965, completely upended the Dodgers and changed the culture of the major leagues. Whereas an ecosystem of cigar-chomping regional scouts, bushwhacking birddogs, militaristic coaches, and tightly prescriptive training philosophies had ruled before the draft, the aftermath not only knocked the über-traditional boys in blue from its perennial pennant pedestal, but pushed the sport toward sharper analytics, new-style player-friendly managers, a restive players union, the first-ever collective players strike, the overthrow of the reserve clause, and the emergence of free agency. Vickrey deftly paints a portrait of these changing times, reaching a climax with the 1981 World Series, when the rebuilt Dodgers and their core draftee class of 1968 come back to defeat the juggernaut New York Yankees and their team of superstar free agents. *Before They Wore Dodger Blue* is an exciting and essential look at how a brave new world emerged out of the primordial, old school baseball soup of the 1960s."

— Michael Fallon, author of *Dodgerland: Decadent Los Angeles and the 1977–78 Dodgers*

"An amazing literary journey through a baseball time capsule thanks to Eric Vickrey's exhaustive research and master storytelling. Relive the behind-the-scenes drama and thrills when an ambitious minor-league manager with a larger-than-life personality and a bumper crop of top prospects eventually became Southern California's beloved Big Blue Wrecking Crew."

— Mark Langill, Team Historian, Los Angeles Dodgers

"In *Before They Wore Dodger Blue*, Eric Vickrey does a masterful job of taking the reader behind the scenes of the Los Angeles Dodgers' famed Amateur Draft of 1968 and how this group of players came together with the Spokane Indians of 1970 and launched highly acclaimed major-league careers. Eric's dedicated work provides insights into an organization known for its scouting and player development departments while providing a look at the talent and personalities of players who reached stardom. All of this while a little-known minor-league manager named Tommy Lasorda made his way from Spokane to the Hall of Fame and remained an influence on the lives of young men who had their baseball dreams come true."

— FRED CLAIRE, LOS ANGELES DODGERS GM AND EXECUTIVE VP, 1969-1998 AND AUTHOR OF *MY 30 YEARS IN DODGER BLUE* AND *EXTRA INNINGS: FRED CLAIRE'S JOURNEY TO CITY OF HOPE*

"Eric Vickrey makes a convincing case for the 1970 Spokane Indians as the greatest minor-league club ever assembled. He shows in dramatic detail how the team was built, and how it was driven to success by Tom Lasorda—irrepressible as a manager and irresistible as a character—in this engaging book."

— KEVIN KERRANE, AUTHOR OF *DOLLAR SIGN ON THE MUSCLE*

"The author's impressive research has unearthed the inside story of Dodger Blue, weaving together Tommy Lasorda's strong influence on a young group of Dodgers. A magnificent work bringing together Lasorda's success, the 1968 draft and the fabulous 1970 Spokane Indians."

— KEN WILSON, FORMER MAJOR-LEAGUE BROADCASTER

"The amateur draft was supposed to let poorer clubs compete with the big-money franchises, such as the Dodgers. But picking winners was about more than money and the 1968 draft proved it. There was the scouting that recognized Steve Garvey, Davey Lopes, Ron Cey, Bobby Valentine, Bill Buckner, Tom Paciorek, Joe Ferguson, Doyle Alexander, Sandy Vance and Geoff Zahn that spring. And there was the player development system, epitomized by Tommy Lasorda, that transformed the talent into major league stars. Vickrey profiles them all, delving into their backgrounds and careers in a crisp presentation that makes the story sparkle."

— ANDY MCCUE, AUTHOR OF SEYMOUR MEDAL-WINNING *MOVER AND SHAKER: WALTER O'MALLEY, THE DODGERS, AND BASEBALL'S WESTWARD EXPANSION*

"Eric Vickrey's *Before They Wore Dodger Blue* is an insightful look at the 1968 MLB amateur draft and the future Dodger stars selected in that draft. He also takes an in-depth look at the 1970 PCL Champion Spokane Indians, a team led by HOF manager Tommy Lasorda and comprised of many of those same players. Whether you're a baseball fan, Dodger fan, or Lasorda fan, this book is a hit!"

— ZACK MINASIAN, AUTHOR OF *LASORDA UNIVERSITY*

"I fell in love with the 1970s Dodgers as a kid in Southern California, studying the backs of their baseball cards. Often the list of teams played for included Spokane. Eric Vickrey adeptly explains the significance of that geographic stop on the success of the Dodger teams that reached four World Series in eight years. Bolstered by dozens of interviews with players and supporting personnel, *Before They Wore Dodger Blue*, details how Tommy Lasorda motivated this group of eager, young, and talented players who would reverse the downward trend the Dodger franchise experienced in the late 1960s. This is an insightful and fun read!"

— STEVE DITTMORE, AUTHOR OF *JIM GILLIAM: THE FORGOTTEN DODGER* (2025)

Contents

Preface   xi

Part One
1964-1969

1. Last of the Bonus Babies   3
2. Major League Baseball Adopts an Amateur Draft   12
3. From Norristown to "The Show"   23
4. Dodgers Draft Hough and Russell   40
5. Turmoil in LA, Another Pennant in Ogden   49
6. The Scouts   58
7. A Philosophy Shift   69
8. June Haul   80
9. The '68 Ogden Dodgers   94
10. An Organization in Transition   104
11. Coconut Snatching   120

Part Two
The 1970 Spokane Indians

12. Termite Palace   131
13. The Opening Homestand   146
14. Jaw Breaker   157
15. Old Jerry   162
16. The Hoodlum Priest   171
17. Hutton to Operating Room, Russell to LA   178
18. The Power of Motivation   184
19. Good Old Days   191
20. Major-League Calls and Banquet Brawls   200
21. Dougie   205
22. Re-Creating Reality   209
23. Heavyweight Fight   216
24. Like Butter   222

Part Three
Show Time

25. 1971	231
26. Dukes and Angels	241
27. The '74 Series	247
28. Loyalty Pays Dividends	252
29. Lasorda at the Helm	262
Notes	283
Acknowledgments	297
Bibliography	301
Index	303
About the Author	327
Also from August Publications	329

"All evidence seems to point to the fact that 'Lady Luck' is, to a large extent, self-generated."—Al Campanis, internal memo to the Los Angeles Dodgers scouting department

Preface

Since its inception in 1965, Major League Baseball's Amateur Draft has been more or less a crapshoot. On average, less than one in seven players selected in the draft ever appear in a big-league game.[*] Roughly 30 percent of first-round picks—players deemed the best of the best by scouts and front offices—never reach the major leagues. Even the number one overall pick sometimes doesn't pan out. For every Ken Griffey Jr., Chipper Jones, and Bryce Harper, there is a Steve Chilcott, Al Chambers, and Brien Taylor. There are myriad reasons why some prospects fizzle. Some get hurt, some fail to harness their physical ability, and some lack the mental fortitude to succeed. On the other end of the spectrum are players who defy expectations. Albert Pujols, one of the greatest right-handed hitters to ever play the game, wasn't drafted until the thirteenth round. Hall of Famers Ryne Sandberg and John Smoltz were selected in the twentieth and twenty-second rounds, respectively. And the Los Angeles Dodgers famously picked Mike Piazza in the sixty-second round as a favor to Tommy Lasorda, a family friend of the Piazzas.[†]

Amateur baseball players are difficult to project because they are typi-

---

[*] Based on players drafted between 1965 and 2009.
[†] Mike Piazza's father, Vince, grew up a few blocks from Lasorda in Norristown, Pennsylvania. Lasorda was a distant cousin of Vince and the godfather of his youngest son, Tommy.

cally years away from competing at the major-league level. Baseball is unique in this way. The NBA and NFL select mostly from a pool of college players whose athletic skills are more translatable to the pro game and are thus easier to project. Baseball players, on the other hand, require varying degrees of minor-league seasoning to compete at the highest level. This is reflected by the fact that in the first fifty years of MLB's Amateur Draft, fewer than two dozen players went directly from high school or college to the majors.

A good draft class can carry an organization to the promised land. The Athletics' drafts of the mid-1960s produced Reggie Jackson, Vida Blue, Gene Tenace, and Sal Bando—key cogs of three consecutive championship teams in the early '70s. In 1982, the New York Mets drafted a record-high seventeen future major leaguers, including Dwight Gooden and Roger McDowell—the ace and closer of the 1986 Mets championship team. A poor draft, on the other hand, can set an organization back for years. The Atlanta Braves drafted forty-eight players in 1981, none of whom reached the majors. The fact that the Braves suffered five straight losing seasons in the second half of the decade was surely no coincidence.

In the early years of the MLB Amateur Draft, teams relied on old-school, naked-eye scouting and rudimentary written reports. Radar-gun technology was years away. If a team's top pitching prospect tore his ulnar collateral ligament, his career was likely over. Back then, one could say the name Tommy John without having to specify whether they were referring to a person or a surgery. Medical advances in the decades since the inaugural draft have extended careers and helped teams extract value from players in whom they've invested dollars and years. More recently, the evolution of analytics has provided teams with a wealth of data and knowledge that scouting directors couldn't have fathomed in the early years of the draft.

Despite these advances, no team has come close to replicating the success of the Dodgers' 1968 draft under scouting director Al Campanis. That year, the Dodgers drafted six future All-Stars—Doyle Alexander, Bill Buckner, Ron Cey, Steve Garvey, Davey Lopes, and Tom Paciorek—who would be selected for a combined 23 All-Star games—both draft records. These six—plus Joe Ferguson, Bobby Valentine, and Geoff Zahn—would proceed to play in the majors for a decade or more, also a draft record. According to Baseball-Reference, the eleven eventual major leaguers signed from the class* would combine for 234.5 Wins Above Replacement—yet another record.† By the ends of their careers, the eight position players collectively compiled 11,231 career hits and 1,139 home runs, while the three pitchers racked up a combined 314 wins. By any measure, the Dodgers' draft class of '68 remains the best in baseball history.

Multiple publications agree. In 2011, ESPN.com's David Schoenfield proclaimed it "the greatest draft haul in history."[1] Five years later, *Baseball America's Ultimate Draft Book*, which took a comprehensive look at the first fifty years of the draft, described the '68 class as the "best in draft annals."[2] More recently, in 2025, MLB.com's Jim Callis dubbed the Dodgers' historic crop the "best draft haul of all time."[3]

And remarkably, it could have been even better. The career of Marv Galliher, a first-round pick in the January draft, stalled at Triple-A because of injuries. Sandy Vance, a top college pitcher whom the Dodgers snagged in the June draft, was limited to 30 career big-league games because of arm trouble. Many in baseball circles viewed fifth-round pick Bill Seinsoth as a surefire future big leaguer, but he opted to return to USC for his senior year and later died in a car accident. And then there was Valentine—the consensus best of the lot. He had Hall-of-Fame ability but endured a catastrophic injury that turned him into a fringe utilityman.

All but three of the future major leaguers the Dodgers inked from the class of '68—Alexander, Buckner, Garvey, Lopes, Paciorek, Valentine, Vance, and Zahn—played together in 1970 for the Triple-A Spokane Indians. There, they joined Tommy Hutton, Charlie Hough, Bill Russell, Bob Stinson, and several other highly touted prospects and big-league veterans, forming one of the greatest minor-league teams in the Expansion Era (1961 to present).‡ In fact, the '70 Spokane Indians ranked number one on

---

* In addition to signing eleven future major leaguers in the 1968 draft, the Dodgers also drafted four players who did not sign but later reached the majors: Ed Crosby, Mike Pazik, Bob Sheldon, and Bobby Randall.

† Wins Above Replacement, or WAR, is a calculation that measures a player's value to his team relative to his peers. The combined WAR of the Dodgers' 1968 draft class has been reported as 235.6, but this figure does not include Bob Gallagher's career WAR of -1.1. The Boston Red Sox 1983 draft class generated the next highest WAR, 191.8, almost entirely because of two players—Roger Clemens and Ellis Burks.

‡ In 2006, baseball historians and statisticians Bill Weiss and Marshall Wright published a book titled *The 100 Greatest Minor League Baseball Teams of the 20th Century*. They devised their list using a formula based on a team's classification, winning percentage, and total wins. The majority of teams on the list played in the first half of the twentieth century

Baseball America's 1993 list of the top minor-league teams of the previous fifty years.*

Based on how aggressively organizations promote their players nowadays, the talent on the '70 Indians may never be equaled. Spokane's roster was on par with some major-league teams at the time. Chuck Tanner, who later piloted the world champion 1979 Pittsburgh Pirates, thought so after watching Spokane's resounding sweep of his Hawaii Islanders in the Pacific Coast League championship series. "They played as well as any Triple-A team I've ever seen," Tanner said at the time. "That's a major-league ballclub ... They're just outstanding."[4]

The Spokane Indians were managed by former major-league pitcher Tommy Lasorda. One of the most dynamic figures in the history of American professional sports, Lasorda was equal parts showman, motivational speaker, father figure, and stand-up comedian. He loved his players, loathed losing, cussed like a sailor, fought with his opponents, despised the Giants, and was unwaveringly loyal to the Dodgers. Lasorda also possessed a brilliant baseball mind, which was at times overshadowed by his audacious antics and larger-than-life personality.

The Dodgers were the National League's most successful franchise from the late 1940s through the mid-1960s. The '68 draft would lay the groundwork for the team's next great era. Cey, Russell, Lopes, and Garvey proceeded to form an All-Star infield that would play together for an unprecedented eight and a half consecutive seasons. That foursome, along with other homegrown stars and pieces acquired through trades involving the '68 draft class, carried the Dodgers to three National League pennants in the 1970s and a World Series title in 1981 under Lasorda.

So how did the Dodgers pull off such an extraordinary draft? Was it the genius of Campanis and his venerable group of eagle-eyed scouts? Was it an astute minor-league development system that maximized prospects' potential? Or was it pure luck? As with many things in life, there isn't one clear answer. Naturally, there was a certain amount of luck

---

because there were more teams at that time. The 1934 Los Angeles Angels (137-50) topped their list. The 1970 Hawaii Islanders ranked 38th, but curiously, the Spokane Indians did not make the cut. According to Wright, the Indians ranked around 115th based on their formula.

* The second and fourth teams on the list (the 1981 Albuquerque Dukes and 1946 Montreal Royals) were also Dodgers affiliates.

involved. But in the words of Campanis's mentor, Branch Rickey, "Luck is the residue of design."

Part One
1964-1969

Courtesy Spokane Indians.

Last of the Bonus Babies

"Scouting is the life blood of a major-league organization. Any organization which expects to remain competitive must have a capable, industrious, and adventurous scouting staff. The major-league scout must have three qualifications: detective, bloodhound, and diplomat."—Fresco Thompson, *Inside the Dodgers*

Tom Keynerd died in Los Angeles, California, on June 12, 1964. His funeral was held eight days later at the church where he had served as a deacon. When Tommy Lasorda arrived at the service, every pew was filled, so ushers directed him to an empty seat at the front of the church. He introduced himself to the preacher and mentioned that he was a scout with the Los Angeles Dodgers.

Lasorda, a round-faced Italian-American with a bulbous nose and prominent chin, came to pay his respects to Deacon Keynerd's daughter, Clara Crawford, and her son Willie, a budding baseball star at John C. Fremont High School in Los Angeles. As the preacher addressed the all-Black congregation, he informed the mourners that they were in the presence of a distinguished guest. As Lasorda looked around with curiosity, the preacher then turned to the Dodgers scout and asked him to say a few words. Now realizing that *he* was the distinguished guest, Lasorda stood slowly, his mind racing. He had done his fair share of public speaking, but this was altogether different than the Kiwanis Club luncheons and sports banquets he was accustomed to.

At first, the words came slowly. "Ladies and gentlemen ... we are all here ... to mourn the passing of Deacon Keynerd." Then, the cadence picked up. "When actually we should be rejoicing because now the deacon is finally going to face his Lord, his master, and his judge."

Lasorda had paid many visits to the dilapidated duplex in South Central Los Angeles where Clara, an assembly line worker at Uniroyal Tire Company, raised her five children. As he thought about the Crawford family, the words rolled off his tongue. Lasorda talked glowingly about Clara's perseverance and spoke of how proud the deacon was of his daughter and grandchildren. "And to see the great number of people who have gathered here today to pay their respects to this man," Lasorda said, "is indicative of the kind of man we all know he was." As he continued his spur-of-the-moment eulogy for a man he met once, shouts of "Amen, brother!" echoed throughout the church.[1]

That was how Lasorda, an amazing storyteller, remembered the memorial service two decades later in his autobiography, *The Artful Dodger*. The eulogy story became part of Lasorda's catalog of fantastic tales, many of which he undoubtedly embellished for effect. He was, however, loquacious enough and so full of self-confidence that his version of events may have been entirely accurate. What is unquestionable is that Lasorda would have moved heaven and earth to sign Willie Crawford.

LASORDA AND FELLOW DODGERS SCOUT KENNY MYERS SPENT TWO YEARS recruiting Crawford, a natural athlete who trained religiously before and after school to hone his athletic skills and chisel a six-foot-one, 200-pound frame. Crawford captained the Fremont Pathfinders football squad in the fall and simultaneously ran track and played baseball in the spring. By his junior year, he was the top high school broad jumper in the country and a standout center fielder on a baseball team that included future big leaguers Bobby Tolan and Bob Watson.

Willie Crawford and Al Campanis at the formal signing ceremony. Los Angeles Times Photographic Collection. Copyright UCLA; used under Creative Commons 4.0 license.

Crawford emerged as a budding star less than ten miles from Dodger Stadium, so naturally the hometown nine took notice. Al Campanis, the Dodgers' director of scouting, wrote a laudatory report on Crawford: "Strong legs. Thin waist. Strong upper body. Unusual speed. A 25-foot broad jumper. A .444 hitter. Graceful fielder. Strong arm. Very religious. Good character. Hits with power of Roberto Clemente and Tommy Davis at similar age."[2] Campanis spoke on good authority when comparing a prospect to Clemente and Davis considering he had scouted and signed both.

It wasn't long before scouts from all twenty major-league clubs pursued Crawford, whom sportswriters dubbed "The Fremont Flash." Unlike professional basketball and football, Major League Baseball did not have an amateur draft at the time, so players like Crawford were free agents who could sign with any organization. This free-for-all system of amateur-talent acquisition had resulted in skyrocketing bonuses over the previous two decades as teams outbid one another in order to remain competitive and, just maybe, land the next Clemente or Davis.

The bonus frenzy began in 1942 when the Detroit Tigers outbid several teams to sign outfielder Dick Wakefield at an unprecedented cost of $52,000. Competition for amateur players only intensified postwar, pushing MLB owners to adopt rules aimed at dissuading one another from overspending on unproven amateurs and prohibiting wealthier teams from hoarding prospects. The first iteration, simply called the Bonus Rule, stipulated that a player who received a bonus over a certain amount—usually $4,000 to $6,000—must be kept on the big-league roster after one year in the minor leagues. The rule failed to tamp spending, so the owners instituted another version of the rule between 1953 and 1957 that required bonus players be kept on the big-league roster immediately. These so-called "bonus babies" often rode the bench and in many cases suffered from the lack of minor-league development.

Signing bonuses soared to six figures despite the Bonus Rule, so the owners came up with the first-year player draft in 1959. Similar to the Rule 5 draft, the first-year player draft allowed teams to buy players with one year of experience from one another at a cost of $15,000. Major-league clubs could select players at Triple-A or lower, Triple-A teams could choose other teams' Double-A players, and so on. The idea behind the first-year player draft was that owners would think twice about giving a player a six-figure bonus if they might lose him for pennies on the dollar after one year.

Nevertheless, teams handed out increasingly lucrative bonuses like Halloween candy. In 1961, the Dodgers signed Texas infielder Bart Shirley for $60,000 and gave a six-figure bonus to high school pitcher-outfielder Roy Gleason; the Red Sox secured the services of Anaheim prep pitcher Jerry Stephenson for $75,000; and the Pittsburgh Pirates blew away the competition by forking over a record-breaking $175,000 bonus to high school shortstop Bob Bailey. At the time, the highest-paid player in the majors was Willie Mays, who earned a salary of $85,000. Teams were spending more on untested amateurs than on proven big leaguers. The owners responded by lowering the first-year player draft price to $8,000 and amended the rule so that, with one exception per team, first-year players on the forty-man roster could not be sent to the minors without passing through waivers.

The Dodgers and New York Yankees, meanwhile, dominated the era. Over seventeen seasons between 1947 and 1963, the two teams met in the World Series seven times and accounted for a combined thirteen championships. The Yankees' deep pockets and winning reputation helped maintain a steady stream of young talent to the Bronx. "Kids wanted to sign with the Yankees, the most glamorous team in baseball at the time," said Yankees president Larry MacPhail years later. "If two or three teams were after them, and one was the Yankees, we generally had the inside track."[3] It was no wonder why the Dodgers and Yankees were perfectly content with the status quo.

THE DODGERS, YANKEES, LOS ANGELES ANGELS, AND KANSAS CITY Athletics were among the teams willing and able to shell out six figures to sign Willie Crawford. The Athletics' owner, Charlie Finley—who was highly involved in scouting, recruiting, and signing his own players—phoned Crawford daily and showered him with gifts, including a signed photograph of himself. "Usually, it was the local scout who developed a relationship with the family and maybe the supervisor would come in," recalled Pat Gillick, who worked with the Houston Colt .45s at the time.* "It was very seldom that owners would get involved. Our scouts thought what Finley did was unusual."[4]

Finley outfitted Crawford with a tuxedo to wear to his senior prom, rented a Ford Thunderbird so he could drive his date, and gave him a cash advance of $600. Crawford, who had never carried so much money, nervously tucked the wad of bills inside his shoe, making it so painful to walk that he feigned an injury when his date asked him to dance.

Campanis tasked Lasorda and Myers with convincing Crawford to sign with the Dodgers. Lasorda and Myers, whose taciturn nature earned him the nickname "Monk," built a rapport with Crawford by attending his games, visiting his home, and taking him to countless Dodgers games. Lasorda skipped spring training to recruit Crawford and spent more time with him than he did with his own family. He often brought over pastrami sandwiches, and on multiple occasions the Crawfords invited Lasorda over to eat food that had been delivered by rival scouts.

---

* The Colt .45s were renamed the Astros prior to the 1965 season.

Crawford graduated from high school on Friday, June 19—the day before his grandfather's funeral. Lasorda ate dinner with the Crawfords following the memorial service and received assurance from Clara that the Dodgers would be granted the final meeting the next day when Willie, Clara, and Willie's high school coach planned to field offers from nearly every big-league club. Getting the last meeting with a potential signee was like having pole position in a car race. It provided a scout with the opportunity to top other every other team's offer.

Meetings began Sunday at 3:00 p.m. in the Crawford's living room at 1447 East 69th Street. By 10:00 p.m., all but two teams had made proposals with the Athletics and Dodgers the last to present their case. Finley took his turn while Campanis, Myers, and Lasorda waited anxiously in the front room. Finley offered Crawford $200,000—higher than any bonus in baseball history—but insisted that Crawford must sign at that moment, or the offer would be off the table. Clara refused to let Willie sign, citing the promise she made to Lasorda and how touched she was that he came to her father's funeral. Finley left the room exasperated and asked to speak to Campanis outside. Finley told Campanis that Willie was leaning toward the Dodgers and that he planned to turn his attention to another top prospect named Rick Reichardt.[5]

It was after midnight when the Dodgers signed Crawford for $100,000. Campanis, dressed in a gray suit with his dark hair slicked back, watched with delight as Crawford, wearing a cardigan sweater and blue Dodgers cap with the white LA logo, signed his contract. Crawford's bonus was half of Finley's offer but still the largest bonus ever paid to a Black player and the second-highest given by the Dodgers behind Frank Howard's $108,000 pact. "We sold him a name product, like … General Motors," explained Campanis. "With our turnstiles, we showed him where he would have no salary worries over the next fifteen years. We also explained the fringe rewards of playing in his hometown."[6] Crawford used his windfall to buy his mother a new home.

Most scouts avoided the limelight, but Lasorda made sure sportswriters were aware of his contributions to the Dodgers' signing of Crawford. Within days, the *Los Angeles Times* and *Kansas City Star* reported on Lasorda's eulogy. Later, the *Pittsburgh Press* and *Baltimore Sun* picked up the story with quotes from Lasorda. Myers, a more senior scout who played an equal hand in the recruitment of Crawford, received little fanfare. Four years later, Myers left the Dodgers and went to work for the Angels, in part because of his contentious relationship with Lasorda.*

CRAWFORD WAS THE SECOND BONUS PLAYER THE DODGERS SIGNED IN THE spring of 1964. A few weeks earlier, Campanis and scout Hugh Alexander had secured the services of Tommy Dean, an eighteen-year-old shortstop from Iuka, Mississippi, for a bonus of $60,000. With a pair of bonus players already under contract, the Dodgers were out of the running for Rick Reichardt, a junior outfielder at the University of Wisconsin and the consensus best college player in the country. Reichardt, who attended Wisconsin on a football scholarship, tried out for the Badger baseball team as a sophomore just to get out of spring football practice and wound up winning the Big Ten batting title. He turned down six-figure, major-league contract offers in the summer of 1963 and returned to Wisconsin for his junior year, further increasing his stock by hitting three home runs and stealing home in a doubleheader versus Illinois in front of dozens of scouts and baseball executives, including Angels owner Gene Autry. Reichardt, the son of an orthopedic surgeon, faced the choice of returning to Wisconsin and fulfilling his obligation to the football team as a potential All-American halfback or signing a lucrative baseball contract. His fallback plan was medical school. He concluded that baseball provided the best opportunity for longevity as a professional athlete. If a club offered what he wanted, he would turn pro.

Autry tried selling Reichardt on the Angels' family-friendly atmosphere and boasted about his plan to build a new ballpark in Anaheim. A St. Louis Cardinals contingent that included Stan Musial and general manager Bing Devine also went to the Dairy State and made their case. When Wisconsin's season ended, Reichardt and his father visited the White Sox, Red Sox, Phillies, and Yankees. At Yankee Stadium, the six-foot-three Reichardt posed for a photo with the Yankees' five-foot-seven manager, Yogi Berra. Gazing up at the young phenom, Berra said, "The kid don't make me feel so tall."[7]

---

* Sadly, Myers's tenure with the Angels was brief. He died of colon cancer in 1972 at the age of fifty-one.

Rick Reichardt in college. Courtesy University of Wisconsin.

Following a brief respite in Wisconsin, Reichardt and his parents boarded Flight 197 out of O'Hare and traveled to the West Coast, where Angels executives put on the full-court press. They drove Reichardt around Los Angeles in a convertible, showed him the team's spring-training facilities in Palm Springs, and brought him to the set of *Ship of Fools*, a film starring Lee Marvin and Oscar-winning actresses Vivien Leigh and Simone Signoret. Marvin's advice to Reichardt: "Ask for more money."[8]

Autry's generous offer, combined with lure of Hollywood and the potential of playing minor-league ball with the Angels' Triple-A affiliate in Hawaii, persuaded Reichardt to choose the Angels. Charlie Finley, who had just lost out on Willie Crawford, swooped in and attempted to outbid the Angels at the eleventh hour, but it was too late. Reichardt had already accepted the Angels' eye-popping $205,000 signing bonus—$30,000 more than the record-setting bonus the Pirates gave Bob Bailey three years earlier. Reichardt signed his contract at a June 24 press conference in the penthouse suite of Autry's lavish Hotel Continental. "I don't think any athlete is really worth all that money," said Reichardt. "But if they're going to pay it, then I'll take all I can get. I'd be foolish not to."[9]

The Dodgers were thrilled with the signings of Crawford and Dean, and the Angels had scored big with the acquisition of Reichardt. But many baseball executives in both leagues were becoming increasingly frustrated by the system where teams doled out $7 million to unproven amateurs in 1964 alone. Finley, owner of the last-place A's, spent more than $600,000 that year.* Major-league front offices continued to outbid one another in order to remain competitive while claiming they were mortgaging their futures. A number of baseball executives viewed soaring bonuses and the uneven distribution of talent as a threat to the national pastime. Some had been saying for years that an amateur draft could solve baseball's woes.

"Maybe we have to be saved from ourselves," said Braves general manager John McHale in 1960. "I think it's unfortunate that this is the system. ... If you're not prepared to pay, you just stand by and watch somebody else sign 'em. ... If a draft system similar to that used by football or basketball would hold up in our Justice Department, maybe that would be the answer."[10]

It had been four years since McHale uttered those words to *The Sporting News*, and the cost of amateur talent had continued to soar. Calls for a draft were growing louder.

---

* Finley's investment paid huge dividends. Among the players he signed in 1964 were future big leaguers Jim "Catfish" Hunter, John "Blue Moon" Odom, Joe Rudi, Skip Lockwood, Ken Suarez, and Chuck Dobson. Less than a decade later, Hunter, Odom, and Rudi formed a key part of the Athletics' nucleus that would win three consecutive World Series titles beginning in 1972.

Major League Baseball Adopts an Amateur Draft

> *"The free-agent draft will help solve our biggest problem: player procurement and development. It'll help equalize our teams. We have to do something to give the weaker teams greater incentive."*—Cleveland Indians GM Gabe Paul

Six months before Rick Reichardt signed his record-breaking pact with the Angels, Major League Baseball began exploring the possibility of an amateur draft. At a meeting of baseball executives in January 1964, the owners collectively asked Commissioner Ford Frick to formulate a proposal for a draft. Reichardt's bonus only added fuel to the fire.

Frick used the National Football League draft as a model for his plan, which he presented on August 11 during a meeting of baseball executives at the Edgewater Beach Hotel in Chicago. Under Frick's proposal, high school graduates and college upperclassmen would be eligible for two drafts—one in January and another in June. Teams would select in reverse order of the previous year's standings and have a specified amount of time following the draft to sign their picks. Having two drafts per year would give players the option of holding out for the next draft (without having to wait another full year) if they chose not to sign. Frick and the owners believed that providing players some degree of agency and negotiating power would reduce any chance of the league facing legal repercussions. In an informal vote to gauge support for the idea, eight of the ten National League teams backed the plan. But only three American League clubs showed support, well short of the three-quarters majority needed to ratify the system. Frick tabled the issue.

THE LOS ANGELES DODGERS STAUNCHLY OPPOSED THE IDEA OF AN amateur draft. And for good reason. Between 1947 and 1964—the period when the Bonus Rule and first-year player draft were in effect—the Dodgers captured eight National League pennants and three World Series titles. The organization's extensive scouting network and robust farm system, installed by Branch Rickey in the 1940s and maintained by general manager Emil "Buzzie" Bavasi and minor-league director Fresco Thompson in the '50s, were keys to the Dodgers' success. The 1963 championship roster—which included Ron Fairly, Maury Wills, Tommy Davis, Willie Davis, John Roseboro, Jim Gilliam, Frank Howard, Sandy Koufax, Don Drysdale, and Johnny Podres—was almost entirely homegrown. Dodger scouts thrived at spotting talent and selling the Dodger brand. Furthermore, owner Walter O'Malley, whose wealth grew considerably after the franchise relocated to Los Angeles, had pockets deep enough to outspend other teams.* Frick's proposed draft threatened to diminish what had become the Dodgers' strengths.

Cleveland Indians GM Gabe Paul was the most vocal of the executives who favored a draft. Although his team won only two pennants during the Bonus Rule and first-year player draft era, it had failed to finish better than fourth place in seven of the last eight years. During the Indians' run of losing seasons, attendance at Cleveland Municipal Stadium had steadily declined, further limiting the team's ability to spend on prospects. The Detroit Tigers, Pittsburgh Pirates, Cincinnati Reds, and Baltimore Orioles were in a similar boat, also voicing strong support for an amateur draft.

---

* According to the February 29, 1960, edition of *Sports Illustrated*, the Brooklyn Dodgers took in $3.8 million in 1956. Three years later, O'Malley made an estimated $7 million during his second year in Los Angeles.

Proponents of the plan saw it as the best way to suppress spending and ensure an equal spread of talent around the league.

Bavasi disagreed. He remained skeptical that an amateur draft would save teams money and predicted that a player who did not get paid what he wanted would simply hold out and test his luck in the next draft six months later. Bavasi also doubted that a draft would create parity. In his view, teams with weaker scouting departments would continue to lag behind.[1] Some owners, including O'Malley, worried that an amateur draft —even if held twice a year—would expose Major League Baseball to anti-trust litigation.

Major League Baseball executives revisited the idea of a draft in late October 1964 during a meeting at the Rolling Rock Country Club in Ligonier, Pennsylvania. Every team was represented except the Dodgers. "I've never seen a group of baseball people so willing to sit around and discuss common baseball problems so objectively, without putting their own clubs before everything else," Orioles GM Lee MacPhail told the *Baltimore Sun* at the time.[2] The GMs and owners met again a week later in Phoenix, Arizona, and took another informal vote. This time, fourteen teams—three more than in August—voted in favor of the draft. The Dodgers remained ardent critics of the plan. The Cardinals, Angels, Senators, Athletics, and Mets joined the Dodgers in voting against a draft. But the proposal—only one vote short of approval—was gaining steam.

In the weeks leading up to the Winter Meetings in Dallas, Gabe Paul and Walter O'Malley exchanged verbal jabs in the *Cleveland Plain Dealer*. Paul called the draft the greatest idea since night games and asserted that there was no doubt in his mind that a draft would equalize talent and reduce operating costs. In response, O'Malley, who remained concerned about the legal ramifications of an amateur draft, called Paul immature and accused him of headline hunting. "It boils right down to this. Is the damned thing going to leave us open to restraint of trade and/or anti-trust litigation?" O'Malley opined.[3] The next day, Paul compared Bavasi and O'Malley to "pied pipers with a flute in their hands, always worried about the boogey man."[4]

Paul consulted with an expert attorney, who expressed confidence that an amateur draft would not jeopardize Major League Baseball's anti-trust exemption. The attorney's written statement, which Paul brought to the Winter Meetings, assuaged the concerns of O'Malley and Bavasi enough to earn the Dodgers' vote. "We'll simply have to learn to live with it," said Bavasi "We were vehemently opposed to it, but now we're in favor of it and will vote for it."[5]

The amateur draft, also known as the Rule IV draft or free-agent draft, was formally proposed and adopted by an 18-2 vote on December 3, 1964. Casting a dissenting vote, Athletics owner Charlie Finley remained resolute in his opposition, predicting the draft would fail and be thrown out within two years.[6] The Cardinals also voted against the proposal.

The new system, which replaced the first-year player draft, was similar to the NFL-style plan first proposed by Frick and included three drafts: January and June drafts for eligible high school and college players and an August draft for American Legion players.[*] Only United States residents would be eligible. Teams had fifteen days to offer contracts to their draft picks, and players could only sign with the team that drafted them. If a player remained unsigned within fifteen days of the next draft, be it January or June, he would re-enter the draft pool in a separate selection process called the secondary phase.[†] In theory, a player could be drafted in the secondary phase of multiple drafts until he signed.

The draft forced teams to beef up their scouting departments. The Giants, for example, hired five new scouts in the month following the Winter Meetings. The draft also changed scouts' priorities. Spending two years building a relationship with a player, like Tommy Lasorda and Kenny Myers did with Willie Crawford, was no longer worth the investment because nineteen other teams could draft the player and own exclusive negotiating rights. Judgment now mattered more than salesmanship.

Over the next six months, teams scoured the country for talent. Area scouts like Billy Capps, who covered north Texas and Oklahoma for the Cubs, searched the backroads hoping to discover an unknown prospect.[‡] One day, Capps stumbled across a high school game in Binger, Oklahoma. He stopped to watch a few innings and was instantly enamored with a brawny, cannon-armed catcher named Johnny Bench. Feeling strongly that

---

[*] The August American Legion draft was eliminated after two years.
[†] Players who had never been drafted were eligible for the main draft, also called the regular phase. The secondary phase, early on called the special phase, existed through 1986. Ahead of '87, the regular and secondary phases were rolled into one.
[‡] Capps, a former minor-league player, spent thirty-eight years as a scout for the Cubs. He would later sign Kerry Wood and be inducted into the Texas Scouts Hall of Fame.

Bench should be the Cubs' first-round pick, Capps sent a glowing report to Cubs farm director Gene Lawing. "Billy Capps of the Chicago Cubs loved me," recalled Bench. "He brought [Lawing] down to watch me, and I had just come off a class trip and hadn't played in ten or twelve days. I went 1-for-4."[7] Capps wanted Lawing to stay for the next day's game, but Lawing opted to see other players instead. Bench would go 4-for-4 with two home runs and two doubles that day. Eventually, Reds farm director Jim McLaughlin heard about Bench through the grapevine. Intrigued, he dispatched area scouts Tony Robello and Bob Thurman to Binger. Based on their reports, Bench rose to nearly the top of the Reds' list.

Once an area scout recommended a player, scouting directors often sent a national cross-checker to offer a second opinion. Cross-checking scouts, sometimes called regional scouting supervisors, evaluated players from coast to coast, giving them a big-picture view of the prospect landscape. "The national cross-checker had the toughest job in baseball," recalled Joe McDonald, who served as the Mets' administrative secretary in 1965 and later had stints as farm director, minor-league director, and general manager. "No one worked harder than them. He would travel the country day after day, on and off planes, enduring disappointments when a pitcher would be scratched after the scout traveled 2,000 miles to see him. It was a thankless job."[8]

In preparation for the draft, some teams formed alliances and shared scouting reports with one another, providing clubs with information on more players than they could have scouted on their own. The Indians, Tigers, Braves, and Pirates formed one coalition; the Cubs, Athletics, and Astros formed another. The Mets were invited to join the latter, but team president George Weiss believed such collaborations tarnished the spirit of competition.[9] Weiss's decision would prove prescient. Pirates GM Joe Brown later recalled that some teams in the co-op withheld information about players they wanted to take.[10]

Most teams accumulated lists of 200 to 500 names of potential draftees. The Indians-Tigers-Braves-Pirates cooperative produced bound copies of more than 2,500 scouting reports on 800 players. During McDonald's preparation for the draft, he realized an alphabetical list would be essential. This minor detail, which was overlooked by some teams, allowed the Mets to eliminate players as they were drafted and avoid the embarrassment of selecting a player who had already been chosen, something that happened multiple times.

The 1965 draft was scheduled for June 8 and 9 in New York City. The Astros' contingent of GM Paul Richards, farm director Eddie Robinson, and assistant farm director Pat Gillick traveled by train because Richards didn't like to fly. "We left the office a week before the draft," recalled Gillick. "We took a train from Fort Worth to Chicago and took another train from Chicago to New York. We were in Fort Worth, and we said, 'This will be great. We can work on the draft on the train. It'll give us something to do.' Lo and behold, we got on the train and found out that the guy we entrusted the reports to accidentally left them on the platform in Fort Worth. So, we had no reports."[11] Luckily, someone found the Astros' documents and sent them by courier to New York in time for draft day.

Around 200 team representatives, reporters, and photographers filed into the East Ballroom of the Commodore Hotel during the early morning of Tuesday, June 8, for the first day of the inaugural event. Many sensed they were on the precipice of something historic. Executives and scouts from each of the twenty teams sat at assigned tables. The Dodgers' four-man entourage included GM Buzzie Bavasi, minor-league director Fresco Thompson, assistant minor-league director Bill Schweppe, and scouting director Al Campanis. When it was their turn to pick, they would write their selection on a card and bring it to Commissioner Ford Frick, who would read the name.

The Kansas City Athletics, by virtue of losing a major league-worst 105 games in 1964, owned the first overall pick. Leading up to the draft, there was little doubt that the A's would select college outfielder Rick Monday, who, like Rick Reichardt a year earlier, was considered the best college player in the country. Monday had turned down a $20,000 offer from Tommy Lasorda and the Dodgers after graduating from Santa Monica High School in the spring of 1963. Lasorda was struck by Monday's physical ability and his character. "He was so polite and proper, very intelligent and humble," Lasorda recalled. "He was the kind of kid that you wanted to see in a Dodgers uniform."[12] But Monday's mother didn't think her son was mature enough at the time. She gave Lasorda her word that after two years of college, Rick would sign with the Dodgers. That was before Major League Baseball instituted the draft. Monday enrolled at Arizona State University, where he hit .359 and blasted a school-record 11 home runs as a sophomore.* "Every now and then a player comes along who's head and shoulders above the crowd ... We zeroed in on him pretty early," said Athletics GM Hank Peters later.[13]

Kansas City kicked off the draft by making the selection of Rick Monday official.† With the second pick, the Mets chose Les Rohr, a six-foot-five southpaw from Billings, Montana. Rohr's high school did not have a baseball program, but he made a name for himself in the summer of 1964 by striking out 23 batters in the American Legion state tournament. Mets assistant GM Bing Devine and scout Red Murff traveled to Montana to see Rohr pitch an American Legion game in late May, but rain postponed the game. Instead, Rohr threw a twenty-minute side session. The report Joe McDonald received on Rohr said, "You wish he was your son." Devine became convinced that Rohr was a future 20-game winner. But as McDonald learned, it's best to judge a player in game situations rather than a bullpen session. "Big, big difference," said McDonald in retrospect.[14] Rohr struggled with his control early in his minor-league career, suffered an elbow injury, and appeared in only six big-league games.

Future All-Stars Joe Coleman and Ray Fosse went to the Senators and Indians with the third and seventh overall picks, sandwiching a trio of relatively forgettable selections by the Astros, Red Sox, and Cubs.‡ Drafting eighth, the Dodgers picked John Wyatt, a six-foot-two high school shortstop§ from Bakersfield, California. Campanis personally scouted Wyatt and advocated for his selection. Ultimately, Wyatt's baseball career fizzled, and he never made it above Single-A. His name resur-

---

* Freshmen were ineligible to play varsity sports, so Monday did not play varsity until his sophomore year.
† The A's gave Monday a $100,000 signing bonus. Turns out the draft held bonuses in check, just like the owners hoped it would. No player topped Monday's bonus until 1975, when the Angels gave the top overall pick, Danny Goodwin, a bonus of $150,000. And until 1988, only one player, Todd Demeter—the Yankees' second-round pick in 1979—bested Rick Reichardt's $205,000 bonus. Demeter, the son of former major leaguer Don Demeter, never played above Double-A.
‡ With the fourth pick, Houston chose Alex Barrett, who maxed out at Triple-A. With the fifth pick, Boston took Tony Conigliaro's younger brother, Billy, whose career ended because of a knee injury at age twenty-six after five seasons in the majors. The Cubs' first rounder, Rick James, would carry a 13.50 ERA in just three big-league outings.
§ Wyatt had a similar build to Corey Seager, the Dodgers' first-round pick in the 2012 June Amateur Draft. Both players were left-handed hitting shortstops.

faced in newspapers during the 1980s when he was charged for his role in a drug-smuggling operation and convicted in a federal court of tax evasion and fraud.

Five collegiate and fifteen high school players were selected in the first round, which took all of twenty-eight minutes. In the second round, the Cubs had the opportunity to take Bench—as Billy Capps had recommended—but instead chose college catcher Ken Rudolph. Later in the round, the Reds pounced. Bench later recounted how disappointed Capps was that the Cubs didn't take his advice: "He used to visit me when he was around. He was such a great man ... I felt so bad for him that he had found me and loved me, and I didn't become a Cub."[15]

The Dodgers used their second pick on high school pitcher Alan Foster, a first-round talent who was passed over in the initial round because his father insisted that he attend USC. The Dodgers flexed their financial muscle, making Foster a too-good-to-refuse offer of $96,000—only $4,000 less than Monday received as the top overall pick.* Foster would go on to compile a 48-63 record over the course of a ten-year major-league career. The rest of the Dodgers' inaugural draft class failed to pan out.†

Of the players the Dodgers chose in rounds three through nine, two did not sign and none of those who did would play higher than Double-A. In the tenth round, the Dodgers selected Tom Seaver based on the recommendation of scout Tommy Lasorda. "Boy has plenty of desire to pitch and wants to beat you," Lasorda wrote in his scouting report. The sophomore pre-dental student was coming off a 10-2 season pitching for Rod Dedeaux's USC Trojans. The Dodgers offered Seaver a modest bonus. When he responded by asking for $50,000, Lasorda allegedly told him, "Good luck in your dental career."[16] Seaver returned to USC for his junior year and later signed with the Mets.‡

---

* The average signing bonus for first-round players in 1965 was $42,516.
† Other than Foster, the only other Dodgers signee to reach the majors was drafted by mistake. In the fifteenth round, Fresco Thompson meant to turn in the card for Jack Glover but instead handed in pitcher Leon Everitt. Everitt pitched in five games for the 1969 San Diego Padres, posting an 0-1 record and 8.04 ERA.
‡ The Atlanta Braves drafted Seaver in January 1966 and signed him a month later. The contract was voided by Commissioner William Eckert, however, because of a rule that teams could not sign a college player while his season was in progress. USC's season had already begun when Seaver signed.

```
SCOUT REPORT    Club_____  League_____     Pos. P     Age 20
                                                               Hgt. 6     Wgt. 185
Name  SEAVER           Tom                                     Bats R    Throws R
       (Last)          (First)         (Middle)
Hitting_____  Arm_____
Power_____  Accuracy_____
Running Speed_____  Base Running_____
Fielding_____  Reactions_____
         Fast Ball  73 with LIFE
PITCHER  Curve      63 could improve with Right instructions    Aptitude    GOOD
         Change (F.B.)_____(Cv.)_____             Aggressiveness GOOD
         Control  FC                                            Attitude
Definite Prospect? ✓    Has Chance?_____  "Away"_____  N.P._____
Physical Description (Build, Size, Agility, etc.) Lean But with Good Actions
Remarks: This Boy Showed A Real Good Fast Ball with Good
LIFE, has Real Good Command of Point of Release.
Boy has Slider Type of Curve But Could improve As
He has Good Arm Action And Should Be Able to come
Up with Good Curve. Boy has Plenty of Desire to
Pitch And wants to Beat you.

Report By:  Tom Lasorda                              Date: March 23, 1965
```

Lasorda's scouting report on Tom Seaver.

The Mets struck gold in the twelfth round with the selection of Nolan Ryan, a right-handed pitcher from Alvin, Texas. Red Murff, the Mets' area scout in Texas, had closely tracked Ryan for three years and knew he was special. "I swear he threw over 100 miles per hour as a [high school] junior," said Murff years later. "There were no radar guns in those days, but he had the best arm I'd ever seen—not just in high school, in my life. And I'd seen [Bob] Feller and [Sandy] Koufax." The Mets did not take Ryan earlier because he had a poor outing on the day the national cross-checker saw him pitch. Ryan's subpar performance came a day after his coach made him throw batting practice and run sprints until he threw up. "Nolan had the best arm I'd ever seen, but because of that one game, I couldn't sell him to our organization," Murff said. "Beyond that, it's always been a mystery to me why other organizations never saw in him what I saw."[17]

Other noteworthy players taken late in the draft included a pair of Genes in the twentieth round, Garber (Pirates) and Tenace (Athletics), and

Steve Renko in the twenty-fourth round by the Mets.* McDonald, who played a hand in the Mets' selection of Renko, paid close attention to the late rounds. During his career as an executive, McDonald recalled myriad examples of late-round draft picks blossoming into quality major leaguers. And then there were players who were completely overlooked. No team drafted Larry Bowa and Don Money, each of whom would ultimately play sixteen seasons in the big leagues. The pair of future All-Stars had to sign as free agents after attending open tryouts.

Prioritizing position players, the Athletics had the most successful draft. In fact, the A's did not select a pitcher until the tenth round and took only four among the first twenty rounds. Besides Monday, the A's landed Sal Bando and Tenace, who became cornerstone players for their championship teams of the early 1970s. Some organizations drafted based on positional need, a strategy that proved less successful. The Cleveland Indians, for example, signed just two players from their draft class who would ever play in the majors, Fosse and Vic Albury.

The inaugural draft had its share of snafus. More than a dozen selections were voided because players were deemed ineligible. Several players were drafted twice under slightly different names, including Bench, who was chosen as John Bench from Binger and Johnny Lee Bench from Anadarko. Several college coaches showed up to the draft and lingered around the ballroom so they could hear the names of the best high school players. "You could see a coach write a drafted player's name down, then get up and leave so he could call and offer him a scholarship," said Chief Bender, then a Cardinals scout. "We gave them an easy way to recruit."[18] Major League Baseball later became more secretive, announcing only first-round picks to the public on the day of the draft and delaying the rest until a week later.†

Though the landscape of amateur-talent acquisition had radically shifted, its impact at the big-league level was still years away. The 1965 Dodgers—built on homegrown pitching, speed, and defense—won 97 games during the regular season to edge out the Giants for the National

---

* Renko was drafted as a first baseman. He converted to pitcher in his third pro season and won 134 games in the big leagues.
† MLB maintained the policy of delaying announcing the full draft results until 1998, when league officials caught wind that *Baseball America* planned to publish a draft list immediately.

League pennant before defeating the Minnesota Twins in a seven-game World Series. The Dodgers' top three starters, Sandy Koufax (26-8, 2.04 ERA), Don Drysdale (23-12, 2.77), and Claude Osteen (15-15, 2.79) logged a combined 931 innings that season. Walter Alston's top relievers, Ron Perranoski and Bob Miller, tossed a combined 207⅔ innings and sported sub-3.00 earned run averages. The staff as a whole posted a major-league best 2.81 ERA. The Dodgers' outstanding pitching carried a pedestrian offense that led the league in stolen bases but finished seventh in batting average, eighth in runs per game, and last in home runs.

To maintain success, the Dodgers would need their farm system to replenish the roster. And to help develop its young prospects, the organization turned to Tommy Lasorda.

From Norristown to "The Show"

"It isn't always the fastest man who wins the race or the strongest man who wins the fight; it is the one who wants it more than the other guy. All I wanted in life was to play baseball in the major leagues." —Tommy Lasorda, *Tommy Lasorda: My Way*

DODGERS EXECUTIVES BUZZIE BAVASI, FRESCO THOMPSON, AND AL Campanis met with scout Tommy Lasorda at Dodger Stadium in the spring of 1965 and offered him a job managing the Pocatello (Idaho) Chiefs—the organization's Rookie-level minor-league team. It was a calculated gamble. There were some within the Dodgers organization who believed Lasorda was not capable of being a successful manager because as a player he couldn't even manage himself. He was braggadocious, profane, and hot-tempered. Putting a quarrelsome man like him in charge of impressionable young prospects was a risky proposition. But the Dodgers brass had seen flashes of Lasorda's potential at Dodgertown a few years earlier when he managed the Single-A Greenville team during spring training and got them so fired up that they clobbered the Triple-A squad. Lasorda had also shown fierce dedication and an innate ability to motivate during his tenure as a scout. He had earned a chance to manage in spite of the naysayers. From Lasorda's point of view, it was a dream come true. He accepted the job without hesitation. At the end of the meeting, Bavasi told Lasorda the same thing that Lasorda's wife, Jo, told him whenever he left for the ballpark: "Please don't start any fights." The words went in one ear and out the other.

Thomas Charles Lasorda, the third of six boys born to Sabatino and Carmella (née Covuto), entered the world on September 22, 1927, in Norristown, Pennsylvania. Their second child, Thomas, had died from a respiratory illness as an infant a year earlier. When their next-born emerged onto the scene, Sabatino and Carmella reused the name. Edward came before the Thomases; Morris, Joey, and Harry followed. The Lasordas lived in a modest three-story house at 713 Walnut Street in Norristown, a small town on the outskirts of Philadelphia. In the summer, the home was cooled by whatever breeze came through the windows. During the winter, the only source of heat was a small coal stove on the first floor. Tommy endured a wide range of temperatures growing up in his third-floor bedroom.

Sabatino immigrated to the United States in 1920 from Tollo, a small town in the Abruzzo region of Italy known for its olive groves and vineyards. He landed at Ellis Island and joined an enclave of Italian immigrants in Norristown, where he met Carmella, whose father hailed from Tollo as well. Sabatino worked twelve-hour days, six days a week as a laborer and truck driver in a local quarry owned by the Bethlehem Steel Company. Tommy would later credit his father for instilling in him a strong work ethic. He also inherited Sabatino's knack for storytelling and entertaining.

Tommy attended Holy Saviour Elementary School and Rittenhouse Junior High. When he was old enough to work, he shoveled snow, shined shoes, sold produce door to door, hauled bushels of apples, laid railroad track, pressed pants in a military uniform factory, and worked as a bellhop at the Valley Forge Hotel. Anything to make a buck. The job he disliked most involved riding in the back of a truck and delivering hundred-pound sacks of potatoes for an old miser who paid him a dollar a day. But Tommy found a way to supplement his income. He'd toss bags of potatoes off the truck at a predesignated location for one of his brothers to pick up. The Lasordas did not have much money, but they always had plenty of potatoes.

Tommy fell in love with baseball before he could tie his shoes. His life revolved around the game. On one particular morning, his father assigned him the task of cleaning the second-floor bathroom. It was a sunny day, and his friends were headed to Elmwood Park to play ball, so Tommy had other ideas. He took a mop and bucket upstairs, then snuck out the window, slid down a drainpipe, and joined his friends. When Tommy came home later that day, Sabatino removed his belt and gave him a whipping. "I'll take a one-minute beating for one day of baseball anytime," proclaimed Tommy.[1]

It was at Elmwood Park where Lasorda formed a competitive drive that would become renowned. He and his brothers and friends played nine-inning pickup games with no coaches or umpires. There were separate teams of Italian, Irish, and Black kids. "We always wanted to win," Lasorda explained, "because if you lost you would have to go wait on the swings till it was time to play again. I never wanted to leave the field. I wanted to beat you. I would throw at my own mother if she was crowding the plate."[2]

When he wasn't playing baseball at Elmwood Park, Lasorda could be found throwing a ball against the side of the house or hitting rocks with a broomstick. He idolized Lou Gehrig and liked Dodgers pitcher Van Lingle Mungo because of his unique name. Lasorda never lacked confidence, even at a young age. Although he was surrounded by better athletes growing up and didn't play organized baseball until ninth grade, Lasorda somehow became convinced that he would someday play for the New York Yankees. In high school, he begged his father to buy him a pair of spikes—a requirement to play varsity. Sabatino relented but bought a pair that was three sizes too big so his son wouldn't outgrow them. Tommy stuffed the newspaper in the toes of the shoes so they would fit properly.

Lasorda's high school career was unspectacular. The stout southpaw later described himself as Norristown High's third-best pitcher on a team that mostly used two. But he could spin a decent curveball, an ability he displayed in the summer of 1944 pitching for a Norristown Parks and Recreation team. After he beat the Connie Mack All-Stars, a team made up of the best high school players in the Philadelphia area, Lasorda received an invitation to play in a tryout game in Philadelphia. That's where Phillies scout Jocko Collins first saw him. Collins described Lasorda as "about 160 pounds, a curveball guy, guts, and not too much ability."[3] It was hardly a glowing assessment, but Collins liked small-statured lefties because in his experience they often outperformed their raw ability. He offered Lasorda $100 a month. Sabatino and Carmella wanted their son to continue his education but trusted him to choose his own path. Tommy wanted nothing more than to play baseball, so the decision to sign was a no-brainer. He was only seventeen, so Sabatino, who couldn't have explained the difference between a double play and a double steal if his life depended on it, signed on his son's behalf.

Because of wartime travel restrictions, Lasorda spent his first spring training with the Phillies in Wilmington, Delaware, just a short train ride from Norristown. He trained alongside Jimmie Foxx, a player he grew up admiring, and had to resist the temptation to ask for an autograph. When Lasorda signed his pro contract, he naively assumed he'd be pitching for the Phillies right away. At the end of camp, he received a rude awakening when the Phillies sent him to the Concord Weavers, a farm team in the Class-D North Carolina State League—the lowest level of the minor leagues.

Lasorda grew up fighting with his brothers over who got the last piece of bread or who was the next to use the bathroom. He packed a good punch, so his Uncle Tony arranged boxing matches between Tommy and other kids his age. If Tommy won, Uncle Tony paid him a quarter. As Lasorda got older, he would brawl at the drop of a hat. At age fifteen, he beat up three drunks who made fun of his bellhop uniform. His reputation as a fighter became so notorious around Norristown that a couple of local professional boxers encouraged him to pursue boxing as a career. Although he stuck with baseball, the two sports—in his mind—were not mutually exclusive. Following his first professional game with Concord, Lasorda socked a teammate whose error cost him a win. The manager, John "Pappy" Lehman, pulled Lasorda aside and gave him a tongue lashing. Lasorda learned an important lesson that day: You win as a team, and you lose as a team. From that day forward, if a teammate made a mistake while he pitched, he would offer words of encouragement rather than scorn.

In addition to pitching in 27 games, Lasorda played some first base for the Weavers and hit .274 in 208 at-bats. On the mound, his inability to throw strikes (100 walks in 121 innings) and his teammates' dreadful defense (306 errors in 114 games) resulted in an unsightly 3-12 record. Lehman told him he should start thinking about a future in something other than baseball. "When all those guys come out of the service, you won't be playing professional baseball anymore," warned the skipper.[4] But Lasorda was undeterred. He used Lehman's words as fuel.

After the season, Lasorda was drafted into the Army and sent to Fort Meade, Maryland. While awaiting his basic training assignment, Lasorda and some fellow inductees killed time by playing a little basketball. Officers saw Lasorda sink several shots, so they kept him at Fort Meade to play hoops and attend the School for Bakers and Cooks. Lasorda's time at Fort Meade proved to be as short as his fuse. His superiors kicked him off the basketball team for fighting and reassigned him to Fort McClellan, Alabama, and then to Fort Jackson, South Carolina, where he ran the athletic program and pitched on the baseball team. Lasorda received his discharge from the Army in the spring of 1947. When he found out he could quadruple his minor-league salary pitching for a semipro team in Camden, South Carolina, he told the Phillies he had suffered a nervous breakdown and needed the year off. They bought it. Lasorda used the surplus he made on the semipro circuit to buy his family new beds and a heater that could reach the third floor.

Lasorda returned to pro ball in 1948 with a Class-C team in Schenectady, New York. "I couldn't spell the name of the city, I couldn't pronounce it, so I told my parents I was pitching somewhere near Albany," he later recalled.[5] Though his season statistics were pedestrian—a 9-12 record and 4.64 ERA—he opened some eyes by striking out 25 batters in a fifteen-inning game against the fantastically named Amsterdam Rug Makers. Lasorda, who also drove home the winning run in the marathon game, later calculated that he must have thrown around three hundred pitches that day. In another game versus the Trois-Rivières Royals, a Dodgers affiliate, he fanned 15 batters. These standout performances compelled the Dodgers to take a chance on Lasorda in the offseason minor-league draft at a cost of $4,000.

In the spring of 1949, Lasorda reported to Vero Beach, Florida, home of Dodgertown, the team's spring-training site that occupied a former US Naval Air Station. The sprawling complex boasted practice diamonds, batting cages, sliding pits, barracks, a dining hall, a lounge with poker and pool tables, a swimming pool, and horseshoe courts.* Walter O'Malley famously paid one dollar a year to rent the deserted complex, which had been turned over to the city of Vero Beach at the end of World War II. He later purchased adjacent land and built his own nine-hole golf course. Dodgertown's self-contained structure promoted a sense of togetherness and allowed for coordinated instruction. "The players relied on each other for fun," said legendary broadcaster Vin Scully years later. "They sat around at night and talked baseball or shot pool. The camaraderie was incredible."[6]

Lasorda's flight from Pennsylvania touched down in Vero Beach following multiple layovers. He arrived weary and exhausted at 10 p.m. Eight hours later, he was awoken by the sound of a whistle. Lasorda splashed cold water on his face and went for breakfast in the dining hall, where he found himself surrounded by more than six hundred ballplayers, roughly a third of whom were pitchers. After breakfast, the players gathered on the ball diamonds and rotated through stations in thirty-minute intervals to practice bunting, hit-and-run, sliding, and fielding. There were so many minor leaguers that they wore color-coded uniforms with a combination of numbers and letters. Coaches referred to players by their jersey color and number. This was nothing like Phillies camp, which had a relaxed vibe and a fraction of the players.

The size and scope of Dodgers camp was enough to shake Lasorda's confidence. With so many guys vying for a limited number of jobs, it seemed that his chances of ever pitching at Ebbets Field were slim to none. That night, Lasorda went to Fresco Thompson, the director of minor-league operations, and asked to be traded or released. When Thompson told him there was no chance of that happening, Lasorda switched strategies and asked for a raise. Thompson told him to go out and earn it.

From sunrise to sundown, the Dodgers received rigorous instruction and endured intense conditioning. At night, every player in the organization gathered in a huge assembly hall for lectures on baseball strategy given by Branch Rickey and the Dodgers coaches. Lasorda learned more about baseball in six weeks than he had in his entire life up until then.

---

* In 1953, O'Malley would build a new spring-training ballpark in Dodgertown, Holman Stadium, with a seating capacity of nearly 5,000.

"Mr. Rickey's theories were drilled into every player on every level, so that we would all be playing Dodger baseball," recalled Lasorda. "I had always been a willing worker, but for the first time I was taught to focus my energy to make my work more effective. And perhaps most important, everyone—from the minor-league rookie to the major-league regular—was made to believe he had an important role to play in the success of the entire organization."[7] Rickey indoctrinated players in the organization with the saying, "I'm proud to be a Dodger." Lasorda took those words to heart as much as anyone.

As camp wound down, the Dodgers planned to send Lasorda to a farm team in Pueblo, Colorado, but he talked his way into an assignment in the familiar locale of Greenville, South Carolina. With the Class-A Greenville Spinners, he played for an authoritarian manager, Clay Bryant, who rarely spoke to his players and showed no interest in getting to know them either. Lasorda observed that his teammates played with a fear of making mistakes, which seemed to hamper their ability. He thought to himself that if he were to ever manage, he would be the antithesis of Clay Bryant.

One day during the 1949 season, Lasorda was pitching for the Spinners against the Augusta Yankees when he heard the public address announcer introduce the next batter as Buster Maynard. Lasorda could hardly believe his ears. When he was in eighth grade—a time in his life when he believed major leaguers walked on water—he asked Maynard for an autograph at Shibe Park in Philadelphia. Maynard brushed him off. Lasorda never forgot that feeling of disappointment. And now the source of his disappointment stood a mere sixty feet, six inches away. Lasorda went into his windup and directed the first pitch at Maynard's noggin. Maynard dove out of the way, got back on his feet, and dug back in. Lasorda buzzed Maynard twice more. After the third knockdown, Maynard started toward the mound but was restrained. Maynard found Lasorda after the game and asked why he threw at him. Lasorda told Maynard the story of being denied an autograph as a star-struck youngster. All Maynard could do was shake his head and walk away.

Lasorda averaged seven walks per nine innings in Greenville but posted a sub-3.00 ERA. In baseball terms, he was effectively wild. Lasorda didn't throw hard; sportswriter Milton Richman once wrote that Lasorda's fastball "couldn't put a dent in a tub of butter."[8] But his excellent curve and erratic control prevented hitters from getting comfortable in the batter's box.

It was a monumental year for Lasorda for reasons other than exacting revenge on his childhood nemesis and taking a step forward in his development as a pitcher. He met a Greenville girl named Joan "Jo" Miller at the ballpark that summer. The petite blonde wasn't a baseball fan at the time and had only gone to the ballpark that day because her mother made her. Tommy asked Jo out numerous times before she finally agreed to go on a date under the condition that he would leave her alone if she didn't like him. Less than a year later, they were married. "She was a perfect complement to her husband," recalled family friend Zack Minasian. "Jo was gentle, patient, kind, beautiful, and the rock of the Lasorda household ... They fit together like a hand in a glove."[9]

In 1950, the Dodgers promoted Lasorda to the Montreal Royals of the Triple-A International League. Unlike Clay Bryant, Montreal's manager, Walter Alston, fostered a loose clubhouse and earned respect by developing relationships with his players. But make no mistake, Alston could be tough when necessary. Lasorda once described him as a volcano because he always had the potential to explode.

Lasorda pitched in Montreal for the next three seasons, compiling an outstanding 35-17 record while evolving from a thrower into a pitcher. Despite his consistent success over a three-year stretch, he never got called up to the Dodgers. The club's talented pitching staff—which included Don Newcombe, Preacher Roe, Carl Erskine, Ralph Branca, Joe Black, Clyde King, and bonus baby Billy Loes—had no room for the soft-tossing southpaw from Norristown. He was optimistic that his luck would change heading into the 1953 season. But just as he was about to leave for Vero Beach, the Dodgers sold Lasorda's contract to the St. Louis Browns on a conditional basis. The Browns could keep him for $50,000 or send him back to the Dodgers. The talent-starved Browns seemingly could have benefited from adding him to their big-league staff, but the team's financially strapped owner, Bill Veeck, couldn't afford to keep Lasorda and exercised the option of returning him to the Dodgers near the end of spring training. Lasorda packed his bags and returned to Dodgertown for what was left of the Grapefruit League, destined for a fourth season in Montreal. While the Dodgers won 105 games and the National League pennant that season, Lasorda compiled 17 wins and posted a stellar 2.81

ERA for the Royals, earning International League Pitcher of the Year honors.

1952 insert from Montreal's French-language La Patrie *daily newspaper.*

That offseason, Dodgers manager Charlie Dressen—coming off back-to-back National League pennants—demanded a three-year deal. Walter O'Malley refused to budge on a one-year offer. Dressen stood his ground, so O'Malley hired Alston. Lasorda's manager the previous four seasons in Montreal was now at the helm in Brooklyn. Alston's presence, Lasorda thought, might help his chances of making the team. He thought wrong. When the Dodgers cut Lasorda from the big-league roster and optioned him to Triple-A yet again, he considered walking away from baseball altogether. His father, who often said, "Because God delays does not mean God denies," encouraged the twenty-six-year-old to keep grinding. Money also factored into the decision. Lasorda was never going to find another job that paid him $9,000 a year to do something he loved. He put aside his frustration and reported to Montreal.*

On July 31, 1954—the same day he won his 14th game of the season for the Royals, a three-hitter versus the Toronto Maple Leafs—the Dodgers promoted Lasorda to the big leagues. Finally. He made his debut five days later, tossing three innings of mop-up relief against the St. Louis Cardinals in the Dodgers' 13-4 loss at Ebbets Field. Then he languished on the bench for the next thirty-one days. When he complained to Alston about his lack of action, Alston said that he planned to sink or swim with his veterans. Lasorda could best contribute, he said, by providing a spark in the dugout. Looking back decades later, Lasorda told author Bill Plaschke that Alston never liked him, which he called one of the greatest disappointments of his life. The bombastic Lasorda put his feelings aside and became his team's biggest cheerleader, rooting on the likes of Roy Campanella, Gil Hodges, Pee Wee Reese, Duke Snider, and Jackie Robinson. The Dodgers failed to win a third-straight pennant, however, finishing in second place behind the Giants. Lasorda appeared in a total of four games, yielding five earned runs in nine innings.

Lasorda pitched for the Mayaguez Indians in the Puerto Rican Winter League that offseason. There, he held Willie Mays to only four hits in 18 at-bats but grabbed headlines for other reasons. In a game versus San Juan, Lasorda threw a fastball near the head of Pirates infielder Gene Freese, who responded by charging the mound. Gene's older brother, George, was playing right field for Mayaguez and rushed to the aid of his brother. Lasorda suddenly found himself taking on both siblings—one of whom was his own teammate. A *Brooklyn Eagle* article about the fracas appeared under the headline, "Tom Lasorda Starts War in Puerto Rico."[10]

---

* Among his teammates that summer was a nineteen-year-old Puerto Rican outfielder named Roberto Clemente. Lasorda, who learned Spanish playing winter ball in the Caribbean, helped translate for Clemente.

This was not Lasorda's first rumble in the Caribbean. Two years earlier, he instigated an epic brawl in Cuba. Lasorda told the story countless times over the years and undoubtedly embellished some of the details, but the basic facts were corroborated by teammate Roy Hartsfield. The fight involved Lasorda, who pitched for the Almendares Scorpios, and Chiquitín Cabrera, a powerful first baseman on the Marianao Tigers. Cabrera got a few cheap hits off Lasorda one game, leading to an exchange of unpleasantries between the two competitors. The next time Lasorda faced Marianao, his first pitch to Cabrera sailed high and inside, sending Cabrera to the ground. Cabrera got up and warned Lasorda not to come inside again. "You know Lasorda," recalled Hartsfield, "nothing ever scared him. The next pitch was just as tight and the big fellow hits the dirt again."[11] Now it was on. Cabrera, who had four inches and forty pounds on Lasorda, charged the mound with his bat. Lasorda instinctively rushed toward Cabrera, slung him to the ground, got him in a headlock, and landed a few punches. Policemen rushed on to the field and pulled Lasorda off Cabrera.

The next day, men in suits and sunglasses showed up and escorted Lasorda into a black limousine. His teammates weren't sure they'd ever see him again. The men drove Lasorda to a large house in the countryside, where he was introduced to President Fulgencio Batista. The dictator wanted to meet the man who took down Cabrera and apologized on behalf of Cuba for Cabrera's unsportsmanlike behavior.

Lasorda made the Dodgers' opening-day roster for the first time in 1955 and watched from the bench as his teammates went 17-2 to start the season. He received a long-awaited starting assignment on May 5 versus the Cardinals in place of Don Newcombe, whom the Dodgers had suspended for refusing to throw batting practice. Lasorda felt good warming up in the bullpen but had trouble finding the strike zone when the game began.

After he walked the leadoff man, Wally Moon, he uncorked a wild pitch that advanced Moon to second base. Then he walked Bill Virdon and threw a second wild pitch, putting runners at second and third. Stan Musial was up next. Lasorda managed to get two strikes on Stan the Man and then unleashed what he later described was the best curveball he ever threw. Musial whipped his bat through the zone but came up empty. Lasorda had just fanned one of the best players to ever don a uniform. He felt a surge of confidence but quickly came back to earth when he threw another pitch to the backstop. Moon tried to score from third, so Lasorda covered home. As the two players converged, Lasorda attempted to block the plate, putting his knee in the direct path of Moon's spikes. Moon scored safely and Lasorda was left with a gash so deep that it exposed a tendon. After limping back to the mound, Lasorda convinced Alston and the trainer that he was okay, then managed to record the final two outs of the inning without allowing further damage. Like the Black Knight from *Monty Python and the Holy Grail*, Lasorda was not going to let a "flesh wound" stop him. When he got back to the dugout, however, the severity of the injury became more apparent. Alston removed Lasorda and sent him to the hospital for stitches.

Over the next month-plus, Lasorda appeared in only three more games, all in relief. In four outings, he tossed four innings, issued six walks, and allowed six earned runs for an ERA of 13.50. In early June, Buzzie Bavasi needed to create a roster spot for a newly signed nineteen-year-old pitcher named Sandy Koufax. Because Koufax signed for $14,000, he was subject to the Bonus Rule and had to remain on the big-league roster, leaving Lasorda the odd man out and sending him back to Montreal. For the rest of his life, Lasorda would boast that it took the greatest left-handed pitcher in baseball history to bump him off the Dodgers roster. And deep down, he felt he never got the shot he deserved. Brooklyn went on to win the World Series without Lasorda, though his teammates voted him a half-share of their World Series earnings.

In the spring of 1956, the Dodgers sold Lasorda to the Kansas City Athletics, perennial bottom feeders of the American League. He made the opening-day roster as a long reliever and spot starter. His pitching ledger for the Athletics—an 0-4 record, 6.15 ERA, and nearly a walk per inning—was nothing to write home about. Lasorda's most memorable moment with Kansas City came on May 21, when the A's hosted the Yankees in front a Ladies' Day crowd of 13,799. In the bottom of the third, with the Yankees ahead, 5-2, the Athletics' Héctor López and Gus Zernial hit back-to-back home runs off Yankees reliever Tom Sturdivant, who responded by throwing brushback pitches to Harry Simpson and Jim Finigan. Players on the Kansas City bench watched their teammates get buzzed and didn't say a word. A's manager Lou Boudreau blew a gasket. From the opposing dugout, Mickey Mantle could hear Boudreau scream, "That's what's wrong with this lousy club. Everyone is afraid of the Yankees!" Lasorda spoke up and said he wasn't afraid of the Bronx Bombers. The skipper appreciated the southpaw's conviction.

With his team trailing 8-4 in the eighth, Boudreau put in Lasorda, who decided to throw at every hitter. He knocked down Andy Carey, then got him out on a pop up. He sent Sturdivant to the dirt, then got him on a fly ball to right. Then he sailed two pitches over the head of Hank Bauer before striking him out to end the inning. Lasorda returned to the mound in the top of the ninth and it was more of the same. He got ahead of Billy Martin with two quick strikes and then threw some chin music. Martin got up and began spewing expletives at Lasorda. After he watched strike three, Martin walked back to the dugout and continued yelling at Lasorda, who said something to the effect of, "Let's go." Martin bolted out of the dugout and Lasorda sprinted to meet him. The two combatants exchanged a few harmless punches while the umpires intervened. Bauer, meanwhile, went ballistic. He wanted a piece of Lasorda. Mantle recalled that Lasorda yelled, "Stay out of this, Bauer. This is an Italian fight!"[12] Mantle escorted Bauer off the field as the umpires restored order. Lasorda finished the game and later paid a $10 fine for his actions.

Less than two months later, the Athletics traded Lasorda to those very same Yankees. He was sent to their Triple-A club, the Denver Bears, who ultimately advanced to the American Association playoffs. There, they faced the Omaha Cardinals in a best-of-seven playoff series. Omaha won the first two contests, including a 22-3 laugher in Game 2. The Bears' manager, Ralph Houk, asked Lasorda to start a fight in the third game in order to shake things up. "What inning?" asked Lasorda.[13] It turned out to be the fourth. Bears outfielder Bob Martyn hit a three-run homer off Omaha starter Frank Barnes, giving Denver a 5-0 lead. Houk didn't intend for his team to start a fight if they were ahead, but he forgot to tell Lasorda. Barnes zipped his next pitch under the chin of Tony Kubek. Later in the at-bat, Kubek tapped a foul ball down the first-base line, where Lasorda was stationed as first-base coach. He picked up the ball and fired it at Barnes. Barnes sidestepped the ball, which rolled to Omaha third baseman Stan Jok, who threw the ball back at Lasorda. When Barnes threw another pitch inside on Kubek, both benches emptied. "We kicked the hell out of them, like I expected," said Houk, a manager Lasorda would later emulate.[14]

As the 1957 season approached, the thirty-year-old Lasorda gave some thought to life after his playing career. He had strong connections in the Dodgers organization and figured that's where he had the best chance of finding employment as a coach or manager. He asked Yankees GM Lee MacPhail to trade him to the Dodgers if possible. On May 26—two days before the proposed relocation of the Dodgers and Giants was formally presented at a National League meeting in Chicago—Lasorda got his wish. He spent the rest of the summer with the Los Angeles Angels, the Dodgers' Pacific Coast League affiliate.

In 1958, Bavasi assigned Lasorda to be a player-coach with the Montreal Royals at the recommendation of scouting director Al Campanis. The downside of the job from Lasorda's perspective was being reunited with the stern Clay Bryant, who was now Montreal's manager. Lasorda opted to skip playing winter ball and began the '58 campaign with a fresh arm. The decision resulted in the best season of his professional career—an 18-6 record, 2.50 ERA, and only 76 walks in 230 innings. Besides conducting infield practice, leading conditioning drills, and winning his second International League Pitcher of the Year Award, he also served as the Royals' traveling secretary.

Lasorda spent another two seasons as a player-coach in Montreal, during which his tenuous relationship with Bryant deteriorated. Because Bryant had little direct communication with his players, Lasorda became the de facto liaison between Bryant and the team. One day during the 1960 season, pitcher Willard Hunter asked Lasorda about the possibility of a raise. Lasorda asked Bryant on Hunter's behalf. He relayed Bryant's firm "no," but then Bryant accused Lasorda of making false promises to Hunter. Bryant proceeded to call the Dodgers front office to complain Lasorda was undermining his authority.

Just days after he notched his 105th career regular-season win in a Montreal Royals uniform, Lasorda received a letter from Bavasi informing him of his release. He called Bavasi, presented his side of the Hunter-Bryant story, and declared his undying love for the Dodgers. Several Montreal players came to Lasorda's defense in a letter to Bavasi, who called Lasorda back and offered him a job as a scout. Lasorda was lukewarm on the idea. After getting a taste of coaching, he really wanted to manage. But then Campanis emphasized the positive aspects of scouting. He described the thrill of finding a player with raw talent and watching him blossom into a major leaguer. He explained that it was the "most important job in baseball" and the "backbone of the organization."[15] The more Campanis talked, the better the job sounded. By the end of the conversation, Lasorda was all in.

Campanis and veteran scout John Carey taught Lasorda the ins and outs of scouting, including grading talent, talking to parents, and digging into a player's background to avoid troublemakers. With Norristown as his home base, Lasorda traveled throughout the northeast, approaching the job with the same enthusiasm with which he approached a plate of pasta. And because of his outgoing nature and gift of gab, he began receiving invitations to speak at banquets and civic luncheons throughout his scouting territory, regaling his audiences with entertaining baseball stories and life advice. When talking to younger audiences, he encouraged loyalty to their parents, neatness of attire, and a positive attitude. He preached that nothing is impossible with hard work and determination.

In the fall of 1962, Al Campanis asked Lasorda to come work as a scout in Southern California. Leaving Norristown and relocating his family wasn't an easy decision, but Lasorda realized it was a great opportunity to advance within the organization. Tommy, Jo, and their children—Laura and Tommy Jr., also known as Spunky—trekked across the country and settled in Fullerton.

Lasorda hung around Campanis and assisted Kenny Myers, a distinguished scout and hitting instructor perhaps best known for signing and mentoring Dodgers center fielder Willie Davis.* Lasorda helped coach the Myers-led Dodger Rookies, a select team of top prep players in the LA area, and worked with scout Ben Wade, his former teammate who later became the Dodgers' scouting director.† Besides the mentorship from his

---

* Myers, who signed a professional contract with the St. Louis Cardinals at age fifteen, played thirteen seasons in the minor leagues. In 1947, as a member of the Class-C Las Vegas Wranglers, he accomplished a feat that will likely never be duplicated on a professional baseball field: He hit four home runs in a game, including two grand slams in the same inning, in the Wranglers' 30-5 thrashing of the Ontario Orioles. Myers's mentorship of Willie Davis, a high school track star with raw baseball talent, was chronicled in the 1961 documentary *Biography of a Rookie: Willie Davis*, narrated by Mike Wallace of *60 Minutes* fame.

† The Dodger Rookies played the Angel Rookies, Giant Rookies, and a handful of other amateur teams throughout California. The program afforded players the opportunity to face elite competition while giving scouts an extended look at prospects and the inside track on signing them. Willie Davis, Ken McMullen, John Werhas, Joe Moeller, Wes Parker, and Rollie Fingers were among the players who participated in the program. Each signed with the

Dodgers colleagues, Lasorda found many of his competitors to be welcoming, including esteemed scouts Rosey Gilhousen, Howie Haak, and Joe Stephenson of the Angels, Pirates, and Red Sox, respectively.

When Lasorda scouted in the Northeast and tried to convince a player to sign with the Dodgers, he told them it was good to get away from home and see a different part of the country. Playing too close to home would present distractions that could keep a player from reaching his potential, he said. In California, he changed his tune, extolling the advantages of playing close to home. That's how he sold Tommy Hutton and his parents on the Dodgers.

Lasorda first heard about Hutton from an unlikely source. One day in the spring of 1964, while in the midst of recruiting Willie Crawford, he had a meeting at Dodger Stadium and tried to park in a lot reserved for executives. A parking attendant said he'd allow Lasorda to park there on one condition, if he agreed to scout his friend, Tommy Hutton. Lasorda followed up on the tip and was impressed by the left-handed first baseman from South Pasadena High School. A couple of other teams had also shown interest in Hutton, particularly the Red Sox. Lasorda and Wade showed up at the Hutton residence and gave their sales pitch. Lasorda—who did the talking and left the paperwork to Wade—asked Hutton's parents, "Do you want your son playing all the way across the country in Massachusetts, or do you want him playing right down the freeway at Dodger Stadium?"[16] Lasorda's spiel convinced Hutton to sign for $8,000.

Between Crawford, Hutton, and left-handed pitcher Jim Strickland out of Lakewood High School, Lasorda signed three players in 1964 who'd ultimately play a combined thirty seasons in the majors. His scouting career was off to an excellent start. But when Major League Baseball adopted the amateur draft at the Winter Meetings, Campanis felt that Lasorda's skills could be better utilized by developing the Dodgers' minor leaguers. When the Dodgers' Rookie-level team, the Pocatello Chiefs, had a managerial vacancy heading into the 1965 season, Campanis campaigned for Lasorda and helped land him the position.

With Lasorda at the helm, the 1965 Pocatello Chiefs played .500 ball over a 66-game schedule in the four-team Pioneer League. The roster

---

Dodgers except Fingers, who signed for less money with the Athletics so he could reach the big leagues faster.

included a handful of players from the Dodgers' inaugural draft class, including first-round pick John Wyatt. Two weeks into the season, Lasorda started his first brawl against the Idaho Falls Angels. Tempers flared after Lasorda fielded a foul ball in third-base coach's box and tossed it out of play. "Hey, what are you throwing the ball out of play for?" barked Idaho Falls manager Fred Koenig.[17] Lasorda shouted some expletives in the direction of the Idaho Falls bench, prompting the six-foot-three, 200-pound Koenig to charge at him. The fight quickly escalated into a full-out donnybrook involving all sixty players from both teams. It took a combination of police, fans, and groundskeepers to break up the fracas. Things got so heated that local authorities escorted Pocatello's team bus to city limits after the game. It occurred to Lasorda that he had already broken his promise to Bavasi, and he worried he may have just blown his chance. When the Dodgers GM called the next day to ask what happened, Lasorda used his power of persuasion to plead his case and was granted forgiveness.

Lasorda survived the season with his job intact and would return for a second one at the same Rookie level, this time with the club's new affiliate in Ogden, Utah. The next crop of prospects would include a couple of young pups named Charlie Hough and Bill Russell.

Dodgers Draft Hough and Russell

"It's a disease, this baseball. It could be a lonesome life, but not for me. I've wanted to quit thirty-five times, but I never did. I never will. I'll die in it." —Leon Hamilton

LEON HAMILTON SCOUTED ON INTUITION. HE HAD NO USE FOR advancements like radar guns and despised the player-grading system that Al Campanis made standard. When Hamilton evaluated a player, there was no gray area. In his mind, a guy could play, or he couldn't. He wore the label "Backwoods Scout" with pride and built a reputation on signing players that other teams overlooked or ignored. Over his decades-long scouting career he signed dozens of players who reached the major leagues. In the world of scouting, Leon Hamilton was a legend.

Born in Birmingham, Alabama, in 1911, Hamilton was raised in Chattanooga, Tennessee, by his grandmother following the death of his mother when he was an infant. His father, a physician, wanted his son to take a conventional path and go to medical school. But Leon was anything but conventional. At seventeen, the pitcher quit high school and signed with the Kinston Eagles in the Class-D Eastern Carolina League, the lowest rung of minor-league baseball. When the team released him a month later, he returned home to obtain his high school diploma, then enrolled at the University of Kentucky and earned a business degree.

After college, Hamilton spent winters playing basketball for the House of David, a prolific team of bearded barnstormers who played hundreds of games each fall and winter. He eventually put his degree to use as the team's general manager. During summers between the late 1930s and World War II, Hamilton worked as a business manager and traveling secretary for minor-league baseball teams in Cordele, Georgia, and Jacksonville, Florida. He served four years in the Navy during the war, then got hired as general manager of the Binghamton Triplets, an affiliate of the New York Yankees, in 1947. Two years later, he requested a move south and began scouting. Hamilton later described himself as a lackey for Johnny Nee and Paul Krichell, a pair of venerable ivory hunters who signed numerous future Hall of Famers.* Hamilton found his estimable colleagues to be anything but welcoming. They'd send him to fetch the lineup and occasionally throw him a nugget of advice, but that was the extent of their niceties.

After a year of performing menial tasks as a Yankees scout, Hamilton jumped to the Dodgers, taking responsibility for a scouting territory that included South Carolina, Georgia, Alabama, and Florida. He attacked the job with boundless energy. Hamilton, slender and tall with a narrow face and receding hairline, spent thousands of hours driving on two-lane roads and hundreds of nights sleeping in his car at highway rest stops and fast-food parking lots. In one year alone, he attended 476 games. He often said that he was gone from home so much that the family dog would bite him when he returned. He saw his wife and six children for a couple of weeks at a time, twice a year. Then he'd hit the backroads and continue his search for the next hidden gem.†

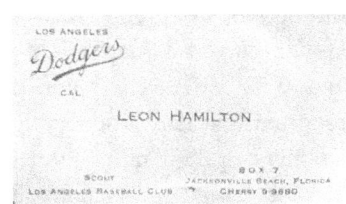

Courtesy Marlee Hanby.

Hamilton socialized with other talent hawks and was popular in the

---
* Johnny Nee signed Bill Dickey, Spud Chandler, Ben Chapman, Dixie Walker, and Atley Donald. Paul Krichell, who played two seasons with the St. Louis Browns, signed Lou Gehrig, Phil Rizzuto, Tony Lazzeri, and Whitey Ford.
† Don Sutton, Charley Smith, Jack Billingham, Jim Fairey, Nate Oliver, and Choo-Choo

scouting fraternity, but at the ballpark he sat by himself so he could concentrate and avoid the influence of his rivals. If he had time to kill before or after a game, he'd walk around town and chat up the locals with his southern drawl, hoping to pick up a tip about a ballplayer. One former baseball executive described Hamilton as equal parts detective, psychologist, budget analyst, raconteur, and military strategist. He observed that fathers did more talking but that the moms were usually the boss, so he always helped wash dishes after having dinner and tried to earn the mother's trust. When the amateur draft came along and teams had to cast a wider net, Hamilton was forced to scout more broadly, which he acknowledged made getting to know players more difficult. "You don't know if a boy smokes pot because you're not around town long enough to find out," Hamilton told author Kevin Kerrane. "You can't tell if he has heart. You don't even get to know his mother."[1]

Leading up to the 1966 June Amateur Draft, Hamilton recommended a high school player named Charlie Hough to Dodgers scouting director Al Campanis. Hamilton had carefully monitored Hough's progress throughout his prep career. As a high school senior in Hialeah, Florida, Hough played corner infield and pitcher, batting .362 with an 11-2 record and 0.52 ERA. He planned to attend Miami-Dade Junior College, a program that had produced Steve Carlton three years earlier, but then the Dodgers drafted him 159th overall. Hough's meeting with Hamilton to discuss terms of his contract was brief. "It took about five minutes," recalled Hough. "Nobody knew much about the draft. I was an eighth-round draft pick, which felt like it was the end of the line."[2]

Baseball executives went into that June '66 draft better prepared after learning from their mistakes the previous year. The Houston Astros, for example, realized they needed to do more crosschecking. Before the draft, they had relied almost entirely on the judgment of the area scout except for cases in which the bonus exceeded $50,000. "We had our West Coast supervisor travel to the eastern United States and see the top ten players," said Pat Gillick, looking back. "And we'd have our East Coast supervisor travel west to see their top ten. This gave some semblance of how players in the West compared to players in the East, and vice versa."[3]

Coleman were among the players Hamilton scouted or signed for the Dodgers in the pre-amateur draft era.

The general consensus amongst front offices heading into the draft was that the overall talent level exceeded the previous year's crop. "Last year, I was wondering whether we could pick up as many as three players," said Paul Richards, who had transitioned from Houston's GM to a Phillies scout. "But this year, give me the entire twenty of the first round, and in three years, I guarantee you that team would make trouble for anybody. And I mean anybody."[4] The assessment of Richards and other talent evaluators would prove to be overly optimistic.

The draft began with the secondary phase, a separate selection process for players who had previously been drafted but didn't sign. One hundred four selections were made over the course of two hours—most notably Andy Messersmith (Angels), Joe Niekro (Cubs), and Del Unser (Senators). The Dodgers' top choice was Miami-Dade Community College outfielder Bob Stinson, another player recommended and signed by Leon Hamilton.

The consensus two best players available in the regular draft were Arizona State University outfielder Reggie Jackson and a high school catcher from Lancaster, California, named Steve Chilcott. One executive who surveyed the draft room found that the twenty teams were evenly split between the two. But only one team's opinion mattered. The Mets, who had averaged 113 losses in their four years of existence, held the first overall pick and went with Chilcott. "Catching was at such a premium," recalled then-Mets executive Joe McDonald. "We took Chilcott because we had good reports, including a report from Casey Stengel. He was destined to be a good catcher, but he had serious injury problems."[5] Charlie Finley's Kansas City Athletics nabbed Jackson with the second pick. Chilcott would never reach the majors, whereas Jackson went on to slug 563 home runs and win five World Series rings over the course of a decorated, Hall-of-Fame career. Chilcott wasn't the only bust. Of the twenty first-round selections, only twelve ultimately played in the majors and just six—Jackson, Ken Brett, John Curtis, Gary Nolan, Richie Hebner, and Carlos May—would ever become established big leaguers.*

The Dodgers used the nineteenth overall pick to select Larry Hutton, a

---

* Curtis was drafted twelfth overall by the Cleveland Indians but did not sign. He then enrolled at Clemson University, later signing with the Boston Red Sox after being selected in the 1968 June Draft-Secondary Phase.

hard-throwing right-handed pitcher from Greenfield, Indiana. "I didn't even know that it was draft day," said Hutton, looking back. "My dad called and said, 'You were drafted number one.'" Hutton was surprised to be chosen by the Dodgers, who were not one of the half-dozen teams that contacted him before the draft. When it came time to discuss terms of a contract, Dodgers area scout Cliff Alexander—who happened to be Walter Alston's brother-in-law—offered him $50,000. Hutton said, "That'll work. When do we start?"[6]

Hutton would later battle control issues when he advanced to Single-A and admittedly went into a tailspin after the Dodgers bypassed him for a promotion. He would ultimately never play above Double-A. In fact, six of the Dodgers' top-seven picks would fail to reach the majors. The one who did, John Gamble, would play in only 13 games for the Detroit Tigers, mostly as a pinch-runner. The Dodgers did, however, strike gold in the later rounds. After taking Hough in the eighth round, they picked future major leaguers Bill Russell (ninth round), Billy Grabarkewitz (twelfth round), Ted Sizemore (fifteenth round), and Ray Lamb (fortieth round).*

According to Baseball-Reference, the eight players from the Dodgers' class of 1966 who made the majors would combine for 99.6 career Wins Above Replacement, the most of any organization that year. Many of the same Dodgers scouts who were involved in the '66 draft under Campanis would contribute to the organization's historic haul two years later.

A week after the draft, Charlie Hough, Bill Russell, and Larry Hutton were among the Dodgers prospects who reported to Ogden, Utah, the new home of the organization's short-season Rookie-league team. After one season in Pocatello, Lasorda would now manage two hours south at the foot of the Wasatch Mountains. Within a few days of arriving in Ogden, the players attended a Chamber of Commerce luncheon in which Lasorda served as the keynote speaker. Speaking without notes, he proceeded to introduce each player, providing details such as where they were from, their position, and where they were taken in the draft. "It was amazing,"

---

* Sizemore won the 1969 NL Rookie of the Year Award. Lamb's claim to fame is being the last Dodger to wear forty-two. Equipment manager Nobe Kawano issued Jackie Robinson's iconic jersey number to Lamb when he was called up to the Dodgers in '69. After the season, Kawano realized his mistake and made Lamb switch numbers. Robinson's forty-two was officially retired in 1972.

Hough recalled. "He knew everybody within the matter of a couple of days ... The best thing I can say is that he cared."[7]

BILL RUSSELL - Outfielder

Courtesy Spokane Indians.

Lasorda sized up his roster during ten days of workouts and intrasquad games leading up to the season opener. The first time he saw Russell try to hit a curve, Lasorda just shook his head. Russell, a seventeen-year-old from Pittsburg, Kansas, looked like a baby attempting to walk for the first time. Russell's inexperience with breaking pitches stemmed from the fact that his high school didn't have a baseball program. He grew up playing Little League but as a teenager only played baseball during the summer with the local American Legion team. During high school, Russell excelled most in basketball. As a senior, the six-foot guard averaged 18.7 points per game, led Pittsburg to the state tournament, and earned all-state honors. Because there was no baseball in the spring, he lettered in track, placing third in the state in the javelin. Despite his relative inexperience on the baseball diamond, in some ways he looked like a natural. Scouts who watched Russell play American Legion ball were tantalized by his quick wrists and foot speed that could set grass on fire. Russell increased his draft stock in the summer of 1965 with hits in 11 consecutive at-bats in front of numerous scouts, including John Keenan of the Dodgers. Based on Keenan's recommendation, the Dodgers drafted Russell and signed him for $14,000.

When it came to Hough, Lasorda initially wasn't sure how to use the young Floridian, who was drafted as a third baseman-first baseman-pitcher. Hough could hit well enough and had the hands to play either corner-infield position. But the fact he was slower than molasses is ultimately what made him a pitcher in Lasorda's eyes. The skipper joked that he timed most players with a stopwatch, but in Hough's case he used a *stopped* watch.

Hutton's and Hough's performances during their first season reflected their respective draft positions. Hutton, the first-rounder, led Ogden with nine wins, struck out 142 batters in 119 innings, and posted a 3.03 ERA while relying almost entirely on his fastball. Hough, the eighth-round pick, pitched mostly in relief and finished the season with a 5-7 record and an uninspiring 4.76 ERA. His repertoire at the time consisted of a decent fastball and a hard-breaking curveball. "Charlie lost more games than he won," recalled Hutton, "but he was always around the plate and had good command of the curve. And he had a huge heart."[8]

The Ogden Dodgers played in a no-frills, prewar wooden ballpark called Affleck Park, where the dugouts resembled bomb shelters and the locker rooms, painted dark green, reeked of pine tar and deodorant. Training facilities? No chance. When a player once asked where the whirlpool was located, Lasorda told him to go stick his foot in the toilet and flush it. On the field, players endured subpar conditions that made seemingly routine plays an adventure. The poorly manicured infield frequently caused bad hops, and the diamond was positioned in such a way that the sun set over the left-center field wall, making it nearly impossible for a batter to see a ball coming from the hand of a right-handed hurler in the early evening. When the sun set, conditions weren't much better. "The lights were far below modern standards," remembered Erik

Jensen, a Brigham City native who attended several Ogden Dodgers games during the summer of 1966. "The games were all at night, and whether an outfielder was going to be able to see, much less catch, a fly ball was always a question. The bottom line—a five-run lead was never safe, and even a ten-run lead could be overcome."[9]

The Ogden Dodgers provided good entertainment value in spite of the ramshackle ballpark. Nearly six decades later, Jensen recalled that players such as Russell and second baseman Rich Thompson flashed potential, but the most memorable performer at Affleck Park that summer was Ogden's manager and third-base coach. "Lasorda obviously loved the game and cared about the players and the fans," said Jensen. "He was dancing, yelling, clapping in the coaching box … he responded to calls from the stands. He was a great salesman for the game."[10]

Lasorda believed in the importance of providing a good show for the fans who paid hard-earned money for admission to the ballpark. It was one of the tenets Lasorda instilled in his players, along with loyalty to Dodger blue and the power of optimism. He repeated his mantra, "You've got to believe!" to players he managed, audiences on the banquet circuit, and—on at least one occasion—a Mormon missionary on the street.

"One time, while we were all assembled outside the hotel in Ogden waiting for the team bus, a young Mormon missionary approached us and made the mistake of engaging directly with [Lasorda]," recounted catcher Mike Criscione. Lasorda scanned over a pamphlet handout and softly asked the young man if he believed in Jesus Christ. When the young man nodded, Lasorda responded a little louder, "Well then say it son, 'I Believe!'" Then Lasorda asked him if he believed in the Virgin Mary. When the guy said he did, Lasorda encouraged him to say it louder, "I believe!" Lasorda asked him several more questions, each time raising the decibel level another notch. "Finally," recalled Criscione, "when Tom had worked this guy up into a frenzy, he handed back the brochure and softly responded, 'Okay, I was just curious.' And the missionary just went off evangelizing down the street waving his arms and ranting, 'I believe … I believe!'"[11]

In addition to giving motivational speeches and teaching baseball fundamentals, Lasorda dispensed life hacks to his players. "He would often take me and other players out to dinner with his family on home game days," remembered Criscione.* "One gem was his suggestion that after eating about 80 percent of a steak you should pluck a hair out of your head and place it on the plate. Then call the waiter and complain that you couldn't eat the remainder in this condition and demand that they get you another steak."[12]

Between the white lines, Ogden performed well down the stretch, reeling off twelve consecutive victories to capture the Pioneer League pennant. Lasorda made such a favorable impression that the team and local businesses honored him with "Tom Lasorda Night" and showered him with gifts, including vinyl records, an electric cigar lighter, savings bonds, golf balls, a painting, and a poodle. His players used their modest wages to buy him a pen and pencil set.

When Ogden's season concluded, Lasorda joined the big-league Dodgers in their march to a second straight National League pennant.† Just as he had done eleven years earlier, Lasorda threw batting practice and helped keep Walter Alston's team loose with his unique sense of humor. One difference between Lasorda the player and Lasorda the manager was his expanded waistline. In the visitor's clubhouse at Connie Mack Stadium in Philadelphia, sportswriter Dick Young observed Lasorda "was a sight, sitting there on the stool, with his baseball cap perched jauntily on his head, and his long white hose on, and practically nothing else. The blubber was pinched over the elastic band of the supporter, creating rolls of flesh around the middle making him some sort of model Buddha."[13] It was a sight Los Angeles sportswriters would come to know all too well.

---

* Darcy Fast, who pitched for the Caldwell Cubs in the summer of '67, recalled coming down for breakfast at the Ben Lomond Hotel in Ogden and seeing Lasorda eating with a dozen of his players. "I had never seen a manager do that with his ball team," recalled Fast. "He was the kind of guy who looked out for the interests of his ballplayers. When I walked by his table, he said, 'Hi, Darcy, how are you doing?' and struck up a conversation. I was surprised that he even knew who I was."

† Among the Dodgers' September call-ups was Willie Crawford, the young phenom Lasorda had signed two years earlier. Crawford spent most of the season in Double-A Albuquerque, where he hit .265 with 15 home runs but struck out a whopping 186 times. He was still a few years from becoming an established big leaguer.

Turmoil in LA, Another Pennant in Ogden

"I used to throw the ball as hard as Koufax, but somehow it didn't get up there as fast."—Tommy Lasorda

In the fall of '65, Sandy Koufax and Don Drysdale, who earned $85,000 and $80,000 that year, respectively, joined forces to demand a three-year, no-cut contract totaling a combined $1 million. Their asking price would make them the highest-paid players in the game, topping Willie Mays's annual income by roughly $50,000. The two pitchers hired attorney Bill Hayes of Executive Business Management in Beverly Hills to serve as an agent and insisted that neither would sign unless the other received fair compensation. The joint holdout was an unprecedented maneuver in an industry where the owners had long wielded unilateral authority.

The situation infuriated general manager Buzzie Bavasi, a ruthless negotiator and loyal lieutenant of Walter O'Malley, who told Koufax and Drysdale that anything more than the standard one-year pact was out of the question. "What you're selling is your physical ability, and how can you guarantee your physical ability three years in advance?" argued Bavasi.[1] The pitchers' asking price, in Bavasi's mind, was equally absurd.

The 1966 budget allowed for salary increases of $100,000 for the entire roster. A substantial raise for the two star pitchers, Bavasi claimed, would ostensibly mean lower raises for their teammates.

O'Malley, baseball's most influential owner, objected to the players' use of an agent. He believed negotiations should strictly remain between the player and team. Even more troubling to O'Malley were the potential consequences of players staging similar joint holdouts in the future. "To an owner, this was breaking a new ceiling," recalled Peter O'Malley, Walter O'Malley's son and heir to the throne. "The biggest thing was, they were doing this together."[2]

As the winter months passed, there was little movement in contract talks between Koufax-Drysdale and the Dodgers. Eventually, the two players lowered their combined asking price by $100,000, but their terms were still way out of line in the minds of O'Malley and Bavasi. Just before the start of spring training, the two hurlers dropped their demand for three-year contracts and hinted that they would sign for $150,000 each on a one-year deal. When Bavasi refused to budge, they held out in tandem. All-Star shortstop Maury Wills, meanwhile, sought a raise of his own and was a no-show to begin camp. He lacked the leverage of Koufax and Drysdale, however. When Bavasi told Wills that O'Malley was going to run him out of the game, a spooked Wills quickly backed off his six-figure asking price and reported to camp the next day.

Because of baseball's reserve clause, which bound a player to his team until the team decided otherwise, the pitchers' only leverage was the threat of walking away from the game. Koufax, who knew his pitching career had a rapidly approaching expiration date because of a balky elbow, later admitted he would have been comfortable hanging up his spikes that winter.[3] To further boost their negotiating power, Koufax and Drysdale signed movie deals with Paramount Pictures. If they couldn't play ball, they were prepared to make a living on the big screen. Neither pitcher would become the next Cary Grant or Paul Newman, however. Shortly before opening day, the two pitchers agreed to terms with the Dodgers, Koufax for $125,000 and Drysdale for $110,000.

Although the situation embittered Koufax, it didn't hamper his effectiveness on the mound. He looked as dominant as ever in 1966 while leading one of the greatest starting rotations in baseball history. Koufax won 27 games, registered a microscopic 1.73 ERA, and struck out 317 batters in 323 innings pitched. Future Hall of Famers Drysdale and Don Sutton and three-time All-Star Claude Osteen rounded out Walter Alston's four-man rotation. The bullpen, which consisted primarily of Phil Regan, Bob Miller, Ron Perranoski, and Joe Moeller, wasn't too shabby either. Regan—whom Koufax nicknamed "The Vulture" because of his knack for poaching wins from the starters—compiled 14 wins in relief and posted a 1.62 ERA. At 2.62, the Dodgers had the National League's lowest ERA in twenty-three years.* The offense, on the other hand, was lackluster. Tommy Davis, Willie Davis, Ron Fairly, Jim Lefebvre, Wes Parker, John Roseboro, and Lou Johnson were all above-average hitters according to OPS+, but none of them struck fear in opposing pitchers. Additionally, Maury Wills's .314 on-base percentage out of the leadoff spot was suboptimal, and third base was an offensive black hole. It all added up to 3.74 runs per game, third lowest in the league.

The Dodgers won 95 games in spite of their anemic offense, clinching the NL pennant on the season's final day behind Koufax's complete-game victory over the Phillies on just two days' rest. In the World Series, the exhausted Dodgers faced the Baltimore Orioles, a power-hitting juggernaut with an excellent bullpen. Led by the dynamic trio of Frank Robinson, Brooks Robinson, and Boog Powell—who finished first, second, and third in American League MVP voting, respectively—the O's won the pennant by nine games, allowing manager Hank Bauer to rest his regulars down the stretch and set his starting rotation for the World Series. Baltimore swept the Fall Classic in four games, holding the Dodgers scoreless over the final 33 innings.

Although it ended in disappointing fashion, the Dodgers' 1966 season marked a continuation of excellence that had reached two decades. Walter O'Malley's club had captured ten of the last twenty National League pennants, including three of the last four. In nine seasons since moving to Los Angeles, the Dodgers had won three World Series titles and four pennants. Furthermore, they had set attendance records and christened a stunning new ballpark. From a 10,000-foot view, the NL's preeminent franchise appeared to be positioned for many more years of dominance. But upon closer inspection, there were growing cracks in the foundation.

After they were trounced by the Orioles in the World Series, the weary

---

* The 1943 St. Louis Cardinals had a team ERA of 2.57.

Dodgers, minus Koufax and Drysdale, traveled to Japan for an eighteen-game goodwill tour. Wills, having dealt with a sore right knee throughout the season's second half, did not want to go but relented under the premise that he would pose for photos, sign some autographs, and play sparingly. Alston, who ran his veteran shortstop out for nine innings every night, apparently didn't get the memo. On a rainy night in Sapporo, Wills aggravated his knee injury while running the bases. He left the team without permission to get medical attention back home and stopped in Hawaii for a few days to relax. When word got out that Wills had been spotted playing banjo in a Honolulu nightclub, O'Malley was furious. He sent Bavasi a wire that said, "Get rid of Wills and get rid of him today."[4]

A few weeks after the Wills ordeal, Koufax shocked the baseball world. Sitting in front of a dozen microphones and a legion of reporters in a hastily organized press conference at the Beverly Wilshire Hotel, Koufax announced his retirement from baseball because of an arthritic left elbow. In order to pitch every fourth day during the '66 season, he had required frequent cortisone injections and large quantities of analgesics. Doctors warned him that continuing to pitch would jeopardize the use of his arm long-term, so the man nicknamed "The Left Arm of God" called it quits at age thirty. Over his final four seasons, Koufax averaged 24 wins and 307 strikeouts, recorded a miniscule 1.86 ERA, and won three Cy Young Awards. He won ERA titles in each of his final five seasons and tossed four career no-hitters, including a perfect game.

Koufax's dedication to baseball had limits, unlike Tommy Lasorda, a fringe big leaguer who fought tooth and nail to remain employed in the game. "[Koufax] never had a love for baseball," Lasorda told the *Montreal Star* in 1967. "What was I without baseball? Nothing. I wouldn't be sittin' here. I wouldn't be anywhere and if Buzzie had said to me that he wanted me to stay around another year, the love for the game would have kept me there. Not Koufax. He made up his mind that he didn't want any more of it."[5]

Losing the irreplaceable Koufax was an enormous blow to O'Malley's club. Without their ace, the weak-hitting Dodgers projected to be a second-division team in '67. They simply didn't have a way of filling the immeasurable void he left. As Charles Maher of the *Los Angeles Times* put it, "On the face of it, this may appear to put the Dodgers in terrible trouble, but it is actually a little worse than that."[6]

At the Winter Meetings, Bavasi complied with O'Malley's demand to trade Wills, sending the shortstop to the Pittsburgh Pirates in exchange for Bob Bailey and Gene Michael. The Dodgers also dealt Tommy Davis to the New York Mets for Jim Hickman and Ron Hunt. Continuity had been a cornerstone of the Dodgers' success since moving to Los Angeles. Now, their highly successful homegrown roster was beginning to look a lot different.

Besides the flurry of trades during the Winter Meetings, major-league executives got together and approved a rule change affecting the draft eligibility of college players. In the first two years of the amateur draft, teams were permitted to select and sign college sophomores. The new rule stipulated that only college graduates or players who turned twenty-one years old within forty-five days of the draft would be eligible. The new mandate benefitted college programs but significantly reduced the pool of college players available in the draft. This was problematic for the Dodgers, who were looking to rebuild quickly.

Because of the new restrictions on college players, the 1967 June Amateur Draft was skewed heavily toward riskier prep players who were further from the big leagues and thus more difficult to project. Of the first forty selections, all but one were high school players. The lone exception, the Dodgers' first-round choice, Donny Denbow, a third baseman from Southern Methodist University, would never play above Single-A. Future All-Stars Bobby Grich, John Mayberry, Ted Simmons, Jerry Reuss, Vida Blue, and Don Baylor all came out of the first two rounds. Rick Dempsey (fifteenth round), Gary Lavelle (twentieth round), and Dusty Baker (twenty-sixth round) were among the late-round picks who would blossom into established big leaguers. In total, however, only 8.7 percent of players in the regular phase of the June draft would make the majors—fewer than any other year in draft history. Compared to the league as a whole, the Dodgers had a below-average draft. Of the seventy players they selected in the regular phase, only four (6 percent) would make the majors. And of the thirty-one who signed, just two—Steve Yeager and Bruce Ellingsen*—ever would.

---

* In 1974, the Dodgers traded Ellingsen to the Cleveland Indians for Pedro Guerrero. Ellingsen appeared in sixteen games for the Indians, whereas Guerrero became a five-time All-Star and played with Yeager on the world champion '81 Dodgers.

The Vietnam War would affect the careers of some players drafted in '67—and throughout the late 1960s. Between 1965 and 1969, more than 1.4 million American men between the ages of eighteen and a half and twenty-five were inducted into the military through the Selective Service System.⁷ Being drafted into the military carried a two-year service requirement, which was often the death knell to the baseball dreams of a fringe prospect. And for those who served, there was, of course, much more at stake. At least seven minor leaguers—Harmon Bove, Udell Chambers, Charles Chase, Eddie Glinnen, Joe McCarthy, Kerry Taylor, and Donny Tidwell*—were killed in the line of duty.

Players who were married with children or full-time college students were granted draft deferments. Others avoided the military draft by joining the National Guard or a federal Reserve unit.† Since 1957, the Army Reserve—created as an expansion of President Dwight Eisenhower's Ready Forces Act—had served as a viable mechanism for ballplayers to fulfill military service while continuing their careers.‡ Teams proactively ensured that their top prospects joined Guard or Reserve units after President Lyndon Johnson instituted an active military draft in July 1965. Members of the Guard served two weeks of active duty per year and one weekend a month, whereas the Reserve had an initial six-month training and two weeks of active duty per year. Players who were in a Reserve unit typically fulfilled their six-month training during the winter to minimize interference with the baseball season. Joining the Guard or Reserve minimized the risk of seeing combat overseas but did not absolve a player from active duty. For example, several big leaguers, including the Tigers' Mickey Lolich, were deployed to help quell race riots in '67 and '68. Similarly, Ken Holtzman of the Cubs was activated because of protests at the '68 Democratic National Convention in Chicago.

Major-league front offices established relationships with recruiting officers as a means of getting their players enlisted in the National Guard

---

* Tidwell, a right-handed pitcher from Diana, Texas, was the Dodgers' forty-second round pick in the 1966 June Amateur Draft. He played one season of Rookie ball in Ogden under Lasorda before voluntarily enlisting in the Army in November 1966.

† As of early 1967, there were 145 professional baseball players in the National Guard or Army Reserve.

‡ The first major leaguers to enter the Army Reserve were the Pirates' Bill Mazeroski and Buddy Pritchard in July 1957. Drysdale and Koufax enlisted in October 1957.

or Reserve, but there weren't enough slots for everyone. "Major-league players were the first priority, then the better prospects in the Class AAA and AA minor leagues, which left the greater draft exposure to players at the Class-A and Rookie-league levels," explained baseball historian Charlie Bevis.[8]

One prospect from the '67 June Amateur Draft who got swept up in the Vietnam War was Kara Hall, an infielder from Dos Palos, California.* The Dodgers' thirteenth-round pick eagerly signed his contract without much negotiating. "It didn't make no difference to me what the amount was," recalled Hall. "I just wanted to play some ball."[9]

Hall hit .246 with five home runs playing for Lasorda's Ogden Dodgers that '67 summer. The following year, he was in Vietnam. "That was the worst break I could ever have," said Hall. "It was a lot of valuable time I missed."[10] He returned to professional baseball two years later but could not get his baseball career back on track and never advanced above Single-A. Decades later, Hall looked back fondly on his time playing for Lasorda. The manager's favorite expression, "You gotta believe," remained etched in his mind.

Larry Burchart, Hall's teammate, also held Lasorda in high esteem. The Oklahoma State product, who was drafted in the 1967 June Amateur Draft-Secondary Phase, could tell Lasorda was a player's manager from the day he met him. "He would always make guys feel like they were better than they really were," recalled Burchart, who later pitched in 29 games for the '69 Cleveland Indians. "We had a seventeen-year-old pitcher from Georgia named Larry King, and Lasorda nicknamed him Killer King. He was never going to make it out of the lower minors, but Lasorda would scream, 'Killer King's future address will be Dodger Stadium!' King would smile, and he really believed it."[11]

Lasorda was nearly forty in the summer of '67. There were streaks of gray in his hair and pouches beneath his eyes, but his youthful energy had not waned. And he needed every ounce of it. Like most managers in the lower minor leagues, he filled the roles of third-base coach, batting-practice pitcher, trainer, and traveling secretary. Minor-league pitching coach Goldie Holt helped with preseason workouts, but most of the work during the season fell on Lasorda and fifteen-year-old Zack Minasian, who was in

---

* Hall was one of more than 100 professional baseball players to serve in the Vietnam War.

his second season as Ogden's clubhouse boy. He'd landed the gig because his father, Eddie, managed the Cocoanut Grove, a supper club at the Ambassador Hotel in Los Angeles that served as a popular hangout for celebrities, including members of the Dodgers organization. Lasorda became friends with Eddie and invited Zack to work with him in Ogden. "I imagined I was the only fourteen-year-old in the world who was doing what I was doing," recalled Minasian. "It was just a fantastic experience that was very, very impactful on my life."[12] The experience was so impactful that Minasian would later manage the Texas Rangers' clubhouse.*

From the first day of practice, Lasorda instilled in his players his love for the Dodgers and his disdain for the San Francisco Giants and their Pioneer League affiliate, the Salt Lake City Giants. "He hated the Giants," said Burchart, "Hated them. He pounded that into your head." In one particular game, Lasorda ordered Burchart to drill Salt Lake City's third baseman with a pitch. He followed his manager's instructions, throwing a fastball up and in. The pitch shattered the hitter's bat and knocked him to the ground. "That started a big brawl," remembered Burchart. "Lasorda said, 'That's the best knockdown pitch I've ever seen. You got a strike, and you broke his bat!'"[13]

Lasorda's club finished sixteen games ahead of the last-place Giants and won a second consecutive Pioneer League pennant. With the league title already clinched and nothing to play for on the final day of the season, he rewarded first baseman Carmine Marceno for getting a game-winning hit earlier in the season by playing him at all nine positions. The gesture made Marceno feel like a million dollars and gave him a cherished memory that would last a lifetime. Lasorda realized that the majority of his players would never sniff the big leagues, so he tried to create experiences and teach lessons that they could carry with them after baseball.

The Koufax-less Los Angeles Dodgers did not enjoy the same success as Lasorda's Ogden Dodgers that season. Los Angeles plummeted to eighth place in the ten-team NL with a 73-89 record. The team's pitching remained solid but not dominant enough to overcome the lineup's short-

---

* Three of Zack Minasian's four children (Rudy, Perry, Calvin, and Zack) would also go on to work in professional baseball. As of 2025, Perry and Zack worked as general manager of the Los Angeles Angels and San Francisco Giants, respectively, and Calvin served as director of equipment and clubhouse services for the Atlanta Braves.

comings. The Dodgers' .236 team batting average and 82 home runs were league-worst, while their 3.2 runs per game barely edged the last-place Mets. The team had been deficient in power for years, but now it also lacked speed, stealing just 56 bases. With neither the prospect capital to make impactful trades nor major league-ready talent to boost a listless lineup, the Dodgers' near-term future looked bleak.

Bavasi blamed his team's struggles on the amateur draft. "The draft rule really hurt us," he told the *Los Angeles Times* in June of 1967. "For two years after the draft was started, we finished first. That meant we got the last shot in the draft. If there hadn't been a draft, we naturally would have made a pitch for boys like Rick Monday. With the draft, we had no chance."[14]

It was hard to argue with Bavasi's assessment. Under the pre-draft system of player procurement, the Dodgers' farm system had churned out prospects like an assembly line. In 1960, the Triple-A Spokane Indians' roster included the likes of Willie Davis, Ron Fairly, and Frank Howard. Three years into the amateur draft era, the Dodgers had fallen back to the pack. "The draft is a good equalizer," said Bavasi at the time, "no doubt about it ... Now you work hard, and it doesn't do you any good."[15]

If the Dodgers were to return to relevance, they would need to replenish a struggling roster and barren farm system by way of the amateur draft. That onus would fall on the scouting department, a group of baseball lifers whose names rarely appeared in newspapers, but whose impact would be felt for years to come.

THE SCOUTS

"Scouting is an occupation where you can be wrong 90 percent of the time and still hold a job. If 15 percent of the players you draft make it to the bigs, you've done a helluva job."—Los Angeles Dodgers scout John Keenan

ALESSANDRO CAMPANI WAS BORN IN 1916 ON THE GREEK ISLAND OF KOS, which had been under Italian occupation since the end of the Italo-Turkish War four years earlier. He was the result of a love affair between a local teenage girl named Aphrodite "Tulla" Hazzis and an Italian army captain named Giuseppe Campani. Ostracized by her family and shunned by the aristocratic Campani clan in Italy, Tulla took her son and boarded the New York-bound SS *Conte Rosso* during the summer of 1922. When they arrived at Ellis Island, an immigration officer added an *s* to Alessandro's surname because it sounded more Greek. Alessandro Campani became Alexander Campanis.

Tulla worked as a seamstress, scraping together enough money to rent an apartment in Manhattan's Upper West Side. She found ways of stretching her meager income during the Great Depression. Campanis later remembered her returning half of a perfectly good watermelon, complaining it was bad so the grocer would give her a new one. Tulla could also turn a few pennies worth of lentils into a delicious soup. "We ate that soup because we were poor," Campanis recalled, "but my friends used to come around and beg for that soup."[1]

Campanis spoke Greek at home, learned English at school, and became fluent in Spanish hanging around Puerto Rican kids in his neighborhood. At one point during his youth, he overcame a leg infection so severe that doctors contemplated amputation. He recovered and ultimately grew to be a solid six feet tall and 185 pounds. Preternaturally athletic, he demonstrated enough skill as a high school ballplayer to garner offers from the Yankees and Giants, but Tulla insisted he go to college. Campanis capitulated to his mother's wishes, attending New York University, where he obtained an education degree and captained the baseball and football teams. The Brooklyn Dodgers signed him after his senior year on the recommendation of Leo Durocher.

Campanis's baseball career would be stalled by a shoulder injury and interrupted by World War II. In 1943, the infielder played in seven games with the Dodgers, recording two hits in 20 at-bats. He would never play in the majors again. As of 2025, he remained the only native of Greece to play in the major leagues. Following two years in the Navy during the war, Campanis played shortstop alongside Jackie Robinson on the Dodgers' Triple-A Montreal Royals, a year before Robinson integrated the major leagues. Campanis worked with Robinson, who had played shortstop for the Kansas City Monarchs, on second-base defense. The double-play partners also roomed together on the road.

Campanis took a managerial job in the Dodgers' minor-league chain in 1948 and began spending winters working in the front office under team president and legendary talent evaluator Branch Rickey. As a member of the St. Louis Cardinals' front office in the 1920s, Rickey had revolutionized baseball by inventing the affiliated minor-league system. His philosophy entailed looking for prospects with raw athleticism and a positive attitude, then teaching them baseball fundamentals through coordinated instruction in the minors. Rickey frequently traded his veteran players while they still had some gas in the tank, replacing them with younger, cheaper alternatives from the farm system. The model had turned the Cardinals into perennial winners and was also successful in Brooklyn. Rickey's willingness to sign Black players and break major-league baseball's color barrier, beginning with Robinson, was a second revolutionary idea that led to the Dodgers' success under his leadership.

Campanis joined the Dodgers' scouting department in 1950, filling a variety of roles, including oversight of the minor-league camp during spring training. At Dodgertown, he taught the organization's prospects baseball strategy and exhorted morality in speeches that had the cadence and inflection of a preacher. The principles he touted became known as "the Dodger Way" and formed the basis of a book he wrote, *The Dodger Way to Play Baseball*. Campanis scouted in the New York City area during the summer and spent winters mining for prospects in Latin America. He developed a numerical system for prospects, assigning a score of 60 to 80 with 70 being major-league average. A similar grading scale, now 20 to 80, is still used today.

Campanis had an impeccable eye for talent. In the winter of 1952, while conducting a baseball clinic in Puerto Rico, he discovered a five-tool teenager named Roberto Clemente. Campanis would eventually sign him for a bonus of $10,000. Major League Baseball's Bonus Rule stipulated that Clemente had to be kept on the Dodgers' major-league roster. Otherwise, he would become available to other teams in the Rule 5 draft. Much to Campanis's dismay, GM Buzzie Bavasi tried to stash Clemente with the Triple-A Royals for the entire 1954 season, limiting his playing time in hopes that no other team would notice his immense talent.* Rickey, who by then had joined the Pittsburgh Pirates' front office, wasn't fooled. The Pirates selected the eventual Hall of Famer in the Rule 5 draft. The Dodgers didn't make the same mistake a year later when Campanis signed another bonus player—Sandy Koufax.

Perhaps equally important as Campanis's ability to spot talent was his salesmanship. His signing of Tommy Davis, a highly touted athlete from The Boys' High School in Brooklyn, was a prime example. As Davis neared graduation, he was leaning toward signing with the vaunted Yankees, the team that had hosted him for a series of workouts. Two days before Davis was eligible to sign, Campanis visited him at his home. As they were talking, the phone rang. The voice on the other end of the line

---

* Clemente received only 155 plate appearances, hitting .257 with two home runs for Montreal in 1954. According to Jim Campanis Jr., Clemente became so frustrated by his lack of playing time that he considered quitting, but Al Campanis talked him out of it.

belonged to Jackie Robinson. Campanis had arranged for Robinson to call and tout the Dodgers, knowing that Davis could not say no to his idol. Campanis was right. Davis, who would become a three-time All-Star and win two batting titles over the course of an eighteen-year big-league career, signed with the Dodgers two days later.*

The Dodgers promoted Campanis to scouting director in the fall of 1957. In his new leadership role, he coached his lieutenants on strategies he had used to become a successful scout. To ensure that they were best prepared to interact with parents and sell the Dodgers brand, he put his scouts through rigorous role-playing scenarios, covering every detail from small talk to contract negotiations. Make the family feel important, he told them. Show genuine interest and ask about trophies and medals. Be a good listener and address each member of the family by name. Ask questions to stimulate a "yes" response. Your son is a big strong boy? You want your boy to go the big leagues? You want him to get there as fast as possible? Campanis believed that getting the parents to answer in the affirmative was like Newton's First Law of Motion. The momentum of yesses would carry over when it came to signing on the dotted line.

Campanis encouraged the use of other psychological tactics during salary negotiations. He instructed his scouts to write the dollar amount in large numbers, then circle it to make the figure seem impressive. He recommended a similar strategy when verbalizing the amount. "Say 'ten thousand dollars' quickly with an air of triviality so that it sounds like a very small sum," he wrote in one department-wide memo sent on September 13, 1961. "Now, say 'five thousand dollars.' Say it slowly. Say it feelingly. Say it as if you were tremendously impressed with the hugeness of the amount. Haven't you now made the five thousand dollars sound larger than the ten thousand dollars?"[2]

Campanis instructed his scouts to use informative descriptions when filling out report cards. Indicating that a hitter has "good form" was not enough. He wanted to be able to visualize a prospect based on a scout's report. Does the hitter have a short, controlled stride? Does he have good wrist snap? Does he swing with an uppercut?

---

* Davis later coached Al Campanis's grandson, Jim Campanis Jr. Until the day Davis died, every time he saw Jim, he told him the story of how Al Campanis arranged for Robinson to call his home that day, a fact that never ceased to amaze him.

Campanis's leadership, combined with Walter O'Malley's pocketbook, proved synergistic. The Dodgers spent more than $2 million on amateur players during Campanis's first three years at the helm, landing a crop that included future All-Stars Frank Howard, Ron Fairly, Willie Davis, Pete Richert, Jack Billingham, and Jim Lefebvre.

By 1968, the Dodgers scouting department under Campanis was a well-oiled machine, consisting of twenty full-time talent hawks whose duties included scouting and coaching. Scouting was divided into amateur and pro ranks. Amateur scouts, also known as production scouts, evaluated high school and college players in preparation for the draft. They watched prospects perform in games, conducted clinics, and ran tryouts. Pro scouts, sometimes called club scouts, were typically more experienced members of the staff. Their task was to gather information on other organizations' players and provide advanced scouting reports, information that proved invaluable when the Dodgers faced unfamiliar American League competition in the World Series. In spring training, during the minor-league season, and in the fall and winter instructional leagues, several Dodgers scouts coached the organization's young prospects. Goldie Holt and Dwight "Red" Adams coached the minor-league pitchers. Monty Basgall taught fielding. And until he jumped ship to join the expansion San Diego Padres in July of '68, Dodgers legend Duke Snider served as a hitting instructor.

All told, the Dodgers scouts had hundreds of years of experience and an encyclopedic knowledge of baseball. Most of them had fleeting major-league careers—if they made it to the majors at all. Several lost their prime playing years because of World War II, some had playing careers cut short by injury and turned to scouting as a way of staying involved in the game they loved, and nearly all had deep roots in the organization. These mostly anonymous men would discover players who later became household names: Lopes, Buckner, Garvey, Paciorek, Cey, and Valentine.

In many ways, the Dodgers roster of scouts resembled a family tree. The oldest was octogenarian Harry "Ted" McGrew, whose seven decades in professional baseball began in 1895 as a batboy for his hometown Indianapolis Indians. McGrew played twelve seasons of minor-league ball, had stints as a coach and manager, and then spent seventeen years umpiring, including six seasons in the National League. When he found out he could make more money as a scout, he took a job with the Brooklyn

Dodgers. McGrew quickly rose to head scout, helping the Dodgers acquire Pee Wee Reese, Whit Wyatt, Hugh Casey, and Pete Reiser, among others. McGrew jumped to the Phillies in 1943, then returned to the Dodgers two decades later after stints with the Braves, Pirates, and Red Sox. In 1964, the Dodgers acquired rotation stalwart Claude Osteen from the Senators on McGrew's recommendation. Osteen, who represented the Dodgers in three All-Star games, became an important cog in the starting rotation behind Sandy Koufax and Don Drysdale. By then, the Indianapolis-based McGrew was semiretired, mostly scouting big-league teams as they came through Chicago.

During McGrew's tenure as head scout in the late 1930s, he hired Bert Wells, who turned to scouting after breaking an arm in a car accident, an injury that ended any aspirations of a playing career. Wells, a native Iowan, settled in Larned, Kansas, where he coached a semipro team and did some part-time scouting for the St. Louis Browns. While scouting some players in Larned, McGrew met Wells to get his opinion and came away so impressed that he hired him as a scout. Nearly three decades later, Wells remained a trusted member of Campanis's staff as Midwest supervisor.

Early in Wells's scouting career, he discovered a slick-fielding second baseman from tiny Pfeifer, Kansas. The player, whose paternal grandparents immigrated to the United States from Russia, was born Anton Romanus Basgall, but everyone called him Monty. Basgall first appeared on scouts' radar as a nineteen-year-old semipro player at the National Baseball Congress tournament in Wichita. Wells made dozens of trips to Pfeifer in an effort to sign him but repeatedly left without a signed contract. When Basgall finally put pen to paper, he said he intended to sign all along but had put off doing so because he enjoyed Wells's company.[3]

During World War II, Basgall served in the Army and played for a service team in Enid, Oklahoma. After the war, the Dodgers sold his contract to the Pittsburgh Pirates. Basgall hit .215 with four home runs in parts of three seasons with the Bucs, played a few seasons with the Hollywood Stars and Seattle Rainiers in the Pacific Coast League, and then managed in the Pirates' farm system. He rejoined the Dodgers in 1958 as a roving minor-league infield instructor and scout, helping cover the Midwest from his home in Sedalia, Missouri.

Leon Hamilton was credited with signing Don Sutton, but it was Wells and Basgall who convinced Sutton to choose the Dodgers over two other suitors, the Athletics and Astros. Sutton once said that he signed with the Dodgers "because Monty Basgall and Bert Wells treated me like an individual rather than a piece of merchandise."[4]

Another scout in the Wells lineage was Wells's own grandson, John Keenan, who had accompanied his grandfather on scouting trips since age five. Keenan accumulated so much baseball knowledge growing up that he began submitting scouting reports for the Dodgers while he was a student at Washburn University in Topeka. The Dodgers hired the twenty-one-year-old as a full-time scout in 1961. A couple years later, the Dodgers promoted Wells to supervisor with Keenan taking over his seven-state territory, which included parts of Kansas, Missouri, Nebraska, Texas, Oklahoma, Colorado, and New Mexico.

Hugh Alexander, another scout on Campanis's staff, covered a territory just as vast as Keenan's. Known as Uncle Hughie or Red, Alexander grew up poor on the oil fields of Oklahoma. For several years during his youth, his family lived in a tent until his father was promoted to oil-field supervisor and made enough money to buy a framed house. Alexander blossomed into a star as a high school athlete in Seminole, Oklahoma, eventually catching the eye of Cleveland Indians executive Cy Slapnicka —the scout who discovered Bob Feller on an Iowa sandlot.* Slapnicka signed Alexander for $250 and promised him another $1,000 if he made the big leagues.

Alexander showed enormous potential during his first two seasons in the Indians' farm system, hitting .347 with a whopping 57 home runs. The outfielder played so spectacularly that Cleveland called him up for a cup of coffee at the end of the 1937 season.† Alexander, still only nineteen, had the makings of a future star. But then an offseason accident altered the course of his life. On December 5, 1937, while working on an oil-well water pump near his family's home, he got his sleeve got caught on one of the cog gears. Before he could react, his left hand was pulled into the machinery. Alexander extricated his hand, wrapped it in a pillow case, and

---

* Slapnicka filled the general manager role for Cleveland under the title of assistant to the president. He also signed Herb Score.
† Alexander recorded one hit in 11 at-bats for the Cleveland Indians in 1937.

drove fifteen miles to the hospital in Seminole. A physician looked at the mangled appendage, gave his patient two shots of whiskey, and cut off the hand with a saw. Alexander's promising baseball career was over.

Alexander spent the first few weeks after the accident moping around and getting drunk. Then Slapnicka offered him a job as a scout. Alexander took the gig but quickly realized he had much to learn. Slapnicka, an industry pioneer known for cutting corners and signing players illegally, gave his new pupil a two-week crash course during spring training.* He taught him how to analyze the five tools (hitting, power, speed, fielding, and throwing), explained the difference between process and results, and reviewed how to break down a pitcher's mechanics. Slapnicka encouraged Alexander to ask each town's newspaper editor—or a local bartender if need be—who the best player in town was. Then he sent the young redhead on his way.

Scouting was a profession still in its infancy when Alexander joined its ranks in the late 1930s. Teams collectively employed fewer than two dozen full-time scouts, often referred to by sportswriters as "ivory hunters." Alexander didn't sign any players during his first year, but he gained valuable knowledge from other scouts, most of whom were old enough to be his grandfather. The elder ivory hunters were a rough-and-tumble bunch who drank too much and split their free time between golf courses and poker tables. Alexander joined them for cards but resisted the lure of the links, opting instead to spend more time in ballparks.

In his second year on the job, he got a tip from Oklahoma State University baseball coach Hank Iba about a pitcher named Allie Reynolds, a star fullback who hadn't played baseball until his senior year. Alexander drove his Chevy to Stillwater, where he saw the hardest throwing pitcher he had seen since Bob Feller. He had pinpoint control and released the ball at full extension—something Slapnicka taught Alexander to look for. The New York Football Giants were also courting Reynolds, who needed some convincing to play baseball. Alexander went out on a limb and offered Reynolds $1,000 without Slapnicka's permission. It was enough to secure

---

* As an example of Slapnicka's conniving methods, he sometimes failed to date contracts, so if a player ended up not being good enough, the player would simply be released without pay.

the young hurler, who went on to win 182 games in the majors and six World Series titles with the Yankees.

During Alexander's sixty-year scouting career, which spanned every commissioner from Kenesaw Mountain Landis to Bud Selig, he signed dozens of players who eventually made the major leagues. But there was one notable prospect who slipped through Alexander's grasp like a wet bar of soap. In the late 1940s, he received a tip about a promising prep outfielder in Commerce, Oklahoma. Alexander wrote the name on a piece of paper and went to talk to the kid's high school principal, who said the boy suffered a football injury and had arthritis in his legs. Alexander didn't pursue him any further. The kid's name was Mickey Mantle. "It's hard enough to make the majors if you're healthy," recalled Alexander, "and when he told me that stuff I walked out of the school. When I got to my car, I took the piece of paper and threw it away. I can still see it blowing across the parking lot."[5]

By the time the Dodgers hired Alexander as a scout in 1960, he had more than two decades of experience under his belt. Covering the southwest, he sometimes traveled as many as 60,000 miles a year. His car was like a second home. It lacked air conditioning, so during summers he often drove at night. While many of his contemporaries took offseason jobs as car salesmen or substitute teachers, Alexander continued to pound the pavement during the winter, visiting high school players' homes and college players' dormitories. The lifestyle was not conducive to a stable homelife. He had as many wives as he had fingers on his remaining hand.

Scouts who covered large swaths of land—like Hugh Alexander, Bert Wells, and Leon Hamilton—relied on a network of so-called bird dogs, part-time scouts who helped the full-timers by giving them tips on local players. If a player recommended by one eventually signed or reached the majors, the bird dog would receive a small commission. Boyd Bartley had worked as a bird dog for Wells before joining the Dodgers as a full-time scout in 1967.

Bartley grew up in the Hyde Park neighborhood of Chicago, where he was raised by his father following the death of his mother from tuberculosis when Bartley was nine. He and his dad lived above a tavern, whose proprietors paid young Boyd a dollar for each rat he killed. As a teenager, Bartley played for the House of David, a barnstorming baseball team, then captained the University of Illinois squad as a strong-armed shortstop. At the end of his senior year in the spring of 1943, he attended a tryout at Wrigley Field. Before the Cubs could secure Bartley's services, Branch Rickey swooped in and persuaded him to sign with the Dodgers for $8,000. Two days later, Bartley made his big-league debut. He appeared in nine games, recording one hit—a single off the Cubs' Claude Passeau at Wrigley Field—in 21 at-bats. After a two-week trial, the Dodgers farmed Bartley out to the Montreal Royals, where he was teammates with fellow middle infielder Al Campanis.

He played a month in Montreal before the Army came calling. While in basic training, Bartley's pregnant wife, Aletha, developed life-threatening complications, so he returned home to Chicago. Aletha and baby Thomas survived. Soon thereafter, Bartley returned to the Army to start basic training over again. While his original unit ended up fighting in the Battle of the Bulge, Bartley—who rose to rank of captain—played baseball as a recreational officer in the Philippines. In a jeep accident during his tour of duty, he suffered an injury to his throwing arm, which required multiple surgeries and dashed any hopes he had of making it back to the majors.

When Bartley returned Stateside, the Dodgers employed him as a minor-league manager for nine seasons. He and Aletha eventually settled in the Dallas-Fort Worth area, where they raised their four children. Bartley went to work for State Farm Insurance but remained involved in baseball as a bird-dog scout, passing along tips and information about local players to Wells. Bartley disliked the insurance business but turned down full-time opportunities with the Dodgers until his youngest son graduated high school. Once the kids were out of the house, he accepted a job as an area scout covering Kentucky, Ohio, Indiana, and Tennessee.*

Boyd Bartley's counterpart in the upper Midwest was Guy Wellman, a former catcher in the Dodgers' farm system. Wellman was an Indiana University graduate and veteran of World War II and the Korean War. He coached football at Valparaiso University and high school baseball in Downers Grove, Illinois, before joining Dodgers as a full-time scout in 1961.

California's dense population and warm climate produced a large

---

* In 1979, Bartley signed a right-handed pitcher named Orel Hershiser.

number of prospects relative to other parts of the country.* Thus, the Dodgers employed a half-dozen scouts to cover the West Coast, including Red Adams, Bill Brenzel, Tommy Lasorda, Greg Mulleavy †, Kenny Myers, and Ben Wade. ‡ Working under Brenzel was Washington state-based scout Dick Calvert, who'd later work for more than a half-century as UNLV's public-address announcer. Adams, a native of Parlier, California, had a playing career that mirrored Lasorda's. At age seventeen, he signed with the Los Angeles Angels of the Pacific Coast League and worked his way up through the low minors. Although his big-league experience would be limited to eight games with the '46 Chicago Cubs, Adams won 179 games over the course of 19 minor-league seasons.

The Dodgers employed Corito Varona in Latin America and a trio of experienced scouts in the Northeast. Ed Liberatore, the Dodgers' Philadelphia-based talent hawk, began his scouting career in the 1930s as a bird dog for legendary Washington Senators scout Joe Cambria. John Carey, a Baltimorean, was a former Dodgers farmhand who showed Tommy Lasorda the ropes early in his scouting career. Rudolph "Rudy" Rufer, a Queens native who had cups of coffee with the New York Giants before ultimately joining the Dodgers' scouting staff in 1959, covered the greater New York City area.

The stakes were high for Al Campanis and the Dodgers' venerable scouting department as they scoured the country for talent ahead of the 1968 January and June drafts. A reasonable goal would have been to find a few prospects who could eventually help the major-league club. Instead, they hit the jackpot.

---

* Nearly 300 of the 1,169 players selected in the 1967 draft hailed from California.

† Mulleavy, a former Red Sox and White Sox player, had worked in the organization since 1946. His son was actor Greg Mullavey, who changed the spelling of his last name to distinguish himself from his father.

‡ Wade, a former pitcher, once homered off Warren Spahn twice in the same game. He won 19 games for the Brooklyn Dodgers over two-plus seasons in the early 1950s. In 1973, he would become the Dodgers' scouting director. The Dodgers would draft and sign Rick Sutcliffe, Dave Stewart, Mike Scioscia, Bob Welch, Steve Sax, Orel Hershiser, John Franco, Eric Karros, and Mike Piazza on his watch.

A Philosophy Shift

"Lopes was a hell of an athlete. We used to play pickup basketball. In fact, I think he's the guy who cut my eyelid and sent me to the hospital."—
Washburn University teammate Gene Reardon

GROWING UP IN EAST PROVIDENCE, RHODE ISLAND, THE ODDS WERE stacked against Davey Lopes. His father, whose family emigrated from Cape Verde—a group of volcanic islands off the West African coast—died when Davey was a toddler. A stepfather came and went. For the most part, Davey's mother, a woman of Irish descent named Mary Rose, raised Davey and his nine siblings in a three-bedroom, one-bathroom tenement on her modest income as a housekeeper. Davey used a bat, not just to hit baseballs, but to stamp out roaches that infested the building.

Sports provided a way for Davey to pass the time and stay out of trouble, an exception being the night he spent in jail for shoplifting. "If it hadn't been for sports, there's no telling what I'd be or where I'd be," he said later. "All I had to do was step off the porch to a choice of all the things you associate with a ghetto ... drugs, vice, stealing."[1] As the oldest of five boys, Davey became the man of the house as a teenager. He tried to steer his younger siblings in the right direction, developing leadership skills that proved useful during his baseball career.

DAVE LOPES - Outfielder

Courtesy Spokane Indians.

Lopes lived in a predominantly Black neighborhood and attended La Salle Academy, a predominantly white private high school in Providence. Because he had light-brown skin, thick black eyebrows, and curly black hair, some people assumed he was Latino. Later, when he entered professional baseball, people would ask, "What the hell are you?"

"When you grow up mixed race, even as a kid you have a tough time identifying where you fit in," said Lopes. "When you're deciding what you are, you're caught in between. When you look in a mirror, what do you see looking back at you? With me, it's a person of color."[2]

Lopes's first love was basketball. At La Salle, he led an up-tempo offense as an all-state point guard and played center field for the baseball squad, although New England's inclement spring weather limited outdoor practices and games. He attacked sports with an intensity and aggression that grew out of his upbringing. Because of these traits, his coaches appointed him team captain.

After graduating high school, Lopes spent a year unloading boxes at a clothing store, keeping in shape by playing basketball in a nineteen-and-under Catholic league. His mother pushed him to go to college. When Davey told her that he planned to join the military instead, she slapped him across the face. Two months later, he was enrolled at Iowa Wesleyan College in Mount Pleasant, Iowa, where a former Providence area basketball coach, Mike Sarkesian, had become athletic director. Sarkesian, who had also grown up poor, not only recruited Lopes to play both basketball and baseball, but he also became a father figure. "He could relate to my problem, my environment," Lopes said. "The drive, the determination not to give in to the ghetto, to make something of my life, stems from my relations with him."[3]

At Iowa Wesleyan, Lopes earned first-team all-conference honors and received honorable mention from the NAIA for his basketball prowess. But the five-foot-nine, 170-pound guard realized that he had a more realistic chance of playing professional baseball. Although he wasn't an imposing presence in the batter's box, his small but sinewy frame packed a surprising amount of power. As a sophomore, he slugged nine home runs in 19 games.

At the end of Lopes's sophomore year, Sarkesian left Iowa Wesleyan to become athletic director at Washburn University in Topeka, Kansas, where he recruited Lopes a second time. "Mike could sell air conditioners to Eskimos," said Lopes. "He convinced me that it would be my best chance to get signed baseball-wise. I didn't know that it was going to be my ticket, but no one else was recruiting me. Mike was offering me the opportunity to go to a bigger school, and the brand of baseball was a little better, a little more difficult."[4]

Lopes displayed five-tool ability as a center fielder for the Ichabods, hitting .380 with nine homers and 20 stolen bases in 29 games as a junior. Bernie Bianchino played football at Washburn and worked out briefly with the baseball team that year. He decided to stick to football after watching Lopes take batting practice. "He hit about one out of every three pitches over the fence," Bianchino recalled. "He had unbelievable wrist action with the bat. I was six-foot-two, 235 pounds, and I could hit maybe one out of ten pitches over the fence. I realized pretty quickly that baseball wasn't going to be my sport."[5]

Lopes's classmates were just as awed by his ability on the basketball court. He possessed quickness, excellent coordination, and absurd jumping ability. His physical attributes, coupled with his no-nonsense attitude, made him a shutdown defender. "Davey was a defensive guru," said Washburn alum Mark Elliott, whose father, Larry Elliott, coached Lopes on Washburn's baseball team.[*] "He could really defend because he was quick and strong. He was short but stout."[6]

The San Francisco Giants selected Lopes in the eighth round of the 1967 June Amateur Draft, but he turned down their offer on the advice of Sarkesian, who told him he could improve his draft position and earning potential by waiting.[7] Lopes returned to Washburn for his senior year, playing one final season of basketball while earning a degree in elementary education.

Because he didn't sign with the Giants, Lopes was among the pool of players eligible for the secondary phase of the next draft the following January. Although the best talent typically came out of the more expansive June pool, a few future stars, including Carlton Fisk and Ken Singleton, were January signees during the few years of the draft. The Dodgers, having signed only one future big leaguer from their first two January drafts,[†] selected Lopes in the second round.[‡] After the conclusion of the college basketball season, Dodgers scout John Keenan, a fellow Washburn alumnus, signed him for a bonus of $10,000.

All told, the Dodgers picked twenty-three players in the two phases of

---

[*] Larry and Mark Elliott both played in the Dodgers organization. Larry signed with the Brooklyn Dodgers in 1955 and played one year in the minor leagues. Mark Elliott was drafted in the sixth round of the 1977 MLB June Amateur Draft and played three years of pro ball. His minor-league teammates included Ron Kittle, Orel Hershiser, Steve Sax, Alan Wiggins, and Alejando Peña.

[†] In January 1966, the Dodgers drafted and signed Stanford catcher Jim Hibbs, who played in three games with the 1967 California Angels.

[‡] The Dodgers' first-round pick in the secondary phase, Marv Galliher, was scouted and signed by Tommy Lasorda. The outfielder/corner infielder hit .286 in eight seasons of affiliated baseball before injuries cut his career short.

the January draft, the most of any team.* Marking a notable shift in philosophy, only five of the Dodgers selections, (22 percent) were pitchers. In the first three years of the draft, they had used 40 percent of their picks on pitchers. Of the ten players who signed, only Lopes and Geoff Zahn, a left-handed pitcher out of the University of Michigan, would make the big leagues.†

IN THE WEEKS LEADING UP TO THE JUNE DRAFT, AL CAMPANIS SOUGHT advice from his friend Al LoCasale, who had experience scouting and drafting in the National Football League. The pair had first met at a coaching clinic in the late 1950s, when LoCasale was a graduate assistant with the USC football team. LoCasale, having read books and articles Campanis wrote on coaching, was already an admirer of the Dodgers executive. After the two met in person, Campanis became a mentor to LoCasale, who went on to serve as director of player personnel for the San Diego Chargers before joining the Cincinnati Bengals front office. As a football executive, LoCasale recognized the inexact nature of the amateur draft but sought to gain an advantage over his opponents through intense preparation and fine-tuned coordination. Recognizing the parallels between the football and baseball drafts, Campanis reached out to LoCasale for advice. The mentor had become the mentee.

"We spent a lot of time talking about organization and preparing paperwork," recalled LoCasale, who later became an executive with the Oakland Raiders, serving as Al Davis's right-hand man. "How do you evaluate your evaluators? You have to know what weight to assign various people, how to break personnel down."[8]

LoCasale told Campanis that everyone in the scouting department and front office needed to be on the same page. Speaking the same vocabulary was essential. The difference between excellent speed and good speed, for example, needed to be clearly defined. LoCasale, a proponent of taking the best athlete rather than drafting for need, also taught Campanis his system

---

* By comparison, the other nineteen major-league teams averaged fourteen picks in the 1968 January Amateur Draft.
† The Dodgers chose future big leaguer Ed Crosby in the January secondary draft, but he did not sign. George Foster (Giants), Garry Maddox (Giants), George Hendrick (Athletics), and Eric Soderholm (Twins) were all products of the 1968 January Amateur Draft.

of ranking players on a 100-scale based on fundamental skills. "He took a neophyte like me and taught me how to approach the draft, and I think this helped us," said Campanis years later.[9]

Campanis adapted LoCasale's ranking system for baseball. When Campanis and his scouts rated potential prospects, they added bonus points for mental toughness and a desire to win. "We told our scouts to look for the cream," said Campanis. "We didn't just want a major-league prospect. We wanted a Dodgers prospect. They learned to look out for the very best."[10] And the very best, in the collective minds of the Dodgers scouting department, were Bobby Valentine and Bill Buckner.

Robert John "Bobby" Valentine was born on May 13, 1950, in Stamford, Connecticut, the second of two boys born to Joseph and Grace Valentine, whose parents immigrated to the United States from Italy in the early 1900s. As Bobby was growing up, Joseph put in eighty-hour weeks as a carpenter while Grace worked full time as an office manager, though she somehow found time to volunteer at church and her kids' schools. And she never missed one of Bobby's sporting events.

Valentine blossomed as a baseball player during grade school. At age ten, he tagged along with older brother Joe to Southfield Park, where all the neighborhood teens gathered for pickup games. "Bobby was always faster and better than everyone, even as a ten-year-old going against fourteen-year-olds," Joe recalled. "You just had to see it—he was special. The second time I brought him to the park, when we chose up sides, my older friends all wanted to take him first."[11]

Valentine routinely made All-Star teams in Little League and led his Babe Ruth League squad to the national championships in California. Stamford fell to a team from El Segundo, California, that included future big-league pitcher Ken Brett. Valentine, a natural extrovert, showed leadership ability early on. "In practice," teammate Frank Abbott said, "if he noticed the other kids losing concentration, he would make up games to keep everyone focused and interested."[12]

BOB VALENTINE — SS & Outfielder

Courtesy Spokane Indians.

He attended Cloonan Junior High School, which, fortuitously, was closed before his ninth-grade year. Instead of returning to junior high for the ninth grade, Valentine completed ninth grade at Rippowam High School. The extra year enabled him to learn the football team's playbook as a freshman and hit the ground running—literally and figuratively—as a sophomore. In his first game, he scored the first four of his 53 prep touchdowns.

During the spring of Valentine's junior year, Lou Lamoriello, an assistant coach at Providence College and the soon-to-be coach of the Cape Cod League's South Yarmouth Indians, visited Stamford to watch him play. "I had one of those crazy games," Valentine recounted. "I hit home runs. I ran the bases. I made plays."[13] After the game, Lamoriello, who went on to a Hall-of-Fame career as a National Hockey League executive, asked Joseph and Grace if their son could play for him in the Cape Cod League, an amateur circuit typically reserved for the nation's best college players. Valentine spent the summer competing against the likes of Thurman Munson, a catcher from Kent State University, and showcasing his skills to pro scouts.

Valentine, the first three-time all-state football player in Connecticut history, possessed talents beyond the gridiron and baseball diamond. He excelled in the classroom, won ballroom-dancing competitions, and landed the lead role in a school play. Scholarship offers poured in from the nation's top universities, including Notre Dame, Miami, Michigan, USC, and several Ivy League schools. Dodgers owner Walter O'Malley, a Penn alumnus, personally reached out to Valentine and encouraged him to attend his alma mater. Another former Quaker, Yankees president E. Michael "Mike" Burke, invited Valentine to Yankee Stadium and arranged for him to meet his favorite player, Mickey Mantle. As a photographer snapped their picture, Mantle whispered in Valentine's ear, "I hope you have to go through this shit someday, kid."[14]

Valentine was offered a full-ride scholarship to play both football and baseball for USC, a powerhouse in both sports. The baseball program fielded perennial College World Series contenders under legendary baseball coach Rod Dedeaux, and the football team, coached by John McKay and led by running back O.J. Simpson, defeated Indiana in the 1968 Rose Bowl and finished as 1967 consensus national champion. McKay planned to replace Simpson with Valentine when the former turned pro. In the fall of '67, USC treated Valentine like a VIP during a recruiting trip. He toured the campus with Simpson, met quarterback Steve Sogge—a two-sport athlete who played catcher on the Trojans baseball team—and enjoyed a performance by Diana Ross and The Supremes at the Cocoanut Grove. While attending a fall baseball game during the same trip, a scout named Tommy Lasorda tapped Valentine on the shoulder and handed him his business card and a transistor radio with "Dodgers" inscribed on the front. "Don't tell anyone where you got this," said Lasorda, "but the Dodgers really like you."[15] Later that day, Valentine and Lasorda encountered each other at a barbecue for baseball recruits at Dedeaux's home. Valentine offered to go outside and demonstrate his swing, showing an assertiveness and desire that impressed Lasorda, who saw a bit of himself in the youngster. Valentine returned to the East Coast and shortly thereafter signed a letter of intent with USC.

STEVE SOGGE - Catcher

Courtesy Spokane Indians.

The Dodgers' other top-ranked prospect was William Joseph "Bill" Buckner, a first baseman out of Napa High School in Napa, California. Bill was six feet tall and 185 pounds with a bushy brown unibrow and prominent cheekbones. He had an older brother named Bob and a younger named Jim. All three were ballplayers.* "We lived out in a subdivision in

---

* Bob, also known as Bobby, was drafted in the thirty-seventh round of the 1966 MLB June Amateur Draft by the Atlanta Braves. He'd play five seasons of pro ball, including three in the Dodgers' farm system. Jim was selected by the Baltimore Orioles in the twenty-ninth round of the 1972 MLB Amateur Draft before playing nine seasons in the minor leagues.

the middle of nowhere," Bob Buckner recalled. "The two things to do were play wiffle ball in the backyard and duck hunt."[16]

When Bill was eight, his parents, Leonard and Marie, wanted him to play on the same team as Bob, so they fudged his age as nine. It worked. Freckle-faced Bill was the youngest and smallest kid in the West Vallejo-Mare Island Little League. He quickly showed confidence and ability that belied his age. "Right field was the sun field," said Bob, looking back. "Every player the coach put out in right field lost the ball in the sun and couldn't catch it. After about six right fielders, Bill went up to the coach and said, 'Put me out there. I can catch it.' Sure enough, the coach put him out there and he never missed a fly ball."[17]

That same summer, Buckner's team faced the top pitcher in the league, a twelve-year-old named Gary Encerti, who later pitched in the New York Mets organization. Encerti had pitched multiple no-hitters that season. Before the game, Bill walked up to him, gestured to the letters on his jersey and said, "Gary, throw me one right here."[18] When Bill came to bat, Encerti indeed threw him a letter-high heater, which Bill drilled it back through the box for a single. It was the only hit Encerti allowed that day.

In Bill's early teen years, his father's life spiraled out of control. Leonard struck another car head-on while driving drunk, causing serious injuries to himself and a couple in the other car. After surgery and a prolonged hospitalization, Leonard's alcohol use escalated, and he abused prescription drugs. Eventually, Marie filed for divorce. In September 1966, Bill had just started his sophomore year of high school when forty-one-year-old Leonard Buckner took his own life by overdosing on sleeping pills.

Bill coped with the unthinkable tragedy by throwing himself into sports and schoolwork. As a tight end on the football team, he set records for receptions and yards in a season and career. He also started at guard for the basketball team. But baseball is where Bill Buckner saw his future. His eye-popping batting averages of .667 and .529 as a junior and senior, respectively, proved that his goal of playing in the major leagues was no pipe dream.*

Boasting a 3.5 GPA in high school, Buckner planned to attend college,

---

* Buckner's statistics came in a small sample size, his high school season consisting of only 12 games.

ultimately narrowing his choices to Stanford and USC. Stanford baseball coach Ray Young visited the Buckners and brought along a young football coach named Dick Vermeil, who had worked at Napa Junior College a year earlier. Young said he had one full scholarship remaining and offered it to Bill. A week later, Bill flew to Los Angeles to visit USC. He attended a barbecue at the home of Dedeaux, the USC coach, along with Casey Stengel and several of the nation's top prep baseball players, including Bobby Valentine. That visit swayed Buckner to commit to USC. But professional baseball teams were also interested. Angels scout Joe Gordon, who had a Hall-of-Fame playing career with the Yankees and Indians, said Buckner "had the finest swing I saw anywhere on the West Coast." Buckner had developed a compact hitting stroke with power to all fields. Gordon observed that the young first baseman had "complete control of his bat and his body."[19]

A week before the draft, Campanis and the Dodgers brass had yet to decide whom they would draft in the first round. One certainty is that they would target bats. The offense-starved club needed to balance out a roster that had been top-heavy on pitching for years. "At the time, we couldn't get a hit," Campanis said later. "If you're hungry, you eat."[20]

Some within the organization pushed for Greg Luzinski, an All-American football star and slugging first baseman from Notre Dame High School in suburban Chicago. Campanis stopped in the Windy City on his way to the draft in New York to see Luzinski play a doubleheader, but the games were rained out. Campanis continued east to see Valentine one last time before draft day.

Besides comparing players' skills and potential, Campanis and company had to consider the likelihood that a player would sign. Five days before the draft, Valentine told the Dodgers that he planned to go to college and would not sign if selected.[21] Campanis, who could be very persuasive, knew that bonus money, the lure of Hollywood, and the opportunity to wear Dodger blue could change a player's mind. Each pick was a calculated gamble. This much became clear: the offense-starved Dodgers needed to sign whomever they chose in the higher rounds. And the clock was ticking.

JUNE HAUL

"Scouting is not necessarily only what you see but what you think you will see. This is what makes our job tough, but it also gives you a deep sense of satisfaction when a player's development concurs with your earlier evaluation."—Al Campanis, internal memo to the Dodgers scouting department, March 8, 1968.

JUST AFTER MIDNIGHT ON JUNE 5, 1968, ROBERT KENNEDY, WINNER OF California's Democratic primary, delivered a victory speech at the Ambassador Hotel in Los Angeles. Days earlier, he had visited the Dodgers' clubhouse and conversed with Don Drysdale. Kennedy opened his speech by congratulating Drysdale, who had blanked the Pittsburgh Pirates at Dodger Stadium earlier in the evening for an unprecedented sixth consecutive shutout. The Dodgers ace had now tossed 54 consecutive scoreless innings, a new National League record. "I hope we have as good fortune in our campaign," said Kennedy, who then went on to thank his dog, Freckles, and his wife, Ethel. "Not in order of importance," he joked.[1] Following his brief remarks, Kennedy made his way through a crush of reporters. While cutting through the hotel kitchen en route to the press room, he was wounded by an assassin's bullet. Kennedy would succumb to his injuries early the next morning of June 6. Hours after he was pronounced dead, with the nation in a collective state of shock, Major League Baseball's June draft proceeded as scheduled in a ballroom at the Americana Hotel in New York City.

Baseball executives gathered with their draft lists and optimism that could perhaps only be matched on Opening Day. No other day of the year provided a better opportunity for an organization to replenish its talent supply. And the Dodgers needed talent. With the fifth pick overall, they targeted Valentine and Buckner, but there was a strong possibility that neither would be available when their turn came. The Mets and Yankees—two teams in close proximity to Valentine, owned the first and fourth picks, respectively. It just so happened, however, that the Mets zeroed in on two prep players from California—shortstop Tim Foli and hard-throwing pitcher Lloyd Allen.* "We didn't decide until after midnight and we had to make a late call to the coast to check on Foli's physical condition," recalled Mets scouting director Nelson Burbrink. "We had been undecided between Foli and Lloyd Allen, a right-handed pitcher, but the fact that we might need a little hitting made the difference and we took Foli."[2]

The Mets gave Foli a bonus of $74,000—the second highest in the '68 draft. He'd go on to have a sixteen-year big-league career as a light-hitting infielder, but a short fuse would prematurely end his Mets tenure. Foli showed his fiery nature during Rookie ball in Marion, Virginia. "He would argue extensively with the umpires, and he'd be kicked out by the third or fourth inning," recalled Mets executive Joe McDonald. "We told him, 'You can't play the game if you're in the clubhouse.'"[3] In '72, the Mets traded Foli to the Montreal Expos as part of the Rusty Staub trade after he engaged in fights with teammate Ed Kranepool and coach Joe Pignatano.

After the Mets picked Foli, the Oakland Athletics chose Pete Broberg, a high school pitcher from Palm Beach, Florida. Many scouts rated Broberg as the top prep arm in the country, but it was well known that he had committed to Dartmouth College, his father's alma mater. Charlie Finley took a chance, but the gamble would backfire. Broberg ultimately

---

* Foli, an elite high school quarterback at Notre Dame High School in Sherman Oaks, was recruited to play football at USC under coach John McKay. As a prep star in Selma, California, Allen pitched a perfect game in which he struck out the first 19 batters.

rebuffed Finley's $175,000 bonus offer in favor of an Ivy League education.

The next two players selected were catchers, the Astros taking high school backstop Marty Cott third, followed by the Yankees' selection of Kent State All-American Thurman Munson. The twenty-one-year-old Munson had detractors, but the Yankees scouts were not among them. "He was our first choice all the way," said Yankees farm director Johnny Johnston at the time.[4] Munson would win the Rookie of the Year Award two years later, earn Most Valuable Player honors in '76, and play in seven All-Star games before his untimely death in a plane crash in '79.

It was now the Dodgers' turn, and Valentine and Buckner were both available. Campanis and his staff rated Buckner as a better hitter but Valentine as a superior runner and all-around athlete. They went with Valentine. Campanis later learned that the Cleveland Indians, who had the sixth pick, planned to take Valentine if he was still available. Cleveland instead settled for prep shortstop Michael Weaver, who'd peak at Double-A.

On the day of the draft, Valentine sat by the phone, waiting on pins and needles as the hours passed. Finally, at around 8:30 p.m., the phone rang. The voice on the other end belonged to Fresco Thompson, who had succeeded San Diego-bound Buzzie Bavasi as the Dodgers' general manager just days earlier. Thompson informed Valentine that the Dodgers had drafted him in the first round. He said Campanis would call the next day and hung up.

As the rest of the first round played out, Luzinski went to the Phillies with the eleventh pick, Lloyd Allen went to the Angels twelfth overall, and the Giants took Gary Matthews seventeenth. When the Dodgers' turn came back around in the second round, Buckner was still on the board. Campanis was elated.

The Dodgers had snagged their top two choices. They continued to prioritize offense as the draft unfolded, taking future big leaguers Tom Paciorek, Joe Ferguson, and Bob Gallagher in the fifth, eighth, and seventeenth rounds, respectively.* In fact, twenty-nine of the team's first forty

---

* Of the fifty-four players the Dodgers selected in the regular phase after round seventeen, only one—Bob Sheldon (fifty-second round)—would play in the major leagues. Sheldon did not sign and was drafted four years later by the Brewers.

picks were position players. Doyle Alexander, a prep pitcher from Alabama recommended by scout Leon Hamilton, went to the Dodgers in the ninth round as only their second pitcher selected.

By the fifty-fourth round, every team had bowed out except for the Dodgers, who kept drafting through the seventy-first round. With no limits on the number of players a team could select, they used the late rounds to build a surplus, echoing an old adage passed down from Branch Rickey: out of quantity comes quality. There was also the question of how many players would actually sign. Better to have negotiating rights with too many players than not enough.

PETE SCARPATI – Pitcher

Courtesy Spokane Indians.

The Dodgers used the late rounds to take fliers on a number of arms from the Northeast. The strategy reflected an organizational belief that pitchers from northern states pitched less and thus had fresher arms. All told, the Dodgers drafted eight pitchers from New York and New Jersey, more than the Mets and Yankees combined.

The late-round selections included sixty-eighth rounder Pete Scarpati, a pitcher from St. Francis College in Brooklyn. The Dodgers had discovered the righty through a tip from Steve Lembo, who worked as a bird-dog scout for Rudy Rufer. Lembo happened to be Scarpati's boss at a Brooklyn department store, Abraham & Straus. Scarpati raised his stock in the spring of '68 by shutting out a St. John's University team that advanced to the College World Series. The Atlanta Braves had expressed interest but never called his name. Thirty-one rounds after the Braves' last pick, the Dodgers did. Scarpati would make it as high as Triple-A.

The Dodgers continued to add offense the following day in the secondary phase, choosing Michigan State University third baseman Steve Garvey in the first round (thirteenth overall). It was a dream come true for Garvey, who grew up a Dodgers fan in his hometown of Tampa, Florida. His parents, Joe and Mildred "Millie," moved to Tampa from Long Island, New York, while Millie was pregnant with Steve. Garvey's paternal grandfather, a Brooklyn police officer whose beat included Flatbush, patrolled the streets around Ebbets Field on game days, relishing in the cheers emanating from the ballpark. Another familiar sound in the neighborhood was the voice of Dodgers announcer Red Barber, which radiated from homes and businesses like a giant surround sound system. In Florida, Joe and Millie, along with Millie's parents, had a short-lived venture in the motel business. The motel was off the beaten path and lost money, so they sold the property. Millie got a job as a secretary and Joe drove buses, first for city transit and then for Greyhound.

Garvey adopted his parents' passion for baseball and his father's love of the Brooklyn Dodgers. In his salad days, Steve played out entire games in the backyard, usually between the Dodgers and Yankees. He'd meticulously lay out lineups using baseball cards and mimic the batting stances of each player. Tossing the ball up in the air, he'd take a mighty hack. If he hit the ball into the tree, it was a single. If it went into the neighbor's lawn, it counted as a home run.

In late March of 1956, Greyhound assigned Joe to drive the Dodgers' charter bus from the Tampa airport to St. Petersburg's Al Lang Field, the Yankees' spring-training home. Joe allowed Steve to play hooky and tag along. They picked up the bus early in the morning and drove to the tarmac. As they stood in front of the bus and waited, the Dodgers' team plane descended from the pink-gray sky. When the team decamped the plane, Steve's baseball cards suddenly came to life. Walter Alston. Pee Wee Reese. Gil Hodges. Duke Snider. Jackie Robinson. Roy Campanella. Steve was in awe. His day got even better when the bus arrived at the ballpark, and the equipment manager asked him to be a batboy for the day. He was living every kid's dream.

For the next six years, whenever the Dodgers came to town during spring training, they requested Joe Garvey as a driver. Occasionally, he got assigned to drive the Yankees or Tigers, too. Each time, he'd bring Steve along to serve as batboy. Hanging around big leaguers, Garvey learned baseball lingo and some words he probably shouldn't have. He observed the players' mannerisms and how they interacted with coaches and fans. He noticed that Reese and Hodges, for example, always found time to sign autographs. Hodges, in particular, left an indelible impression on Steve. The soft-spoken superstar asked Steve about school and played catch with him during pregame warmups.

Garvey didn't get a hit during his first year in Little League, but he kept practicing and improved his hand-eye coordination by hitting grapefruits with a stick. Within a few years, he made his league's All-Star team. When his mother asked what he wanted for Christmas, he picked out a $25 glove. "That's a lot of money," she said. Steve responded, "Mom, look at it this way. Twenty-five dollars now will bring you $25,000 later on."[5]

In grade school, Garvey, an only child, helped care for his maternal grandmother, who suffered from a neurological disorder. He'd go to her house after school to vacuum, make dinner, and even help her to the bathroom. Garvey was equally dedicated to his chores at home and was obsessively fastidious. "His bed was always made, and his small room was kept just so, each of his little things in its proper place," wrote Peter J. Boyer of the *Los Angeles Times*. "His little shoes were all nicely paired, toes pointing in the same direction; his shirts hung neatly together in the closet, separate from his crisply creased pants."[6]

As a student at Chamberlain High School in Tampa, Garvey wore loafers, starched button-down shirts, and Hagar slacks. Every hair on his head was always in the right place. He was polite to classmates and treated his teachers with respect. The honor roll student played quarterback on the football team and manned the hot corner for the baseball team. Garvey was the kind of guy fathers hoped their daughters would bring home.

Like ants on sugar, scouts began showing up to Garvey's games during his sophomore year. He hit .425 that season and continued to improve as an upperclassman, eventually capturing the county batting title with a .465 average as a senior. As a five-foot-nine, 178-pound senior quarterback, he earned all-city and all-conference honors.

Despite Garvey's impressive baseball credentials and the interest of scouts, he and his parents agreed that it would be best to further his education and use college as a vehicle for professional baseball. After all, he'd be the first person in his family to earn a college degree. Curiously, neither the University of Florida nor Florida State showed much interest. Years later, Garvey learned that some schools shied away because they figured he would turn pro within a year and didn't want to waste a scholarship. Chamberlain's assistant baseball coach had played for Michigan State University coach Danny Litwhiler when Litwhiler worked at Florida State and put in a good word for Garvey, who traveled to East Lansing with his parents for a campus visit. Because of an airline strike in the spring of 1966, the trip involved a sixty-four-hour roundtrip bus ride. The arduous journey proved worthwhile. Garvey came away impressed by the campus and liked the idea of getting away from home. He received a full-ride baseball scholarship offer and was asked to play football by coach Duffy Daugherty. Despite making his intentions clear to scouts and the press, the Minnesota Twins drafted him in third round of the 1966 June Amateur Draft. Garvey turned down the Twins' modest offer without hesitation.

Garvey continued to thrive on the baseball field as a Spartan, especially with a bat in his hands. He hit .450 with the freshman team and .376 with the varsity squad as a sophomore while tying the school record with nine home runs. Garvey was strikeout-prone, but he had an uncanny ability to accept failure and remain even-keeled. If an umpire made a bad call, it wouldn't faze him. If he struck out in his first three at-bats, he would get a clutch hit in his fourth.

"He hit the ball as hard as anyone I'd ever seen," recalled teammate Bill Linne. "If somebody threw it down the middle, the pitcher was in trouble because he would just drill it back at him. If the pitcher threw it inside, it was gone."[7] Garvey's massive arms, which he began sculpting with barbells in high school, supplied his considerable power. His fifteen-inch forearms were Popeye-like, and his biceps were equally impressive. A half-century later, Shirley Linne—Bill's wife and a fellow Michigan State alum—recalled that she hadn't seen many people in her lifetime with arms like Garvey's.

"He knew he was going to be a great player," said Bill Linne. "Some people would say it was cockiness, but if you don't have confidence, you're probably not going to play major-league ball. My jersey number was nineteen, so I put that in my helmet. Steve didn't put his number in his helmet—he put a Superman *S* in his helmet. He deserved it. He was the best player I ever played with or against. And a clutch hitter."[8]

Scouts liked Garvey's hitting ability, but they questioned his throwing arm, which he hurt during an intrasquad football game during his freshman year. He didn't project as outfielder, was suspect at third base, and didn't have the prototypical height of a first baseman. Jim Fanning of the newly formed Major League Scouting Bureau wrote in his report of Garvey that his "bat and desire will have to carry him."[9]

Garvey's power and aggressive approach at the plate are what impressed Dodgers scout Guy Wellman, who watched Garvey play several times. The Dodgers rated prospects as either "chance" or "definite." Players labeled as definite prospects were projected to be in the majors within three years. Wellman graded Garvey as a definite prospect. "You knew he wanted it," said Wellman. "I rated him as an outstanding hitter, with average running speed and below-average arm. But he had power to all fields, and that's hard to find. We feel we can teach someone to hit, but we can't teach power."[10]

Bert Wells traveled to Iowa City in late May 1968 to cross-check Wellman's glowing report. In the doubleheader against Iowa, Garvey homered and doubled in each game, and Wells was sold. The Dodgers took him thirteenth. Half of the twelve players selected ahead of Garvey never reached the majors.*

In round two of the secondary phase, LA nabbed right-handed pitcher Sandy Vance, a hard-throwing junior from Stanford University who had

---

* Of the six players taken ahead of Garvey who reached the majors, only Bart Johnson (White Sox) and John Curtis (Red Sox) had productive major-league careers.

been a highly regarded prospect since his prep days in Pasadena. The Angels had selected Vance in the second round of the inaugural 1965 draft, but he felt he wasn't physically or emotionally ready for pro baseball. He enrolled at Stanford and fashioned a record of 26-3 over three seasons.

The Dodgers selected third baseman Ron Cey (pronounced *Say*) in the third round of the secondary phase. The former Tacoma, Washington, prep star was originally drafted by the Mets in the nineteenth round of the 1966 June draft but opted to attend Washington State University on a baseball scholarship rather than risk exposure to the Vietnam War draft. As a full-time student, he received a military draft deferment and enlisted in the Army Reserve. At five-foot-ten and 180 pounds with short arms and legs, Cey did not possess a prototypical athletic build. Washington State baseball coach Chuck Brayton nicknamed him "Penguin" because his running stride resembled a waddle. Cey's unusual gait and atypical physique didn't seem to pose any limitations. He hit .396 as a freshman and gained national exposure playing in back-to-back Stan Musial AABC World Series as a member of a summer semipro team called the Cheney Studs.* During his sophomore season with the Cougars, he hit .362 and led the Pac-8 Conference with eight home runs.

The San Francisco Giants took a close look at Cey but shied away. Giants farm director Jack Schwarz, who once called Cey "a dumpy little fellow," sent three of his top scouts to check him out.[11] None would recommend him because of his body type. Dodgers area scout Dick Calvert and his supervisor, Bill Brenzel, formed a more favorable opinion.† They liked Cey's quick, explosive swing. Brenzel had once signed six-time All-Star Jim Gentile, who swung with such force that he would bruise his back.‡ "My father always thought a fast bat was a barometer of

---

* The Studs were so named because their sponsor was the Cheney Lumber Company, launched by Ben Cheney, the Tacoma Rainiers owner whose claim to fame and fortune was the invention and marketing of the uniform eight-foot 2×4 stud used in construction. Among Cey's teammates on the Studs was future big leaguer Rick Austin.
† Brenzel, a former catcher, played in parts of three seasons with the Pittsburgh Pirates and Cleveland Indians and once barnstormed with Babe Ruth. He spent seventeen seasons in the minors, mostly in the Pacific Coast League.
‡ In a 2025 interview with the author, ninety-year-old Jim Gentile confirmed that he indeed swung so hard he routinely bruised his back. Dodgers coaches tried breaking him of the habit by having him take half swings in the batting cage. They even outfitted him with a pad to

a good ballplayer," recalled Brenzel's son, Gary. "If you could run fast, and you had a good arm, and you bruised your back, he was for you."[12] Al Campanis personally evaluated Cey when the Cougars played a twin bill at UCLA. The Penguin swatted five hits, including a home run, in eight at-bats, cementing his place on the Dodgers' draft board.

Another notable player the Dodgers chose in the secondary phase was fifth-rounder Bill Seinsoth, a power-hitting first baseman who led USC to the 1968 NCAA College World Series title, earning the tournament's Most Outstanding Player Award just days after the draft. Seinsoth opted to return to USC for his senior year and would be drafted again by the Dodgers as a first-rounder in 1969. He would sign and play in Single-A Bakersfield that summer, hitting .276 with 10 home runs. Tragically, Seinsoth would die in a car accident while driving back to his hometown after the season. Many thought the six-foot-four Seinsoth was the Dodgers' first baseman of the future. "I've always felt, had the accident not occurred, we might not have had Steve Garvey playing first base for the Dodgers all those years," said USC baseball coach Rod Dedeaux.[13]

FOLLOWING THE DRAFT, THE DODGERS BEGAN NEGOTIATIONS WITH Valentine, Buckner, Paciorek, Garvey, and the rest of the team's draft picks. Choosing whom to draft was one thing. Agreeing to terms and securing a signature on a contract was another. In fact, four of the Dodgers' first ten picks in the regular phase did not sign.

It was a confusing time for Bobby Valentine. He had to choose between college and professional baseball, both of which were completely foreign concepts to him and his family. Valentine's father enlisted the help of someone experienced in contract negotiations—former pro football player Andy Robustelli, a Stamford native who made seven Pro Bowls during his fourteen-year Hall of Fame career. Robustelli sat with Bobby, Bobby's parents, and Campanis in the Valentines' living room the day after the draft. "Al Campanis said I had a big decision to make," recalled Valentine. "I could either go to USC and play against the best players in the Pac-8, or I could sign professionally and play against the best players

---

protect his back, but he didn't like how it felt and quickly discarded it. Gentile hit 179 home runs over the course of his nine seasons in the majors.

in the world. I figured playing against the best was the choice I had to make."[14]

Robustelli initially asked the Dodgers for $135,000 on Valentine's behalf. He ended up signing for a bonus of $65,000, more than double what his parents paid for their house. Rudy Rufer, the area scout who signed Valentine, had no doubts about the first-rounder's future. "I never met a boy as determined as he was," said Rufer years later. "He was aggressive but polite. He knew what he wanted to do. In other words, he was almost a lock to be a success at whatever he did."[15]

Most high school players would have been ecstatic about being a second-round pick. But not Bill Buckner. He was ticked off at not being taken in the first round. Campanis went to Vallejo and offered Buckner $44,000. Buckner said in no uncertain terms that he wasn't going to sign. Campanis angrily left with a blank contract. Things got so heated that Marie Buckner vowed she'd never let Campanis in her house again. A short time later, Cleveland Indians scout Loyd Christopher, who signed Bob Buckner for the Atlanta Braves two years earlier, called Bob and said, "If your brother is getting offered more than $28,000, tell him to take it because we wanted to draft him and that's all the money we were allotted to give him." After Bob told Bill what Christopher had said, Bill had a change of heart. Bill said he'd try to get another thousand bucks and also a contract for Bob, who had been released by the Braves.

Things went more amicably when Dodgers scout Bill Brenzel went to Buckner's home for the second round of negotiations. Buckner got his extra grand and signed for $45,000—the highest amount given to any second-round pick that year. After Buckner put pen to paper, Brenzel said, "I've signed the best left-handed hitter and the best right-handed hitter I've ever signed. Bill, you're the best left-handed hitter I've ever signed. And I just signed a third baseman out of Washington, and he's the best right-handed hitter I've ever signed. His name is Ron Cey. But they call him the Penguin because he runs kind of funny."[16]

Unlike his high school counterparts who contemplated signing with the Dodgers versus college, Tom Paciorek faced a choice between the Dodgers and the Miami Dolphins. The six-foot-four, 215-pound outfielder from Hamtramck, Michigan,* had attended the University of Houston on a

---

* Paciorek came from a family of athletes. Three of his four brothers played professional

football scholarship and played baseball on a whim. "The coach said, 'If you can start on the baseball team, you don't have to go through spring football,'" recalled Paciorek. "All the guys on the football team who played baseball in high school went out for baseball."[17]

Houston's baseball team of football players made it to the College World Series, finishing second to Arizona State. The brown-haired, square-jawed Paciorek, who possessed an easygoing personality and quick wit, was a three-year starter on the football team, set a school record with a .435 batting average as a junior, and earned All-American honors twice in both baseball and football. The defensive back may have turned pro in football after an excellent junior-year season, but NFL rules dictated that college players could not enter the draft until they had completed their eligibility. Paciorek returned for his senior year but missed several games because of injury and fell to the ninth round of the joint NFL/AFL draft. Paciorek had not yet signed with the Dolphins when the Dodgers selected him in the fifth round of the '68 June Amateur Draft.

Dolphins general manager Joe Thomas only called him once. "He offered a $2,000 signing bonus, a $3,000 bonus if I made the team, and a $15,000 salary, which was also contingent on making the team." recalled Paciorek. "The Dodgers offered a $20,000 bonus, so I took that instead. Every once in a while, I'll think, 'If I would have signed with the Dolphins and made the team, I could have been on that unbelievable 1972 team that went undefeated.'"

Legendary one-armed scout Hugh Alexander signed Paciorek. "I would run into Hugh every once in a while," said Paciorek, "and I'd say, 'You bandit, you got me for nothing!'"[18]

Unlike Paciorek, who had exhausted his college eligibility, Steve Garvey had the option of returning to college, giving him some leverage during his negotiations with the Dodgers. Guy Wellman was tasked with convincing Garvey to leave Michigan State. Wellman flew to Tampa to meet with Steve at his parents' ranch-style home in Lake Egypt Estates. Wellman ate dinner on the plane and then arrived to find that Millie Garvey had prepared a feast of stuffed pork chops, steak, pasta, and lemon

---

baseball. His older brother, John, famously played in a single major-league game in which he recorded three hits and two walks in five plate appearances for a perfect 1.000 batting average. A congenital spine problem that required fusion surgery ended his career prematurely. Tom's younger brother Jim played one season for the Milwaukee Brewers.

meringue pie. Wellman felt it would be rude to turn down a meal, so he ate again. As he gorged himself to the point of nearly feeling sick, he made small talk with the Garveys. He asked if they went to church and where they liked to vacation. When they finished eating, Wellman, Joe, and Steve moved to the living room and sat on plastic-covered furniture while Millie washed dishes in the kitchen. Wellman then launched into his sales pitch.

"We're supposed to pick out the parent we think is the boss and try to win him over," said Wellman years later. "I'm giving Joe and Steve my best effort, working on their sentimental feelings for the Dodgers—I'd done my research—building up my offer. Finally, I tell Steve, 'And I'm going to give you $25,000 and send you out as a Dodger!'"

Steve and Joe were pleased with the offer, but then Millie piped in from the kitchen that she would personally give Steve that much to stay in college. "Right then I knew who the boss was, and it wasn't Joe," said Wellman, who called Campanis from the Garvey's rotary phone and got approval to bump up the offer. Garvey signed for a bonus of $39,000 plus $10,000 for college tuition.

Gene Vance was perhaps not as tough of a negotiator as Millie Garvey. The traveling salesman served as a de facto agent during his son's signing-bonus meeting with Al Campanis and Tommy Lasorda. "There wasn't much negotiation … I was ready to sign because of being drafted previously," recalled Sandy Vance, who signed for $28,500 and received a succinct "no" when he asked Campanis for a used car.[19] During the meeting, Campanis mentioned to Lasorda that Vance needed to develop a more aggressive attitude toward opposing hitters. "Tommy's eyes got wide," remembered Vance, "and he said, 'Sandy, you come to me as a lamb, and you'll leave as a tiger!'"[20]

Like all teams, the Dodgers more or less employed a take-it-or-leave-it approach with players drafted in the later rounds. Their eighteenth-round pick, Arizona State University second baseman Fred Nelson,* had a year of college eligibility remaining,† so he was able to negotiate an extra three

---

* Nelson earned First Team All-America honors in 1968 after hitting .351 for the Sun Devils. A Giants fan growing up in Phoenix, he was "shocked" to be drafted by the rival Dodgers.

† ASU coach Bobby Winkles encouraged Nelson to forgo his senior year and sign with the Dodgers. "It turned out the guy who took my place was Lenny Randle, so maybe he was trying to get rid of me," quipped Nelson.

grand above the Dodgers' initial $8,000 offer. Sixty-eighth rounder Pete Scarpati, a college senior with zero leverage, received a courtesy $1,000 bonus. "I would have given them money," recalled Scarpati. "When they offered the contract, I was so willing to sign that it didn't matter."[21]

The ink had barely dried on their contracts when the players from the Dodgers' class of '68 received airline tickets from director of minor-league operations Bill Schweppe. Within a matter of days, they would report to their respective teams. Doyle Alexander, Ron Cey, and Joe Ferguson were dispatched to the Tri-City Atoms in the Northwest League. But the majority—including Bobby Valentine, Bill Buckner, Tom Paciorek, Steve Garvey, and Sandy Vance—would converge in Ogden, Utah, where they would begin their professional baseball careers playing for Tommy Lasorda.

The '68 Ogden Dodgers

"The Rookie league is their first look at professional baseball, and it gets to some of them. If they're not guided right, some future greats can be lost forever. My job is to build their confidence."—Tommy Lasorda, February 1968

DAYS AFTER CHOOSING THE DODGERS OVER USC, BOBBY VALENTINE arrived at Salt Lake City International Airport, where he was greeted by a pudgy middle-aged man who looked vaguely familiar. "Remember me?" asked the man. "I'm the guy who gave you the transistor radio. I'm Tommy Lasorda, and I'm going to be your manager."[1]

Lasorda personally chauffeured the Dodgers' first-round pick to Ogden, but other players, including Tom Paciorek, had to make the forty-mile trek by bus or taxi. Paciorek debussed in downtown Ogden and found the Ben Lomond Hotel, his home for the next three months. He hadn't yet checked into his room when Lasorda strutted through the front door accompanied by a handsome young man with a tan complexion, sideburns, and a wide smile. Lasorda greeted Paciorek and mentioned he had just returned from the airport. "The young guy who'd walked in with Tommy stepped over and introduced himself," recalled Paciorek. "It was

Bobby Valentine. Tommy told us Bobby and I were going to be roommates."[2]

Valentine was a bit awestruck. "I thought I was the hot shot, being the two-sport guy," he said decades later, "and then I realized my roommate was Tommy Paciorek. He had just played in a bowl game and went to the college baseball World Series!"[3]

Lasorda, Valentine, and Paciorek grabbed seats in the lobby and talked over the next couple of hours. More accurately, Lasorda and Valentine did the talking. Paciorek, the most reserved of the three, couldn't get a word in edgewise. "I sat there and had to listen to these two Italians go on and on with Bobby telling me what a great player he was and Tommy telling me he would soon be managing in the big leagues," remembered Paciorek. "Finally, I asked Tommy why he didn't pick me up at the airport like he did Bobby. I told him I had to take the damn bus. Tommy looked at me and said with a smile, 'Because you're not Italian.'"[4]

While they were getting acquainted, Steve Garvey walked in wearing a starched monogrammed shirt, pressed pants, and shiny shoes. He heard a booming voice across the sun-drenched lobby. At first, he couldn't see because of the glare. But as he got closer, he saw that the voice belonged to a stout man who was holding court with a couple of strapping young lads. "Are you the Garv?" asked Lasorda. After Garvey confirmed his identity, Lasorda introduced himself and said, "Your life is about to change forever."[5] He wasn't wrong.

The next morning, Lasorda decided to have a little fun at the expense of his friend Rod Dedeaux. He summoned Valentine to his room and dialed Dedeaux's number. "He told me he wanted to get on the phone with Rod," recalled Valentine, "and for me to tell him personally that I had signed with the Dodgers, just to bust his chops." When the USC baseball coach answered, Lasorda said, "Rod, I got your boy," before handing the phone over to Valentine. "I told Rod I was sorry but that I had signed a contract with the Dodgers," remembered Valentine. "I thanked him and told him I appreciated the opportunity he had given me to attend USC."[6] Lasorda then grabbed the phone and took additional pleasure in telling Dedeaux that the Dodgers had also landed another of his top recruits, Bill Buckner.

On the first day of practice, the Ogden players, ranging in age from seventeen to twenty-five, were divided into two teams for an intrasquad game. The team's rubber-armed manager pitched for both sides. In Buckner's first at-bat, he blasted one off the right-field wall. "Lasorda takes his glove off, throws it on the ground, and starts screaming at me, 'If you ever hit another ball like that off me, I'll cut my throat!'" recalled Buckner years later. "That was my first hour in professional baseball. I had no idea what to think."[7]

For the next week and a half, Lasorda led two-a-day workouts, pushing his players harder than they'd ever been pushed on a baseball diamond. He tutored Garvey on footwork and throwing, worked with Paciorek on hitting curveballs, and coached Valentine on handling pitches at the top of the strike zone. Although the Dodgers' top draft picks had flaws, their raw ability was evident. Zack Minasian immediately noticed how the ball seemed to jump off the bats of Garvey and Paciorek. Ogden's sixteen-year-old clubhouse boy knew right then that these were a pair of future big-leaguers.

Lasorda established a set of team rules early on. Infractions resulted in fines that funded an end-of-season team party. One of the costliest penalties involved bench-clearing brawls. In the event of a brouhaha, the last man off the bench had to pay $25, a hefty amount relative to the players' daily meal-money allotment of $3. The rule had the desired effect. Rather than risk a hit to their wallets, players quickly joined the fray when tempers flared.

Lasorda enforced midnight curfew by performing occasional room checks. That method wasn't foolproof, however. After hearing rumors that a few guys were burning the midnight oil, the skipper turned to an old managers' trick. He recruited an elderly gentleman who worked the night shift at the hotel and had him ask players for their autograph as they strolled in during the early morning hours. The players assumed the old guy was just a big fan, so they happily signed their names on a baseball without giving it a second thought. Minasian would retrieve the ball each morning and bring it to Lasorda, who fined the offenders when they arrived at the ballpark. The players never did figure out how their manager knew about their late-night carousing.

The players' eagerness to sign autographs may have stemmed from advice Lasorda dispensed to his team early on. To drive home his point, he told the story of Buster Maynard snubbing him at Shibe Park decades earlier. Reflecting back, Paciorek vividly recalled Lasorda's words of advice: "Make sure that when a kid asks you for an autograph, you sign it. If you blow him off, he's going to go through his life hating you and he's going to tell all his friends what a jerk you are."[8]

Both in Ogden and on the road, the team, including Lasorda, ate meals together and became fast friends. Their favorite local haunt, Chuck-a-Rama, served an all-you-can-eat buffet for $1.99.* "Tommy would round up a dozen of us and off we would go," recalled Minasian. "We would follow him as if he were General Patton leading us into battle."[9]

Over team meals and on bus rides through rural Utah and Idaho, Lasorda regaled his players with stories from his playing and scouting career. "Tommy's storytelling during the long bus rides was legendary," recalled outfielder Jim Doran. "He knew how to captivate an audience." Lasorda's story of attending the funeral of Willie Crawford's grandfather remained etched in Doran's mind decades later.[10]

Lasorda loved to eat. Moreover, he loved to eat for free. During batting practice, he'd bet his players a steak dinner that they couldn't hit a home run off his curveball. More often than not, he won the bet. On road trips, Lasorda devised a scheme to get his meals comped. When the bus arrived at a roadside diner, Lasorda would send Minasian in to speak with the manager. Minasian would explain that a bus full of ravenous baseball players was parked outside, ready to spend their meal money under one condition—that Lasorda and Minasian got to eat for free.

During one team dinner early in the season, Lasorda gave Paciorek a nickname that stuck with him like peanut butter on bread. "We all went out to eat, and everyone was ordering steaks," said Paciorek. "I really hadn't had any steaks up to that point in my life. So, I ordered these big double cheeseburgers. And from that point on I became Wimpy."[11]

Gene Covington Vance's maternal grandfather nicknamed him Sandy as an infant because of his hair color. Lasorda gave him a different moniker. "Tommy gave me the nickname Dazzy so that the fans could come to the ballpark and see 'a reincarnation of the great old-timer Dazzy Vance,'" recalled Vance. "Also, Koufax had just retired two years earlier, and I think Tommy likely felt that there should be only one Sandy, especially since my first and last names were the two greatest pitchers in

---

* As of 2025, the Chuck-a-Rama was still in business. The all-you-can-eat buffet costs around $18.

Dodgers history at that time. When I took the mound in spring training for the first time in a major-league game, Vin Scully thought someone was playing a joke on him. He had to double-check the name to be sure."[12]

Courtesy Spokane Indians.

Lasorda spent nearly every waking hour teaching and nurturing the young Dodgers prospects, dedicating extra time to Valentine, Buckner, Garvey, and Paciorek. On days of home games, Lasorda would round up the foursome for morning batting practice. After games, he took them bowling at Hilltop Lanes. "The loser had to pay for the beer and hot dogs," remembered Paciorek, who often partnered up with Lasorda.[13] During one game at Affleck Park, Paciorek injured his wrist in a collision while sliding into third base. "As I laid there in the dirt thinking I had broken my wrist," remembered Paciorek, "Tommy came running over from the third-base coaching box to check on me. 'Wimpy, Wimpy!' he yelled. 'Are you all right?' I said I was, and he said, 'Thank God. I thought it might have been your bowling hand!'"[14]

Lasorda believed in the power of self-confidence and constantly sought ways to build up his players. One night at dinner, he told a few of them to write letters to the Los Angeles Dodgers who played their same positions. "The letters said, 'Congratulations on a great career, but I'm coming to take your job soon,'" recalled Paciorek.[15] Valentine wrote to center fielder Willie Davis, Buckner penned a note to first baseman Wes Parker, Garvey addressed his letter to third baseman Bob Bailey, and Paciorek sent one to outfielder Ron Fairly. Except for Garvey, each of the players sent their letters, never stopping to consider the ramifications of openly challenging their big-league counterparts. After all, these were guys they could be sharing a locker room with someday. Naturally, the letters gave the big-league Dodgers the impression that the kids down in Ogden were a bunch of young punks. "Everyone hated us when we got to spring training!" said Paciorek, looking back.[16]

When the press caught wind of the players' bold declarations, Lasorda deflected credit for them, saying they were Buckner's idea. "I told them I didn't think they'd better write the letters," he told the *Los Angeles Times*. "It might create some ill feelings in the organization. But I sure liked their attitude."[17] Parker, nonplussed about the note he received from Buckner, later said he believed the letters were all Lasorda.[18]

Buckner, known as Mad Dog or Buck, never lacked confidence. He arrived in Ogden expecting to get a hit every time he stepped into a batter's box. "He was such a competitor right from the beginning," recalled Garvey. "Nobody was more competitive than Billy."[19] Lasorda encouraged Buckner to go up hacking, an approach that suited him well. He almost always made contact and could hit to all fields. Buck hated making outs but absolutely loathed striking out. On the rare occasion that he struck out (16 times in 275 plate appearances during the 1968 season), he'd throw his equipment or punch a water cooler in a fit of rage. Over the course of the summer, Lasorda helped Buckner control his emotions, encouraging him to take his aggression out on the opposing pitcher instead of his batting helmet.

Lasorda helped Sandy Vance in a similar way. Vance struggled early in the season and in one start against the Magic Valley (Twin Falls) Cowboys coughed up a three-run lead by loading the bases, walking in the tying run, and yielding a two-run double. When Lasorda sauntered to the mound and signaled to the bullpen for a reliever, Jack Jenkins, he asked Vance if he knew why he was coming out of the game. "Yeah, because that last guy hit a two-run double," responded Vance. Lasorda said, "No, Daz, I took you out because of the hitter before him, the one you walked. You were so angry, stomping around out here on the mound. You lost your concentration and composure, and you ruined yourself for the next hitter who hit the double."[20] Vance learned a valuable lesson that day: focus on the next pitch, not the previous one. From that day forward, Vance dominated the Pioneer League. "[Lasorda] knew which players needed encouragement and which needed a kick in the ass, and when to deliver what they needed most to help them perform," said Vance.[21]

Midway through the season, the Dodgers promoted Paciorek, raking at a .386 clip, up to Single-A Bakersfield. Even though he was climbing one step closer to the big leagues, the news devastated him. He hated to leave teammates who had become like family in just a matter of weeks. "I remember when I got called up to Bakersfield, I was crying," Paciorek said decades later. "Tommy took me to the airport in Twin Falls, Idaho. We didn't have any suitcases on our bus trips. I had two plastic Kroger bags. Tommy looked at me and said, 'Hey Wimpy, is that your Polish Samsonite?'* I was laughing through the tears."[22]

A few days after Paciorek departed, Ogden added Fred Nelson, the Dodgers' eighteenth-round pick from the June draft. The former Arizona State infielder had delayed signing while mending a broken hand suffered in his final college game. Nelson did not possess the physical strength of Garvey, the charisma of Valentine, or the athleticism of Buckner, but he played fundamentally sound baseball. He had refined his skills competing on a Sun Devils team that won the 1967 national championship. Because he made fewer mistakes than his younger, less experienced teammates, Nelson mostly avoided Lasorda's wrath. After losses, the skipper would jump on guys who missed cut-offs or made baserunning blunders. "Tommy could work them over pretty good with his ranting and raving," recalled Nelson. "I had played for [ASU coach] Bobby Winkles, who was a tough guy and disciplinarian, so I was used to it."[23]

---

* Paciorek was of Polish descent.

Nelson's ability would ultimately take him as high as Double-A. After three years in the Dodgers organization, he entered the college coaching ranks and eventually worked in player development and scouting with the Houston Astros for thirty years. Nelson came to realize that many players like himself—guys who play on the West Coast or at top college programs like Arizona State—enjoy the best facilities, most knowledgeable coaches, ideal weather, and longer schedules. Such prospects may have more advanced skills, but their potential may be tapped out by the time they reach pro ball. The Dodgers, Nelson learned from Lasorda and Monty Basgall, looked for guys in the Midwest or Northeast who had physical ability and room to develop. Players like Bill Russell, Davey Lopes, and Valentine fit that mold.

ENTERING THE LAST WEEK OF THE SEASON, OGDEN AND THE IDAHO FALLS Angels were neck and neck atop the five-team Pioneer League. Because there was an odd number of teams that year, the Angels had already wrapped up their schedule as the Dodgers played their final series against the Magic City (Twin Falls) Cowboys—an affiliate of the Atlanta Braves. Ogden, trailing Idaho Falls by one game, needed to win two of the last three games to clinch a third consecutive pennant.

On the morning of August 28, Minasian called Lasorda to deliver some unfortunate news. Starting catcher Pat Burke had caught a stomach virus and could barely move. He looked like death warmed over and felt even worse. Lasorda knew having Burke in the lineup would give Ogden its best chance to win, so he devised a plan. He told Minasian to let him rest for a bit and then bring him to the ballpark. When they got to the clubhouse, Minasian and Lasorda pushed some benches together so Burke could lie down. Lasorda suggested that Burke put his uniform on so his clothes wouldn't get wrinkled. Burke changed into his Ogden flannels and laid back down while his teammates went through their pregame routine.

Just before first pitch, Lasorda burst into the clubhouse and barked at Burke to get up because he was in the starting lineup. Dumbfounded, Burke told his skipper he couldn't play. Lasorda wasn't having it. "You're in the lineup!" he shouted. "You're catching! Let's go! Get up! The ballgame's gonna start. Get your ass up. Let's go!"[24]

A wobbly Burke got up, put on his catching gear, and hustled out to the field. He proceeded to catch Sandy Vance, who fired six scoreless frames before Magic Valley broke through with three runs in the seventh. Burke came to the plate in the bottom of the eighth with a man on base and Ogden trailing 3-2. The guy who could barely move hours earlier mustered enough energy to smash a long home run over the left-field wall, giving Ogden the lead. Vance closed the door in the ninth to seal a crucial victory.

"Tommy was a double-edge sword," said Burke. "He could be the meanest bastard you could ever imagine, or the nicest guy in the world. I got to experience both, but really, he was the greatest teacher, and he treated me and all the other guys fairly. I really loved the guy. I'd walk a mile through dog shit for him if he asked me to."[25]

Ogden suffered an 8-6 defeat the following night, setting up an all-important season finale. A victory would mean a third consecutive league pennant for Lasorda. A loss would give the Angels the title. The Dodgers scored the first five runs of the contest and built a 9-3 advantage after six frames. Magic Valley then came storming back, scoring six runs in the eighth inning to take a 10-9 lead. Lasorda's never-say-die club responded with eight runs in the bottom half of the inning. Vance, who had thrown a complete game two days earlier, came on in relief to seal the victory, recording the final four outs. The trio of Valentine, Buckner, and Garvey combined for eight runs, seven hits, and five RBI.

As the players celebrated their championship, they hoisted Lasorda on their shoulders. The manager pointed to the fans in the stands and said, "Fellas, you see those people back there? They are the most important people in your life. Don't *ever* let them down!"[26] The celebration continued in the clubhouse, where players doused each other with champagne and shaving cream. "You ain't seen nothin' yet," exclaimed Bucker during the revelry. "Wait 'til we get 'em in the World Series in Los Angeles!"[27]

Buckner won the Pioneer League batting title with a .344 average, finishing just ahead of Garvey, who hit .338 with 20 home runs in 62 games. Valentine, the team's center fielder, hit .281, posted a .402 on-base percentage, stole 20 bases, and won the league's Most Valuable Player Award. Vance won ten straight decisions on the heels of Lasorda's advice and finished the season with a 14-3 record. In 118 innings, the Stanford product compiled a league-high 150 strikeouts. The Dodgers promoted him all the way up to Triple-A for what was left of Spokane's season.

Elsewhere in the Dodgers' farm system, Davey Lopes hit .247 and swiped 26 bags in Daytona Beach. Bill Russell cranked 17 round-trippers and stole 23 bases for Bakersfield. And third baseman Ron Cey (9 HR, .878 OPS) and outfielder Joe Ferguson (12 HR, .946 OPS) showed pop with the Tri-City Atoms. The Dodgers' future was beginning to look a little brighter.

Lasorda had won three Pioneer League pennants in four seasons, so it surprised many when news circulated upon season's end that he planned to quit managing and return to scouting. A few weeks later, Dick Young wrote in *The Sporting News* that Lasorda had floated the possibility of joining Buzzie Bavasi in San Diego. Had either rumor come to fruition, the trajectory of Lasorda's life and the history of the Los Angeles Dodgers could have been vastly different. But Lasorda changed course after the Dodgers offered him a promotion he couldn't refuse. He would continue to manage, but it wouldn't be in Ogden or San Diego. Nor would it be in Single-A or even Double-A. Instead, Al Campanis entrusted Lasorda to make a huge leap from Rookie ball to Triple-A.

Next stop: Spokane.

An Organization in Transition

"You have to grow players yourself, down on the farm, like rutabagas. Trading for them is a vastly overrated technique. The Dodgers don't like to trade, and if we didn't make another trade in the next ten years it would be too soon."—Buzzie Bavasi, June 5, 1967

COMING OFF A DISASTROUS 1967 SEASON, DODGERS GENERAL MANAGER Buzzie Bavasi overhauled the roster through a series of trades aimed at improving the team's abysmal offense. Out were John Roseboro, Ron Perranoski, Bob Miller, Ron Hunt, Gene Michael, and Lou Johnson. In came Zoilo Versalles, Mudcat Grant, Len Gabrielson, Paul Popovich, and Tom Haller. It was antithetical to the Dodger way. "We make trades rarely and under special circumstances," wrote Bavasi in *Sports Illustrated* just months earlier.[1] An eighth-place finish and .236 team batting average qualified as special circumstances. There was hope within the organization that the multitude of transactions would get the Dodgers back to winning baseball in '68. After all, it had been thirty years since the franchise had endured back-to-back losing seasons. Arthur "Red" Patterson, the Dodgers' vice president of public relations and promotions, optimistically dubbed the '68 campaign "Operation Bounce Back."

Two months into the '68 season, there was more change afoot—this time involving the Dodgers front office. Bavasi, who had been in the organization for thirty years, including seventeen as GM, left to become part-owner and president of the expansion San Diego Padres, who, along with the Montreal Expos, were preparing to join the National League in '69. Walter O'Malley tapped Fresco Thompson, who had been in charge of minor-league operations, to fill the Dodgers' GM vacancy. Thompson, a former big-league second baseman and Branch Rickey disciple, had worked in the Dodgers front office since the mid-1940s.

Between the white lines, Operation Bounce Back fell flat. The revamped Dodgers lineup performed about the same as the '67 iteration. Zoilo Versalles, just three years removed from an MVP season, fell off a cliff. The former Twins shortstop hit a paltry .196, lacked power, played erratic defense, and displayed a "poor mental attitude," according to Thompson.[2] Versalles wasn't the only Dodger who failed to meet expectations, however. Infielder Jim Lefebvre, who averaged 15 home runs his first three seasons, battled injuries and showed diminished power in limited action. Ron Fairly had a second consecutive subpar season, hitting .234 with only four home runs.* First baseman Wes Parker played his usual Gold Glove-caliber defense but posted the worst offensive season of his nine-year career. The Dodgers had added aging stars Ken Boyer and Rocky Colavito, but they were shells of their former selves. Offense was down across the league in the so-called "Year of the Pitcher." The Dodgers accordingly hit 13 points below league average and finished dead last in the NL in runs scored, averaging just 2.9 runs per game.† The entire roster hit just 67 home runs with only one player, Gabrielson, reaching double digits. One of the few bright spots among the Dodgers' position-player group was the late-season emergence of twenty-one-year-old Willie Crawford, receiving his first extended look in the big leagues.

---

* In a 2012 interview with Paul Hirsch of the Society for American Baseball Research, Fairly blamed his diminished production on taller grass at Dodger Stadium. "After Sandy retired, Drysdale told Buzzie that we should lengthen the grass and slow down the infield," said Fairly. "I thought that was crazy. We were a ground-ball/line-drive team. We didn't hit the ball in the air. Well, Buzzie lengthened the grass, and it killed me. I didn't have the speed to beat out infield hits and ground balls that had been getting through for me were winding up in infielders' gloves."

† In 1968, the Dodgers team OPS+ of 90 (i.e. 10 percent below average) was one point higher than the 89 registered in 1967.

While the Dodgers offense continued to sputter, the pitching remained elite despite the loss of Sandy Koufax. Their 2.69 staff ERA ranked second in the NL behind the pennant-winning St. Louis Cardinals, whose ace, Bob Gibson, put together one of the all-time great seasons in baseball history with 28 complete games, 13 shutouts, and a preposterous 1.12 ERA. With more run support, Don Drysdale could have easily won 20 games but had to settle for a 14-12 mark. In any other year, his career-best 2.15 ERA and record-breaking streak of 58⅔ scoreless innings would have made him a frontrunner for the Cy Young Award, but Gibson won the honor unanimously.* Two other Dodgers starters, Bill Singer and Don Sutton, suffered similar fates as Drysdale. Both registered sub-3.00 ERAs but tallied losing records because of a lack of run support.

The Dodgers' longtime nemesis, Willie Mays, gave a candid critique of the Giants' arch rival. "They just don't seem to have any spark left," said the future Hall of Famer. "It looks to me like they're just waiting for October to come so they can forget about baseball. It looks like they're going through the motions. I'm sorry to see it this way because all the other Dodger teams I've seen always had plenty of fire no matter how good or bad they were going."[3]

At the end of August, the Dodgers were nineteen games under .500 and in danger of finishing in last place for the first time in sixty-three years. They ultimately avoided the cellar by winning 18 of their last 27, finishing tied with Philadelphia for seventh place with a 76-86 record.

Former Dodgers star Duke Snider, who had jumped ship to join Bavasi in San Diego as a scout, expressed pessimism about the Dodgers' immediate future. He told the *Los Angeles Times* that, in his estimation, it would take several years for the Dodgers to return to playoff contention. "The organization is in shambles," said Snider.[4]

The Dodgers front office was forced to undergo additional restructuring during the offseason. Fresco Thompson, who had been diagnosed with cancer just a few months after stepping into the GM role, died on November 20, 1968, at the age of sixty-six. To take his place, Walter O'Malley promoted Al Campanis to GM under the official title of vice president, player personnel and scouting. Campanis, another Branch

---

* Drysdale broke Walter Johnson's thirty-five-year-old record of 55⅔ scoreless innings on June 8, 1968—the first day of the June Amateur Draft.

Rickey protégé, was the definition of a baseball lifer. "Growing up, I'd be swimming in my grandpa's pool, and I'd come in for dinner," recalled his grandson, Jim Campanis Jr. "While we were waiting, he'd show me the four ways to turn a double play at second base. He showed me that a thousand times. He was always coaching. He was basically a coach who was a scout who had an eye for tools he could develop. I think that's why he was put in the GM role. He was the best fit for the way the Dodgers were operating at that time."[5]

In addition to changes in the executive ranks, the Dodgers had turnover in the minor leagues. Roy Hartsfield, who had piloted the Spokane Indians to the Pacific Coast League playoffs in back-to-back seasons, joined Walter Alston's coaching staff in Los Angeles. Further down the chain, Albuquerque manager Roger Craig and Bakersfield skipper Don Williams took jobs with the Padres, leaving the Dodgers with managerial vacancies at Single-A, Double-A, and Triple-A. Rumors swirled that the two National League expansion teams, San Diego and Montreal, might be interested in Tommy Lasorda. But Walter O'Malley's son, Peter, the Dodgers' vice president of stadium operations and soon-to-be executive vice president, wanted to keep Lasorda in the organization and told him so early that offseason.

One of Campanis's first acts as GM was to offer Lasorda a promotion to manage the Spokane Indians.* Lasorda, who had considered a return to scouting, reminded Campanis that he had been the one who had originally convinced him to become a scout. But Campanis's thinking had evolved after witnessing Lasorda's success in Pocatello and Ogden. Campanis now valued him more as a manager, although a promotion from Rookie ball to Triple-A was no small order. Handling a blend of veterans and prospects in the Pacific Coast League would be vastly different than mentoring a group of teenagers in the Pioneer League. Some people, both inside and outside of the organization, were skeptical that Lasorda's rah-rah speeches and buddy-buddy managerial style would work with more experienced players. But having some three pennants under his belt and the backing of

---

* Another of Al Campanis's first decisions as GM was to trade his son, Jim—a Dodgers catching prospect who had played sparingly during a few cups of coffee with the big club—to the Kansas City Athletics. The trade served two purposes. It gave the younger Campanis a greater chance of regular playing time and avoided any potential charges of nepotism.

Campanis and Peter O'Malley gave Lasorda the confidence to tackle to the challenge head-on. He accepted the job on November 30.

A few days later, Lasorda attended the Winter Meetings in San Francisco, where he ran into old friend Billy Martin, new manager of the Minnesota Twins. In a true pot-calling-the-kettle-black moment*, Martin told Lasorda, "You're gonna be a big-league manager someday. The only thing you gotta learn to do is control that temper of yours."[6]

When Lasorda and Campanis met over the winter to plan for the '69 season, they discussed the Dodgers' shortstop depth, or lack thereof. The organization lacked a clear long-term solution and had an immediate need at the position following the Padres' selection of Versalles in the expansion draft.† Tommy Dean, the bonus player that Campanis and Hugh Alexander identified as the heir apparent to Maury Wills four years earlier, had struggled to hit Triple-A pitching during his two full seasons in Spokane. Billy Grabarkewitz had performed well in Double-A in '68 but was coming off a serious ankle injury. That left Ted Sizemore, a converted catcher, as one the few viable shortstop options entering spring training. It became apparent to Lasorda and Campanis that Bobby Valentine might be more valuable to the big-league club as a shortstop rather than a center fielder. The Dodgers still had Willie Davis in the prime of his career, after all. Lasorda had already begun working Valentine out at shortstop in Ogden during the summer of '68 with a potential position change in mind. Valentine continued to take shortstop reps during the offseason with Rod Dedeaux. The USC coach told Lasorda and Campanis that, in his opinion, Valentine could handle the conversion. A decision was made. The Dodgers would play Valentine at shortstop during spring training and then send him to Single-A Bakersfield for further seasoning.

When assessing the Dodgers' other top prospects, Lasorda felt strongly that some players from his Ogden club—namely Buckner, Paciorek, and Garvey—were ready to compete in Triple-A. According to Lasorda, Bill Schweppe, the Dodgers' VP of minor-league operations, disagreed. Schweppe followed the Dodgers' usual practice of advancing players one level at a time. The general thinking was that rushing prospects could hurt

---

* Ironically, Martin would be fired after a single season with the Twins after brawling with his own player, Dave Boswell.

† Versalles never played for the Padres. San Diego traded him to the Cleveland Indians during the Winter Meetings.

their confidence if they struggled. Schweppe got his way. Lasorda's nucleus from Ogden would be divided amongst Bakersfield and Albuquerque.

The spring of '69 marked the first Dodgertown camp for players from the '68 June Amateur Draft. Sandy Vance, just a year removed from pitching for Stanford, was now rubbing elbows with Don Drysdale. Tommy Lasorda introduced the pair following a workout early in camp. Drysdale took one look at Vance's battered cleats and joked, "Hey kid, who gave you those shoes, Ty Cobb?" Drysdale went to his locker and returned a few minutes later with a pair of his own spikes. "Here, see if you can fill these shoes," he said. "I hope to see you pitching with me someday." Vance pitched with Drysdale's shoes on until he wore them out. "When my dad and mom found out that instead of saving them for posterity or a trophy case, I wore them out and threw them away, they couldn't believe it," recalled Vance. "But they were good shoes and a great fit!"[7]

It was also the inaugural spring training for Fred Claire, a sportswriter who had recently been hired by the *Long Beach Independent Press-Telegram* to cover the Dodgers. While socializing in the Dodgertown lounge one night, Claire, who played baseball in high school, mentioned to Lasorda that he'd like to shake off the rust and take infield practice some time. A few days later, as Claire prepared to board the Dodgers' team bus for a road trip to Orlando, Lasorda bellowed for him to come over to one of the practice fields, where Lasorda's Spokane squad was about to play Bakersfield. Lasorda mentioned what Claire had said before about playing with his team. "Why not today?" he asked.

"I said I wanted to take infield," said Claire. "I didn't say anything about playing in a game."

"Okay," replied Lasorda, "get on that bus, you chicken shit, and don't mention anything to me again about playing for my team."

The master of motivation had struck a nerve with the sportswriter. Claire blew off his newspaper assignment and made a beeline for the clubhouse to suit up for the game. He found clubhouse man Jim Muhe, who gave him a heavily worn flannel uniform that appeared to be left over from the 1940s. Now dressed for his first baseball action in nearly two decades, Claire hustled out to Field 2 and found Lasorda, who told him to go coach first base.

"Listen, you chicken shit, I didn't come here to coach first base," said Claire with confidence.

"Okay, pal" said Lasorda, "next inning, you replace Bobby Valentine at shortstop."[8]

Claire, whose crowning achievement in baseball had been making junior varsity at Torrance High School, replaced the Dodgers' top prospect in the third inning. In the fourth, he came to bat and whiffed on three straight pitches. The next time up, same result. Claire's third and final at-bat came in the ninth inning with the game still scoreless. Catcher Steve Sogge doubled to start the inning and was on third with one out when Claire stepped into the box. "Just the guy you wouldn't want to see up in this spot," wrote Claire in an article he penned in the next day's *Press-Telegram*.[9]

After two failed bunt attempts, Claire swung away and made contact, sending a squibber to the first baseman, who stepped on the bag for out number two. Sogge would remain stranded on third, the game ending in a draw. The headline of Claire's *Press-Telegram* article read, "Scribe Blows Chance to Wow Dodger Brass."

Claire's name did not appear in Spokane newspaper stories about the game, however, nor did the actual final score. When Lasorda phoned in a report to the desks of the *Spokane Daily Chronicle* and *Spokesman-Review*, he said that Sogge singled home Roy Gleason to give Spokane a 1-0 victory.* Lasorda wanted to get fans in the Inland Northwest excited about the upcoming season, so after every exhibition game that spring he called the Spokane papers and reported a victory, regardless of whether his team won or lost. Indians general manager Elten Schiller eventually realized what Lasorda was doing after he read conflicting game accounts in the Albuquerque and Spokane papers. Schiller told Lasorda to start reporting accurate information.

BY THE TIME SPRING TRAINING WRAPPED UP IN EARLY APRIL, SEVERAL Dodgers prospects—including Valentine, Buckner, and Garvey—had

---

* Gleason, who appeared in eight games for the Dodgers in 1963, was attempting a comeback from shrapnel injuries sustained in Vietnam but never pitched again in the majors. He was the only serviceman with previous major-league experience to serve in the Vietnam War.

already left camp to finish their spring semester college classes. They, like many players in the late 1960s, maintained a full course load, which allowed them to qualify for a student deferment and avoid the military draft. Valentine planned to report to Bakersfield after his final exams. Meanwhile, Buckner and Garvey—along with Ron Cey, Charlie Hough, and Geoff Zahn—were assigned to Double-A Albuquerque to start the season.

The Dodgers broke camp with a roster mostly resembling the previous year's squad that finished in seventh place. The four-man starting rotation of Drysdale, Sutton, Singer, and Osteen remained intact. Pete Mikkelsen, acquired in an offseason trade with St. Louis, and rookie Alan Foster were new additions to the bullpen. The lineup also remained largely unchanged with the exceptions of new outfielder Andy Kosco and a pair of rookies—Bill Russell and Ted Sizemore. Russell would begin the season as a regular outfielder in place of the injured Willie Davis.

A mix of veterans and up-and-coming prospects were assigned to Lasorda's Spokane club, including a position-player group that possessed good speed and positional versatility. The infield included Cleo James, Billy Grabarkewitz, Bart Shirley, and Tommy Hutton. Hutton, whom Lasorda had signed five years earlier, was beginning his third full season with the Indians. The outfield consisted of Jim Barbieri, Von Joshua, George Lott, and player-coach Dick McLaughlin. Thirty-three-year-old Jimmie Schaffer and Bob Stinson handled the catching duties. The Indians' pitching staff included thirty-six-year-old reliever Jack Spring, several hurlers in their mid-to-late twenties with Triple-A or big-league experience (Bruce Brubaker, Fred Norman, and Larry Staab), and a few guys on their way up (Sandy Vance, Mike Strahler, and Ray Lamb).

When the PCL season began, sportswriters covering Lasorda for the first time quickly discovered that he was a bit unconventional. "Words, unfortunately, don't do justice in describing the Spokane Indian manager," wrote Chuck Stewart, who had been on the Indians beat for nearly a decade. "You can call him dynamic, spontaneous, personable ... they all fit, but they don't capture the complete 'him.' About the best phrase we can think of is 'You've got to see him to believe him.' And at times that's even hard to do."[10]

On the Indians' season-opening road swing through Tucson and Phoenix, Lasorda pushed his team to be aggressive on the bases. Spokane swiped five bags in Tucson and another 12 in Phoenix. "I got a look at [Phoenix catcher John] Stephenson in infield practice and decided we would go," said Lasorda. "A couple of times when he threw down to second against us, I was surprised the umps didn't call the infield fly rule."[11] No one could deliver a barb like Tommy Lasorda.

Six of the Indians' 17 steals on the opening road trip belonged to shortstop Billy Grabarkewitz, leaving no doubt that his ankle had fully healed. It turned out to be fortuitous timing for Grabarkewitz, a twelfth-round pick from the '66 June Amateur Draft. Jim Lefebvre sprained a foot, leaving Los Angeles with a vacancy at shortstop.

On the night of April 21, while the Dodgers were beating Juan Marichal and the Giants, Al Campanis sat in his Dodger Stadium office and called Lasorda, whose club was rained out in Tacoma. Campanis wanted to discuss options for Lefebvre's replacement. Lasorda recommended the team promote Grabarkewitz, who, in addition to terrorizing PCL catchers on the bases, was hitting .405 through 10 games.

In attendance at Dodger Stadium that same night was Bobby Valentine, who had just finished his final exams at USC. He took advantage of free tickets to the game and brought along his pal Zack Minasian. As they were leaving the game and walking to the player's parking lot, Valentine and Minasian passed the team's executive offices. Campanis's secretary, Marge Roundtree, saw Valentine and encouraged him to say hello to Campanis. Valentine peered through the window and saw Campanis sitting with a cigarette in one hand and a telephone in the other. Campanis waved for Valentine to come in and motioned for him to have a seat. Valentine had only met Campanis twice—once in his living room when he signed his contract and another time during spring training. His heart began to race.

Just as Valentine entered, he heard Campanis ask Lasorda, "Who do you want to replace Grabarkewitz on your team?"

Without hesitation, Lasorda said he wanted Valentine.

It was a crazy idea, which is precisely what Campanis told Lasorda. "They'll run you both out of town!" exclaimed Campanis, as Valentine sat just a few feet away.[12]

Lasorda held firm. He believed in Valentine implicitly. And he got his wish.

Campanis then informed Valentine of his new destination. Valentine had planned to report to Bakersfield the next day, so his car was already packed. Instead of a short jaunt two hours north, he now had a 1,200-mile trek to Spokane ahead of him. Valentine wanted some company for the trip, so he stopped at Burroughs High School in Burbank on his way out of town the next day and invited Minasian. Valentine didn't have to ask twice.

As they headed north on Interstate 5, Minasian was at the wheel when Valentine directed him to take a detour near Woodland, California, where Valentine had played in the Babe Ruth League World Series five years earlier. Valentine navigated Minasian through a series of turns until, finally, they reached a driveway. A woman came running out and threw her arms around Bobby. "She was his host mother during the Babe Ruth World Series, and he remembered where she lived," recalled Minasian. "I couldn't believe it!"[13]

When Valentine got to Spokane, Lasorda made him the Indians' starting shortstop and leadoff man. It did not go well. He committed five errors in his first six games. In one contest against Hawaii, he airmailed a throw into the stands that struck a female fan, breaking several bones in her face. "He could field the ball and had a strong arm, but he made a lot of throwing errors," recalled first baseman Tommy Hutton, a superb defensive first baseman who undoubtedly saved Valentine from many errors on top of the 38 he was charged with over the course of the '69 season.*

Lasorda played Valentine in the outfield on occasion but kept running him out at shortstop regularly despite the miscues. He knew that the only way for the youngster to improve was to play. The unearned runs and losses mounted, however. Spokane had a 7-6 record when Valentine joined the team. Three weeks later, they were 12-22. Lasorda was willing to suffer with the shortstop through growing pains—even if it meant losing some games. He believed it would pay dividends in the long run for both Valentine and the Dodgers.

Several pitchers on Spokane's roster lacked Lasorda's patience. "They wanted me there like they wanted the plague," said Valentine, looking back. "They wanted someone there who could catch the ball and throw it

---

* Hutton's 141-game errorless streak from 1967-68 and .997 fielding percentage in 1968 set Pacific Coast League records.

across the diamond."[14] Valentine's errors were costing the Indians' pitchers wins and potentially hurting their chances of making it to—or in the cases of veterans Bruce Brubaker, Fred Norman, and Jack Spring, getting back to—the big leagues. This was a big deal. In late June, a group of hurlers—led by Brubaker—decided they had had enough.

Lasorda arrived at the ballpark later than usual because of a speaking engagement at the Kiwanis Club and noticed that his pitchers weren't shagging fly balls with the rest of the team. Lasorda asked player-coach Dick McLaughlin where they were. "They're up in the clubhouse, Tommy," said McLaughlin. "They want to meet with you because they don't want to pitch if Valentine is at shortstop."[15]

Lasorda's blood boiled. He called the entire team into the clubhouse, then went into his office to put on his uniform. He emerged a few minutes later and began pacing the room. "Okay, so what I hear is that pitchers don't want to pitch when this kid is playing shortstop," he said, pointing at Valentine, who sat with his eyes fixed to the ground. "Well, I'm going to tell you what we're going to do. Not only is this kid going to play shortstop, but everybody in this room, right now, is going to stand in front of this fuckin' guy's locker ... and you're going to get his fuckin' autograph because when you're all home carrying a lunch bucket, he's going to be playing in the big leagues."[16]

As Lasorda's tirade continued, Valentine wanted nothing more than to disappear. If his teammates weren't fond of him before, he thought, they must really hate him now. When Lasorda finally finished his diatribe, he stormed into his office and slammed the door. And then something remarkable happened. Valentine looked up slowly and saw his teammates lining up for his autograph. From that day forward, no player openly questioned Lasorda's authority during his tenure in Spokane. He came to town with a reputation as a player's manager, but the incident proved he was no pushover.

Lasorda was, in fact, the same manager in Spokane that he had been in Ogden. He still cracked jokes, showed limitless enthusiasm, and oozed positivity with his oft-repeated motto "You gotta believe!" To instill that positivity, he carried around a book titled *Psycho-Cybernetics: A New Way to Get More Living Out of Life* by Dr. Maxwell Maltz. Published in 1960, the self-help book described how to achieve success by changing one's self-image, boosting self-esteem, and eliminating false beliefs and negativity. Chapter titles include "The Self-Image: Your Key to a Better Life," "Discovering the Success Mechanism Within You," and "How to Get That Winning Feeling."

Lasorda summarized the book in an interview with Mike Lynch of the *Spokesman-Review*: "Have you ever told a story so often over a time that you finally believed it yourself? Have you ever picked out a successful man in your field that you want to be like? ... You tell yourself you're the best. I wake up in the morning, and I believe. I tell myself I'm the best manager in baseball. You see a situation and ask yourself how that man you admire for his success would handle it. I speak before thousands of people every winter, and I have confidence that I can without preparation entertain those people because I believe."[17]

Some of the veterans who thought Lasorda's rah-rah style was only suited for younger players came to appreciate his methods, but not everyone drank the Kool-Aid. One pitcher who declined to go on record for this book described Lasorda as more of a politician than a manager. Some guys who had played for Roy Hartsfield a year earlier preferred his more traditional style and thought Hartsfield possessed a higher baseball IQ. "Hartsfield was a better manager than Lasorda," Brubaker said, looking back. "Tommy was at the right place at the right time. He was a fantastic PR guy. He was great at giving speeches and telling jokes. The sportswriters loved him. But he didn't always make the right decisions managing."[18]

Indians general manager Elten Schiller spun a more positive tune at the end of the '69 season. "Never have I seen a baseball club anywhere with more harmony," said Schiller. "Lasorda was tough, but his players loved him, the rookies and veterans alike."[19]

Valentine looked back on his manager's baseball savvy and intuition for the game with high regard. "Lasorda developed into a master," said Valentine. "His baseball acumen, his ability to manage a game is always overshadowed by his persona. He was a spectacular in-game manager. He knew when to put on a hit-and-run. When a guy was in a slump, he'd give him a high-five when he came into the dugout. That would boost the guy's confidence for the next at-bat. He knew when to take a pitcher out, when to leave him in, when to challenge him, when to take a kid out for a private dinner, and when to scold a kid in front of the entire team."[20]

The confidence Lasorda showed in Valentine and the countless hours

Valentine spent taking extra ground balls paid off as the summer wore on. He cut down on his errors significantly while raising his batting average from the low .200s to .259 by season's end. Lasorda's unwavering support of Valentine through a difficult season left a lasting impression on the youngster, who would eventually embark on a managerial career of his own. "Sometimes I think about how that experience I had with Tommy influenced how I dealt with young players when they weren't successful in the beginning," Valentine said, reflecting back on the experience. "I think it had everything to do with how I dealt with them and how I stuck with them and believed in them. It was incredible on his part. It was unprecedented. My play from that day on was amazingly better."[21]

Something else Lasorda did in the summer of '69 may have stuck with Valentine. It happened during a Sunday afternoon game in Tacoma. "I was pitching and Lasorda got thrown out of the game in the second or third inning," recalled Brubaker. "In the sixth or seventh inning, there was a man on base. I was kneeling in the on-deck circle when I hear, 'Bru, Bru.' It sounded like Lasorda. I looked around, and I couldn't see him anywhere. Then I hear him again say, 'Bru, Bru.' I looked around again, and there he is in full disguise sitting in the front row twenty feet from me. He was wearing a black raincoat, hat, fake beard, and sunglasses. He saw that I heard him and said, 'I want you to fake a bunt and swing away.' The fans around him heard him and started yelling, 'Hey, this is Lasorda!' They stopped the game, and the police came down and escorted him out of the park."[22]

Thirty years later, Brubaker was watching television one day and saw his former teammate, New York Mets' manager Bobby Valentine, pull off a nearly identical ruse following an ejection.

IN LATE JULY OF '69, THE DODGERS PROMOTED BILL BUCKNER TO Spokane. The Indians' regular first baseman, Tommy Hutton, had been called up to Los Angeles to replace Wes Parker, who had required an emergency appendectomy. Buckner, a .307 hitter in Double-A, took Hutton's spot on Spokane's roster.

Two weeks later, the Indians visited Honolulu to play the Hawaii Islanders. During the national anthem, Valentine and Buckner, who were hitting one-two in the batting order, stood side by side next to Lasorda near the on-deck circle. During the anthem, Buckner mumbled expletives under his breath as he mentally prepared to face Lloyd Allen. The nineteen-year-old righty, who possessed a mid-90s fastball and excellent breaking ball, was making his Triple-A debut after dominating the Single-A California League. The Angels had picked Allen in the first round of the '68 draft, a fact that did not sit well with the ultra-competitive Buckner, who always felt that he should have been a first-rounder. As Buckner continued to mutter obscenities, Lasorda asked what all the grumbling was about. Buckner replied that he intended to hit Allen in the forehead with a line drive.

After Valentine singled to start the game, Buckner stepped to the plate. Just as he predicted minutes earlier, he squared up Allen's heater and redirected it back through the box like a laser. The ball caromed off Allen's cranium, rolling far enough away for Buckner to reach second base. Remarkably, Allen stayed in the game. And even more remarkably, Buckner had called his shot—in this case a line drive off the pitcher. His teammates couldn't believe it. "The incident became legendary," said Valentine. "It was Buck 101 as a hitter."[23]

Looking back more than a half-century later, Allen, who never once spoke to Buckner, remained skeptical that Buckner truly called his shot. "What are the chances that Bill Buckner, or any hitter for that matter, could say he is going to hit a pitch off my forehead? If Buckner called that shot, he belongs in a higher club than the Hall of Fame."[24]

One certainty is that Buckner raked after his promotion to Spokane. There, he maintained his aggressive approach, batting .315 in 36 games with the Indians. True to form, he rarely struck out and almost never worked a base on balls—nine strikeouts and three walks in 148 plate appearances.

While Valentine and Buckner were cutting their teeth in Triple-A, other players from the Dodgers' 1968 draft made similar strides in their development. Although his third-base defense remained a liability, Steve Garvey had no problem handling Double-A hurlers, hitting .373 with 14 home runs. Outfielder Davey Lopes improved in his second season at Single-A Daytona Beach, batting .280 with nine home runs and 32 stolen bases. In Bakersfield, Ron Cey and Tom Paciorek lit up California League pitching, posting batting averages over .300 with double-digit home runs. Pitchers Geoff Zahn and Doyle Alexander, meanwhile, showed flashes of potential, registering winning records for Albuquerque and Daytona Beach, respectively.

Davey Lopes at bat. Courtesy Spokane Indians.

When the minor-league season ended and big-league rosters expanded, the Dodgers called up Valentine, Garvey, and Buckner for their first taste of "The Show." Because Los Angeles was in contention for a division title in the newly formed National League West, the youngsters saw little action. So little, in fact, that Walter Alston failed to learn Valentine's first name, repeatedly referring to him as Billy. Buckner, the guy actually named Billy, got into one game as a pinch-hitter. Buckner's lone at-bat came in the ninth inning of a tie game against Gaylord Perry at Candlestick Park in San Francisco. With two on and one out, Buckner had a chance to be the hero. "He hit a looping line drive," recalled Bill's brother, Bob Buckner. "It looked good off the bat, but the second baseman caught it. I asked him after the game what he hit. He said, 'What do you think I hit? It was a spitter!'"[25]

The Dodgers were a half-game out of first place on September 18 but proceeded to lose 10 of their next 11 to fall out of the race. They finished fourth in the NL West with an 85-77 record, missing the postseason for a third consecutive year. Although it ended on a sour note, the season served as a step forward following a pair of losing campaigns. The turnaround came in large part because of the contributions of Rookie of the Year Ted Sizemore and the mid-season additions of Maury Wills and Manny Mota (acquired in a trade with the Expos for Ron Fairly and Paul Popovich) and Jim Bunning (obtained in a deal with Pittsburgh for infielder Chuck Goggin, minor-league pitcher Ron Mitchell, and cash).*

While the Dodgers returned to respectability in '69, the club's Triple-A affiliate in Spokane finished with a losing record (71-73) despite leading the Pacific Coast League with a .281 team batting average and setting a league record with 207 stolen bases. It marked Lasorda's first losing season in five as a minor-league manager. Sportswriters criticized him for his team's slipshod defense, which committed a league-high 198 errors, and its overaggressive baserunning, which resulted in numerous failed hit-and-run plays and rally-killing outs on the basepaths. Lasorda defended his club's mistakes by calling them errors of enthusiasm. He realized that the only way to quiet the naysayers and end the criticism would be to win the 1970 PCL championship.[26]

"Tommy knew there was a lot that he had to prove," said Valentine, "and 1970 was the year to do it. If he had another lousy year in Triple-A, the ending of this story would be different.[27]

---

* Goggin, a native Floridian signed by Leon Hamilton in 1964, missed the '66 and '67 seasons after he was drafted into the Marine Corps. He and the aforementioned Roy Gleason were the only two major leaguers who sustained combat wounds in Vietnam. Goggin suffered shrapnel wounds to his legs and back from stepping on a landmine. He would spend parts of three seasons with the Pirates, Braves, and Red Sox.

Coconut Snatching

"Boys, I want you to think about this weather. Feel the sun. Let it sink in. You're going to work hard here, but you could be shoveling snow, or you could be down in a coal mine. The great Dodger in the sky made all this possible. It's a tremendous opportunity. Take advantage of it."—Tommy Lasorda, November 1969

ON APRIL 5, 1993, FORTY-FIVE-YEAR-OLD CHARLIE HOUGH STARTED THE first-ever game for the expansion Florida Marlins, outdueling Orel Hershiser and the Los Angeles Dodgers to earn his 203rd career win. All told, Hough pitched twenty-five seasons in the major leagues, a milestone reached by ten players in baseball history, six of whom are enshrined in the Hall of Fame. What makes Hough's achievement even more remarkable is the fact that he may have never pitched in the major leagues at all if minor-league pitching coach Goldie Holt had not asked him a simple question on an Arizona baseball diamond in 1969.

Hough had just completed his fourth season of pro ball. His career had stagnated. His future in baseball appeared bleak. Shoulder problems had diminished the zip on his fastball, turning the former eighth-round draft pick into a fringe prospect, at best. In two seasons in Double-A, he had registered a combined 16-19 record and 4.02 ERA. In the parlance of Tommy Lasorda, Hough was on the verge of playing in the lunch-bucket league.

Charlie Hough. Courtesy Spokane Indians.

In October 1969, Hough played for the Dodgers' Arizona Instructional League squad. Lasorda managed the team with Holt serving as pitching coach. "Goldie taught everybody pickoff moves, how to back up the bases, and defensive stuff you do pitching," Hough recalled. "He was terrific at it. He was a fabulous baseball guy, the kind of guy who devoted their life to helping minor leaguers play ball."[1]

On one autumn day, as Hough played catch under the desert sun, Holt strolled by and asked him if he had ever tried throwing a knuckleball. Hough had not. Certainly not in a game. Few pitchers in baseball history have mastered the pitch. A good knuckleball moves erratically and unpredictably—much like the flight pattern of a butterfly—making it difficult to both catch and hit. The term knuckleball is, in fact, a bit of a misnomer. It is typically thrown using the fingertips to push the ball so that it floats to the plate without spin. Maintaining consistent fingernail length and shape is crucial to throwing the pitch effectively. Holt showed the knuckleball grip to Hough, who gave it a try. After all, he had nothing to lose. "I picked it up in five minutes," said Hough, looking back. "And then I spent twenty-five years trying to get it over the plate."[2]

Hough walked off the practice field and informed Lasorda he intended to become a knuckleball pitcher. "Tommy said, 'You better try something, because you're on your last chance,'" Hough recalled. "I was really close to not playing for the Dodgers anymore."[3]

Hough started incorporating his new pitch in the Instructional League that fall. He described his performance, in retrospect, as "awful." When he threw the knuckleball right, batters couldn't touch it. The problem was that most of the time he didn't throw it right. "I could strike out the side and give up four runs," recalled Hough. "It was walk, hit batter, home run, strikeout, strikeout, walk, hit batter. It was ugly."[4] Even though he had added a new weapon to his arsenal, he still wasn't sure he would have a job when the 1970 season rolled around.

Another member of the 1966 June Amateur Draft class, Bill Russell, played with Hough in Arizona that fall. Coming off a full season with the '69 Dodgers, Russell had hit a meager .226 with five home runs in 98 games. He played excellent outfield defense, but the Dodgers brass thought his quick hands and strong arm could serve him well at the hot corner. Management sent Russell to the desert to learn third base under Monty Basgall, a former big-league infielder who coached with a calm demeanor and unending patience. The legendary instructor had his hands full between Russell and converted shortstop Bobby Valentine. A year earlier, Basgall had helped catcher Ted Sizemore transition to second base. Sizemore not only filled LA's keystone vacancy in 1969, but he also won the NL Rookie of the Year Award.

The Dodgers liked to put their eggs in many baskets. More so than most clubs, they did not hesitate to switch a player's position to match his skill set or fill an organizational need. They called it "coconut snatching," a term coined by Branch Rickey. "Mr. Rickey got it from the islands, or

Hawaii, or some tropical place," Al Campanis once explained. "He noticed that one native would climb to the top of the coconut tree and hold on with his legs and snatch the coconuts, throwing them to a native below. When the coconut snatcher's legs got tired, he would climb down, and the coconut catcher would climb up to become the coconut snatcher. They were filling a position of need."[5]

The Dodgers employed the practice of coconut snatching myriad times over the years. In 1951, they signed Maury Wills as a pitcher and converted him to second base and then shortstop. A year later, the Dodgers inked catcher John Roseboro, moved him to the outfield, and then returned him to catcher to succeed the aging Roy Campanella. Fast-forward to 1970 when the club again had needs at shortstop and catcher. The front office pegged Valentine, a former outfielder, as Wills's eventual replacement. To build catching depth, the Dodgers moved third baseman Bill Sudakis and outfielders Bob Stinson and Joe Ferguson behind the dish. Ferguson, the club's eighth-round pick in the '68 draft, donned the tools of ignorance in the '69 Arizona Instructional League at the suggestion of Lasorda, who liked the Bay Area native's "tremendous arm" and "hands of a basketball player." The solidly built University of the Pacific product became a willing guinea pig. "I had done everything else in baseball, including some pitching in college," Ferguson said years later, "so the challenge was okay with me."[6] Former big-league catcher Del Crandall taught him catching fundamentals that fall and the following summer in Albuquerque. Crandall emphasized the importance of backstop defense to the team's success. Take satisfaction from your defense, he said, not your offensive totals.

BOASTING A YEAR OF SHORTSTOP EXPERIENCE UNDER HIS BELT, VALENTINE arrived at Vero Beach a more confident player in the spring of 1970. The twenty-year-old impressed everyone from front-office executives to big-league veterans with his combination of raw ability, poise, and positive attitude. Ross Newhan of the *Los Angeles Times* predicted that Valentine would be the Dodgers' next captain, a title held by only two players—Pee Wee Reese and Maury Wills—since the team moved to LA. After the Dodgers re-acquired Wills from the Expos the prior June, he hit .297 and stole 25 bases, proving he still had some gas left in the tank. Now thirty-seven, he would maintain a firm grip on the shortstop position for at least another year. The Dodgers planned on having Valentine spend the majority of the season in Triple-A so he could continue to work on his defense.

Other spots on the Dodgers roster were not as set in stone, a fact not lost on two of Valentine's buddies from the '68 draft cohort. Steve Garvey accumulated 11 extra-base hits and led the Dodgers in Grapefruit League RBI to win the opening-day third-base job. And Bill Buckner impressed so much during spring training that Gold Glove first baseman Wes Parker offered to give up his position to get Buckner's bat in the lineup. Walter Alston instead kept Parker at first and made Buckner his starting left fielder to begin the season. Buckner's fluid, line-drive swing even wowed Senators manager and Red Sox legend Ted Williams, who predicted that Buckner would win the National League batting title within three years.

Some Dodgers prospects did not have an opportunity to participate in spring training. Ron Cey, Geoff Zahn, and Von Joshua were among those who missed most or all of camp because of Army Reserve or National Guard obligations. A number of other players in the organization, including Davey Lopes, Charlie Hough, and Bill Russell, would miss time periodically during the season.

Vero Beach bustled with the usual annual traditions, including pitchers' fielding practice, bunting drills, and an unmistakable air of optimism. But there was plenty of levity in Dodgertown in the spring of 1970, mostly at the expense of Lasorda, whose outspokenness and love of attention made him a natural target of practical jokesters. The antics began early that spring, a day after the rotund Norristown native took a dip in the whirlpool to soothe some sore muscles. Lasorda had often ridiculed players who used the whirlpool as being soft, a bit of irony not lost on many in the Dodgers clubhouse. The next day, Lasorda entered the trainer's room to find that someone had painted "U.S.S. *Lasorda*—The Green Phantom" on the side of the whirlpool. A couple of days later, the Green Phantom struck again. Lasorda found bottles of ant and weed killer in his locker with labels that read "Lasorda's Deodorant" and "Lasorda's After Shave Lotion."

The pranks continued throughout the spring, each more elaborate than the one before. Following the team's annual St. Patrick's Day shindig, Lasorda returned to his room in the Dodgertown barracks to find that all his furniture was gone. The only item left in the room, a green baseball, contained a message directing him to the Dodgers clubhouse. Lasorda woke up equipment man Nobe Kawano and asked him to unlock the clubhouse door. Once inside, Lasorda followed a trail of clues that led him to a player's shoe, then another player's warmup jacket, and then finally to the top drawer of Walter Alston's desk. It was 3:30 a.m. when Lasorda finally found his furniture in a storage room.

"The Phantom's pranks have been so well conceived and so skillfully consummated that on most occasions Lasorda has been left speechless, a first according to reliable sources," wrote Ross Newhan in the *Los Angeles Times*.[7]

The Green Phantom's most audacious stunt involved Walter O'Malley, who had handed over the reins of team president to his son, Peter, on March 17. The elder O'Malley, who would remain on as chairman of the Dodgers' Board of Directors, awoke one morning to discover that the wheels on his prized golf cart were missing. A note left on the cart implicated Lasorda, who was sawing logs when O'Malley and a security guard knocked on his door and conducted a morning raid. Unbeknownst to Lasorda, someone had stashed the tires under his bed the night before.

At the annual cookout on the last day of camp, the players behind the Green Phantom revealed themselves, including ringleader Jim Lefebvre and accomplices Joe Moeller, Don Sutton, Tommy Hutton, and Wes Parker. Lefebvre read a poem written for the occasion, which ended with him yelling, "Attack!" as a group of players threw Lasorda into the pool. Decades later, Moeller chuckled as he recalled helping Lefebvre remove the wheels from O'Malley's cart. "I'm not sure how smart that was," said Moeller in hindsight.[8]

Besides being the target of a spring-training caper, Lasorda busied himself with preparing the players he would take to Spokane. The Indians' twenty-one-man roster crystallized after the big-league club finalized its opening-day roster. Spokane's ten-man pitching staff would include three players with big-league experience (Jerry Stephenson, John Purdin, and Jack Jenkins) and four who pitched for Spokane a year earlier (Sandy Vance, Mike Strahler, Larry Staab, and Dick Armstrong). Lasorda filled the final three spots with hurlers he handpicked from the lower minor leagues—Charlie Hough, Pete Scarpati, and Bob O'Brien.

Although he made the Triple-A roster, Hough's status in the organization remained tenuous. When he left for spring training, he told his wife, Sharon, that he'd either be home in a few weeks or pitching in Double-A

Albuquerque or Spokane, all three scenarios in the realm of possibility. He had a few shaky outings in the Grapefruit League, but Lasorda planned to give him every chance to succeed out of Spokane's bullpen.

Scarpati, the Dodgers' sixty-eighth round pick in the '68 draft, was coming off a superb second pro season in which he registered a pristine 8-0 record and 1.75 ERA. He cemented his spot in Lasorda's bullpen with a strong spring, including an impressive three-inning outing against the Washington Senators. His Italian heritage didn't hurt either. Scarpati would miss the first week of Spokane's season, however. As a result of the U.S. postal workers' strike in mid-March, the National Guard had activated him, sending Scarpati home to sort mail for three weeks.

Like Scarpati, Bob O'Brien, the Dodgers' fourth-round pick in the 1969 January Amateur Draft, recorded a spectacular 1969 season in which he posted a sparkling 1.65 ERA while breaking a Pioneer League record with 186 strikeouts. On a spring road trip, he tagged along with the big-league club as a batting-practice pitcher but wound up tossing three scoreless frames against the defending champion New York Mets. Lasorda chose O'Brien, a left-handed starter, in large part because of that one impressive outing.

Another player Lasorda plucked from the lower minor leagues was outfielder Davey Lopes, who had spent his first two seasons of pro ball with the Dodgers' Single-A affiliate in Daytona Beach. Similar to how Steve Garvey had heard Lasorda's voice moments before they met, Lasorda heard Lopes's bat before he saw him. The skipper was behind the clubhouse near one of the practice diamonds when he heard the unmistakable sound of solid contact. As he rounded the corner of the clubhouse, the field came into view. Lasorda looked out and saw a blur speeding around the bases. Right then and there, Lasorda told spring training director John Carey that he wanted that guy, Lopes, on his Spokane club.

Lopes joined an outfield mix that included Tom Paciorek and a couple of holdovers from the '69 club—Von Joshua and George Lott. The Indians' opening-day infield consisted of Bill Russell at the hot corner, Bobby Valentine at shortstop, Bart Shirley at the keystone, and Tommy Hutton at first. Bob Stinson and former Division I quarterback Steve Sogge would split the catching duties. The Dodgers signed the latter as an undrafted free agent in January 1969. Sogge had played three years of football at USC, including two as the Trojans' starting QB.* He and running back O.J. Simpson led USC to a national title in '67 with a Rose Bowl victory over Indiana.

Spokane's bench included Marv Galliher, Gustavo "Gus" Sposito, and player-coach Dick McLaughlin.† Galliher, a first-round pick in the 1968 January Amateur Draft-Secondary Phase, was scouted and signed by Lasorda, so the skipper had a personal stake in his success. "Lasorda treated me like a son and wanted me to play in LA," recalled Galliher. "He told me a few times that someday my mail would come to Dodger Stadium."[9]

Typical of any Triple-A season, there would invariably be many roster changes throughout the summer to fill the needs of the big-league club. And in 1970, the demands of the Army Reserve and the National Guard would come into play too. Just because his team existed to meet the needs of the Los Angeles Dodgers didn't diminish Lasorda's desire to win, however. He pushed his players hard in spring training, setting the tone for what he hoped would be a championship season. "We're going to win, and the way we're going to win is to pay the price," he told his players. "We're gonna work like my wife shops ... all day long."[10]

After three weeks of training and a dozen practice games against other Dodgers minor-league clubs, the 1970 Spokane Indians left the sunshine of Florida for Salt Lake City, where snow loomed in the forecast.

---

* Sogge was a native Angeleno and graduate of Gardena High School. In 2021, *USA Today* named him one of the ten greatest quarterbacks in California high school football history. As a sophomore at USC, Sogge won a Pacific-8 Conference batting title.
† McLaughlin later served as a Dodgers scout, minor-league manager, and renowned organizational instructor. He taught outfield defense, baserunning, and bunting.

Part Two
The 1970 Spokane Indians

Courtesy Spokane Indians.

TERMITE PALACE

"Managing is like holding a dove in your hand. Squeeze too hard and you kill it; not hard enough and it flies away." —Tommy Lasorda

IN 1970, THE PACIFIC COAST LEAGUE CONSISTED OF EIGHT TEAMS divided into two divisions. The Spokane Indians, Portland Beavers, Eugene Emeralds, and Tacoma Cubs played in the Northern Division. The Salt Lake Padres, Phoenix Giants, Tucson Toros, and Hawaii Islanders comprised the Southern Division. Each team would play a 146-game schedule. Off days were rare. Doubleheaders were not. A league champion would be determined at the end of the season by a playoff series between the two division winners.

The Indians opened the campaign 4,300 feet above sea level in Salt Lake City, Utah, home of the San Diego Padres' new Triple-A affiliate.[*] Don Zimmer, a five-foot-nine, round-faced, dimple-chinned former infielder, piloted the Salt Lake Padres. Nicknamed "Popeye" because of his resemblance to the comic-strip character, Zimmer spent seven of his

---

[*] Remarkably, unlike the other three expansion franchises, the San Diego Padres did not have a Triple-A team in the franchise's inaugural season of 1969.

twelve major-league seasons as a player with the Dodgers. He and Tommy Lasorda were pals from their days as teammates in spring training and winter ball. Both were fierce competitors who had squeezed the most out of their own abilities. They did the same with players they managed. "Zimmer let you play the game, but you had to play hard," recalled Padres second baseman Walt Hriniak.* "That was the number one thing. As long as you kept running ground balls out and played hard, he didn't get on your ass. If you didn't hustle or play the game right, he'd let you know. He was a great baseball man."[1]

Zim, as his players called him, wore his emotions on his sleeve. Like his counterpart in the Spokane dugout, he was fiery and prone to fighting. Looking back decades later, Salt Lake first baseman Jeff Pentland † remembered breaking up several skirmishes between Zimmer and his players over the course of the 1970 season. One such altercation involved pitcher Darcy Fast. "He took me out, and I was disgusted at myself," Fast remembered. "I came into the dugout and fired my glove at the bench. I walked into the clubhouse, and he followed me in and jumped on me. A couple other players had to pull him off me. He was a hothead. But I never felt for one moment that he didn't care about me or didn't want me to succeed. He showed that fire in many different ways."[2]

Having stout, volatile former Dodgers at the helm is where the similarities between the Indians and Padres began and ended. Spokane's roster was chock-full of former big leaguers and high draft picks. Salt Lake's roster, on the other hand, mostly consisted of prospects who had been rushed to Triple-A because the newly hatched San Diego franchise lacked better options. Salt Lake's pitching staff was particularly green. Besides

---

* Hriniak played catcher for most of his career, including parts of two seasons with the Atlanta Braves and San Diego Padres. Beginning in 1971, he spent six seasons with the Montreal Expos as a player, coach, manager, and big-league first-base coach. When the Boston Red Sox hired Zimmer to manage in 1976, he tapped Hriniak to be his bullpen coach. During his twelve seasons with the Red Sox, Hriniak became the de facto hitting coach, a role he later held with the Chicago White Sox. Frank Thomas and a minor-league outfielder named Michael Jordan were among his pupils.

† The five-foot-ten Pentland once tried out for the Dodger Rookies—an amateur team of high school and collegiate players from the Los Angeles area sponsored by the Dodgers—when Lasorda was a scout. "Lasorda told me I wasn't tall enough to play on the team," he recalled. "It kind of upset me. Every time I played against a Dodgers affiliate, I felt I needed to do as good as I could. I had a vendetta against them." Pentland never played in the majors but later enjoyed a long career as a major-league hitting coach.

former White Sox lefty Jerry Nyman and ex-Phillies/Reds reliever Jack Baldschun, most of the hurlers on Zimmer's staff had never played above Single-A. The San Diego Padres had only began drafting players two years earlier. Even then, the four expansion teams (Padres, Expos, Pilots, and Royals) weren't allowed to participate until the fourth round. By the time the Padres made their first picks in the regular and secondary phases of the 1968 June Amateur Draft, the Dodgers had already selected Bobby Valentine, Bill Buckner, Steve Garvey, and Ron Cey. It was no wonder that a canyon-sized talent gap existed between the Spokane and Salt Lake rosters.

On Friday, April 10, the Indians and Padres commenced the 1970 season in Salt Lake City. Lasorda was no stranger to Derks Field, having managed there in the Pioneer League. During the pregame ceremony, he and Zimmer introduced their respective rosters to the crowd. Lasorda grabbed the microphone and confidently proclaimed, "Ladies and gentlemen, I'd like you to meet the 1970 Northern Division champions of the PCL, the Spokane Indians!"[3] The Salt Lake City fans responded with a chorus of boos.

John Purdin, a six-foot-two righty with 58 big-league games under his belt, toed the rubber for Spokane.* The lanky hurler showed midseason form, going the distance while surrendering just two runs in the Indians' 6-2 victory. Thirty-year-old Bart Shirley, the Indians' elder statesman, delivered the key hit of the game—a wind-blown, bases-loaded double that scored three runs, providing Purdin all the support he would need.

The next night, the Indians defeated the Padres again, 7-4, amidst plummeting temperatures, swirling winds, and snow flurries. Catcher Steve Sogge and outfielder George Lott each homered to lead the Spokane charge. On April 13, at Derks Field, a miniscule Monday night crowd of 181 braved elements more befitting of dogsledding than baseball. Those who stayed away missed seeing Tom Paciorek hit his first Triple-A home run, Bobby Valentine tie a PCL record with three triples, and Charlie Hough unveil his fluttering knuckleball. During Hough's two innings of relief, he faced six batters, each of whom flailed helplessly at his new

---

* Purdin played in parts of four seasons with the Dodgers between 1964-69. Pitching mostly in relief in the majors, he registered a 6-4 record and 3.90 ERA. In 1967, he led the Spokane Indians in wins (15) and strikeouts (158).

weapon. He was the pitcher of record in the Indians' 6-5 victory. Snow postponed the finale, providing Lasorda a rare day off and the opportunity to celebrate he and Jo's twentieth wedding anniversary in Los Angeles before the Indians' next series in Hawaii.

JOHN PURDIN

Courtesy Spokane Indians.

THE HAWAII ISLANDERS WERE A CO-OP TEAM OWNED BY SELF-MADE millionaire Chinn Ho. Their roster comprised mostly California Angels prospects, but the co-op arrangement between the Angels and Islanders allowed general manager Jack Quinn* to supplement the team each season with a half-dozen-or-so independently contracted veteran players, most of whom had major-league experience. The arrangement was common in the first half of the twentieth century but nearly obsolete by 1970. Having the ability to augment the roster with big-league veterans gave the Islanders a competitive advantage and helped boost attendance, bringing in revenue needed to cover the team's travel expenses and the $30,000 fee the Islanders had to pay the league to subsidize visiting teams' airfare.

John Werhas typified the sort of player whom Quinn targeted: thirty-two years old, some big-league experience, and a proven track record in Triple-A. The then-Minneapolis Lakers (two weeks before a move to Los Angeles) drafted Werhas, a former All-Conference basketball star at USC, in the eighth round of the 1960 NBA draft.† He turned down the Lakers' offer of a two-year, no-cut contract. Instead, he signed with the Dodgers for $30,000. Werhas then spent most of the next decade toiling in the minor leagues, including five consecutive seasons with the Spokane Indians. He received scant playing time during a few different stints in LA before the Dodgers dealt him to the Angels for Len Gabrielson in May of 1967. After the '68 season, Werhas turned thirty. The grind had worn him down. He decided to hang up his cleats in favor of selling stocks and bonds. That is, until Quinn made him an offer he couldn't refuse.

"He called four times, and the fourth time he doubled his offer," recalled Werhas. "I was making more than some players in the major leagues. The Islanders had more money than they knew what to do with."[4]

Other former big leaguers on the Islanders roster to start the 1970 season included thirty-seven-year-old Jim Coates, who had pitched in three World Series with the Yankees, thirty-year-old hurlers Phil Ortega and Dennis Bennett, who had earned a combined 89 wins in the majors, and ex-Phillies outfielder Rick Barry.‡ Hawaii's roster also included an excellent crop of Angels prospects who would later play in the majors, including second baseman Doug Griffin, shortstop Marty Perez, outfielder

---

* Jack Quinn's grandfather, Bob Quinn, once owned the Boston Red Sox. Jack's father, John, served as general manager for the 1957 World Champion Milwaukee Braves.
† The Lakers' first-round pick in 1960 was Jerry West.
‡ Later in the 1970 season, the Islanders would add forty-two-year-old Elroy Face, who pitched 10 innings across eight appearances.

Tomás Silverio, super-utilityman Winston Llenas, and pitchers Greg Washburn, Tom Bradley, Dave LaRoche, and Steve Kealey.

Perhaps no player on the Islanders possessed more talent than the Dominican-born Llenas (pronounced *YAY-noss*), who had signed with the Kansas City Athletics a decade earlier. A's scout Félix Delgado had heard whispers about the talented sixteen-year-old. Delgado showed up at Llenas's house one day to offer him a tryout. The kid was skin and bones but demonstrated a good arm and a surprising pop for someone his size. Llenas's father accepted Delgado's offer of a $500 bonus and signed on his son's behalf.

Llenas made his professional debut in 1961 with a Class-D team in Albuquerque. He had a decent enough year for a raw prospect, but the A's released him the following season after he struggled against better competition in the Florida State League. Shortly thereafter, however, Angels scout Tufie Hashem, who had seen Llenas play in Albuquerque, signed him to a free-agent contract. The Halos assigned the franchise's first Dominican player to the Single-A Quad Cities Angels, a team helmed by first-year manager Chuck Tanner. A natural infielder, Llenas showed incredible versatility by filling in at catcher for twenty-five games after the team's first- and second-string backstops went down with injuries. At the end of that season, the Angels promoted him three levels to the Hawaii Islanders. More than a half-century later, Llenas proudly characterized the jump as kismet: "When something is meant to be yours, that's what happens."[5]

Llenas played another two seasons under Tanner with the Double-A El Paso Sun Kings. Although he grew to be just five-foot-ten and 165 pounds, his quick wrists allowed him to extract every ounce of power from his wiry frame. In 1966, he hit 25 bombs, tying six-foot-three, 220-pound Moose Stubing for the Texas League home-run title. Nearly sixty years later, Llenas laughed when remembering a photograph that ran in *The Sporting News* that showed Stubing carrying Llenas like a baby. Llenas spent parts of the 1968-69 seasons with the Angels in Honolulu, marking the third city in which he played for Tanner. In the highly competitive Pacific Coast League, the ten-year pro earned the respect of his teammates and opponents alike. Jeff Pentland, who later worked as a big-league hitting coach, said Llenas was as good of a hitter as he ever saw—minors or majors.[6]

Chuck Tanner, a veteran of eight major-league seasons as a reserve outfielder, had steadily climbed the minor-league ranks as a manager before his promotion to the Islanders dugout in 1969. As a former player who spent more time on the bench than on the field, he could relate to his players' struggles and understood the power of positive thinking. Tanner was quiet but intense. He possessed an innate knack for motivating his players, though his methods were much more subdued than Lasorda's. When John Werhas joined the Islanders, Tanner knelt beside him before the first game of the season and said, "You're going to hit fourth for me, and you're going to play every day. You'll never have to look at the lineup card." With that, Tanner got up and went back to his seat. Those few words took all the weight off the third baseman's shoulders, allowing him to perform at his best. "That was his magic," recalled Werhas. "He knew how to drive a guy and make him believe in himself."[7]

Islanders reliever Harvey Shank* had similarly fond recollections of Tanner: "Chuck was such a positive guy and an outstanding leader. His mantra was 'Don't make excuses, make plays.' He could get in your face if you weren't doing what you should be doing."[8]

There was an abundance of talent in the Islanders dugout, but the broadcast booth wasn't too shabby either. The team's lead play-by-play announcer was twenty-five-year-old Al Michaels. The Arizona State University product landed the Islanders' radio gig in 1968 after his father-in-law, who owned a vending-machine business in Honolulu, helped set up a meeting with Jack Quinn. Michaels earned $15,000 a year broadcasting Islanders games while working a second job as a sports anchor at the local ABC affiliate. He emulated the cadence and delivery of Vin Scully, whom he had grown up listening to—first in Brooklyn and then in Los Angeles after his family moved there in 1958. Islanders fans would regularly bring transistor radios to the ballpark. According to Tucson Toros pitcher Gene Rounsaville, it sounded as if Al Michaels was in surround sound—much like Scully at Dodger Stadium.[9]

At some point during Lasorda's tenure in Spokane, he touted Michaels to his bosses. Lasorda routinely called Campanis to provide updates on the team. During one call, between going over his team's statistics, Lasorda

---

* Shank's major-league career consisted of one relief appearance with the 1970 Angels. He later enjoyed a long career as an executive with the NBA's Phoenix Suns.

said, "By the way, the Islanders have this kid who does a great job announcing the games. I know Scully's the best, but you might want to keep this kid in mind if there's ever an opening. His name is Michaels—Al Michaels."

Lasorda continued with his daily recap. Later in the conversation, Campanis circled back: "Wait a second, Tommy. This Michaels guy—the announcer ... how do you know he's any good?"

"Well," Lasorda replied, "I've been thrown out of the last four games, and I've been in the clubhouse listening to him on the radio."*,10

Michaels's partner in 1970 was first-year broadcaster Ken Wilson, a recent graduate of the University of Michigan who later enjoyed a long broadcasting career in MLB and the NHL.†

The two young announcers called games in a tiny booth atop the grandstand at Honolulu Stadium, a mostly wooden multi-purpose stadium nestled amongst homes and businesses at the intersection of King and Isenberg Streets, just a couple of miles from Waikiki Beach. Built in 1926, the stadium had a seating capacity of around 25,000. It had a single tier of seats surrounding all four sides of the diamond. A waist-high chain-link fence separated fans from the infield. The grass was an intensely lush green and the outfield wall was plastered with billboards promoting local businesses like Zippy's and Bea's Drive-In and national and international entities such as Coppertone, Continental Airlines, and Datsun. Diamond Head, Honolulu's most recognized geologic landmark, loomed beyond the center-field wall.

During its half-century of existence, the multi-purpose facility hosted

---

* In his autobiography, *You Can't Make This Up*, Michaels notes that this was a slight embellishment. The umpires ejected Lasorda in three out of four games, including one while presenting the lineup card. The umpiring crew that series included Bruce Froemming.

† Wilson landed the Islanders broadcasting job through incredible happenstance. He had a low draft lottery number after graduating from college, so he moved to Honolulu to enlist in the Reserve and avoid being sent to Vietnam. He failed his physical because of an old knee injury, so instead of joining the Reserve he got a job as a disc jockey. He went to some Islanders games during the summer of '69 season and sold Coca-Cola as a vendor for a couple of nights. During one game, he approached Quinn about a broadcasting job. The GM politely told him there was nothing available. Several months later, Wilson was living in Philadelphia and got a letter in the mail from Hawaii. Quinn had an opening for the 1970 season and was requesting a sample tape. Wilson sent a tape to Quinn, who offered him the job. "It was a lot of good fortune to say the least," said Wilson. In recent years Wilson has served as commissioner of three summer-collegiate leagues.

football games, track and field, concerts, carnivals, polo, parades, and hula festivals. Elvis Presley performed there. Jesse Owens once raced a horse there—and won. And countless baseball legends played exhibition games there, including Babe Ruth, Lou Gehrig, Joe DiMaggio, and Jackie Robinson. "The first time I saw Honolulu Stadium, I thought it was a little bit of Brooklyn in the tropics, with an old ramshackle Ebbets Field kind of flavor," Michaels recalled.[11] The ballpark's baseball-field-in-a-football-stadium configuration reminded Southern Californian Dave LaRoche of the Los Angeles Memorial Coliseum—the Dodgers' home ballpark during the team's first four seasons in LA.

Honolulu Stadium was affectionately nicknamed "Termite Palace." On game nights—when the aroma of wood, cigarette smoke, and beer permeated the tropical air—termites that infested the wooden park congregated around the stadium lights by the millions. After the game, when the lights went dark and the only illumination in the stadium emanated from the press box, the termites swarmed around the sportswriters as they feverishly typed up their game stories.

Parking around the stadium was almost nonexistent, so many fans walked or took the bus, creating a parade-like atmosphere before games. Vendors outside the ballpark sold boiled peanuts in brown paper bags, and concessionaires inside sold corn on the cob, barbecue, fish cakes, and a Hawaiian noodle soup called saimin. During rain delays, the Islanders relief pitchers would take cover under the right-field bleachers and get a bowl of saimin from the concession stand. The bullpen also enjoyed macadamia nuts that a lady brought to every game, recalled Dave LaRoche.

The postgame clubhouse spread, which included such offerings as spicy pork and Primo beer, was one of the many things opposing teams loved about playing in the Termite Palace. Another was the mouthwatering fresh pineapple that the Islanders kept stocked in an old Coca-Cola cooler in the visitors' dugout. This posed a couple of problems. One was that pineapple is 85 percent water. A second was the visitors' clubhouse sat in a parking lot beyond center field. "By the fourth inning you'd have to go the bathroom, and you had to wait until in between innings," recalled Indians pitcher Bob O'Brien. "Our players would be beelining out to center field. The Hawaii players would be laughing at us. They knew exactly what they were doing."[12]

Unsurprisingly, Hawaii was the favorite road destination of players in the Pacific Coast League, including Indians pitcher Pete Scarpati. He recalled, "That was a trip that everybody wanted to make. You were hoping you didn't get released or sent down or even sent *up*. Everyone wanted to go to Hawaii."[13]

Visiting teams stayed in a hotel located a stone's throw from Waikiki Beach. Tommy Lasorda's rule was that his players had to be off the beach by noon. According to Bobby Valentine, "That's because he would start walking the beach to check out all the girls, and he didn't want to be seen."[14]

During one trip, Valentine and Zack Minasian took rafts out in the water so Lasorda wouldn't catch them on the beach. They drifted out too far, however, and before they knew it the waves were above them and surfers were coming down on them. Valentine, not the strongest of swimmers, struggled to hold on to his flimsy raft. "It took me about two hours to kick myself in," remembered Valentine. "The next thing I know, it's a half-hour before the bus is leaving for that night's game. The tops of my shoulders were so sunburned that I showered with a T-shirt on so Tommy wouldn't see how sunburned I was."[15]

Those lucky enough to call Honolulu home for the summer loved playing there. In addition to paying excellent wages, Chinn Ho housed his players in the posh Ilikai Hotel and provided each of them with a Datsun to drive around all season. The owner promised his players they'd get to keep the cars if Hawaii won the PCL championship.*

Because it was built for football, Honolulu Stadium had unusual dimensions. The center-field wall stood 420 feet from home plate, while the lines were short—320 feet to left and a tantalizing 305 feet to right. Coast League managers loaded their lineups with left-handed hitters to take advantage of the short porch. In fact, Lasorda once started southpaw

---

* Another perk was free food. The Hawaii players received a complimentary steak dinner at the Columbia Inn for hitting a home run or pitching a shutout. The restaurant's baseball-loving owner, Tosh Kaneshiro, was a huge Dodgers fan. He erected a banner above Honolulu Stadium's right-center field wall that read, "Columbia Inn. Fine Foods. Top of the Blvd." The banner had a four-foot hole (or puka in Hawaiian) with a net behind it. If a player from the home team hit a home run through the puka, he'd win $1,000. Only one player, Walter "No Neck" Williams, ever hit a home run through the puka. The five-foot-six outfielder accomplished the feat in 1968.

Tommy Hutton at third base during the 1969 season to get an extra lefty hitter in the lineup.

IN THE SERIES OPENER ON APRIL 15, BILL RUSSELL AND BOB STINSON had no problem clearing the center-field fence, each hitting gargantuan blasts off Jim Coates to put Spokane ahead early. Indians starter Sandy Vance, who had uncorked six wild pitches in a game at Honolulu Stadium a year earlier, held the Islanders scoreless through the first six frames. The Islanders sent Vance to the showers in the seventh and evened the score on Doug Griffin's two-run single. Charlie Vinson's eighth-inning wallop off Indians reliever Larry Staab proved to be the decisive blow.*

John Werhas took advantage of the short fences in the Islanders' 9-5 victory the following night, hitting a pair of homers, including an opposite-field blast off a Charlie Hough knuckleball.

The Indians then rebounded to win the next three games and take the series. The first victory came at the expense of lefty Dennis Bennett, who struck out 11 but lost because of home runs by Tom Paciorek, Tommy Hutton, and Bobby Valentine. Spokane starter Jerry Stephenson improved to 2-0 with a little help from Staab and then Jack Jenkins, who recorded the final two outs with the tying run on base. The next night, the Islanders pounced on Indians starter Mike Strahler with seven runs early, but Spokane came storming back, scoring nine unanswered runs to send 11,273 fans home disappointed. Hough worked six innings of scoreless relief for his second win.

In the rubber game on Sunday, April 19, the Indians overcame a pair of home runs by Winston Llenas to squeak out a 5-4 triumph, in no small part due to winning pitcher Pete Scarpati, who put up five innings of goose eggs. Tommy Hutton took full advantage of the short right-field screen, homering in each of the final four games of the five-tilt set. Bill Russell and Tom Paciorek also flexed their muscles, combining for five home runs in the series.

---

* Staab was reportedly not happy about being relegated to the bullpen before the Dodgers sold him to Rochester of the International League in June.

Tommy Hutton. Courtesy Spokane Indians.

In just nine games, Hutton had already eclipsed his home-run total from the year prior. The former Lasorda signee, who would soon turn twenty-four, was beginning his sixth season in the Dodgers' farm system. He had spent nearly all of the previous three in Spokane, except for a brief sixteen-game stint in LA during the '69 season. Though he lacked the size and power of a prototypical first baseman, Hutton played phenomenal defense. At the plate, he rarely struck out, consistently reached base at a .400 clip, and had improved his batting average each of the previous three seasons. Hutton's ability was not lost on opposing hurlers. Tacoma Cubs pitcher Larry Colton remembered him being just as tough to face as any hitter on the '70 Spokane Indians. Unfortunately for Hutton, the Dodgers' regular first baseman, Wes Parker, had a similar skill set and was still in his prime. Plus, the Dodgers had Buckner, a natural first baseman just as eager to take Parker's job. Barring an injury to Parker, Hutton was destined for another season in Triple-A.

THE INDIANS TRAVELED FROM SUNNY HONOLULU TO SOGGY TACOMA, Washington, for a three-game set versus the Cubs to complete the three-city, season-opening road trip. The Cubs played at Cheney Stadium, a 6,500-seat ballpark that opened in 1960.* Tacoma hosted the San Francisco Giants' Triple-A affiliate from 1960 through '65 and had been the home of the Chicago Cubs' top farm club since '66. Whitey Lockman was in his fourth year as Tacoma's manager. The former New York Giants first baseman-outfielder did not share Lasorda's jovial nature. "Whitey Lockman was a cold individual," recalled pitcher Darcy Fast, who played for him in '69 and the first few weeks of the '70 season before the Cubs dealt him to the Padres. "He never spoke to his players. Maybe one or two words. When I was traded to the Padres, he called me in to his motel room in Tucson and said, 'You've been traded. Here's your airline ticket. Good luck.'"[16]

Lockman led the '69 Tacoma Cubs to the PCL playoffs, in large part because of an outstanding pitching staff that posted a 3.01 ERA. But Jim Colborn and Joe Decker had since graduated to the majors, and veteran relievers Bobby Tiefenauer and Ron Piche had moved on. The '70 Tacoma Cubs sorely lacked pitching. Looking back, starting pitcher Larry Colton called it the "worst team in Pacific Coast League history."[17] The '70 Salt Lake Padres, who registered a league-worst 5.35 ERA, might have something to say about that.

Sandy Vance started the first game for Spokane and stymied Tacoma's offense with a four-hit shutout. In his first two starts, Vance had fanned 16 and yielded only one run in 15⅔ innings. Two days later, the Dodgers lost starting pitcher Bill Singer to a bout of hepatitis and called up Vance to take his place. Unlike Lockman's terse goodbye to Darcy Fast, Lasorda escorted Vance to the airport limousine for an emotional send-off. With tears in his eyes, Lasorda told Vance, "You're going to make it big because I believe in you."[18]

---

* Cheney Stadium still exists today, serving as the home of the Tacoma Rainiers, the Seattle Mariners' Triple-A affiliate.

Armed with Lasorda's confidence and a three-pitch arsenal—fastball, changeup, and a twelve-six curveball—Vance stepped into the Dodgers rotation like a seasoned veteran. In his first three starts, he lost a low-scoring affair to Tom Seaver and the Mets, tossed a complete-game victory against the Expos, and outdueled Nolan Ryan. After four starts, Vance owned a sparkling 1.71 ERA. In his fifth outing, he opposed Juan Marichal and the San Francisco Giants, whose lineup included Willie Mays. Fortunately for Vance, another future Hall of Famer, Willie McCovey, sat out that day with a minor injury. Though Mays was thirty-nine and past his prime, he remained an imposing presence in the batter's box. Vance bested Marichal that day and retired Mays in each of his four at-bats. The young hurler had a close call, however. Vance recalled that one of the outs "was easily the highest, longest out at the warning track in Dodger Stadium history."[19]

Thirteen days later, Vance and Marichal matched up again at Candlestick Park in San Francisco. Before the game, the Dodgers pitchers discussed how to pitch each Giants hitter. When it came to McCovey, Claude Osteen told Vance to pitch him down and inside. The rookie thought about it for a moment. "Wait, isn't McCovey a low-ball pull hitter?" he asked. Osteen replied, "That's right, and you don't want him to hit the ball back at you, so pitch him down and in, and let someone else get in the way of the ball."[20]

Vance lucked out again, however. The Giants' new manager, Charlie Fox, rested McCovey because of a pulled muscle. But Vance still had to deal with Mays. The Say Hey Kid came to bat in the bottom of the first inning with the bases empty. As he stepped up to the plate, he glared out at Vance. Mays had clearly not forgotten about wearing the collar against the rookie earlier in the month. "I went 3-1 on him and had to come in with a fastball," remembered Vance. "The next thing I knew the ball was circling the earth as Willie circled the bases.* As I came off the field at the end of the inning, a fan sitting over our dugout yelled, 'Hey rook, his name's Mays.' I tipped my cap in thanks for the information."[21]

While Vance got his first taste of the major leagues, the Spokane Indians carried on, concluding the opening road trip with an 8-4 record. Ten games into the season, the Indians had already lost one of the team's

---

* The home run was the 612th of Mays's career.

most promising young hurlers. But there was good news on the horizon. The booming bat of Steve Garvey would soon be added to the lineup.

The Opening Homestand

"When we were at home, Tommy had a workout every morning. We'd have a workout from 11 a.m. to lunchtime, hustle back to get something to eat, and then head back to the ballpark. Road trips were our time to get some rest."—Bobby Valentine

WALTER O'MALLEY ATTENDED THE NEW YORK BASEBALL WRITERS' dinner at the Hotel Astor on February 3, 1957. He sat across from Philip K. Wrigley, owner of both the Chicago Cubs and the Pacific Coast League's Los Angeles Angels. At some point during the night, O'Malley jotted a question on the back of an envelope: "How much will you take for the Los Angeles Angels and Wrigley Field?"* He slid the note across the table to Wrigley, who pondered the question for a moment and then scribbled his response: "Two million for the real estate and ballpark and one million for the franchise." He passed the envelope back to O'Malley, who added one word: "Deal!"[1]

---

* The Angels' home ballpark in South Los Angeles was Wrigley Field, designed by architect Zachary Taylor Davis, who also designed Wrigley Field in Chicago. With a seating capacity of 21,000, Wrigley Field in LA was a scaled-down version of the Cubs ballpark.

It was that easy.*

O'Malley had been on a quest to replace aging Ebbets Field with a privately built domed stadium in Brooklyn for more than a decade. A number of potential sites were considered, but O'Malley's preferred location was the corner of Atlantic and Flatbush.† In order to acquire the land, he needed city officials to enact Title I of the 1949 Housing Act, a provision that allowed cities to obtain land and clear slums for redevelopment. Robert Moses, Parks Commissioner for the city of New York, wielded authority over parks, bridges, and construction projects. The powerful bureaucrat disliked baseball and worried about traffic congestion in Brooklyn. In his view, a privately owned ballpark didn't meet the legal requirements to enact a law aimed at prioritizing new construction of public housing. Moses instead recommended that O'Malley relocate to Flushing Meadows, Queens. O'Malley began to more seriously consider moving the team elsewhere.

Days after his back-of-the-envelope deal with Wrigley, O'Malley told sportswriter Dick Young that the city of New York had six months to come up with definitive plans for the financing and construction of a new ballpark or else he would "have to make other arrangements."[2] O'Malley's purchase of the Angels and Wrigley Field (the one in Los Angeles, not the one in Chicago) served dual purposes. As author Andy McCue succinctly put it in his book, *Mover and Shaker*, "It gave him entrée into the most desirable market for a move, if that became necessary, while increasing pressure on New York officials to come up with a reasonable offer."[3]

The O'Malley-Wrigley deal became public knowledge on February 21. The next day, New York Giants owner Horace Stoneham announced that if the Dodgers were leaving New York, so were the Giants. The Giants played home games at the Polo Grounds, another decrepit ballpark that lacked parking for its increasingly suburban crowd. Poor attendance also compelled Stoneham to consider relocation. The Giants were coming off a season in which they ranked last in the National League in attendance with an average of barely 8,000 fans per game. Stoneham had planned a move to Minneapolis for several years. He owned the Triple-A Minneapolis

---

* Wrigley also acquired the Dodgers' minor-league franchise in Fort Worth, Texas, and its home, LaGrave Field, as part of the deal.
† The corner of Atlantic and Flatbush is the present-day site of the Barclays Center, home of the NBA's Brooklyn Nets and WNBA's New York Liberty.

Millers, so he already possessed territorial rights there. Plus, a new ballpark, Metropolitan Stadium, opened in 1956, in the hope of landing an MLB team. Ultimately, however, the opportunity to break ground on the West Coast in tandem with O'Malley lured Stoneham to San Francisco. On May 27, National League owners voted to allow the Giants and Dodgers to move to San Francisco and Los Angeles, respectively, under the stipulation that both clubs move together. The Giants officially announced their intention to relocate to San Francisco on August 19. O'Malley confirmed his plan to move the Dodgers to Los Angeles on October 8.

As part of the Dodgers and Giants' joint relocation, O'Malley and Stoneham each agreed to pay the other Pacific Coast League owners $450,000 for territorial rights. Plus, O'Malley had to find a new home for his PCL franchise, the Los Angeles Angels. In the fall of 1957, Angels team president Dick Walsh met with government officials in two potential relocation cities—Long Beach, California, and Spokane, Washington. Several PCL franchises, including Vancouver, Seattle, and Portland, opposed Long Beach as a potential site because of its proximity to Los Angeles. At a meeting in Spokane on November 27, Spokane officials, led by County Commissioner Bill Allen, proposed a plan to update the city's existing ballpark, Ferris Field. Dodgers executives verbally committed to Spokane on December 2. A few days later, Spokane county and city commissioners agreed to put up $400,000 for the construction of a new ballpark at the Interstate Fairgrounds, four miles east of downtown. The Angels' relocation to Spokane became official in mid-December. The Inland Empire, as Spokane is known (not to be confused with the Inland Empire region of Los Angeles, centered on San Bernardino/Riverside/Ontario), would now have Triple-A baseball for the first time. Previously, Spokane had been home to Class-B teams under the old minor-league classification.

The local papers held a vote to name the team. Readers chose the name Indians, a moniker that had been used by minor-league baseball teams in Spokane since the early twentieth century. It paid homage to the Spokane Tribe for which the city was named.

Spokane's new 9,600-seat ballpark, officially named Fairground Recreational Park but commonly known as the Fairgrounds, was hastily built in three months at a cost of $534,700.* Its lights came from Gilmore Field, former home of the Hollywood Stars, while its batting cage came from Ebbets Field. Upon the stadium's opening on April 29, 1958, the Indians beat the Seattle Rainiers with a lineup featuring Maury Wills at leadoff and Jim Gentile hitting fifth. Two years later, Spokane would win its first PCL title with a loaded roster that included Willie Davis, Ron Fairly, and Frank Howard.

THROUGHOUT THE 1960S AND EARLY '70S, MANY OF THE SPOKANE Indians players rented rooms from Frank and Katy Saccomanno in their five-bedroom brick Tudor home on the north side of town. Frank, a beer and wine wholesaler, and Katy, a homemaker, began hosting players in 1960. Their first tenant was Dodgers prospect Charley Smith, who was related to Frank and Katy's cousin. The Saccomannos continued to rent out rooms long after Smith had embarked on a decade-long major-league career. Their house had a large room downstairs that accommodated a few players and another room upstairs that held one or two more. Marv Galliher, Bob O'Brien, Gus Sposito, and Mike Strahler all stayed there in 1970. Bart Shirley, John Werhas, and Geoff Zahn also rented rooms over the years.

By 1970, Frank had health problems and couldn't get around too well. Katy took on the role of host mom to "her boys." Occasionally, she barbecued for her tenants and loved to slip a rubber hamburger in someone's bun as a prank. She sometimes took the boys across the border to Idaho for some water skiing at the Saccomannos cabin on Priest Lake, much to Tommy Lasorda's chagrin. If her renters were out past curfew and Lasorda called to check in, she always covered for them.

Frank and Katy's grandsons, Frank and Robert Steidl, frequently visited their grandparents' home around the time the players left for the ballpark. Then they'd hitch a ride to the Fairgrounds, shag fly balls during batting practice, and sit in the bleachers for the game. Robert was a lefthanded first baseman and soaked up pointers from Tommy Hutton. Hutton

---

* Fairground Recreational Park still exists today under the name Avista Stadium. In 2024, the ballpark underwent renovations at an estimated cost of $16.8 million.

even gave Robert his extra Spalding first baseman's mitt, which he used throughout college baseball.

THE DODGERS EMPLOYED GERMAN-BORN, OHIO-RAISED ELTEN SCHILLER as the Spokane Indians' president and general manager. Schiller had served in the Navy during World War II, drawing an assignment as a stenographer in the legal department because he knew shorthand. As it so happened, the typing and stenography classes he begrudgingly took in high school may have saved his life. The ship to which he had originally assigned was destroyed in the Bougainville campaign.

After the war, Schiller and his new bride, Valorie, moved to her hometown of St. Paul, Minnesota. While working with the Veterans Administration helping other vets find employment, Schiller came across a listing for a part-time position with the St. Paul Saints, a Triple-A affiliate of the Dodgers. Instead of finding someone else to fill the Saints' vacancy, he applied for it himself. Schiller got the job and had been with Dodgers ever since.

In 1961, he was put in charge of the Dodgers' new affiliate in Omaha. Having only a few months to launch and promote the team, he approached the challenge with boundless enthusiasm. Although Omaha would finish in last place, *The Sporting News* named him Minor League Executive of the Year because of how effectively he promoted the team and stirred up fan interest. Schiller's image appeared on the front page of America's premiere sports publication alongside the likes of Roger Maris and Warren Spahn.

As GM of the Double-A Albuquerque Dukes/Dodgers in the mid-'60s, Schiller served as a mentor to Buzzie Bavasi's son, Peter, who was looking to break into baseball out of college.

"They didn't teach you how to sell scoreboard ads in college," recalled the younger Bavasi, "nor how to stretch the mustard at the concession stands (cut it with white vinegar), or how to talk to the city public-works department out of gallons of green and yellow striping paint so we could paint the old ballpark ... He was the best professor I'd ever had."[4]

In 1970, Schiller oversaw the Spokane Indians' business operations, including ticket sales, promotions, and budgeting. He worked eight-hour days during the offseason and as many as sixteen hours on game days. The front-office staff was bare boned. Schiller typically had only a couple of full-time employees, including the team's longtime secretary, Barbara Klante. Ticketing and concessions managers worked part-time during the season. During games, Schiller sat with Valorie for an inning or two, then roamed around the ballpark and observed various stadium operations for the remainder of the game.

Before the start of each season, Schiller hired a pair of batboys—one for each dugout. In order to narrow the pool of applicants for such a highly desirable job, he enlisted the help of the *Daily Chronicle*, one of the Spokane's two daily papers. On March 26, 1970, the paper ran an article in the sports section under the headline "Indian Bat Boy: Contest Set." The article detailed how five finalists from the pool of applicants would be selected to attend a luncheon, where the two winners would be chosen to serve at batboys. The other three finalists would receive season tickets as a consolation prize. The contest was open to kids between the ages of ten to seventeen. Applicants were asked to submit a written statement of thirty words or fewer explaining why they wanted the job. Having good grades and reliable transportation to the ballpark could help an applicant as well.

Fourteen-year-old Dave Vaughn was a paperboy for the *Daily Chronicle* and happened across the article. He had played Little League growing up in Southern California before his family relocated to Spokane. Vaughn *loved* baseball. Applying was a no-brainer. He wrote "something sappy" for his written statement and put the application in the mail. A couple weeks later, the *Daily Chronicle* notified him that he had been selected as one of the five finalists.

Schiller took them to lunch as a de facto job interview and picked Vaughn to work the visitors' dugout.

The batboys made $3.50 per game—roughly $0.50 an hour. For Vaughn, the pay couldn't have mattered less. He was embarking on what would be the best summer of his life. It began on Friday, April 24—the day of the Indians' home opener versus the Phoenix Giants. Opening-day festivities began at 11 a.m. with a parade through downtown. A luncheon at the Ridpath Motor Inn followed. Luncheon tickets cost $1.50 and included admission to the Giants-Indians game, which began at 3 p.m.

1970 - SPOKANE INDIANS - 1970
Pacific Coast League – Northern Division Champions

Top Row: Trainer Herb Vike, Jerry Stephenson, Doyle Alexander, Mike Strahler, Tom Paciorek, George Lott, Dick Armstrong, Charlie Hough, Clubhouse Boy Kent Schultz
Center Row: Bill Buckner, Geoff Zahn, Sandy Vance, Coach Dick McLaughlin, Manager Tom Lasorda, Coach Bert Shirley, John Purdin, Marv Galliher, Jack Jenkins
Bottom Row: Batboy Dave Vaughn, Bob Valentine, Bob Stinson, Bob O'Brien, B. P. Pitcher Rev. Tom Mulcahy, S.J., Dave Lopes, Steve Sogge, Gus Sposito, Batboy Mike Wilson

The Giants had won their first nine games, arriving in Spokane with a league-best 11-2 record under manager Charlie Fox, who would replace Clyde King in the San Francisco Giants' dugout a month later. Temperatures that day dropped to the forties. Gale-force winds made it feel even colder, keeping many fans at home. The crowd of 1,706 would be the smallest for a home opener in Spokane's thirteen seasons as a Triple-A franchise.

The game started inauspiciously for the Indians, whose starting pitcher, Mike Strahler, allowed four of the first six batters to reach base. Lasorda displayed a quick hook. He yanked Strahler and brought in Charlie Hough, who quickly discovered that the wind made controlling his knuckleball nearly impossible.* The twenty-two-year-old hurler issued six free passes over six and a third innings of long relief but somehow minimized the damage to two runs. Trailing 3-2 in the seventh, the Indians mounted a rally with the help of Mother Nature. Fly balls were already an

---

* Hough noted that his knuckleball generally moved better in the heavier Pacific Northwest air. In Phoenix and Tucson, he had to throw it slower to get the same action.

adventure because of the swirling winds. And then the sun started to set behind the first-base line. Giants left fielder Jim McKnight lost a pair of routine fly balls in the glare, resulting in a pair of doubles off the bats of Tommy Hutton and Bart Shirley that led to a three-run seventh inning. Indians center fielder Davey Lopes provided an insurance tally with his first home run of the season—a wind-aided blast to left field. Spokane won the game, 6-3.

Two days later, Hough tossed another five-plus innings of long relief, picking up his third win in the Indians' last four games. In 27 innings pitched, Hough had allowed just three earned runs for a 1.00 ERA. His knuckleball was moving so much that Steve Sogge and Bob Stinson were having as much trouble catching it as batters were having hitting it. The team sought an oversized mitt to make it easier for the catchers, but the search had so far come up empty.

"Being a catcher was almost always a lot of fun," Sogge recalled, "but trying to catch Charlie, especially when he was trying to learn how to control his knuckleball, was not fun. In the early days, no one, including Charlie, knew where it was going or what movement it would have. All you could do was get into your catching position and prepare for an adventure."[5]

The Indians came away from their five-game set against Phoenix with four wins and had now won 13 of 18. Spokane pitchers shined throughout the series, holding a Giants lineup that included Jim Ray Hart and George Foster to three or fewer runs in each contest. Lasorda's offense thus far had been satisfactory, averaging 4.5 runs per game. And it was about to receive a shot in the arm in the form of Steve Garvey, demoted to Spokane after a slow start in LA.

JUST A FEW WEEKS EARLIER, GARVEY HAD BEEN ON CLOUD NINE. HE SPENT his day off before the Dodgers' season opener filming a commercial for Vitalis Hair Tonic with Maury Wills and Pete Rose. When the Dodgers hosted Rose and the Cincinnati Reds the next day at Dodger Stadium, Garvey was in the starting lineup, playing third base and hitting sixth. Until then, his baseball career had been on a steady upward trajectory.

Expectations were high that Garvey—the Dodgers' twelfth different opening-day third baseman in thirteen years—would stabilize a position that had been in flux since the Dodgers moved to Los Angeles. The outlook for the 1970 squad was equally promising. On paper, the additions of rookies Garvey and Bill Buckner to a talented veteran lineup gave the Dodgers the look of a legitimate contender to win the National League West.

Under the assumption they'd be spending the entire season in LA, Garvey and Buckner rented an apartment together in Marina del Rey. "We were on our way to the Hall of Fame," Garvey thought.[6]

Panic set in quickly, however, when the Dodgers lost their first five games, including a pair to the hapless San Diego Padres—a team coming off a 110-loss inaugural season. None of the Dodgers regulars were hitting, including Garvey, who recorded just one hit in his first 18 at-bats. Walter Alston benched him in favor of Jim Lefebvre after just five games. "Five games?" wrote John Hall in the *Los Angeles Times*. "Even Babe Ruth might have been hard-pressed to prove himself in five games."[7]

Following the 0-5 start, the Dodgers starting rotation stepped up, allowing two or fewer runs in nine of the next fifteen games. Two of the nine were started by rookie Sandy Vance. By the end of April, the Dodgers had climbed back to .500. Garvey, meanwhile, sat on the bench for two weeks, appearing in just four games as a pinch-hitter. Such little playing time for one of the organization's brightest prospects was suboptimal. Al Campanis realized this. On April 29, he demoted Garvey to Spokane so he could get regular at-bats. The demotion disappointed and embarrassed Garvey. Three weeks earlier, he had filmed his first commercial and started on opening day for his childhood team. Now, he was being sent far from the bright lights of Hollywood to Spokane, Washington. When he broke the news to his parents, his father encouraged him to go to Spokane and have some fun.

Lasorda greeted the youngster at the airport—just as he had with Valentine in Ogden. Garvey figured they were going to grab lunch and catch up, but Lasorda had other ideas. They drove straight to the Fairgrounds for batting practice.

GARVEY WAS NOT THE ONLY DODGERS ROOKIE TO STRUGGLE OUT OF THE gate. Over his first six starts, Bill Buckner registered just three hits in 24 at-bats. He, too, was benched and optioned to Spokane a day after Garvey.

Because he was taking a full course load at USC to maintain his Vietnam draft deferment, Buckner wouldn't report to Spokane until a week later. The Dodgers replaced Buckner with outfielder Von Joshua, a .370 hitter through 15 games for Spokane.*

With the addition of Garvey, Lasorda shifted Bill Russell from third base to center field. Once Buckner arrived, Spokane's regular starting outfield would consist of Buckner in left, Russell in center, and Paciorek in right. For much of the season's first half, Davey Lopes was relegated to the bench. In fact, because of call-ups, injuries, and military obligations, there were only four games all season when Garvey, Buckner, Russell, and Lopes were all in the same starting lineup.

Garvey made his presence felt immediately. In his Indians debut on April 30 against the Tucson Toros, the muscular third baseman went 2-for-6 and scored the game-winning run in the bottom of the sixteenth inning on Tommy Hutton's RBI single. Charlie Hough continued to flummox opposing hitters, pitching nine scoreless innings in relief of starter Mike Strahler. With the exception of one curveball to the opposing pitcher, Hough threw nothing but knuckleballs.

"Tommy told me to throw a knuckleball every pitch until it was a 3-0 count," recalled Hough. "He said, 'If it's 3-0 and you believe you're going to get it over, then throw another knuckleball.' That's the way he approached me. He said, 'Look, you've got a pitch they don't hit good. Throw it every pitch.' He showed a lot of confidence in me."[8]

Hough finished April with six wins and a minuscule 0.75 ERA. "It seemed like our starting pitchers early in the year pitched so-so," he recalled. "And it seemed like every time Tommy put me in, we'd rally. And when we rallied, we scored a lot of runs."[9] Looking back, Hough humbly credited the offense for his amazing start, which downplays his value to the team. His ability to throw effective long relief on consecutive days made Lasorda's job much easier and was a key reason the Indians finished April with an excellent 13-5 record.

The Indians wrapped up the opening homestand by winning three of the next four versus the Toros, the Chicago White Sox' top affiliate. Garvey and Bobby Valentine each registered nine hits in the series, and

---

* The roster juggling also included the demotion of Marv Galliher from Spokane to Double-A Albuquerque and the activation of Dick McLaughlin to fill a spot on the Indians bench.

Bill Russell chipped in eight. Davey Lopes recorded a four-hit game in the series opener before leaving for a weekend of Reserve duty. Lasorda's club had performed superbly thus far, winning eight of 10 at home and 16 of 22 overall. Up next loomed a fourteen-game road trip through Phoenix, Tucson, and Portland. All cylinders were firing, and Bill Buckner was on his way.

Jaw Breaker

"They talk about the big bonus players, the spoiled young players. I don't see any here. I see a lot of young talent that's going to the bigs ... they're all throwbacks to the old-fashioned, tough players that give it everything they've got." —Bart Shirley, May 1970

THE 1980s BOSTON RED SOX WERE ONCE DESCRIBED AS A TEAM OF twenty-five guys, twenty-five cabs. The 1970 Spokane Indians could have been dubbed "twenty-one guys, one buffet." On road trips, they ate meals together at $1.99 all-you-can-eat smorgasbords and killed time at bowling alleys and movie theatres. And their manager often joined them. Tommy Lasorda was an extrovert who thrived on camaraderie, friendship, and fun.

A manager fraternizing and developing personal relationships with his players was far from the norm. Baseball's management culture had traditionally been very militaristic. Managers didn't care if a pitcher's shoulder was sore or if the third baseman's wife was sick. They cared that a player performed well. And if he didn't perform, they'd find someone else. As a rule of thumb, managers kept a distance from their players, particularly away from the field. Lasorda was different. He broke down the invisible barriers that had existed for decades and developed relationships with his players. As Bobby Valentine put it, "Tommy changed the entire culture of managing a baseball team."[1]

While eating with his players, Lasorda often ate food off of their plates. It was part of his shtick. He'd ask a player what he was eating. The player would respond, "I'm eating a steak, skip." Lasorda would then grab a fork, take a bite of food from the player's plate, and respond, "Yep, that's a steak alright." He took similar liberties at players' homes. "We invited him for dinner," recalled Pete Scarpati, "and he met my wife for the first time. She made a pot of gravy with meatballs. He felt so at home that he walked up to the stove, took a fork and dipped it right in the gravy."[2]

Another time, Lasorda visited several of his players who were hanging out one afternoon during an off day. He walked up to catcher Bob "Scrap Iron" Stinson, grabbed his Coke bottle, and said, "What're you drinking, Scrap?" Before Stinson could answer, Tommy put the bottle to his lips and took a huge swig. Of tobacco juice. For the next fifteen minutes, recounted Sandy Vance, the players gleefully watched their manager dry heave and curse the heavens.[3]

In Phoenix—the Indians' first stop on a three-city road trip—Lasorda's bit backfired. He walked into a restaurant where a group of players were dining and spotted whom he thought was pitcher Jerry Stephenson. Lasorda snuck up behind him, reached over his shoulder, and grabbed a hunk of meat off his plate. "What's this you're eating?" Lasorda asked. When the man turned around, Lasorda realized that he was neither Jerry Stephenson nor anyone else he knew. Several Spokane players dining nearby watched the scene unfold and fell on the floor with laughter. Lasorda, meanwhile, deescalated the situation by apologizing profusely.

ON MAY 4, THE INDIANS BEGAN A FIVE-GAME SERIES AGAINST THE GIANTS at malodorous Phoenix Municipal Stadium. The foul stench that wafted from nearby stockyards remained seared into Tom Paciorek's olfactory memory decades later. Hitting home runs in the spacious ballpark—410 feet to center and 345 down the lines—required a prodigious blast. The Indians found plenty of other ways to score, winning the first three games by putting up eight, nine, and ten runs, all without the benefit of the long ball.

Skip Pitlock, a second-year pro out of Southern Illinois University, subdued Spokane's offense on May 7, allowing just four hits in the Giants' 4-1 victory. The southpaw was riding a wave of invincibility after pitching in the 1968 College World Series championship game, then compiling a 10-2 record during his pro first season. Following his win over the Indians, Pitlock would win his next seven decisions, earning a promotion to the big leagues in early June.*

In the series finale, three Spokane players—left fielder Bill Buckner, center fielder Davey Lopes, and shortstop Bobby Valentine—collided while pursuing a shallow fly ball at high speeds. Buckner got the worst of it, the impact knocking him unconscious before he awoke with a sore jaw. The young Californian staggered to his feet and exited the game. Lopes and Valentine were shaken up but escaped serious harm. Adding insult to injury, Phoenix won the game, 9-3.

Buckner still played in two of three games over the weekend in Tucson, going 7-for-9. His jaw remained sore and swollen for a few days after the collision, so Lasorda sent him to Los Angeles for an examination on the team's rare day off. When X-rays revealed a fractured mandible, doctors wired Buckner's jaw shut that very day. The Dodgers front office told Lasorda to sit Buckner for five weeks while he healed.

At around 11 a.m. the next morning, the skipper received a knock on his motel room door. As Lasorda later recounted to Dodgers scout Brian Stephenson, he opened the door to a blast of warm desert air and the sight of Bill Buckner standing in silence. Lasorda had canceled batting practice that day because of the heat, but Buckner wanted to go to the field and hit anyway. He couldn't talk with his jaw wired shut, but Lasorda knew exactly what he wanted.

Much to his teammates' amazement, Buckner returned to the Indians lineup that same night. Decades later, Valentine still marveled at the fact that he never missed a game: "Jo Lasorda had to make Buck's food in a blender, and he drank it with a straw. He couldn't open his mouth to brush his teeth. His breath smelled so bad, it became renowned."[4]

---

* Pitlock shared June PCL Player of the Month honors with Bill Russell and Juan Pizzaro. In his big-league debut on June 12, Pitlock lost to Bob Gibson and the Cardinals and would finish the season with a 5-5 record and 4.66 ERA for the San Francisco Giants. In retrospect, Pitlock attributed his mediocrity in San Francisco to overuse in Phoenix. Shortly before his callup, he threw an estimated 175 pitches during an eleven-inning game. He arrived in San Francisco with a sore shoulder but didn't dare mention it and risk his roster spot.

BILL BUCKNER - Outfielder

Courtesy Dave Eskenazi.

If Buckner's fetid breath was renowned, his competitive drive was legendary. In the clubhouse and away from the ballpark, he joked around, but as soon as he walked down the tunnel and on to the field, he flipped a switch. "You'd play pepper with him, and he's there to win at all costs," remembered Indians clubhouse boy Kent Schultz. "He had that ability more than anyone else to turn the competition switch on." And it wasn't just baseball. Buckner's intense desire to win manifested itself during any form of competition. "We'd play cards on the road, and he'd kick your ass," added Schultz. "No ifs, ands, or buts. Once you got into a contest, Billy Buck was out to win."[5]

Several of Buckner's teammates shared a similar desire to succeed on the diamond. Starting their careers together in Rookie ball, Valentine, Garvey, Paciorek, and Buckner quickly became like brothers who endlessly wanted to outdo one another on the field. Lasorda taught them to enjoy one another's success—or at least pretend they were. As Valentine described, "We were all young, we were rather selfish, some more than others. When you played for Tommy, you had to fake it. When somebody else did good, you had to be happy."[6] Similarly, Steve Sogge observed, "The minor leagues can be a little dog eat dog because everyone's goal is to the make it to the majors, but we played together and were a cohesive unit."[7]

After Spokane won four of five in Tucson, the road trip concluded with four games in Portland against the Beavers, Triple-A affiliate of the Milwaukee Brewers.* In the opener, Valentine and Garvey each hit solo home runs, as Mike Strahler and Charlie Hough tossed a combined four-hitter to produce a 2-0 Indians triumph. Through thirty-three games, Hough had already amassed eight wins and four saves. But he would miss the next three games because of military duty. His absence, plus sloppy Indians defense and solid pitching by erstwhile Spokane hurler Bruce Brubaker, resulted in three straight Portland victories. The series loss, Spokane's first of the season, left the Indians with a mere two-game lead over Portland in the Northern Division standings. Perhaps the Beavers and their manager, Al Federoff, came away feeling they could compete for the division crown. Little did they know, it was as close as any team would get to the Spokane Indians for the remainder of the 1970 season.

---

* The Beavers played home games at Civic Stadium. Built in 1926, the ballpark had a j-shaped grandstand built for football. Because it was built into the side of a hill, left field sat below street level while the main grandstand entrance sat at street level. Today, the stadium is known as Providence Park and houses the Portland Timbers, an MLS team.

Old Jerry

"We belong to the 4-H club. You hope to find a prospect. You hope you get him in the draft. You hope you can sign him. And you hope he can play."
—Joe Stephenson, Boston Red Sox scout and father of Spokane Indians pitcher Jerry Stephenson

Kent Schultz's last class ended at 1:30 p.m. on Monday, May 18, 1970. An hour later, the Ferris High School junior walked into the Spokane Indians clubhouse at the Fairgrounds and began preparations for that night's game against the Salt Lake Padres. Schultz had started working for the Indians three years earlier. After one season as a batboy, he earned a promotion to home clubhouse boy. In 1970, Schultz was in his third season on the job. His pregame duties, which began five hours before first pitch, included shining shoes and stocking the clubhouse with concessions that he purchased on his own. He bought candy, bubble gum, and sunflower seeds from a local wholesaler and went to Coeur d'Alene, Idaho, for cigarettes because they were a bit cheaper across the border.[*]

---

[*] Looking back, Schultz estimated that 70 percent of the team smoked. This was six years after the Surgeon General published a landmark report linking smoking to an increased risk

When players grabbed drinks, snacks, or cigarettes from the clubhouse concession area, they marked a swindle sheet. At the end of each homestand, Schultz would tally up the amount each player owed and collect payment.

During games, the clubbie would walk back and forth from the dugout to the locker room, filling a variety of duties while catching glimpses of the game when he could. On the not-so-rare occasion when Tommy Lasorda was ejected from a game, the skipper would loiter in the tunnel out of the umpires' line of sight. Unbeknownst to the men in blue, he'd relay signs to Schultz in the dugout, who'd pass them along to the players. In the later innings, Schultz would wheel cases of beer from the ballpark office to the clubhouse and put them on ice so the players could enjoy a few cold ones after the game. Postgame, he'd knock mud off cleats and collect soiled uniforms, which he then took to a commercial laundromat. The teen often didn't get home until well after midnight. He maintained the demanding schedule with the support of his parents, who helpfully lived just a few blocks from the Fairgrounds. Sometimes Schultz's father came to the ballpark and helped clean spikes. His mother chipped in by sewing holes in the players' pants and driving Kent to buy the cigarettes he sold in the clubhouse.

Like Schultz, visiting clubhouse attendant Jerry Kuntz had gotten his start as a batboy before earning a promotion at the end of the '68 season. During his tenure as a clubbie, the Gonzaga Prep student had the good fortune of rubbing elbows with hundreds of visiting players. Looking back decades later, he fondly recalled playing catch with Bobby Bonds and watching an up-and-coming Phillies third baseman named Mike Schmidt. Kuntz also encountered dozens of prominent PCL managers, including Warren Spahn, Billy Martin, Bob Lemon, and Chuck Tanner. The teen observed how each skipper shepherded a blend of personalities and experience levels. From his point of view, Tanner stood on a pedestal above the rest.

Schultz and the two batboys, Dave Vaughn and Mike Wilson, had lockers amongst the Indians players. Before games, they'd shag fly balls, play pepper, and throw long toss. Schultz, a southpaw, sometimes pitched

---

of lung cancer and overall mortality and five years after Congress required that cigarette packages carry a health warning.

batting practice. Lasorda protected them like he did his players. One time, concessions manager Dorian Chastain shoved a batboy who was pestering Chastain's sister, a popcorn vendor. A short time later, Lasorda approached Chastain and asked why he was roughing up his batboys. The skipper then dispensed a piece of advice that Chastain would carry for the rest of his life. "Anytime you confront somebody, put your hands in your back pockets," said Lasorda. "That way, you don't push or hit someone you shouldn't."[1]

At one point during the summer of '70, Vaughn broke his left wrist at a church camp. Despite having to wear a cast for several weeks, he continued to participate in pregame warmups. To play catch, he'd snag the ball with his gloved right hand, tuck the mitt under his left arm, and then throw with his right arm à la Jim Abbott. Lasorda made a huge deal of it before a game. "You gotta have desire and a love for the game," Lasorda told his players. "Look at this boy. He broke his arm, and he's still out here playing!"[2]

Things weren't always fun and games, however. Minor-league baseball could be cutthroat. Careers were on the line. And because Schultz and the batboys were in the middle of it all, they were privy to some intense clubhouse meetings and difficult conversations. Schultz learned an important adage: what you hear here stays here. Lasorda also taught the clubhouse boy that "pitchers get paid by the out, not by the hour" and to "think you're the very best; just don't tell anybody."[3] Schultz later realized he had translated these principles learned from Lasorda into his professional career in banking.

The Indians' fourteen-game homestand that spanned May 18 through 30 began with a visit from Don Zimmer's Salt Lake Padres. When the teams met up, old friends Lasorda and Zimmer would invariably enjoy a round of golf, during which there would be ample laughs and the occasional practical joke. In one instance, recalled Vaughn, Lasorda brought along a hoagie to eat after the round. Each time Lasorda went to putt, Zimmer pulled out the sandwich and took a bite. At the end of the round, Lasorda went to eat his lunch. There was nothing left.

The Indians manager, however, got the last laugh when Spokane won three of five against Zimmer's team of novices at the Fairgrounds. Steve

Garvey blasted a pair of two-run homers in the opener and batted 10-for-17 in the series. With pitchers John Purdin and Dick Armstrong nursing injuries and Pete Scarpati away on National Guard duty, Lasorda called a team meeting where he implored his players to give a little extra. Charlie Hough, who could chuck a seemingly limitless number of knuckleballs, certainly gave all he could, appearing in all five games of the series. He recorded a four-out save in one outing and suffered his second loss of the season on Fred Kendall's walk-off home run in another. "I couldn't throw hard," said Hough later, "but I had conditioned myself enough to throw batting-practice speed every day, and basically that's what I tried to do."[4]

Jerry Stephenson made sure Hough wasn't needed in the next series opener, the first of five against the Hawaii Islanders. The twenty-six-year-old righty spun a five-hitter against one of the Coast League's top offenses. It was the fifth win of the season for Stephenson, who stood at a different place in his career than many of his comparatively younger teammates. After yo-yoing between Triple-A and the majors for several seasons, the Southern California native was just trying to hang on.

Jerry grew up in Hermosa Beach and went to high school in Anaheim. His father, Joe, was a former big-league catcher who had cups of coffee in the 1940s with the Giants, Cubs, and White Sox before embarking on a long scouting career with the Red Sox. Jerry inherited both his father's lean stature and his love of baseball. Early on, he played catcher. Eventually, he shed the tools of ignorance in favor of pitching. His arm was simply too good. The younger Stephenson, who sprouted to six-foot-two, struck out 74 batters in 32 innings as a high school senior, cementing his status as a legitimate major-league prospect. Joe didn't feel it was right to recommend his own son to his superiors. But when Tom Yawkey heard that the Yankees offered Jerry a $100,000 bonus, he took matters into his own hands. The Red Sox owner flew the young fireballer to Boston for a workout and matched the Yankees' offer. Jerry was signed by Red Sox scout Neil Mahoney.

Stephenson enjoyed an excellent first year in pro ball pitching for the Class-B Winston-Salem Red Sox, winning 11 of 16 decisions while averaging more than a strikeout per inning. The nineteen-year-old made Boston's opening-day roster in 1963 but pitched in only one game before the Red Sox sent him to the minors to get regular work. Struggles in Triple-A resulted in another demotion to Double-A. Between the two stops, Stephenson amassed an unsightly 4-20 record and 4.81 ERA. After a sore elbow cut his '64 season short, he spent the entire '65 campaign in the majors, but the Red Sox used him sparingly. For the next two years, he bounced between Boston and the minors. He did, however, experience the thrill of pitching in the '67 World Series, throwing two innings of relief in Boston's Game 4 loss to the St. Louis Cardinals.

JERRY STEPHENSON — Pitcher

Courtesy Dave Eskenazi.

Shoulder problems contributed to a subpar 2-8 record and 5.94 ERA with the Red Sox in '68. "I had a terrible year," assessed Stephenson years later. "I just couldn't do the job. By that time, I was an old man. Really!

The Red Sox told me the next year that I was too old ... I mean, I'd been around a long time, but I was all of twenty-five."[5]

The Red Sox released Stephenson a week into the '69 season. The expansion Seattle Pilots then took a flier on the "old man" and assigned him to their Triple-A affiliate in Vancouver, British Columbia, the Siberia of baseball. There, he reunited with former high school teammate Frank Peters. But Stephenson remained hampered by a sore shoulder. "We were playing in Eugene, and Jerry couldn't comb his hair because his arm hurt so bad," recalled Peters. "He hadn't pitched in a while and got a call that [manager Bob] Lemon wanted to see him. We thought he was probably getting released. He comes back to the room and says, 'They're sending me to the big leagues!' And of course, he did not do too well because his arm was hurting."[6] Stephenson made two relief appearances in mop-up duty, registering a 10.13 ERA for the one-and-done Pilots.

Stephenson's future as a professional pitcher looked bleak heading into 1970. He ended up on Spokane's roster because of his father's connection to Tommy Lasorda. When Lasorda had first arrived in Southern California as a young scout in the early '60s, Joe Stephenson helped Lasorda by telling him where to go and which players to see. Lasorda never forgot that.

After the 1969 season, Lasorda was determined to jettison pitcher Bruce Brubaker from the Dodgers organization. Brubaker's '69 statistics were excellent—a 3.03 ERA in 175 innings—but he cemented his place in Lasorda's doghouse when he spearheaded the effort to have Valentine benched because of his shaky defense. Brubaker further incensed his manager by failing to show complete loyalty to Dodger blue. Lasorda later recalled that when the scoreboard showed that the Dodgers were losing, Brubaker would pump his fist and cheer. He figured if the Dodgers were losing, he had a better chance of getting called up.

Lasorda loved his players, but if you got on his bad side, look out. "You wouldn't want Lasorda as an enemy," recalled Ron Cey, who later played for him in both Triple-A and Los Angeles. "He'd make up his mind about an issue or a person, and there was no middle ground. ... Lasorda was opinionated about just about everything. He didn't waver ... he could make you or he could break you."[7]

Agreeing to take Brubaker off the Dodgers' hands, the Pilots supplied a list of a half-dozen players whom they would trade. Lasorda looked at the list and saw Jerry Stephenson's name. Joe Stephenson had treated him well years earlier, so Lasorda wanted to return the favor.

It just so happened that Jerry and Tommy lived near each other in Fullerton during the offseason. The two met at Dodger Stadium one day in early 1970 after the trade went down. As they stood on the third level looking down on the field, Lasorda predicted that Stephenson would be pitching on the mound below by September. Given the trajectory of his career, Stephenson thought Lasorda was crazy.

With nearly a decade of pro experience under his belt, Stephenson developed into a veteran leader on the Spokane Indians. He was also one of the more intellectual players on the team. On days he wasn't pitching, Stephenson would perch in the corner of the dugout with a book and a cigarette, recalled batboy Mike Wilson. Between innings, umpires would yell at him to put his cigarette out.[8] Eventually, Stephenson would earn his college degree, fulfilling a promise he made to his parents when he signed with the Red Sox out of high school. It only took him fourteen years.

MIKE STRAHLER, A HIGH-STRUNG SORT WHO SMOKED TWO PACKS A DAY, followed Stephenson's shutout of the Islanders with a complete-game victory of his own, giving Lasorda's shorthanded, overworked bullpen a second day of rest. Hawaii bounced back to win the next two contests behind the pitching of two-time All-Star Juan Pizzaro (another veteran acquired by GM Jack Quinn) and the hitting of John Werhas and Winston Llenas, who combined for six runs, eight hits, and eight RBI.

Lasorda tapped Charlie Hough to make his first start of the season in the series finale on May 27. Hough's catcher that night, Bob Stinson, got to break in the team's new oversized catcher's mitt. The new glove, six inches larger than the standard size, gave Stinson a better chance of getting leather on Hough's unpredictable knuckleballs. Both he and Steve Sogge had trouble catching the pitch early on, resulting in several passed balls.* "It's fantastic how far the ball moves, maybe eight inches one way or the other," said Stinson at the time. "That doggone thing, it might break three

---

* Years later, Dodgers pitcher Rick Sutcliffe would learn firsthand how much Hough's knuckleball moved. "He played catch with Charlie without a cup on," recalled Doug Rau, "and the ball moved so much that the ball hit him square in the nuts. The last time I saw Sutcliffe that day, he was in the locker room with a bag of ice on his balls."

ways coming to the plate. It darts. Like a hummingbird, only faster. You can get up a sweat catching it, especially with a runner on third."[9]

Hough scattered seven hits, struck out four, and walked only one to earn his ninth win in eleven decisions. Every position player in Spokane's starting lineup recorded a hit off Islanders starter Greg Washburn, a former first-round pick in the 1967 MLB June Amateur Draft-Secondary Phase. Washburn had pitched in eight games for the Angels a year earlier, giving him some perspective about the talent on the Spokane Indians roster. "They could have beat half the teams in the big leagues with no problem," assessed Washburn.[10]

Jerry Stephenson and Bruce Brubaker, who were traded for each other in the offseason, both started the opener of the Indians' next series against Portland. That same day, Stephenson's wife, Yvonne, gave birth to a daughter named Shannon. Ironically, Brubaker, the same pitcher who complained about Valentine's defense a year earlier, yielded eight unearned runs as a result of three Beavers miscues. Valentine, meanwhile, turned a slick double play that helped Stephenson escape a sixth-inning jam. With Spokane's 11-5 victory, Stephenson improved his record to 6-3.

Frank Peters, Stephenson's childhood friend and former roommate, played first base for Portland that day. Looking back fifty-four years later, Peters vividly remembered one particular at-bat against his childhood pal. "He threw me a fuckin' 3-2 curveball and froze me," said Peters, a former two-sport star at Oregon State University and a member of the school's 1963 Final Four basketball team. "I played with him for fifteen years and he hadn't thrown a 3-2 curveball! I'll never forget it. I still dream about it."[11]

Timely hits by Bill Buckner and Steve Garvey plus aggressive baserunning by Valentine made the difference in the Indians' 4-3 victory in the finale of the rain-shortened two-game series. A third of the way through the season, Spokane owned a 31-17 record and held a six-game lead over Portland in the PCL Northern Division. The Indians lineup was proving to be a gauntlet for opposing pitchers. Valentine and Bill Russell each had 18 multi-hit games and Garvey had hit in 26 of 29 games since joining the team. Tom Paciorek had hit a half-dozen home runs and ranked amongst the league leaders in RBI. Tommy Hutton was hitting .300 and playing his usual impeccable defense. Even the number eight hitter, Bart Shirley, was a tough out.

Spokane's pitchers were no slouches, either. Stephenson, Strahler, and Bob O'Brien notched a combined 14-5 record, while Hough, the PCL Player of the Month in May, led the league in wins, saves, and ERA. Things were going swimmingly for the über-talented Indians as they departed Spokane for a short four-game trip to Eugene. And then came the news that Doyle Alexander—another member of the Dodgers' draft class of 1968—was being promoted from Albuquerque, providing a boost to a team that hardly needed one.

The Hoodlum Priest

"Tommy was ever betting $5 on things. I was kind of his sideshow. George Lott was a big southern guy on our team. After one game, Tommy bet guys that I could drink a beer faster than George. Tommy really tried to make it fun, and he succeeded."—Bobby Valentine

Butte, Montana, has not historically been a hotbed of baseball talent,* but the small town in Big Sky Country did produce Tom Mulcahy, a right-handed pitcher who averaged 13 strikeouts per game for the Gonzaga University Bulldogs in the mid-1950s. Bing Crosby—a Spokane native, one-time Gonzaga baseball player, and part-owner of the Pittsburgh Pirates—signed Mulcahy to a professional contract in 1956. The pride of Butte played two seasons of pro ball, including a stint with the Spokane Indians, before giving up the game to enter Mount St. Michael's Seminary. Eleven years later, he was ordained as a Catholic priest of the Jesuit Order.

In 1970, Mulcahy worked as the director of student activities at Gonzaga and coached the Bulldogs baseball team. In his spare time, he

---

* Butte has produced three major leaguers: Brennan King, Scott Brow, and Rob Johnson.

scouted for the San Diego Padres and pitched batting practice for the Spokane Indians.* Tommy Lasorda nicknamed Mulcahy "Hoodlum Priest" after the title of a 1961 film about a Jesuit priest who dedicates his life to helping ex-convicts in the slums of St. Louis. The Spokane players shortened Mulcahy's moniker to "Hoodlum." Batting-practice pitchers typically groove easy-to-hit tosses, but Hoodlum hadn't lost his competitive edge. If a player hit a home run off him during BP, the twenty-seven-year-old priest would drill the batter with his next pitch. "We'd say, 'we're on the same team, aren't we?'" remembered Tom Paciorek. "He was tough. Nobody messed with Hoodlum."[1]

On a night off during the '70 season, Mulcahy and Lasorda took a group of players to a boxing match. Paciorek noticed one of the fighters making the sign of the cross before the fight and asked Mulcahy if the gesture would help him win. "It'll help him if he can fight," responded Mulcahy. "If he can't fight, he's going to get his ass kicked."[2]

Perhaps Hoodlum's batting-practice fastballs had helped Paciorek find his groove on June 1, the day the Indians outfielder launched his seventh home run of the season and drove in four of Spokane's nine runs in a victory over the Eugene Emeralds. Nineteen-year-old Doyle Alexander scattered nine hits and went the distance to win his Triple-A debut.

Alexander, a six-foot-three righty from Birmingham, Alabama, threw with a quick overhand delivery. The unorthodox motion, coupled with his willingness to pitch inside, kept opposing hitters on their toes. Bob Buckner, Bill's older brother and Alexander's former teammate on the Tri-City Atoms, got a taste of the tall righty's killer instinct when they faced each other during a spring intrasquad game. "He got ahead of me with two sliders on the outside corner," recalled Buckner. "I leaned over the plate to protect the outside corner, and he threw a fastball under my chin. The next pitch was a slider on the outside corner. I gave it a wobbly swing and struck out. That's the kind of competitor he was. If that was his mom, he would have done the same thing."[3]

Alexander, who would eventually pitch in nineteen major-league seasons, never fully bought in to Lasorda's rah-rah style, though he did keep his teammates' egos in check. The young Alabaman possessed a bite-

---

* Mulcahy eventually left the priesthood to work in the San Diego Padres front office. He would serve as the director of group sales and season tickets for twenty years.

your-head-off personality and would comfortably get in the middle of any clubhouse disagreements despite being the youngest player on Spokane's roster. "He was simply grounded from day one," recalled Kent Schultz. "I believe that was a reason he stuck in the majors so long."[4]

DOYLE ALEXANDER - Pitcher

Courtesy Spokane Indians.

Five days after his complete-game win over Eugene, Alexander replicated the feat during Spokane's three-game sweep of the Tacoma Cubs. This extended the Indians' streak to six. Spokane's relentless lineup smacked 43 hits in the series, not needing a single home run to secure the sweep. Tommy Hutton, Steve Garvey, Bill Russell, and Bobby Valentine collectively hit .579 in the series.

The young studs were performing well, but some of the unsung veterans stepped up too. When the Cubs chased John Purdin in the first inning on June 5, veteran reliever Jack Jenkins, who had pitched abysmally over the season's first six weeks, contributed to Spokane's winning ways in long relief. The native Virginian* pitched around six walks in seven and a third innings to earn the win. During one inning when Jenkins ran into trouble, Lasorda went to the mound and queried his reliever about deer hunting. "What kind of shotgun should I bring when we go hunting this winter?" he asked.[5] Following their brief discussion of firearms, Lasorda retreated to the dugout. The moment of levity helped Jenkins settle down and escape the jam.

A combination of winning baseball and warmer weather attracted larger crowds to the Fairgrounds as the season marched along. Lasorda and his players' community engagement may have also helped at the turnstiles. The Spokane players signed autographs for seemingly every kid in the Pacific Northwest. And no player showed a more affable personality than Bobby Valentine. Before every home game, the youngster would sit on top of the dugout steps and talk with kids while signing their baseballs, gloves, and hats.

On one Saturday afternoon in early June, the Indians hosted a youth baseball clinic and signed autographs for the youngsters. More than a half-century later, Barbara Hopkins-McGee, who began attending games at the Fairgrounds as a six-year-old in the mid-1960s, fondly recalled Davey Lopes, Bill Buckner, Steve Garvey, Bobby Valentine, and Tom Paciorek all signing her baseball glove. Unfortunately, her brother later borrowed the glove and left it outside in the rain, rendering the signatures illegible. Barbara never forgave her brother for it.

Viky Englund's memento from the 1970 season met a similarly tragic end. She and her brothers would pack into the back of her parents' Volkswagen bug and head to the ballpark. Pregame, they'd gather near the dugout to ask the players to sign their baseballs. Decades later, Englund regretfully recalled the fate of her autographed ball: Her dog ate it.

Autograph-seeking kids weren't the only ones vying for the players' attention. Jeff Schiller, the son of Indians general manager Elten Schiller, recalled that teenage girls and baseball groupies frequently hung around

---

* Jenkins played high-school and two seasons of minor-league baseball with future golfing legend J.C. Snead.

the clubhouse exit. Some of the same women frequented player hangouts around town. During games, the batboys sometimes passed notes to players from girls in the stands. "I'm sure to the players it was like being a kid in a candy store," said Schiller.[6]

As the son of a baseball executive, Jeff Schiller grew up around ballparks, including five years spent in Spokane. Over time, he worked nearly every job imaginable at the Fairgrounds—vendor, concessions seller, press-box attendant, scoreboard operator, groundskeeper, and ball boy. In his various roles at the ballpark, the impressionable teen overheard players bragging about their sexual exploits. "This was the early '70s and the sexual revolution was in full swing," said Schiller. "I suppose some of this boasting could have been embellished, but as a teenage kid coming of age, I took it as gospel at the time. I remember Bill Buckner once telling me that if he ever made it to LA, he hoped to date Raquel Welch."[7]

THE INDIANS CONCLUDED THE HOMESTAND WITH A SERIES AGAINST THE Eugene Emeralds, the Phillies' Triple-A affiliate, beginning June 7.[*] Bob O'Brien registered his league-leading third shutout in the opener, extending the Indians' winning streak to seven games. Russell, Valentine, and Garvey each hit .400 or better during the streak. Charlie Hough even got in on the action, blasting his first and only home run of the season.[†] In the midst of the streak, Lasorda proposed that his Indians should meet the Los Angeles Dodgers in a three-game series to determine which team should compete in the National League West. No one ever accused the Spokane manager of lacking confidence.

While the Indians were flying high, Major League Baseball held its sixth annual June amateur draft in New York.[‡] The Padres picked first, selecting seventeen-year-old catcher Mike Ivie, whom scouts had anointed

---

[*] Willie Montañez, John Vukovich, and Joe Lis were among the Emeralds regulars who later played in the majors. Lis, a power-hitting outfielder, would lead all PCL hitters in 1970 with 36 home runs.
[†] Hough would hit four home runs in the minors but only one over his twenty-five-year major-league career.
[‡] Three future Hall of Famers were chosen in the 1970 June Amateur Draft. The White Sox picked Goose Gossage in the ninth round, Dave Parker went to the Pirates in the fourteenth round, and the Senators picked Bruce Sutter in the twenty-first round. Sutter did not sign with the Senators and later inked a contract with the Cubs.

the second coming of Johnny Bench. Ivie would later develop a case of the yips in the minor leagues, ultimately refusing to catch. He would eventually have a few productive seasons as a first baseman but battled anxiety and depression and never lived up to the expectations of a number-one overall pick.

After the Cleveland Indians selected Stanford pitcher Steve Dunning second, two more catchers were taken off the board—Barry Foote and Darrell Porter to the Expos and Brewers, respectively. With the ninth pick, the Dodgers chose pitcher Jim Haller out of Creighton Preparatory School in Omaha.

Looking back, Haller characterized himself as a "young guy who threw hard." The six-foot-six righty had caught scouts' attention with a stellar performance against an American Legion team featuring elite prospect Dave Winfield, who had just completed his freshman season at the University of Minnesota. "Every scout in the country was there to see him," recalled Haller. "I struck out like fifteen guys that night, and my stock went through the roof."[8]

The Dodgers assigned Haller to Ogden for the summer of '70. He pitched decently, posting a 5-4 record and 3.83 ERA. Reality would set in, however, when he reported to Dodgertown the following spring. Watching Bobby Valentine gave him a sense of where he stood in professional baseball. "He was the best baseball player I ever saw," said Haller. "He could run, he could hit, and he played the game with joy. I looked at him and thought, 'I've got no chance in this game.'"[9]

Haller would advance as high as Triple-A but developed elbow trouble. In September 1974, he underwent an ulnar nerve transposition operation with Dr. Frank Jobe, the Dodgers' team physician. Immediately following Haller's procedure, Jobe scrubbed up to perform a novel elbow reconstruction surgery on Tommy John. The operation saved John's career and would come to be known as Tommy John surgery. "I always told Dr. Jobe I thought maybe he had taken something out of my arm and put it in Tommy's," Haller said.[10]

Haller's elbow problems would prevent him from reaching the majors, but four others from the Dodgers' crop did rise to the top. Lance Rautzhan (third round), Mike Vail (seventeenth round), and Greg Shanahan (thirty-third round) would emerge from the regular phase to spend time in "The

Show." And from the first round of the secondary phase came Doug Rau, who would soon make his way to the Inland Northwest, where he would make one memorable appearance for the 1970 Spokane Indians.

Hutton to Operating Room, Russell to LA

"One time, we were conditioning and running sprints in the outfield. Tommy, who was always coming up with something to entertain us, told us to work hard because 'you guys make good money ... there's not a lot of it, but it's all GOOD!'"—Steve Sogge

Major leaguers in the twenty-first century drive Audis, Bentleys, Ferraris, Range Rovers, and similar top-of-the-line vehicles. The 1970 Spokane Indians, on the other hand, drove a bunch of jalopies. Tom Paciorek, for example, owned an early '50s Pontiac that could comfortably seat eight grown men. Similarly, roommates Tommy Hutton, Dick McLaughlin, and Jerry Stephenson each chipped in and bought an old Lincoln for $150. Whoever drove would wear a chauffeur's hat. At the end of the season, they sold the car and broke even. They considered it a great investment.

The Pacific Coast League schedule did not include many off days, so the occasional rainout provided a welcome respite from the daily grind and an opportunity for some tomfoolery. After one postponement, Paciorek and Gus Sposito staged a drag race in the pothole-pocked Fairgrounds parking lot. "We revved up the engines, and they sounded like a couple of tanks," Paciorek remembered. "We got them up to about thirty miles an hour. Elten Schiller and Lasorda came out and yelled at us. They said, 'What the hell is wrong with you? If you do that again, you'll be fined!' I said, 'So, I guess demolition derby is out at the end of the season?'"[1]

A spring shower washed out the Indians-Emeralds game on June 8, the same day doctors removed the wires from Bill Buckner's jaw. He went straight home and brushed his teeth, then ate a couple of hamburgers—his first solid food in a month. "You really don't appreciate the little things like that until you can't have them," he said at the time.[2]

Buckner's lack of sustenance had coincided with a drop in his batting average. After his hot streak in Tucson immediately following the injury, he cooled off considerably before missing a week of games to take his final exams at USC. He returned to the lineup on May 26 but had yet to hit his stride. Buckner's batting average stood at a meager .235, and he still hadn't hit a home run.

When weather in Eugene eventually cleared and the series resumed the following night, the Indians did seemingly everything in their power to end their seven-game streak. Tommy Hutton, one of the best defensive first basemen of his era—or any era—made two rare miscues, accounting for half of his team's four errors. On top of shoddy defense, Spokane pitchers issued seven walks, and the offense stranded eleven men on base. Spokane prevailed in spite of its flaws, in large part because Eugene pitchers walked nine. The Indians' hottest hitter, Bill Russell, extended his hit streak to nine games, strengthening his case for a promotion to LA. Meanwhile, Spokane improved to 39-18, expanding its commanding divisional lead to nine and a half games.

The Indians traveled to Salt Lake City, where they played back-to-back seven-inning doubleheaders against the Padres to make up for earlier postponements. In the lid lifter of the first twin bill, a Spokane lineup that included three former college football players and two blue-chip high school football recruits cranked four home runs, including a pair by former defensive back Steve Garvey. Appropriately, Spokane annihilated Salt Lake by a football score of 14-0. In the nightcap, Padres starter Jerry Nyman blanked the Indians to snap their nine-game win streak. It would be one of only four games all season in which Spokane failed to score. Besides losing the game, Spokane also lost Tommy Hutton. The first baseman collided with baserunner John Sipin while trying to catch Russell's tailing throw from third and suffered a broken thumb. Hutton would require surgery and miss the next six weeks.

The Indians played the next day's doubleheader shorthanded. With Hutton out and four others gone for military duty, Lasorda penciled in the names of player-coach Dick McLaughlin, reserve outfielder George Lott, and seldom-used utility infielder Gus Sposito on his lineup card. Spokane didn't miss a beat, winning both games by an aggregate score of 19-1. Bill Buckner, Steve Garvey, and Tom Paciorek combined for 17 hits in 20 at-bats in the twin bill—a video-game-like .850 batting average.

The pair of defeats dropped Salt Lake's record to a 19-40. It was proving to be a futile season for Don Zimmer's roster, half of whom had been pitching in A ball a year earlier. "We got our lips ripped off," said Nyman in retrospect. "We had a couple guys who developed into big-league players, but at that time they were puppies playing against bulldogs."[3]

Salt Lake's pitching was particularly dreadful. Outside of Nyman, who would lead the Padres with nine wins, Salt Lake's five most frequent starters posted a combined record of 9-35 and a 6.56 ERA. One of the starters, nineteen-year-old Eli Borunda, San Diego's second-round pick in the 1969 June Amateur Draft, went 0-9 before quitting to join the Jehovah's Witness ministry. Salt Lake struggled so mightily that first baseman Jeff Pentland, who doubled as a mop-up reliever, appeared in twenty games as a pitcher. During several thrashings, Zimmer told him to throw at the opposing hitters out of frustration. Pentland would argue, "Hey Zim, I didn't give up the 11 runs!"[4]

Zimmer did not need to employ a mop-up man on Sunday, June 14, when Salt Lake and Spokane played their third doubleheader in four days. The overmatched Padres showed some fight, pulling out a pair of one-run victories with veteran reliever Jack Baldschun notching saves in both contests. "I'm as excited as a twelve-year-old," said an ecstatic Zimmer afterward. "I feel like we've just won a pennant instead of a doubleheader."[5] Salt Lake's surprise series split came despite herculean series performances by Tom Paciorek (.737, 2 HR), Steve Garvey (.545, 3 HR), and Bill Buckner (.450). After taking what amounted to batting practice in Utah, the Indians made the long flight to Oahu for their second of two regular-season trips to the Aloha State.

The Hawaii Islanders roster had undergone significant turnover since the Indians' first trip to the island two months earlier. The Angels dictated some of the roster churn, calling up Jarvis Tatum, Tomás Silverio, Steve Kealey, and Dave LaRoche, sending down shortstop Marty Perez, and promoting starting pitcher Tom Bradley from Double-A. Hawaii's middling 12-12 start, during which the starting rotation combined for a 3-10 record and 5.63 ERA, had also spurred some changes. Quinn attempted to fortify his starting rotation through a series of transactions in May and early June, acquiring thirty-three-year-old Juan Pizzaro and thirty-eight-year-old knuckleballer Ron Kline, two pitchers with a combined 231 career major-league wins. Quinn also bought the contracts of outfielders Jim Hicks and Wayne Redmond, added veteran reliever Bob Allen, and upgraded at catcher with the addition of Merritt Ranew. Quinn desperately wanted to field a winning team and boost attendance. The state legislature's recent appropriation of $11.5 million for the construction of a new 34,000-seat stadium and the opportunity to demonstrate Honolulu's viability as a major-league city provided Quinn with extra motivation. The roster machinations had proven effective, and the locals were turning out in droves. On May 31, Hawaii had owned a 26-22 record. When the Spokane Indians arrived at Termite Palace to begin a five-game series on June 15, the Islanders had won 11 of 14.

In the opener, Charlie Hough entered the game in the seventh with the score tied at three and promptly walked the bases loaded. He then fell behind to the next batter, Charlie Vinson. Hough couldn't find the strike zone with his knuckleball, so he tried sneaking a fastball by Vinson. The Islanders first baseman wasn't fooled, blasting a grand slam that dealt Hough his fourth loss of the season.*

Bobby Valentine and Bart Shirley shined on both sides of the ball the next night in Spokane's 8-4 victory. The middle-infield duo turned four double plays and provided the bulk of the Indians' offense. Valentine launched a pair of home runs and Shirley stroked three hits, including an opposite-field home run over the short right-field screen.

---

* Vinson's only major-league home run came four years earlier against Baltimore Orioles knuckleballer Eddie Fisher.

BART SHIRLEY

Courtesy Spokane Indians.

At age thirty, Barton Arvin Shirley was the oldest player on a relatively young Spokane roster that averaged twenty-three years old. The former University of Texas halfback signed with Dodgers scout Hugh Alexander in 1960 and used his $60,000 bonus to buy his mother a new house. By 1970, Shirley had spent parts of four seasons in the big leagues during his decade in the organization. He never received extended playing time at the major-league level but formed lasting memories during his cups of coffee, including his first at-bat. "There was this lady sitting by our bat rack and she said, 'Come on Bart, get a hit,' recalled Shirley. "It was Doris Day."[6]

During Shirley's first call-up with the Dodgers in September 1964, the Corpus Christi, Texas, native experienced the thrill of hitting an RBI triple in front of hundreds of family members and friends in Houston against the

Colt .45s. Other special moments included getting a hit off Bob Gibson during Gibson's otherworldly 1968 season and hitting a hole-in-one during a round of golf with Duke Snider. But of all his fond memories, Shirley singled out watching Sandy Koufax pitch as the highlight of his career.

Shirley never hit enough to stick with the Dodgers, but he was the type of player all successful organizations need—a guy who could fill in at the big-league level in a pinch and help mentor younger players in Triple-A. For that reason, Lasorda anointed him a player-coach for the 1970 season. "He was like a dad in the locker room," recalled Kent Schultz. "He was a grinder. He didn't make many mistakes, led by example, and was a team player. Not a rah-rah guy but consistent and professional."[7] Having a veteran at the keystone was particularly helpful to a novice shortstop like Bobby Valentine, who called having Shirley as a double-play partner "a godsend."[8]

After splitting the first two games of the series, the Islanders bulldozed Spokane over the next three nights, winning all three contests by a collective score of 38-13. Vinson, Redmond, Rich Barry, and Doug Griffin combined for 26 hits, seven home runs, and 24 RBI in Hawaii's three victories.

The Indians had lost six of seven. Not only did they suddenly appear fallible, but they would now be without their starting center fielder. During the Hawaii series, the Dodgers called up Bill Russell—a .517 hitter in his last 13 games—to replace the injured Ted Sizemore. Russell would stick with the Dodgers for the remainder of the season, slashing .259/.303/.363 in 81 games. In fact, he would never play in another minor-league game for the rest of his career.

The Indians were now without Russell, Tommy Hutton (broken thumb), and Davey Lopes (Army Reserve duty). At 43-25, they maintained a firm grip on the Northern Division, but the Hawaii Islanders were shaping up to be a formidable foe in the Indians' quest for the Pacific Coast League title.

The Power of Motivation

"[Tommy Lasorda] was the best motivator of people I have ever seen in my life."—Tommy John

On October 12, 1983, Tommy Lasorda ate lunch with President Ronald Reagan at an Italian embassy celebration of Columbus Day. Later that afternoon, he stood behind a podium at the daily White House briefing and delivered fifteen minutes of jokes and inspirational stories to the press corps, leaving the room roaring with laughter. That was Lasorda in his element.

He possessed a remarkable ability to control a room, whether his audience consisted of political dignitaries, athletes, or schoolchildren. Over his long career, Lasorda delivered keynote addresses to Fortune 500 companies and spoke at business seminars, earning thousands of dollars per appearance. He also spoke at churches and schools at no cost and addressed troops at dozens of military bases around the world. Even after he had become one of the most recognizable faces in America, he never turned down a request for a speaking engagement, no matter the size of the organization. And he never prepared notes. "I just show up, check out the kinds of people in the audience, and talk from the heart," Lasorda told author Bill Plaschke. "Ain't that what motivational speaking is all about?"[1]

Tommy Lasorda cheering on the troops. Courtesy Spokane Indians.

Lasorda didn't become an accomplished public speaker overnight. Long before he became one of the most sought-after voices in the country, he polished his joke telling and motivational speeches in church basements, civic luncheons, and minor-league clubhouses. Lasorda, whose natural voice was loud and gravelly, used his words to get the most out of his players. He developed a sixth sense for when to hold a team meeting and what tone to use when he spoke. Sometimes, he dispensed words of encouragement. Other times, he bawled his players out. And unlike his Kiwanis Club and sports banquet appearances, Lasorda's clubhouse monologues were famously full of expletives.*

---

* During his tenure as Dodgers manager, Lasorda unleashed legendary expletive-filled rants that have received millions of views on YouTube. His response to a sportswriter's question about Dave Kingman's three-homer game in 1978 and his retort to some unkind words from San Diego Padres utilityman Kurt Bevacqua were legendary. Ron Cey wrote in his autobiography, *Penguin Power*, that Rick Monday used a pitch counter to tally up the number of f-bombs Lasorda dropped during his clubhouse diatribes. Monday would give a thumbs up or thumbs down to his teammates depending on whether the record was broken.

"His meetings were spectacular," recalled Bobby Valentine. "You'd almost want to buy a ticket to be able to sit in these little rooms and have him parade in front of your locker. He didn't stand in the corner. He marched and preached. The volume started loud and then got *louder*. No one moved. You were paralyzed sitting on benches in little lockers. The room would vibrate with his voice. He could use a curse word as an adjective, verb, or noun and make it fit perfectly in the sentence. He used it like he was reciting Dante's Inferno. It was poetry."[2]

On June 22, Lasorda sensed his team needed a pep talk. The Indians were reeling, losers of five in a row and eight of nine, including the first two games against the Tucson Toros to start the homestand. Decades later, Valentine vividly recalled that day. How could he forget? During the meeting, Lasorda put his finger in Valentine's face and called him out. The skipper's words stung. But they had the desired effect of lighting a fire under the young shortstop. When he stepped into the batter's box in the first inning, Valentine had an overwhelming feeling—one he had never experienced before—that he would hit a home run. Sure enough, he barreled a pitch from Toros starter Darrell Brandon that soared over the 411-foot mark in center field. Valentine sprinted around the bases and stomped on home plate. One to nothing, Indians.

Dick McLaughlin, the next man up, channeled his inner Babe Ruth. Though he had hit just one home run the previous season and had yet to go deep in limited playing time in 1970, McLaughlin told his teammates that he would hit a home run in his first at-bat. And incredibly, he did. Back-to-back homers to start the game.

But then Spokane's bats went quiet, Doyle Alexander scuffled, and the Indians' losing streak reached six games. Remarkably, mired in a tailspin of their own, the second-place Portland Beavers hadn't gained a single game during Spokane's skid. The Indians maintained a nine-and-a-half-game lead in the Northern Division standings.

The next morning, Lasorda took Tom Paciorek to the ballpark for early extra batting practice. The skipper wanted him to do a better job of turning on inside pitches. Lasorda's tutelage paid dividends. That night, Paciorek singled twice and pulled an inside pitch off the left-field foul pole, his eleventh home run of the season, propelling the Indians to a 6-1 triumph. Bob O'Brien spun nine innings of one-run ball to earn his sixth victory in seven decisions. After six consecutive losses, the Indians were finally back in the win column.

Two days later, the Indians (45-28) and Phoenix Giants (49-26) began a five-game series at the Fairgrounds. Sandy Vance, recently demoted from the parent club following the return of Bill Singer, made his first start for Spokane since April. The Stanford product had gone 4-3 with a 3.00 ERA for the Dodgers and was fresh off two weeks of Reserve duty. Despite barely pitching in a month, he held Phoenix to two runs over seven and two-thirds innings in the Indians' 5-2 series-opening victory. Bobby Valentine and Bill Buckner scored all five Spokane runs and Steve Garvey drove in three, increasing his league-leading RBI total to 61. Charlie Hough got the final out of the game to notch his 14th save.

The Indians dropped the next three games before O'Brien halted a losing streak for the second time in five days, tossing his fourth shutout of the season and third against the Giants. The stumbling Indians averaged just three and a half runs per game on the homestand while losing six of 10. Going back further, they had lost 13 of 21. Lasorda liked to point out that even the vaunted 1927 Yankees struggled at times, although he usually exaggerated the facts.* The Babe Ruth and Lou Gehrig-led '27 squad, who finished the season with a record of 110-44, did lose 10 of 19, including four in a row, at one point during that historic season.

The Indians resembled Murderer's Row on June 30 in the opener of a four-game series in Portland, scoring 12 runs on 15 hits, including home runs by backup outfielder George Lott and pitcher Jack Jenkins. Over the next three games, Mike Strahler, Sandy Vance, and Doyle Alexander limited the Beavers to a combined three runs. The Indians swept the series and returned to Spokane with a commanding thirteen-and-a-half-game division lead.

During the Portland series, the Dodgers called up Garvey to fill in for Bill Sudakis and Bill Russell while each fulfilled two-week stints of mili-

---

* Paciorek recalled that with the Albuquerque Dukes in 1972, Lasorda called a team meeting during a losing streak and said, "You guys aren't having any fun. Your heads are down; you're acting like it's the end of the world. Did you know that the 1927 Yankees, led by Lou Gehrig, Babe Ruth, and Tony Lazzeri, lost seven games in a row?" The Dukes destroyed the other team that night, starting a long winning streak. "Later," said Paciorek, "I asked Tommy if '27 Yankees really lost seven games in a row. He said, 'How the hell would I know? I wasn't even born yet.'"

tary duty. Garvey's promotion created playing time for outfielder Davey Lopes, who had just returned from his own two weeks of Reserve obligations.* As an indicator of the depth the Spokane Indians possessed, Lasorda had the luxury of replacing one future big-league All-Star with another.

Lopes, a quiet and stoic type, felt out of place. Perhaps it was because, unlike most of his teammates, he came from the ghetto. Or that he frequently missed time fulfilling Reserve duty back on the East Coast. Or that he served as a backup outfielder behind more highly touted prospects. Lasorda later said that Lopes rarely strung more than two words together during that season in Spokane. "I had to yell at him, 'Say something ... say anything ... just holler,'" Lasorda recalled.[3] Eventually, Lopes would come to feel like he belonged. He would follow his manager's example and develop into an outspoken leader. But in the summer of 1970, his bat did the talking.

Lopes went 2-for-4 in the Indians win over the Eugene Emeralds on Independence Day, then made a pair of sensational catches and chipped in two more hits in their doubleheader sweep on July 5. Spokane took four of five from the Ems, boosting their record to a season-high twenty-three games over .500 heading into a ten-game swing through Tucson and Phoenix. Bob O'Brien remained locked in versus Eugene, twirling his third consecutive complete-game victory while improving his record to 8-1.

Spokane cooled off in the sweltering heat of Tucson, dropping four of its next five. Things went marginally better in the stagnant confines of Phoenix Municipal Stadium. The series started favorably enough for the Indians, who scored 20 runs over the first two games. In the opener—a mid-July day that reached 113 degrees†—Lopes hit for the cycle and Bart Shirley recorded four hits in a 7-6 victory. The next night, Bobby Valentine's four hits and George Lott's fourth home run of the season carried the Indians to a 13-3 rout.

---

* Marv Galliher, hitting over .300 at the time, had been playing the outfield but moved to third base and split time with Gus Sposito at the hot corner during Garvey's call-up.

† Tucson Toros pitcher Gene Rounsaville recalled numerous instances in which the thermometer on the center-field scoreboard at Tucson's Hi Corbett Field read 110 degrees at the start of an eight o'clock game. "I look back now and think, 'How did we ever do that?'" said Rounsaville in 2024. "When you're young, I guess you have a way to get through it."

On July 15, runs were at a premium, but late-inning drama was not. The two equally productive starters—Spokane's Jerry Stephenson and Phoenix's Miguel Puente—effectively canceled each other out. At the end of regulation, the game stood tied at one. Things got interesting in the bottom of the tenth when Spokane reliever John Purdin ceded a two-out double to Bernie Williams and then walked George Foster. Lasorda went to the mound and summoned southpaw Geoff Zahn from the bullpen to face Steve Whitaker, a left-handed hitter. As Lasorda returned to the dugout, a fan in the first row dumped ice water on Lasorda's head. Considering that the gametime temperature was 109 degrees, perhaps the guy thought he was doing Lasorda a favor. Spokane's skipper did not see it that way. He picked up a chair and tried climbing into the stands to confront the culprit. It took four ushers and two police officers to restrain him. Once cooler heads prevailed and the game resumed, Zahn hung a 1-1 curveball that Whitaker blasted over the right-field wall, giving the Giants a 4-1 victory.

The Indians lost the next two and limped home having lost seven of 10 on the road trip. Spokane played shaky defense in the desert. In particular, Valentine struggled, committing nine errors in the ten games.[*] He didn't carry his defensive struggles to the plate, as evidenced by a .367 average on the road trip.[†] Two of Valentine's teammates were equally dialed in. Buckner hit .404 during the ten games, this time leaving Arizona with his jaw intact. And Davey Lopes took advantage of increased playing time with four multi-hit efforts.

But perhaps the most memorable moment of the Arizona trip involved a mound visit Lasorda paid to starter Bob O'Brien on July 9 in Tucson. The southpaw, whom Lasorda nicknamed "Baby Robin" because of his skinny legs and big torso, was getting battered around and had to contend with a couple of runners on base. Lasorda went to the mound and said, "Baby Robin, I want to ask you a question. If the skies opened up right now and the big Dodger in the sky spoke down to you and said this is the last hitter you're going to face on earth before going to the big leagues in the sky, how do you want to be remembered?" O'Brien thought about it

---

[*] By season's end, Valentine would lead the Pacific Coast League with 54 errors.
[†] Valentine finished the season with five four-hit games. The Spokane players received a portable television each time they got four hits in a game, so Valentine's apartment must have resembled Radio Shack.

for a moment and said he wanted to be remembered as a successful pitcher. Lasorda responded, "Okay. Get this guy out," and walked back to the dugout. The next batter doubled home two runs. "Tommy came to take me out and asked me what happened," recalled O'Brien. "I said, 'Skipper, you had me so afraid of dying that I couldn't concentrate!'"[4]

BOB O'BRIEN - Pitcher

Courtesy Spokane Indians.

Lasorda later said that was the day he fully grasped the power of motivation. "I actually convinced him that he might die if he didn't get this guy out," recalled Lasorda. "Now *that's* motivation!"[5]

Good Old Days

"Tommy kept us in the clubhouse all night one time after a loss in Eugene. The clubhouses were separated by a thin wall, so we could hear the guys in the Emeralds clubhouse celebrating their victory. He said, 'Listen to those guys. They're laughing and having a good time!' So, we ordered pizza and beer and stayed in the clubhouse the whole night." —Tommy Hutton

In the late afternoon of Monday, July 20, 1970, Bill Singer threw a no-hitter against the Phillies in front of 12,454 fans at Dodger Stadium, becoming the first Dodger to throw a no-no since Sandy Koufax's perfect game in 1965 and the first righty to do so since Brooklyn's Sal Maglie in '56.* Later that night in Spokane, the Indians held a "Good Old Days" promotion, which included heavily discounted tickets and concessions. Box seats cost a buck, popcorn and sodas were a nickel, and hot dogs and beer sold for a dime. The promotion, spearheaded by

---

* Singer's no-hitter was the third in the majors in 1970, following Dock Ellis (Pirates) and Clyde Wright (Angels). Because of a scheduling quirk, the game started at 4 p.m. Shadows crept on to the field around home plate during the game, making it difficult for hitters to pick up the ball.

general manager Elten Schiller, attracted a season-high crowd of 7,369. Like overzealous Black Friday shoppers, fans arrived in droves two hours before first pitch to get their fill.

GEOFF ZAHN - Pitcher

Courtesy Spokane Indians.

During pregame warmups, batboy Dave Vaughn, relievers Geoff Zahn and Charlie Hough, and a couple other players engaged in a round of pepper down the right-field line. Vaughn had the bat and tapped throws from the Spokane players. He whiffed on a knuckleball from Hough and ran to retrieve the ball. The fourteen-year-old was excited about the big crowd and wanted to show off his arm, so he threw a seed to Zahn. Just as Vaughn released the ball, he realized Zahn wasn't looking. The batboy yelled to get his attention and Zahn looked up just as the ball struck him on the mouth. He went down as if Muhammad Ali had delivered a right cross. To Vaughn's horror, blood began pouring out of the pitcher's mouth. Medics quickly rushed to the scene, loaded Zahn on to a stretcher, and rushed him to the hospital. In that moment, Vaughn thought he had just ended Zahn's career, or worse. "I'm crying in the Indians dugout … Bill Buckner puts his arm around me and says, 'It's not your fault.' I'm praying the whole game in the other dugout, 'Let him live.'"[1]

While Vaughn was in hysterics before the game and fraught with guilt during it, the patrons at the Fairgrounds were having the time of their lives. The ravenous crowd, which consumed more than 8,000 beers and 5,000 hot dogs, undoubtedly would have gone home happy regardless of the outcome. Tom Paciorek's game-tying homer and rally-killing diving catch that secured a 3-2 win for Jerry Stephenson was icing on the cake. Vaughn, meanwhile, exhaled a huge sigh of relief when Zahn returned to the ballpark during the game. Before the batboy could apologize, Zahn said, "Not your fault."[2]

Davey Lopes went off the next night against the Padres, blasting a three-run, sixth-inning homer off starter Gary Ross and then replicating the feat an inning later against Jerry Nyman, who was pitching in relief on two days' rest. Lopes's second round-tripper, his fourth of the season, put the Indians ahead, 7-6. Hough recorded the final seven outs to earn his 11th win of the season. Lopes continued his hot hitting the following day, raising his average to .296 with two doubles and a single in Spokane's 7-1 triumph. After playing in fewer than half of the Indians' games during the first three months of the season, he had found his groove.

"I didn't have the pressure on me to produce that some of the others had," said Lopes years later. "That worked in my favor. So did the fact that being overshadowed made me even more determined to do well, to show that I deserved a chance."[3]

THE INDIANS FACED TOUGHER COMPETITION WHEN THE HAWAII ISLANDERS rolled into town on July 23. Chuck Tanner's club had steamrolled the Pacific Coast League since the start of June, winning 43 out of 53 while building a seven-and-a-half-game lead over Phoenix in the Southern Division. In the opener, the Indians faced a familiar foe in the form of John Purdin, whose contract had been sold to Hawaii the week before. Earlier in July, the Islanders had traded Juan Pizarro—who was undefeated in nine decisions with Hawaii—to the Chicago Cubs for Archie Reynolds and cash. Jack Quinn then used the money from the Pizarro deal to buy Purdin's contract from the Dodgers.

Facing a former teammate and the league's hottest team brought out the best in Bill Buckner, who doubled twice, tripled, and drove in five runs, propelling the Indians to a series-opening victory. Lasorda spewed hyperbole after the game, declaring that the Indians' performance "was the greatest exhibition of desire to win I've ever seen."[4]

The Indians apparently used up all their desire because the following night Hawaii's Greg Washburn held them to three runs over eight and a third innings. The Islanders, meanwhile, scored five runs on 14 hits, including three by Winston Llenas. Indians starter Bob O'Brien hit the showers in the third inning. "The Hawaii Islanders were always my nemesis," O'Brien recalled. "Llenas and the other guys wore me out."[5] Indeed, O'Brien lost both decisions and registered an 8.10 ERA in four starts against Hawaii during the regular season. Against the other six PCL teams, he had gone a perfect 9-0.

The two division leaders squared off for an "Aloha Night" doubleheader the following day. Fans arriving to the Fairgrounds wearing Hawaiian garb received $0.50 off admission. Sandy Vance started the lid-lifter for Spokane. Like O'Brien, he had trouble with the Islanders, and Llenas in particular. "No matter how I pitched to him, I couldn't solve him," Vance remembered. Llenas went 2-for-4 with a pair of RBI while another Dominican, Tomás Silverio, fell a home run shy of the cycle. Lasorda pulled Vance in the third inning after he yielded five runs. "After having had a taste of the major leagues earlier that year, I was über-frustrated," Vance said. "I was thinking, 'How am I having so much trouble in Triple-A when I did so well in LA?'"[6]

Vance suffered the loss after the Islanders held on to win, 8-4. In the nightcap, Spokane's offense knocked around Hawaii pitching, but the Islanders did the same to Jerry Stephenson, Charlie Hough, and Geoff Zahn. At the end of regulation—in this case, the seventh inning—seeing an opportunity for Vance to redeem himself, Lasorda told the righty to warm up. As Vance loosened in the bullpen, he began experimenting with a Koufax-style wind-up, reaching much farther back and throwing directly over the top. When he entered the game, it seemed that he had found something. "I was a different pitcher from the first game, striking hitters out with my fastball and twelve-to-six curveball," recalled Vance. "Even Islander players commented to me about the change."[7]

Wearing Drysdale's shoes and using Koufax's windup, Vance threw four scoreless innings before allowing four unearned runs in the twelfth. Bob Allen closed the door on the Indians in the bottom half of the frame, sealing Hawaii's 11-7 victory and hanging another loss on Vance. The second game ended after midnight, so Vance technically didn't lose two games in the same day, but it stung, nonetheless.

Looking back, Vance theorized why he sometimes had more trouble in Triple-A than the majors: "It was largely because young Triple-A hitters tend to be free-swingers, and you never knew how to pitch them. In the majors, hitters are generally known, and you had a road map as to how to pitch most of them. As a result, you were never sure how or where to pitch the young, strong Triple-A hitters who often didn't care where the pitch was—they just swung away."[8]

Tom Paciorek discovered a similar paradox from a hitter's perspective. Although many minor-league pitchers possessed similar velocity and movement to guys in the majors, they lacked control, making for some uncomfortable at-bats at the Triple-A level.

THE ISLANDERS-INDIANS SERIES FINALE PROVED TO BE ONE OF THE wildest games of the season. It started auspiciously for Spokane with Valentine hitting the first pitch he saw from Islanders starter Gary Kroll over the fence. Dick McLaughlin followed with a double and came around to score on a Bill Buckner RBI single. A wild pitch and errant pickoff attempt by catcher Merritt Ranew allowed Buckner to score the Indians' third run. Chuck Tanner had seen enough of Kroll—who was making only his second start of the season—and went to the mound for an early pitching change. The six-foot-six, 220-pound pitcher fittingly nicknamed "Tarzan" was none too pleased with being replaced four batters in. Instead of handing his manager the ball, Kroll threw it at his chest. Tanner's face turned red, and his carotid arteries bulged from his neck. He told Kroll to pick up the ball and hand it to him. Kroll said something to the effect of, "Get ripped," before walking off the field and into the clubhouse. Tanner followed. When the Islanders manager caught up to the towering hurler, he grabbed him by the jersey, threw him on the trainer's table and said, "If you ever show me up again, I'll kill you!"⁹ Kroll wouldn't get the chance. The team suspended him the next day, and he never threw another pitch for Hawaii.

A game's worth of drama had occurred, and it wasn't even the second inning. Later, the Islanders chased Mike Strahler with a four-run sixth inning, then added another tally off Charlie Hough in the seventh to take a 6-3 lead. Lasorda had already used Gus Sposito and George Lott—the only two position players on his short-handed bench. As Chuck Stewart wrote in the *Spokane Daily Chronicle*, "It could have been demoralizing. Most clubs would have folded at that point. But not the Indians."¹⁰

Lasorda's undermanned, never-say-die crew rallied in the eighth. Sposito singled and Buckner walked to start the inning. Islanders reliever Jim Coates retired the next two, but then Bob Stinson singled and Steve Sogge doubled. Tie game. With first base open, Tanner intentionally walked Bart Shirley to get to the pitcher's spot. Lasorda sent up Jerry Stephenson to hit for Dick Armstrong. A lifetime .234 hitter in 64 big-league at-bats to that point, Stephenson drilled a two-strike pitch to the right-center-field gap for a triple, giving the Indians the lead. Valentine followed with an RBI single, making it 9-6 Spokane.

Things got even more interesting in the top of the ninth. Lasorda brought in right-handed reliever Jack Jenkins, who recorded a pair of outs but walked two. The next man up, lefty Tomás Silverio, represented the potential tying run. Lasorda then summoned southpaw Geoff Zahn from the bullpen for the more favorable left-on-left matchup. Instead of using straight-up pitching change, however, Lasorda deployed the rarely used Waxahachie Swap.* He sent Jenkins to right field and replaced Tom Paciorek with Zahn. Tanner countered with a right-handed pinch-hitter,

---

* Dating back to the nineteenth century, venturesome managers occasionally shifted a pitcher to another position, brought in an opposite-handed reliever, and then returned to the original pitcher. The tactic allowed managers to deploy pitchers against same-handed batters without burning multiple arms. Paul Richards, known as "The Wizard of Waxahachie" after his hometown in Texas, used the maneuver four times in the 1950s as manager of the White Sox and Orioles. Sportswriter and author Rob Neyer later popularized the term "Waxahachie Swap" as an homage to Richards. In 1970, Lasorda used the tactic three times (July 15 versus Phoenix, July 26, versus Hawaii, and August 3 versus Eugene). In his twenty-three seasons managing in the big leagues, he used it only once—on October 1, 1991, in the thick of the pennant race. MLB essentially rendered the Waxahachie Swap obsolete when it instituted a three-batter minimum in 2020.

Dave Adlesh, who reached on a Valentine error. Now, the bases were loaded for the Islanders' best hitter, right-hand hitting Winston Llenas. Lasorda's chess match continued. He moved Zahn to first base, sent Buckner from first to right field, and brought Jenkins back in to pitch. For a moment, Llenas sucked the wind out of the stadium with a long fly ball to right-center, but center fielder Davey Lopes managed to track it down for the final out. The Fairgrounds crowd collectively breathed a sigh of relief.

JACK JENKINS - Pitcher

Courtesy Dave Eskenazi.

Despite playing sub-.500 ball over the course of three weeks, Spokane still held a twelve-and-a-half-game lead over Portland with thirty-five to play. The remainder of the Indians' games would come against their three Northern Division foes, all of whom had losing records. For all intents and purposes, winning the division would be a cinch. And the way Hawaii was playing, it seemed likely the two teams would meet again in the playoffs.

The Indians concluded July with a resounding sweep of the Tacoma Cubs at Cheney Stadium. Steve Garvey, who hit .296 in 13 games during his three-plus weeks with the Dodgers, rejoined the Indians in Tacoma, instantly reclaiming the starting third-base job. The Indians then got first baseman Tommy Hutton back for their next series in Eugene. Lasorda had his full complement of players for the stretch run.

Spokane returned home on August 4 and promptly executed another dominant four-game sweep of the Cubs. In a span of eleven days, Spokane had defeated Tacoma eight times by a combined score of 60-13. Spokane's starting pitchers allowed three runs or fewer in each of the eight contests.

The Indians' defeat of Tacoma on August 5 included a Morganna-the-Kissing-Bandit-type situation involving Bill Buckner, followed by a dramatic ending. A couple of hours after police escorted the female fan off the field, the Indians led 7-1 entering the top of the ninth. Sandy Vance, three outs away from a complete-game victory, allowed a single to Brock Davis before walking Roger Metzger. The next man up, Garry Jestadt, scorched a line drive up the middle just to the left of second base. Both runners instinctively took off running, unaware that shortstop Bobby Valentine was positioned in the ball's path. Jim Price, a sportswriter and track announcer at Playfair Race Course, witnessed the play unfold from his seat along the first-base line. He shouted to his wife, "He's going to get an unassisted triple play!" Valentine caught the ball, stepped on second, and ran toward Metzger, who was dead to rights between first and second. Instead of tagging the runner, however, Valentine tossed the ball to Tommy Hutton to complete an *assisted* triple play. Years later, Price asked Valentine why he threw to first instead of turning an exceedingly rare unassisted triple play. "I must have been thinking about my next at-bat," Valentine replied.[11]

In the midst of a 1-for-20 slump, Valentine probably was thinking about his offense. But he quickly regained his stroke with hits in all four games of the Indians' next series versus the Portland Beavers. In the homestand finale, the Indians rallied from an 8-1 deficit to tie the score and send the game to extra innings. Unfortunately, Charlie Hough allowed the winning run to score in the tenth inning on a passed ball that knuckled too much for catcher Steve Sogge to handle. The loss dropped Hough's record to 12-8, but his 1.95 ERA still led the league. The agony of defeat quickly turned to elation, however, when Hough learned after the game that his lifelong dream was coming true. He was headed to the big leagues.

Major-League Calls and Banquet Brawls

"I think I was kind of lucky that I was never so good that winning a game wasn't a struggle. I really had to work to win a game."—Charlie Hough

ON WEDNESDAY, AUGUST 12, 1970, THE DODGERS AND PIRATES FACED off at recently opened Three Rivers Stadium in Pittsburgh. Although each team had accumulated sixty-four wins, their respective positions in the standings differed dramatically. The Pirates sat atop the NL East, two and a half games in front of the Mets, whereas the Dodgers had fallen twelve games behind the Reds in the NL West. With its playoff odds somewhere between slim and none, LA needed to scratch out every win possible.

Charlie Hough watched from the bullpen that night as his new teammates broke a 2-2 tie in the eighth and then poured it on the next inning. The ninth began with Maury Wills and Bill Russell singles. Then Willie Davis doubled, Wes Parker walked, Jeff Torborg and Ted Sizemore singled, and Willie Crawford doubled. When the inning ended, the Dodgers led the Bucs by nine. If Walter Alston was looking for a soft landing for his new knuckleballer, he couldn't have scripted a better scenario. When Pete Mikkelsen ran into trouble in the ninth, the skipper strolled to the mound and signaled for the rookie.

Four months earlier, Hough had debuted his knuckleball in front of 181 shivering spectators in Salt Lake City. At that time, his head was full of doubt. His baseball career had hung by the fingernails he now so meticulously manicured. But in the interim, he had flummoxed Pacific Coast League hitters with his newfound weapon. And now he was standing on the mound at Three Rivers Stadium in front of 34,000-plus.

The first man he faced, Pirates cleanup man Al Oliver, watched four consecutive knuckleballs flutter out of the strike zone. Hough had inherited two runners, so now the bases were packed. Up came Willie Stargell, a future Hall of Famer who would eventually retire with 475 home runs. "I went 3-2 and threw a fastball," recalled Hough. "For some unexplainable reason, he swung and missed it. I threw that pitch harder than any other pitch I've ever thrown, which might have made it 83 miles per hour. I was shocked he didn't kill it."[1]

By season's end, Hough would appear seven more times, mostly in mop-up duty. He'd lost control of his knuckleball, so he often reverted to his low-eighties fastball when he needed to throw a strike. In 17 innings, he walked 11, struck out eight, and served up seven home runs. It was a far cry from his dominance in Spokane, where he had posted a league-best 1.95 ERA and either won or saved 30 of his team's 76 victories.

When Hough pitched for Tommy Lasorda, the skipper encouraged him to throw nothing but knuckleballs regardless of the situation. "He didn't care if I walked five in a row," recalled Hough. The messaging in LA was quite different. Alston constantly reminded him not to walk the leadoff hitter. "That's an automatic 3-0 count," Hough explained. "When you're trying to not do something wrong, it's really hard."[2]

A few days after the Dodgers promoted Hough, they called up his Triple-A roommate, Sandy Vance, to replace Bill Singer, who had broken a finger. Less than three weeks earlier, Vance had suffered the embarrassment of losing both games of a doubleheader. But it just so happened that a Dodgers scout was in the stands that night and liked what he saw in the righty's revamped Koufax-like delivery. Later in life, Vance would often tell the story to show that "no matter how bad things look like they are turning out for you, you never know what might be around the next corner."[3]

Vance excitedly flew to Chicago and took a cab to Wrigley Field, where the Dodgers and Cubs were playing the second game of a twin bill.

He threw on his uniform and rushed to the dugout. Within a few minutes, Alston told him to warm up. Vance pitched an inning and a third of scoreless relief that afternoon, then twirled a complete-game victory three days later against the Cardinals. He would finish the season 7-7 with a 3.13 ERA.

WITHOUT TWO OF ITS BETTER ARMS, SPOKANE WOULD BE MORE RELIANT on its offense down the stretch. No problem. When Indians pitching ceded 24 runs during a four-game series in Eugene,* Spokane scored 31 while winning three. Bobby Valentine led the charge with three bombs. A few days later, the teams met in Spokane. Before the opener, Valentine held court with a couple dozen young fans near the Indians dugout. One of the kids asked the charismatic shortstop when he was going to hit his next grand slam. "Oh, the next time I come up with the bases loaded," Valentine responded with confidence.[4] About an hour later, he found himself in that very situation. As he stood in the batter's box, Valentine remembered what he had told the youngsters before the game. He dug in, put a good swing on a pitch, and deposited his 13th home run of the season over the left-field fence.

By mid-August, the Indians and Hawaii Islanders had each clinched their respective divisions. The two PCL powers would next meet in a best-of-seven postseason series.† As the Indians played out the last two weeks of the schedule against Tacoma and Portland, they showed no signs of letting up. In their final road series, they won three of four in Tacoma, including a 12-0 rout behind Tom Paciorek's four hits and team-leading 15th home run. That same night, Jerry Stephenson won his tenth consecutive decision, improving his record to 17-5. Lasorda's bold February

---

* During one of the Indians' trips to Eugene, Steve Sogge borrowed a car from one of his high school coaches, who was coaching at the University of Oregon. The salmon summer run was underway, so Lasorda allowed Sogge and a couple other players to drive to the coast and go salmon fishing. "We caught the fish and brought them back to the hotel, and the chef cooked a wonderful meal for all of us to share," recalled Sogge. "As I recall, Tommy ate his fair share."

† The series was originally planned for five games. Because of the travel involved with Hawaii winning the Southern Division, league officials made it a seven-game series so that each team would be guaranteed two home games.

declaration that Stephenson would pitch at Dodger Stadium before season's end seemed not so far-fetched after all.

The pitiful Cubs, fifty-two games under .500 after losing the first three games of the series, salvaged the finale on the shoulders of starting pitcher Larry Colton, who tossed a three-hitter and hit a home run. "I was the best hitter on that team," recalled Colton. "I came up after that with runners on second and third and Lasorda intentionally walked me to get to the leadoff man. That's how bad we were."[5]

A day after the Spokane series, the beleaguered Cubs held their end-of-the-season banquet at Cheney Stadium. Colton wrote a poem for the occasion titled "Ode to Whitey."* It was a tribute to his manager, Whitey Lockman, who in Colton's words "had the patience of Job to put up with our team." He had been working on the piece in secret for a couple of weeks. "I knew this was going to be the first poetry reading any of these guys had ever been to," recalled Colton. "I was the emcee and roasted some of my teammates while doing a Howard Cosell impersonation. I'd say, 'You struck out four times against the Spokane Indians. How do you feel about that?' I had done it with a couple of other teams, including Eugene when we won the league, so it was all in good fun, and everyone got in the spirit. It didn't turn out that way in Tacoma because we were so bad and had no team unity. As I was doing this, guys started yelling at each other, and it turned into a brawl. Punches were thrown. Guys were spilling their beer and slipping and falling while trying to fight each other. It was chaos for ten minutes and then finally calmed down. Then, I called Whitey up to the stage and was about to read this poem to him. I asked him, 'What do you have to say about your team fighting?' He looked at me and said, 'You're a fucking asshole.' He thought I was the instigator!"[6]

Despite his manager's harsh words, Colton proceeded to pull out his poem, which was written in calligraphy. He read aloud his beautifully written composition praising Lockman. The players, bloodied and drenched in beer, stopped and listened. Some even started to cry.

While the Cubs were beating up one another, the Indians were pulverizing the Portland Beavers—Spokane's opponent to begin the final homestand of the season. In the Indians' doubleheader sweep to start the series,

---

* Colton later taught high school, authored several non-fiction books, and wrote for *Esquire*, *Sports Illustrated*, and *New York Times Magazine*.

Valentine, Garvey, and Buckner collectively registered 18 hits. Beavers starter Bruce Brubaker served up a home run to Garvey that he vividly remembered decades later: "I threw him a hanging slider, and he hit that thing to center field. I think it was the longest home run I've ever seen in my life. He grinned at me as he rounded second base. Garvey had a short, powerful stroke."[7]

Spokane defeated the Beavers the next two nights, setting up the opportunity for a five-game series sweep in the finale on August 29. Lasorda gave the starting assignment to a twenty-one-year-old lefty just up from Single A. His name was Doug, but Lasorda called him Dougie.

DOUGIE

"I learned a lot about baseball from Tommy. He's right up there with my dad and college coach as far as encouraging me and letting me do my thing."—Doug Rau

WITH HIS TEAM TRAILING THE YANKEES TWO GAMES TO ONE IN THE 1977 World Series, Dodgers manager Tommy Lasorda tapped twenty-eight-year-old Doug Rau to start Game 4. The southpaw won 14 games during the regular season but hadn't started in eighteen days and had only thrown one inning of relief in the NLCS. Rau shook off the rust with a scoreless first inning but ran into trouble in the second. Reggie Jackson, whose Series heroics would earn him the nickname "Mr. October," poked an opposite-field double to start the frame. He came around to score when the next man up, Lou Piniella, slapped a single to right field. The left-handed-hitting Chris Chambliss then inside-outed a Rau delivery the opposite way for another double.* New York led 1-0 and had two runners in scoring

---

* Rau had reverse splits for his career. Left-handed batters hit .285 with a .766 OPS against him, whereas right-handed batters hit .256 with a .681 OPS. This could at least partly be explained by Rau's changeup, which tailed down and in on lefty batters, right into their typical wheelhouse.

position with no outs. "He can't get them left-handers out for Christ all-fuckin'-mighty," Lasorda said to pitching coach Red Adams in the home dugout.¹ Six batters into a game the Dodgers could ill-afford to lose, the skipper had seen enough.

Lasorda called time and slowly jogged to the mound, stalling so that right-hander Rick Rhoden could toss a few more warmup pitches in the bullpen. As his manager approached, Rau told him that he felt good. "I don't give a shit you feel good," replied Lasorda. "There's four motherfuckin' hits up there!"² Rau pointed out that all three hits that inning were to the opposite field. Lasorda wasn't hearing it. "I don't give a fuck," he said.³ Rau continued his plea to stay in the game, declaring that he'd strike out the next guy, Graig Nettles. As Lasorda signaled to the bullpen for Rhoden, he told Rau to shut up, that he was the one making the decisions. CBS had outfitted Lasorda with a microphone that night, so the expletive-laced exchange was captured on tape. A few years later, someone leaked and circulated the recording, giving fans a rare glimpse at an unfiltered on-field conversation in a high-stakes situation.*

"You could have an opinion with Lasorda and talk to him about it and get in his face and cuss each other out and then go to dinner that night," recalled Rau. "Once he got to know you and learned what your intentions were and what you were made of, you could let it all hang out."⁴

Lasorda and Rau forged a close friendship with mutual respect while living together in Venezuela during winter ball. "We would walk five miles one way in Caracas at midnight to get a glass of grapefruit juice because Tommy was on a diet," recalled Rau. "I had one pair of leather shoes, and I wore them out walking to get him grapefruit juice and humoring him almost every night. We talked about everything. Having lived with him and dealt with him on a personal level, I felt like I could say anything around him, and he'd understand. We were from two different worlds, but there were a lot of commonalities, and we clicked."⁵

They didn't exactly get off on the right foot, however.

When Rau deboarded a plane in Spokane in late August 1970, he had swagger. A few months earlier, he had completed his junior season at Texas A&M University, where he set the school record with a 0.86 ERA.

---

* As of 2025, a video of the Rau-Lasorda exchange had over a half-million views on YouTube.

He was named All-American, Academic All-American, All-Conference, and team MVP. That June, the Dodgers drafted him in the first round of the secondary phase. In Bakersfield that summer, he dominated the Single-A California League, winning 12 of 14 decisions while registering a 1.75 ERA and 140 strikeouts in 113 innings.

Rau was a farm boy from Columbus, Texas—a small town seventy-five miles west of Houston. He spent his youth tending crops, feeding hogs and chickens, and repairing fences. When his legs were long enough to reach the pedals, he drove a tractor. At eight years old, he began playing organized baseball and quickly gravitated to pitching. A year later, he taught himself how to throw a curveball while playing catch with his brother under a pecan tree on the family farm.

Rau excelled in baseball during high school. The Orioles chose him in the twentieth round of the 1967 June draft, but he had already made up his mind. Texas A&M had offered a full-ride scholarship he couldn't pass up. By the time Rau got to College Station, he had perfected his breaking ball, mixing it with a low-90s four-seam fastball and changeup. The model student majored in business. He was methodical about his studies and just as dedicated on the baseball diamond, displaying a work ethic that he established on the family farm in Columbus.

When Rau first walked into the Indians clubhouse in Spokane, clubhouse boy Kent Schultz greeted him and said, "Your locker is over here. You're sharing it with me."[6] Rau had other ideas. He pointed to an occupied locker near the front of the clubhouse and said he'd take that one. Schultz was taken aback. He told the assertive southpaw that there were no extra lockers and that he'd have to share for now. Rau was peeved. "He had this air about him," remembered Schultz. "The whole team could read and feel it."[7]

Most players would have been thrilled with getting promoted to Triple-A so soon, not to mention possibly pitching in the PCL playoffs. But not Rau. He had signed up to take twenty-four hours of senior-level finance classes at A&M, and the fall semester had already begun. When he got to Spokane, he told Lasorda that he intended to call Al Campanis and tell him that he needed to get back to College Station. If Rau stayed with the Indians through the PCL playoffs, he'd miss the first few weeks of classes. "Don't do it, Dougie," warned Lasorda.[8] Rau felt he couldn't miss that much school, so he ignored his manager's advice.

Before he left for Texas, Rau took the mound against the Portland Beavers for what would mark his only appearance for the 1970 Spokane Indians. And the Beavers lit him up like a Christmas tree. The first three batters hit two doubles and a triple. By the time he recorded the third out of the first inning, four runs had scored. As the frame unfolded, Lasorda said to the guys in the dugout, "I'm gonna let him fry. He needs to learn what this is about."[9]

Rau returned to the mound in the second. According to Chuck Stewart of the *Spokane Daily Chronicle*, he was "as tight as a violin string."[10] The top of the Beavers order came back around and went single, double, double. With his young southpaw sufficiently fried, Lasorda sauntered to the mound and signaled for reliever Jack Jenkins. Rau departed with a ledger of seven hits and six runs allowed (five earned) in an inning and a third.

As he walked down the tunnel leading to the clubhouse, Rau reached up and jerked on one of the overhead pipes, causing it to come crashing down. He then proceeded to the trainer's room as water poured out of the broken pipe and began flooding the Indians dugout. While the lefty soaked his bones in the jacuzzi, his teammates rallied to score 16 runs on 19 hits, defeating the Beavers handily. Tom Paciorek recorded his fifth four-hit game of the season and Bobby Valentine added three base knocks to his season total, becoming the first PCL player to reach 200 hits since Jesús Alou in 1963.

After the game, the cheerful Spokane players filed into the clubhouse, their uniforms caked in dirt and sweat, only to find that Rau's fit of anger had rendered the showers out of order. "Lasorda was especially disturbed with me," Rau recalled.[11] The young Texan would eventually redeem himself through a combination of hard work and late-night walks through Venezuela.

Re-Creating Reality

"Winston Llenas was over 100 RBIs ... During a pregame interview, I asked him what he thought about going for the league record, and he responded with some cliché answer. The next day, I go out into the clubhouse and Chuck Tanner said to me, 'Why would you ever ask Llenas that question?' And he slugged me in the stomach with a left."—Hawaii Islanders broadcaster Ken Wilson

HERB HUNTER, THE SPOKANE INDIANS RADIO ANNOUNCER, BROADCAST more than 2,100 games during the team's fourteen seasons in the Pacific Coast League. His exuberant voice became synonymous with summer in the Inland Northwest. He called home games in a radio booth at the Fairgrounds and re-created broadcasts of road games from a studio in Spokane.* The re-creations were based on simply play-by-play information delivered by phone or telegram. Hunter once estimated that his re-

---

* Re-creation broadcasts were common throughout baseball in the 1930s and '40s. In fact, one of Ronald Reagan's first jobs out of college was re-creating broadcasts of Chicago Cubs games on WHO radio in Des Moines, Iowa. Major-league announcers eventually traveled to road games, but in the minor leagues budgets were tighter, so re-creations remained in vogue in 1970.

creations were 5 percent information and 95 percent imagination. He'd receive a brief report that would read, "Valentine: Double to LF" and then invent a vivid description of Valentine pulling a grounder down the third-base line, rounding first, digging for second, and sliding headfirst just ahead of the tag.

Courtesy Spokane Indians.

Hunter struck a wooden block with a pencil to mimic the sound of the bat, punched a leather pouch to simulate a catcher's mitt, and played a reel of crowd noise for ambiance. Baseball fan David Eyre, who grew up in Spokane listening to Indians games on KHQ radio, had no idea at the time that Hunter re-created road games. "Once this was revealed to me," recalled Eyre, "I could hear crowd noise that repeated rhythmically on cue about every minute."[1]

Al Michaels and Ken Wilson did similar re-creations for the Hawaii Islanders' road games. They'd begin their broadcasts ninety minutes after the actual first pitch, relying on periodic updates from a sportswriter at the game. "And then we'd go from there—occasionally taking some creative license," Michaels recalled. "Since there was a considerable time delay, if it was 10-1 in the eighth inning, and we got an account of an inning where every batter had taken a full count, sometimes our audience heard a nice, crisp three- or four-pitch inning."[2]

In late August of 1970, as the Islanders played their final regular-season series in Salt Lake City, Michaels and Wilson performed their usual re-creation broadcast from a studio in Honolulu. Although the games were meaningless to the Islanders, Don Zimmer's Padres entered the four-game set with a 43-96 record and desperately wanted to win at least one to avoid the dreaded 100-loss mark.

The Indians, meanwhile, hosted the last-place Tacoma Cubs, whom Spokane had beaten 16 times in 18 tries. Between his team's abysmal play and team-banquet brawl, Whitey Lockman couldn't wait for the misery to end. In the opener, Jerry Stephenson mowed down the Cubs with a complete-game, ten-strikeout performance, earning his 18th win. Over his final 14 starts, the righty posted a pristine 11-0 record and sterling 1.44 ERA. When he accepted Athlete of the Week honors at an Inland Empire Sportswriters and Broadcasters luncheon a couple of days later, Stephenson credited his manager with turning around his career: "Last year, if I'd been invited to a luncheon like this it would have been to clean tables or wash dishes. Tom Lasorda helps you with the physical aspects of pitching, the mechanics, but so do a lot of managers. He helped me mentally. He made me ready to pitch. I want to thank him personally and publicly."[3]

Entering the final series of the season, the PCL batting title remained up for grabs. The Islanders' Winston Llenas sat in the driver's seat with a .338 batting average—four points ahead of Bobby Valentine. The Indians shortstop inched closer, however, by rapping four base hits over the first two games against Tacoma. In Salt Lake City, Llenas went 1-for-3 in the series opener before sitting idle the next night because of a rainout.

With two games to play, Bart Shirley's batting average stood at .299. Before the Indians' penultimate game, Tommy Lasorda devised a plan to help his veteran second baseman reach the coveted .300 mark. "Tommy went over to [Lockman] and said, 'Let Bart lay a bunt down, and then you can pick him off first base,'" recalled Shirley. "I laid a good bunt down, and the guy threw the ball over the first baseman's head. I had to run to second and ended up scoring a run. Tommy looked after his players. He wanted to take care of us."[4] The official scorer gave Shirley a single, raising his average to .300.* Lasorda then pulled him from the game before his next at-bat and benched him in the finale to ensure he maintained baseball's mark of excellence.

In the same game, Tom Paciorek went 2-for-3 but failed to bring home the lone runner he had in scoring position, holding him to 99 RBI, at least for now. Valentine, meanwhile, recorded a fifth consecutive multi-hit game, moving to within one point of Llenas, who went 1-for-4 in Salt Lake City. The batting race would now come down to the final day of the season. League president Bill McKechnie ordered the Islanders and Padres to make up their rainout from two days prior as part of a doubleheader. The Padres, who were two losses away from 100, would have gladly played just the one game.

Later that night, Tacoma's Larry Colton, the next day's scheduled starter, went out drinking with several Spokane players, including Paciorek. The former Phillies hurler, whose major-league career consisted of one game, had gotten off to a terrific start to the season for Tacoma. At one point, he owned a 6-1 record and sub-2.00 ERA and felt confident the big-league Cubs would call him up soon. Instead, the Cubs bought the contract of Juan Pizarro from Hawaii, leaving the twenty-eight-year-old Colton frustrated. Heading into the season's final day, he had lost 13 of his last 19 decisions, and his ERA had ballooned to north of 4.00. Colton had made up his mind that the next day's start would be his last. "I didn't want to play anymore," he recalled decades later. "I made the big leagues, and then I got hurt.† I was disenchanted by Vietnam. The whole zeitgeist was getting me down. Plus, I was having marital problems.‡ Tom Paciorek said he had 99 RBIs, and he wanted to get 100. I said, 'Well, I'll see what I can do.' I know this was unethical and contrary to baseball, but I had just seen a riot on my own team, and I was quitting."[5]

The regular season concluded on Wednesday, September 2. The

---

* Multiple newspapers at the time listed Shirley's batting average as .300 after the bunt single. On Baseball-Reference, his average is listed as .299.

† Colton dislocated his non-throwing shoulder in a bar fight a month after his big-league debut. The injury altered his mechanics, and he was never the same.

‡ At the time, Colton was married to the daughter of actress/inventor Hedy Lamarr.

Islanders-Padres doubleheader in Salt Lake City began at 5:30 p.m. PST, more than two hours before first pitch in Spokane. Llenas batted 1-for-2 in the first game—a Padres victory that took all of ninety-five minutes. Looking back, Salt Lake's Jeff Pentland believed Tanner threw the game to spare Zimmer the embarrassment of 100 losses.[6] In the nightcap, Llenas singled in his first at-bat, giving him a batting average of .340, or .3395 to be precise. Chuck Tanner assumed Llenas had the batting title in the bag, so he removed him from the game before his next at-bat.

Around the same time, the Cubs-Indians game began. In Valentine's first at-bat, he hit a clean single up the middle off Colton. The next time up, he bounced a two-hopper to third baseman John Lung, who bobbled the ball before launching it over the head of the first baseman. In Lockman's estimation, a good throw would have gotten Valentine, but official scorer Frank Herron ruled it a base hit. In his third at-bat, Valentine pulled another sharp grounder to third. This time, the ball skipped off Lung's glove, and Herron again awarded Valentine with a generously scored single. With three hits in as many at-bats, Valentine's average was now .3398—a fraction above Llenas's. Lasorda got word from the press box that Tanner had already pulled Llenas, so the Spokane skipper removed Valentine to guarantee his batting title.* Up until then, the Indians shortstop had played every inning of every game.

Colton, meanwhile, decided to go out in a blaze of glory. Trailing 5-4 in the bottom of the fifth, the poetry-writing pitcher took a page out of Charlie Hough's chapbook and threw Steve Garvey nothing but knuckleballs—a pitch Colton had never thrown before in a game. Lockman fumed in the visitors' dugout as Garvey watched four straight pitches sail out of the zone. Paciorek then stepped in the batter's box, still searching for his 100th RBI. "I wild pitched Garvey to second," recalled Colton. "As I came in toward the plate, I said to Paciorek, 'Fastball down the middle.' I delivered, and he hit one that when last seen was headed to Idaho. He

---

* It marked the second time in Llenas's career that he lost a batting title on the final day of the season. Six years earlier in the Northwest League, he finished the season two points behind Bill Robinson, who would eventually play sixteen seasons in the majors. Llenas looked back on both batting races with great pride. "I ended up being second to two great ballplayers by a fraction of a point," he said years later. "So, that puts me in the same league they were."

killed it. Two-run homer."[7] Colton never threw another pitch in a professional baseball game.

After Spokane hung on to win a 10-8 slugfest, Lockman vented to Ed Honeywell of the *Tacoma News Tribune* about what he viewed as generous official scoring by the home team, calling it a "disgrace to baseball." Lockman added, "This shabby and undisguised attempt to win a batting title leaves me extremely disgusted, which is exactly what I'm informing President McKechnie. My sympathies are certainly all with Llenas in this controversy."[8]

As the Cubs-Indians game played out in real time, Al Michaels sat in a Honolulu radio studio and re-created the Islanders-Padres doubleheader. Michaels got word, possibly from Honeywell, that Valentine had been awarded a pair of hits on some questionable hometown scoring. "When I heard about this," wrote Michaels in his autobiography, "I made a big deal of it during our re-creation. 'Llenas should have won the batting title, but because of some local-yokel scoring decisions, Valentine has won the batting title!'"[9]

A day later, the *Spokane Chronicle* printed the following quote from Valentine: "I didn't want to come out, but Tommy persuaded me to. He said the batting championship was more important than playing every inning. After all, I did play every game. But I don't think I would have come out if Llenas hadn't in Salt Lake. I'm sure he came out thinking he had it won. I thought I would just give him a taste of his own medicine."[10] That last sentence, plus Michaels's description on the re-creation broadcast, drew the ire of Hawaii Islanders fans.

Valentine finished the regular season with a slash line of .340/.389/.522. Primarily leading off, he hit 14 home runs and drove in 80 runs. His 27 stolen bases bested everyone but the Islanders' Doug Griffin. Valentine led the league in batting average, runs, hits, doubles, and triples, and total bases. Naturally, the league's sportswriters and broadcasters voted him the Most Valuable Player, marking the first time a Spokane player had won the award since Willie Davis in 1960. It had barely been a year since some of the young shortstop's teammates had staged a coup in an effort to have him benched. Now, he was a capable defender, batting champion, and MVP, monumental accomplishments for a twenty-year-old whose future seemed limitless.

The same could be said for several of Valentine's teammates. Bill

Buckner overcame his jaw-wired slump to finish with the league's third-best batting average at .336. Tom Paciorek carried a .326 mark while becoming only the second Spokane Indians player to top 100 RBI. Tommy Hutton boasted an impressive .323/.402/.490 slash line while maintaining a .990 fielding percentage. Steve Garvey batted .319, smacked 15 home runs, and drove in 87 runs in 95 games. And Davey Lopes hit .262 with six homers and 11 steals as a semi-regular.

The Indians led the PCL Northern Division wire to wire and concluded the regular season with a 94-52 record—twenty-six games ahead of the second-place Portland Beavers. The Indians' .299 team batting average shattered the league record,* and only the Phoenix Giants bested their 3.31 team ERA. Yet, for as talented and dominant as the Indians were, they did not own the circuit's best record. That distinction belonged to the Islanders, whose final mark of 98-48 topped Phoenix by thirteen games in the Southern Division. The Islanders' .671 winning percentage fell short of just two previous teams in the sixty-eight-year history of the PCL. Spokane's and Hawaii's preposterous run differentials of +209 and +217, respectively, stood far above the rest of the league.

The unabashedly confident Tommy Lasorda liked his team's chances in the forthcoming best-of-seven series. "We're gonna beat 'em," he declared, showing the same conviction that he did on opening day in Salt Lake City. As a follow-up question, a reporter asked how many games the series would go. Lasorda barked, "As many as it takes."[11]

---

* The record was previously held by the 1966 Tulsa Oilers, a Cardinals affiliate, who hit .289.

Heavyweight Fight

"Anything can happen in a short series like this. Especially when two outstanding ballclubs are bucking heads."—Tommy Lasorda, September 3, 1970

"These two clubs are like a heavyweight title fight ... We have the knockout punch; they are the boxer with speed."—Chuck Tanner, September 3, 1970

ON PAPER, THE SPOKANE INDIANS AND HAWAII ISLANDERS LOOKED FAIRLY even. If anything, the Islanders seemingly possessed a slight edge. After all, Hawaii won four more games than the comparatively inexperienced Indians and held an 11-9 advantage in head-to-head play. But a surface-level comparison would overlook several factors. The Indians had played nearly half of their games against the Islanders without the trio of Bill Buckner, Steve Garvey, and Tommy Hutton. All three had returned to full health and entered the playoffs red-hot. Also, both teams had lost key members of their respective pitching staffs to the big leagues over the course of the season. The Islanders had lost three top hurlers—reliever Dave LaRoche and starters Juan Pizarro and Tom Bradley—who combined for a 26-1 record and 2.48 ERA. For their part, the Indians would be without the services of Sandy Vance and PCL Pitcher of the Year Charlie Hough.

As the teams prepared for Game 1 at the Fairgrounds in Spokane, Tommy Lasorda had to be a little jealous. The opposing manager, Chuck Tanner, had just signed a contract to manage the Chicago White Sox (much to the chagrin of the Angels). Tanner would begin his new gig at the conclusion of the Islanders-Indians series. Lasorda's dream was coming true—for his PCL rival.

Hawaii's first-ever PCL playoff appearance stirred so much excitement in the Aloha State that its first two road games were televised live in Hawaii via satellite, a rare occurrence at the time. "Usually everything was taped, flown over, and shown a week later," recalled Islanders broadcaster Ken Wilson. "To have two games from Spokane and have them live was a huge story itself."[1] The telecast had its share of hiccups, however. First, viewers saw Chuck Tanner's lips moving during a pregame interview but heard no sound. Once the game started, the audio feed worked but Hawaii fans missed much of the action due to insufficient camera angles.

Before Game 1, Wilson visited Tommy Lasorda in his office to obtain some intel for the broadcast. "Nobody's in there except for Tommy, and he's got a wooden cutting board and a thing of salami," recalled Wilson. "He looks at me and says, 'Hey, do you want some salami?' I ate a couple pieces and asked him about his starting pitcher. That was the only time in my career that any manager ever offered me slices of salami."[2]

It felt like autumn had come early in the Inland Northwest. At game time, the mercury hovered around fifty degrees as a cold drizzle fell from the dusk sky. Spokane baseball fans weighed the pros and cons of watching their hometown team vie for a championship versus staying in the warm and dry confines of their homes. A crowd of 4,589 braved the elements, leaving the ballpark half-empty—or as Lasorda likely saw it, half-full.

Tanner tapped former Spokane hurler John Purdin to start Game 1, adding an interesting wrinkle to the opener. Purdin had registered a 6-6 record for the Indians with five saves before the Dodgers sold him to Hawaii in late July. He posted a 5-4 mark for the Islanders and lost his only start against Spokane, allowing five earned runs in six innings. Eighteen-game winner Jerry Stephenson, riding an eleven-game unbeaten streak, toed the rubber for the Indians.

Spokane's ace set down the Islanders on fifteen pitches in the first, giving his offense a chance to strike first. And they did. After Winston Llenas robbed Bobby Valentine of a base hit (an ironic start to the game given how the last weekend of the season played out), Bob Stinson reached on catcher's interference, stole second, and scored on Steve Garvey's single. Garvey then swiped second and came around to score on Tommy Hutton's base knock. Later in the inning, Bart Shirley delivered a two-run single to cap off a four-run opening frame. Two innings later, Garvey added a fifth run with a solo homer. Stephenson wasn't as sharp as he had been in recent weeks but managed to limit Hawaii to three runs. He showed signs of fatigue in the ninth, loading the bases with two outs. Lasorda summoned reliever Jose Peña (the pitcher sent down when the Dodgers recalled Charlie Hough), who retired Doug Griffin on one pitch to secure Spokane's 5-3 win. "That was some ball game," said Lasorda afterward. "I feel like a wet dish rag."[3]

In the words of Yogi Berra, Game 2 was déjà vu all over again. In similarly unseasonably cool weather, the Indians again jumped on the Islanders early. Bobby Valentine, who had been held hitless in Game 1, led off with a single, advanced to third on Davey Lopes's base hit, and scored on Bill Buckner's sacrifice fly. With Garvey at the plate, Lopes stole second and took third on an errant throw by catcher Merritt Ranew. Garvey then hit a grounder to shortstop Marty Perez, who threw wild in his attempt to nail Lopes at home. Garvey, safe on a fielder's choice, scampered to second. Tom Paciorek and Tommy Hutton then walked, and Steve Sogge and Bart Shirley singled. By the time Islanders starter Archie Reynolds recorded the third out, the Indians had scored five runs and given starter Mike Strahler a comfortable lead.

Spokane added another run off Reynolds in the third and kept pouring it on against a trio of Hawaii relievers that included Harvey Shank, Bob Allen, and Ron Kline. The Indians banged out 19 hits and scored in every inning except the second en route to a 12-4 shellacking. Buckner hit 4-for-4, and Hutton, Sogge, and Shirley chipped in three hits apiece, with Hutton's sixth-inning solo blast the game's only home run. Strahler went the distance, scattering 11 hits while striking out eight. He got some help from his defense, which turned four double plays behind him. Postgame, the mood in the home clubhouse was jovial. On the visitors' side, you could hear a pin drop. Visiting clubhouse attendant Jerry Kuntz recalled Tanner and his disappointed players sitting dejected afterward. Kuntz, who considered the '70 Islanders to be the most talented team he saw in his three years on the job, was just as shocked. Neither team had time to dwell on the outcome of the first two games, however. Game 3 would be played the following night.

Twenty-four hours later at Honolulu Stadium, the saimin simmered and the Primo beer flowed. A boisterous crowd of 18,032 filed through the Termite Palace turnstiles to witness Hawaii's first-ever playoff game.* The locals did not show Bobby Valentine the Aloha Spirit. When the PCL batting champion and MVP took the field for warmups, the spectators unleashed a torrent of boos. When he led off the game against 18-game winner Dennis Bennett, the jeers grew louder. The hostile reception stunned Valentine. He had never been booed in his life. Perhaps pressing a bit, he popped out to start the game.

In the second inning, Paciorek and Hutton accounted for the game's first run with back-to-back doubles. An inning later, Valentine doubled and scored on Buckner's two-run homer over the right-field screen, making it 3-0 Indians. Solo home runs by Valentine and Paciorek in the seventh and eighth, respectively, gave Spokane more cushion. A locked-in Doyle Alexander had all the support he needed, and more. The Alabaman kept the Islanders off the board for nine innings, striking out six and scattering four singles and three walks. "He would have won in any league, including the majors the way he pitched tonight," said Chuck Tanner after the game. "It was one of the best games we've seen all year."[4]

After the game, Valentine learned that his quote in the *Spokane Daily Chronicle* days earlier had riled up the Hawaii faithful. That quote as printed wasn't entirely accurate, however. Valentine had actually said, "Tommy said, 'Let's give him some of his own medicine.'" The *Daily Chronicle* attributed the quote directly to Valentine. "I wouldn't say anything like that about Winston," said Valentine. "I respect him as a great hitter."[5]

---

* The Islanders outdrew six big-league teams that night—the Braves, Astros, Yankees, Athletics, Senators, and Cardinals.

Valentine's 3-for-4 performance in front of an antagonistic crown impressed his manager. "I believe in him more than any kid I've ever seen in baseball," said Lasorda. "And what he did tonight ... That proves what he's made of ... He's a champion."[6] Almost. Valentine and the Indians still had to win one more game.

Down three games to none, the Islanders' hopes hinged on the right arm of Greg Washburn, the Angels' first-round pick in the 1967 MLB June Amateur Draft-Secondary Phase. Born and raised in Coal City, Illinois, a blink-and-you'll-miss-it town twenty-five miles south of Joliet, Washburn was a highly touted pitcher in high school and at Lewis College in Romeoville. His stellar ledger as a sophomore—a 9-1 record and 1.93 ERA—slingshotted him to the top of the Angels' draft board. Nick Kamzic, the same scout who signed Rick Reichardt in '64, inked Washburn to his first professional contract. The Angels viewed the young righty as the second coming of Dean Chance.*

Washburn enjoyed a terrific first two seasons in the minors, earning an invitation to big-league camp in '69.† He appeared in eight games for the Angels that year, posting a disappointing 0-2 mark and 7.94 ERA. "I made two starts, and I had great stuff," recalled Washburn, "but they hit a bunch of Texas leaguers, swinging late and hitting them down the right-field line. I'd have rather they hit five home runs off me. I pitched fairly well in relief, but then I hurt my elbow, and that was before Tommy John surgery."[7] He underwent ulnar nerve transposition surgery with Dr. Frank Jobe, but his arm never fully recovered.

Washburn went 8-8 with a 4.63 ERA for Hawaii during the '70 season and would now face a Spokane team on the precipice of a championship. Chuck Tanner would not let his team go quietly, however. Before first pitch, the soon-to-be White Sox pilot told Washburn to back Valentine off the plate to start the game. He wanted to send Spokane a message that the series wasn't over yet. "Give him a little chin music," said Tanner.[8]

---

* Between 1961-66, Chance won 74 games with the Angels. In his Cy Young Award season of '64, he won 20 and posted a 1.65 ERA.

† In one memorable Cactus League outing against the Chicago Cubs, the first three hitters Washburn faced were future Hall of Famers Billy Williams, Ron Santo, and Ernie Banks. Just a few years earlier, the young hurler had used Banks in his Cadaco All-Star Baseball board game. Unfazed, Washburn tossed three scoreless innings that day. During a side-by-side interview with Banks postgame, an interviewer asked the legendary shortstop what pitch he was looking for when he faced Washburn. Banks said, "I was just looking for a baseball."

With the Islanders on the brink of elimination, the Hawaii fans' excitement had waned. Five thousand fewer fans showed up for Game 4. Valentine, public enemy number one a day earlier, occupied his usual spot atop the batting order. Wearing his gray road uniform with the number 2 on the back, the twenty-year-old strolled to the plate with his usual swagger. But then something remarkable happened. When the public address announcer said his name, the Termite Palace crowd gave him a standing ovation. The warm reception likely stemmed from a column in that morning's *Honolulu Star-Bulletin* in which sports editor Jim Hackleman argued why the previous night's booing was unwarranted.

Valentine, slated to be called up to the Dodgers at the conclusion of the series, dug in and stared out at Washburn. The pride of Coal City, Illinois, rocked back, raised his right arm, and unleashed his best fastball. As Valentine lunged forward, the pitch rode up and in, following him like a heat-seeking missile as he tried to duck away.

Like Butter

"Bobby had a lot of confidence, a lot of energy. He had the most swagger of any player I played against. You either hated him or loved him. He was a heck of a player."—Jeff Pentland

EVERYONE AT HONOLULU STADIUM ON THE NIGHT OF SEPTEMBER 7, 1970, remembers the sound. A horrific thud. Greg Washburn's 94-mile-per-hour heater struck Bobby Valentine's left cheek just below the temple. The stadium audibly gasped. From the tiny broadcast booth perched above the grandstand, Al Michaels winced. "To this day," Michaels recalled over four decades later, "I can still hear the sound in my mind's ear. It was just sickening."[1]

Tommy Lasorda, Indians trainer Herb Vike, and players from both teams rushed to home plate, where Valentine laid splayed like a chalk outline at a crime scene. He remained conscious, but his left cheek was indented, and blood streamed down his face. Tom Paciorek was so horrified by the sight of his friend that he threw up. Eddie Minasian, Zack's father and Lasorda's friend from the Cocoanut Grove in LA, became enraged over what he considered obvious head hunting. He jumped on to the field and tried going after Washburn. Security intercepted him and escorted him away. Vike, meanwhile, covered Valentine's deformed face with a towel to control the bleeding. Someone called for a stretcher. "Get me up," said Valentine. "I'm not going to give them the satisfaction of seeing me carried off."[2]

Valentine walked off the field to the Indians dugout along the first-base line. His left eye had already started to swell shut. Astonishingly, he tried to convince Lasorda to let him stay in the game. The plea was reminiscent of Lasorda's unwillingness to leave his first big-league start despite a deep knee gash. It didn't take a medical degree to understand that the Indians shortstop was in no condition to play baseball. He needed to go to a hospital sooner than later. But his competitiveness inspired his teammates. "That really did something for us," said Bart Shirley at the time. "Seeing him standing there with tears in his eyes and wanting to play ... it really gave us a lift."[3]

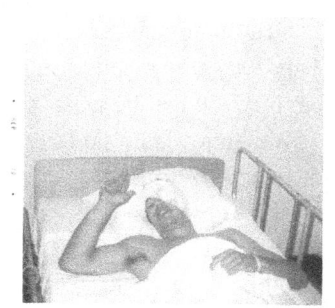

Bobby Valentine in the hospital.
Courtesy Spokane Indians.

Vike and Minasian escorted Valentine to the visitors' clubhouse, located in the parking lot of a bowling alley beyond center field. Tears streamed down Valentine's face as he said, "Tell them I'm not crying because I'm hurt; I'm crying because I'm mad."[4] It just so happened that an esteemed Japanese plastic surgeon attended the game that night. He took a look at Valentine in the locker room, then called the Dodgers' team physician and received permission to operate. While Valentine waited for paramedics, someone in the Indians clubhouse said they hoped Spokane's starter, Bob O'Brien, would retaliate. "I don't care about that," said Valentine. "Just win the ballgame."[5]

Bobby Valentine in the hospital.
Courtesy Spokane Indians.

An ambulance took Valentine to Queen's Hospital, where X-rays showed multiple fractures of his left cheekbone. He listened to Al

Michaels and Ken Wilson's broadcast of the game on KGU until the moment an orderly wheeled him into the operating room.

Back at Termite Palace, a palpable tension permeated as the game resumed. The Indians dugout was furious. "We all thought it was intentional," recalled Tommy Hutton.[6]

"It was quite clear that he threw at him," said broadcaster Ken Wilson. "This was not a letter-high inside fastball. I don't think anyone could convince me that he wasn't throwing at him."[7]

Washburn later said he meant to brush Valentine off the plate but did not intend to hit him. "Nobody ever throws at somebody in the head," he said. "The ball just took off."[8]

O'Brien, whom Hawaii beat like a drum during the regular season, took the bump for Spokane. He was already eager to avenge the previous beatings he took from the Islanders. Valentine's beaning galvanized both him and his teammates. "I was pumped up after that," said O'Brien, looking back.[9] That's an understatement. The southpaw proceeded to strike out eight of the first nine batters he faced.

The game remained scoreless when the Indians came to the plate in the top of the fourth. First, Bill Buckner singled. Then Steve Garvey reached on an error by third baseman John Werhas. Tom Paciorek followed with a single to left field that drove home Buckner. Winston Llenas bobbled the ball, allowing the runners to advance to second and third. With first base open, Washburn intentionally walked Tommy Hutton, loading the bases for Steve Sogge. Washburn jammed the Indians catcher, but the ball found a hole, plating Spokane's second run. Chuck Tanner then sent Washburn to the showers and brought in John Purdin, who promptly wild-pitched home another run before ceding a two-run triple to Marv Galliher, Valentine's replacement in the batting order. Midway through the fourth inning, the Indians held a 5-0 lead.

In the fifth, Paciorek pulled a homer into the left-field stands and Hutton yanked a dinger over the right-field screen as part of a six-run inning. 11-0, Spokane. At this point, the Indians' championship was a foregone conclusion. Many fans started heading for the exits.

In the sixth, Galliher, who hadn't appeared in any of the first three games of the series, topped his earlier triple by blasting a three-run homer to extend the lead to 14 runs. He also registered a single and a double, finishing the day 4-for-5 with six RBI. The Spokane Indians roster was so deep that the man who replaced the Pacific Coast League MVP hit for the cycle. "I still have the bat in my trophy case," said Galliher fifty-four years later.[10]

O'Brien, meanwhile, dotted the strike zone with fastballs and curves. Doug Griffin's fifth-inning, two-run home run would prove to be his only blemish. He allowed just five hits, walked a pair, and struck out 14.

Solo home runs by Garvey and Buckner in the seventh and ninth, respectively, made it 16-2. It was the first time all season that the Indians had walloped five homers in a game. After O'Brien recorded the final out, the Spokane players, minus Valentine, mobbed one another on the field, then continued the celebration in the clubhouse, where they sprayed one another with champagne and Primo beer while chanting, "We're number one!" One player raised a glass of champagne and said, "Happy Valentine's Day to the Hawaii Islanders."[11] An elated Lasorda called it the greatest achievement of his life.

In the four-game sweep, the Indians outscored the Islanders 38-9, while outplaying them in every facet of the game. In the four games, Spokane batted .351; Hawaii hit .205. The Indians outhomered the Islanders 10-1. The five Indians pitchers who appeared in the series posted a combined 2.25 ERA, a fraction of the Islanders' ghastly 7.41 mark. Tommy Hutton, Bart Shirley, Bill Buckner, and Bobby Valentine all hit over .400, Steve Garvey batted .368, and Tom Paciorek hit .313. Winston Llenas, Jim Hicks, and Charlie Vinson—three Islanders who torched Spokane pitching during the regular season—combined to hit .108.

"They were the best accumulation of athletes we ever played against," said John Werhas, with the benefit of years of hindsight. "They were young and spectacular. That team was great, and Tommy made it great. Those guys owe so much to Lasorda. He was a wonderful manager for young players. They were rock solid. They had good pitching, and they could score runs. In the Coast League championship, they went through us like butter."[12]

Once the champagne bottles and beer cans were empty and things settled down in the visitors' clubhouse, the bedraggled champions changed into dry clothes and prepared to visit Valentine at the hospital. Chuck Stewart, the Indians' beat writer for the *Spokane Daily Chronicle*, wanted to tag along with the team. The *Chronicle* was an evening paper, so his deadline wouldn't arrive until the next morning. But Stewart had one problem. His clothes were soaked with booze, and he didn't have anything else to wear with him. Herb Vike pointed to Valentine's locker, which contained a dry set of clothes covered in plastic. "He's not going to be needing these tonight," said Vike.[13] Stewart, in his early thirties at the time, changed into the twenty-year-old's dry threads.

"Valentine was a pretty snazzy dresser," recalled Stewart. "His pants were bell-bottoms, and he had a bright shirt. I went into his hospital room. At some point I mentioned that I was wearing his clothes, and he said, 'I thought those looked familiar!'"[14]

The team flew back to Spokane the following morning except for Dick McLaughlin, who stayed behind until doctors discharged Valentine from the hospital a few days later. Just like that, the season was over. The Indians received no victory parade or hero's welcome. The team did, however, take home $8,000 for winning the championship, which equated to a couple hundred dollars per player. The group also received gold championship rings, which featured a cubic zirconia atop a red gemstone surrounded by the words "Pacific Coast League Champions." The Spokane Indians logo and the player's name and jersey number were engraved on the flanks.* Similarly, the Dodgers issued rings to their other league-winning affiliates as well.†

Most of the roster dispersed for the winter, but a handful of guys on the Dodgers' forty-man roster—Steve Garvey, Bill Buckner, Tom Paciorek, Mike Strahler, and Bob Stinson—received promotions to Los Angeles for the final weeks of the season. The Dodgers also purchased the contract of twenty-six-year-old Jerry Stephenson. Six days after he defeated the Islanders in Game 1 of the PCL playoffs, Stephenson took the mound at the Dodger Stadium—just as Lasorda said he would six months earlier—and logged two innings of relief against the Cincinnati Reds. Being back in the majors, albeit briefly, signaled the cherry on top of an incredible season during which Stephenson won 19 games—eight more than any other season in his twelve-year professional career. "A lot of it was Tommy and the confidence he built in him," said Brian Stephenson,

---

* Steve Garvey's ring sold in an online auction in 2013 for $5,019.60.
† The Dodgers' Double-A affiliate in Albuquerque and Single-A affiliate in Bakersfield also won their respective leagues in 1970.

Jerry's son and a Dodgers scout. "He said stuff with such conviction you would believe it."[15]

The Sporting News named Lasorda Minor League Manager of the Year. In the publication's article announcing the award, Indians GM Elten Schiller pointed out Lasorda's rare ability to get close to his players while maintaining discipline. "Since Tom outwardly shows such personal interest, his players are willing to break their back to go out on the field and do the job for him," said Schiller.[16]

The playoff money and rings were nice, but the real payoff were the memories that would last a lifetime. "There isn't a day that goes by that I don't think of Tommy or Bobby and what we did, mainly in the minor leagues," said Paciorek more than a half-century later. "We had so much fun in the minors that the big leagues seemed somewhat inconsequential. We strove to play in the major leagues, but we had more fun in the minor leagues."[17]

Paciorek's sentiments were echoed by the team's MVP. "It was as much fun as I ever had in baseball," said Bobby Valentine. "We were lucky. We had a good group of guys, and we had a good leader."[18]

Part Three
Show Time

Tommy Lasorda, Bobby Valentine, Steve Garvey, Bill Buckner, Tommy Hutton, and Bob O'Brien. Courtesy Spokane Indians.

1971

"I never really had a relationship with Walt Alston. For the two years I was there, he called me Bill."—Bobby Valentine

FOLLOWING SUCCESSFUL FACIAL SURGERY IN HONOLULU, BOBBY Valentine returned to Los Angeles and resumed classes at USC before transferring to Arizona State University so he could play in the Arizona Fall Instructional League. The Dodgers wanted to see if he had any lasting effects from the injury—physically or mentally. That November, Valentine nervously stepped into a batter's box to face live pitching for the first time since Greg Washburn's heater cracked his cheekbone like an eggshell. On the second pitch of the at-bat, the young phenom leaned in and punched a base hit to right field. Any lingering self-doubt evaporated in that instant. The former first-round pick and reigning Pacific Coast League MVP was back.

Well, not so fast.

Two months later, Valentine took a blindside hit during an intramural flag football game at ASU, suffering torn ligaments and cartilage in his right knee. He told sportswriters and the Dodgers brass that the injury resulted from stepping on a sprinkler head. Although the papers printed it, the Dodgers didn't buy it for one second. Valentine's carelessness disappointed Al Campanis and company. The youngster underwent another surgery—this time on his knee—and showed up to spring training in a cast. Valentine recovered enough to make the opening-day roster but required a bulky knee brace and had lost a half-step. Because of his limited range, Campanis and Walter Alston decided he could no longer play shortstop. Valentine had worked doggedly to learn the position and was determined to prove them wrong.

THE '71 DODGERS RETURNED MAURY WILLS AT SHORTSTOP, JIM Lefebvre at the keystone, Wes Parker at first, Willie Davis in center, and Willie Crawford in right. To bolster an offense that had finished last in the league in home runs in '70, Al Campanis traded Ted Sizemore and Bob Stinson to the Cardinals for slugger Dick Allen, who had averaged 30 home runs over his previous seven seasons. Campanis also added a veteran to the rotation in the form of Al Downing, obtained in a trade with the Brewers for Andy Kosco. Both of Campanis's key offseason acquisitions performed remarkably well. Allen slashed .295/.395/.468, clubbed 23 home runs, and drove in 90 runs. Downing bounced back from a miserable '70 campaign to win a career-high 20 games, finishing third in the Cy Young Award voting and taking home the NL's Comeback Player of the Year Award.*

Although the Dodgers remained veteran-laden, a wave of youth began to descend upon Chavez Ravine that summer. In addition to Valentine, several players from the '70 Spokane Indians—Bill Buckner, Steve Garvey, Bill Russell, Charlie Hough, Sandy Vance, and Bob O'Brien—made the opening-day roster. Tommy Hutton and Tom Paciorek, meanwhile, remained stalled in Triple-A. There was simply not enough room on the big-league roster.

Davey Lopes also returned to Spokane, splitting his time between outfield and second base—a position he reluctantly began learning over the winter at the behest of Lasorda and the Dodgers brass. The Rhode Islander initially fought the suggestion of a position change. He saw

---

* Downing would later etch his name in the history books by allowing Hank Aaron's record-breaking 715th home run.

several experienced infielders on the Dodgers depth chart and no path to regular playing time. At one point, Lopes threatened to go back to Providence rather the play second base. "That's a good idea," responded Lasorda. "Maybe they'll let you play the outfield on the thread factory team."[1]

With some convincing from infielder instructor Monty Basgall, Lopes came around to the idea. From the get-go, the Washburn alum demonstrated excellent range and a strong arm, but his hands were like stones, and he struggled with double plays. Under Basgall's steadfast patience and constant encouragement, Lopes's confidence grew, and his second-base defense rapidly improved. Eventually, he would come to realize how the switch benefitted his career. "When you think of outfielders, you think of [six-foot-five] Dave Parker, not a guy five-nine," he said later.[2]

Spokane's roster also included returning pitchers Doyle Alexander, Jerry Stephenson, Pete Scarpati and a few members of the '68 draft class who moved up from Double-A—third baseman Ron Cey, catcher Joe Ferguson, and outfielder Bob Gallagher. The player who hit for the cycle as Valentine's replacement in the clinching game, Marv Galliher, required surgery to remove bone chips from his elbow and would miss considerable time. Several other members of the '70 championship team had moved on. Bart Shirley jumped the pond to play in Japan, Jack Jenkins opened a sporting-goods store in Florida, and Steve Sogge signed with the White Sox after the Dodgers released him during spring training. The former USC quarterback would play one season with the Tucson Toros before hanging up his chest protector and shin guards to coach football at the University of Oregon.

In '71, neither Buckner nor Garvey would be demoted as they had been a year earlier. In fact, neither would ever play in the minors again. Buckner played semi-regularly for Alston's Dodgers, batting .277 with five home runs in 108 games. A hamate bone fracture interrupted Garvey's season, sidelining him for nearly six weeks. In 81 games, the third baseman hit .227 and homered seven times. Although neither player enjoyed the breakout season he had hoped for, they both benefitted from the experience. As Garvey later explained, "What the Dodgers were operating in 1971 was a graduate-level class in baseball ... The baseball knowledge that veteran players had developed over the length of their careers was quietly and informally being passed on to younger players."[3]

The mentorship of Wills and Allen proved particularly impactful to Garvey.

Charlie Hough appeared in only four games with LA before team brass sent him back to Spokane. "The Dodgers had a veteran manager, and it was a veteran team, so it was hard to break in," said Hough, looking back. "I didn't get to pitch much, and when I did, I didn't pitch very well. It's difficult as a knuckleballer to sit for two weeks and not get in a game."[4]

The silver lining of Hough's demotion was the opportunity to work with legendary knuckleballer Hoyt Wilhelm, who signed with the Dodgers midseason following his release by the Braves. The forty-eight-year-old* Wilhelm agreed to pitch in Triple-A in hopes of working his way back to the majors. It was a win-win situation. The veteran received an opportunity to show he could still pitch, while Hough got to learn from the one of the best knuckleball pitchers in baseball history. "What a thrill," recalled Hough. "I had no idea what I was doing, and a guy on his way to the Hall of Fame is now spending every day with me."[5]

Wilhelm appeared in eight games with Spokane before the Dodgers called him up in mid-August. During his month in Triple-A, Wilhelm taught his young protégé how changing his arm angle and switching sides of the pitching rubber could alter the movement of his knuckleball. The advice would help Hough make necessary in-game adjustments and harness the fickle knuckleball. For the rest of his career, he would pay homage to Wilhelm by wearing his original jersey number, 49.

Hough stayed in Spokane for the remainder of the season. Two years later, he would finally cement a spot in LA's bullpen, where he remained through the end of the decade. In his seven full seasons with the Dodgers, Hough worked mostly as a reliever, averaging eight saves and more than 100 innings pitched. After the Dodgers released him during the '80 season, Hough signed with the Texas Rangers and became a full-time starter. There, he reached double-digit wins in nine consecutive seasons, including his lone All-Star campaign of '86, before finishing his career with the White Sox and Marlins. Had a degenerative hip not forced him to retire at age forty-six, Hough seemingly could have heaved knuckleballs

---

* Wilhelm turned forty-nine during his stint in Spokane, although at the time he was thought to be a year younger. After Wilhelm's death in 2002, it was discovered that his birth certificate showed a birth date of July 26, 1922.

well into his fifties. He concluded his career with a 216-216 record and remains one of ten players to appear in twenty-five major-league seasons and the only pitcher in major-league history to make 400 starts and 400 relief appearances. After his playing career, Hough served as a pitching coach with the Dodgers and Mets, later joining the Dodgers' staff as a special assistant and roving instructor.

TOMMY HUTTON FAILED TO MAKE THE OPENING-DAY ROSTER DESPITE hitting .400 in spring training. Campanis denied his request to be released, so he languished in Triple-A for a fifth consecutive season. With Parker entrenched at the first sack and Buckner and Garvey in the mix, Hutton's chances of seeing regular playing time in LA were bleak. "I started thinking it might be best if I get traded somewhere," he said later.[6] Hutton took out his frustration on Pacific Coast League pitching, hitting .352 with 19 homers and 103 RBI. In doing so, he replicated Valentine's feat of capturing both the batting title and MVP Award. Yet, the parent club did not promote him in '71 because he was out of options. After the season, the Dodgers dealt Hutton to Philadelphia,* where he received a long-awaited opportunity to play semi-regularly in the majors. Over parts of twelve seasons with the Dodgers, Phillies, Blue Jays, and Expos, Hutton batted .248 with 410 hits and 22 home runs. In 2,435⅔ innings as a first baseman, he committed a mere 12 errors.† Following his playing career, Hutton began a new chapter as a television color analyst, eventually spending many years in the Marlins TV booth.

Another stagnated prospect, Tom Paciorek, produced an equally stellar '71 campaign in Spokane, batting .305 with 15 homers and 105 RBI. The following year, he hit over .300 with double-digit home runs and 100-plus RBI for a third consecutive Triple-A season in Albuquerque. In retrospect, Paciorek harbored no ill feelings about getting frozen in the minors. On the contrary. "Tommy convinced us that it was better for us to play in Triple-A than Los Angeles," Paciorek recalled. "We weren't making any

---

* In return, the Dodgers received outfielder Larry Hisle, later a two-time All-Star with the Twins and Brewers.
† Hutton, who played 178 career games in the outfield, never played more than 87 games at first base in a season, so he was never considered for a Gold Glove.

money, but we were having a lot of fun. I thought everybody had to put in five years in the minor leagues."[7]

TOM PACIOREK - Outfielder

Courtesy Spokane Indians.

Beginning in '73, Paciorek stuck in the majors as a reserve outfielder and pinch-hitter. After three seasons in Dodger blue, Campanis traded him in November 1975 to the Atlanta Braves with Lee Lacy, Jerry Royster, and Jim Wynn for Dusty Baker and Ed Goodson. Once he received the opportunity to play every day in the majors—first with the Braves and then the Mariners and White Sox—Paciorek put up excellent offensive numbers, including three consecutive seasons hitting over .300. His best season and lone All-Star nod came at age thirty-four with the '81 Mariners when he batted .326. Paciorek played the final two of his eighteen major-league seasons with the Rangers as a teammate of Hough under the team's young manager—Bobby Valentine. For his career, Paciorek accumulated 1,162 hits and owned a .282 batting average. After retiring as a player, Wimpy spent more than a decade on White Sox television broadcasts with Ken "Hawk" Harrelson, later working in the same capacity for the Braves.

While Hutton and Paciorek were biding their time in Triple-A, Sandy Vance and Bob O'Brien showed their wares in the majors. Each experienced early success that proved fleeting. Vance entered the '71 season looking to build on his solid rookie campaign and become a rotation mainstay. His season began auspiciously with only two runs allowed in his first start. But after a rocky second outing, Alston banished him to the bullpen. Vance developed a sore arm, struggled as a long reliever, and soon found himself back in Spokane. The 204 innings he threw during the '70 season, plus his workload in the Dominican Winter League, had taken their toll. Vance's arm would never recover. Two years later, he stepped away from the game he loved at twenty-six years old. "I put my whole heart and soul into baseball," he said years later. "Then one day it was over ... No one knew enough back then to help me re-strengthen my arm and rehab. There was much they didn't know back then."[8] The Stanford grad found success away from the pitcher's mound, earning a master's in landscape architecture and working in environmental land planning and development for the next four decades.

Bob O'Brien also earned a spot on the Dodgers pitching staff to begin the 1971 season. After pitching out of the bullpen early on, he threw a shutout in his first big-league start against the Cardinals on June 21. But then he failed to make it through four innings in two of his next three outings. Although his overall numbers (2-2, 3.00 ERA) were respectable, the Dodgers sent him down to Triple-A at the All-Star break. O'Brien struggled after the demotion, registering a 3-5 record and 6.35 ERA in 10 starts for Spokane. That offseason, the Dodgers packaged him with Doyle Alexander, Sergio Robles, and Royle Stillman in a blockbuster trade with the Orioles for Pete Richert and Frank Robinson.

O'Brien had no chance of cracking an Orioles rotation that boasted four twenty-game winners.* He pitched well at the start of spring camp, but then an incident during a team meeting with MLBPA director Marvin

---

* Mike Cuellar, Pat Dobson, Jim Palmer, and Dave McNally all won 20 or more games for the 1971 Orioles.

Miller pushed him down Baltimore's depth chart. In the meeting, Miller discussed the players' ask of $5 more per day in meal money, an issue that had become a sticking point in labor talks. When Miller opened the floor for questions, O'Brien raised his hand and asked, "Why not just take the $5 and divvy it amongst the minor leaguers?" Earl Weaver looked at the young lefty with daggers in his eyes. The fifth-year manager had spent his entire playing career in the minors and wanted his share of the pie now that he was in the majors. "Two weeks later, they sent me down to Triple-A," recalled O'Brien. "That was pretty much the end of my career. They buried my ass."[9]

O'Brien never stepped on a major-league mound again. Although his pro career ended on a sour note, the southpaw looked back on his years as a Dodger with great pride. "One thing I can take to my grave is that I wore the same uniform as Jackie Robinson, and I pitched on the same mound as Sandy Koufax," said O'Brien in 2024. "I will appreciate and cherish that for as long as I live."[10]

While O'Brien toiled the minors, a player he was traded with, Alexander, stuck in Baltimore as a swingman before joining the O's rotation full-time in '73. Over the course of his nineteen-year big-league career, Alexander pitched for eight different organizations and accumulated a lifetime record of 194-174. In 1988, he made his lone All-Star appearance at age thirty-seven, a year after the Atlanta Braves had traded him to the Detroit Tigers for a young hurler named John Smoltz.

JERRY STEPHENSON NEVER MADE IT BACK TO "THE SHOW." HIS ERA ballooned to 5.18 in '71, a far cry from the 2.82 mark he compiled during Spokane's championship season. He continued to pitch in Triple-A under Lasorda through '73 before embarking on a twenty-one-year stint as a Dodgers scout. In 1988, Stephenson scouted the Oakland A's in advance of the World Series, providing reports that helped Dodgers pitchers hold the heavily favored A's—a lineup featuring Bash Brothers José Canseco and Mark McGwire—to a .177 batting average.* Seven years later, he returned to his original organization, the Red Sox, working as major-

---

* LA pitchers held Canseco and McGwire to a combined two hits in 36 at-bats, an .055 average.

league scout until 2009. Jerry Stephenson died of cancer on June 6, 2010. His son Brian, a second-round pick of the Chicago Cubs in 1994, pitched seven seasons of pro ball, making it as high as Double-A before a pair of UCL surgeries derailed his career. Brian later followed in the family tradition, becoming a third-generation scout with the Dodgers.

Pete Scarpati, the Dodgers' sixty-eighth round pick from the '68 draft, also scuffled in his return to Spokane in '71, posting a 5-7 record and 6.35 ERA in 36 games. He would never fulfill his dream of pitching in the majors but enjoyed a memorable pro career, nonetheless. Following his subpar '71, Scarpati walked away from baseball in favor of a steadier income. "I had a wife and a child," he said later, "so I decided that at the end of the season if I got a job and it was more money than I was making playing ball, I would take it."[11] He doubled his baseball salary working for a textile company and later ran his own manufacturing business.

Stephenson and Scarpati weren't the only hurlers who failed to find their footing for Spokane in '71. The Indians' team ERA rose to 4.96, a jump of nearly two runs. As a result, Lasorda's team accrued a losing record in what would be Spokane's final season as the Dodgers' Triple-A affiliate. A year later, the Dodgers moved their Pacific Coast League franchise to Albuquerque, a locale that provided warmer spring weather, higher attendance figures, and a newer ballpark.

Spokane's parent club, meanwhile, increased its win total for a fourth consecutive season, finishing '71 with an 89-73 mark. But it wasn't enough to top the rival Giants, who clinched the NL West on the final day of the season. Despite missing the playoffs again, Dodgers fans had reasons to be optimistic about the future. Several of the organization's top prospects had climbed the ladder to Los Angeles, and more were knocking on the door.

VALENTINE'S ROOKIE SEASON PROVED TO BE ONE OF FRUSTRATION AND middling success. After barely playing in LA's first 25 games, the front office sent him down to Spokane. Alston told him he was being demoted to work on his underhand feed to the second baseman, reasoning that baffled the young shortstop. Fortunately for Valentine, the Indians were playing in Hawaii at the time.

"Penguin, Gallagher, Valentine, and I borrowed Joe Moeller's car and drove to the north side of the island," Paciorek recalled. "These waves were beating us to death, throwing us on to the shore. We're getting ready to quit, and I see Bobby getting ready to catch a wave. I look at this wave, and it looked like a hotel coming at him. I yelled, 'Look out!' and started running for the shore. All of a sudden, I see this body coming flying by me like Superman. It was Valentine. He hit the shore like a bullet, and I swear I thought he was dead. We had had the worst sunburns ever contracted in Oahu and struck out like ten times between the four of us."[12]

Valentine recovered from his sunburn and returned to the majors a week or so later. Alston bounced him around the diamond throughout the remainder of the season. Valentine hit .249 with a .597 OPS in 281 at-bats. By season's end, he had shed his knee brace and returned to full speed. With Wills nearing age forty, Valentine envisioned winning the starting shortstop job in 1972. He envisioned playing in an infield with Garvey, Lopes, and Buckner under Alston's likely heir apparent, Tommy Lasorda, for years to come.

Dukes and Angels

"I always tell my players ... when you go to the major leagues and you're in Dodger Stadium and you get a base hit to win a ballgame and they're shaking your hand, just look over your shoulder, because there's old Tom somewhere with a tear in his eye."—Tommy Lasorda, 1972

Even after Steve Garvey, Bobby Valentine, Bill Buckner, Doyle Alexander, and Bill Russell had graduated to the majors, the Dodgers' farm system remained loaded. The talent on the 1972 Albuquerque Dukes—the organization's new Triple-A affiliate*—rivaled that of the '70 Spokane Indians. The infield included Ron Cey at third, Davey Lopes at second, and Tom Paciorek at first. Larry Hisle and Von Joshua roamed the outfield. Steve Yeager and Joe Ferguson split the receiving duties. And the pitching staff included Charlie Hough, Geoff Zahn, Rick Rhoden, and Doug Rau. Those eleven would go on to play an average of fifteen and a half years in the majors. Shrewd scouting and savvy drafting had supplied the Dodgers organization with an embarrassment of riches.

---

* Albuquerque moved up a level from the Double-A Texas League, while the Spokane Indians dropped to Short Season A in the Northwest League for a season.

The '72 Dukes led the Pacific Coast League in runs per game, batting average, and stolen bases, while finishing second in home runs, ERA, and strikeouts. They won 92 games—two fewer than the '70 Indians—and defeated Mike Schmidt's Eugene Emeralds to win the PCL championship, Tommy Lasorda's fifth title in eight seasons as a minor-league manager.

Rau won 14 games that year for Albuquerque, earning a start in the Dodgers' Hall of Fame exhibition game versus the Yankees in August.* The Dukes were in Portland when the parent club summoned him to Cooperstown. Midgame, he went into the bleachers and used a pay phone to make travel arrangements. While in the phone booth, he looked out and suddenly saw the entire Albuquerque team, led by Lasorda, running up into the bleachers. Some obnoxious Portland fans had been heckling the Albuquerque players, and Lasorda had had enough. "All I could hear was cleats clanging on the metal bleachers," recalled Rau.[1] If the same scene played out in the twenty-first century, it would have gone viral and resulted in lengthy suspensions, or worse. But in August 1970, it got a brief mention in the ninth paragraph of the *Oregon Journal's* game story.

AFTER NARROWLY MISSING THE POSTSEASON IN '71, THE DODGERS TOOK A step backward in '72. They boasted the league's best pitching staff, led by Don Sutton (19-9, 2.08 ERA) and Claude Osteen (20-11, 2.64), but struggled defensively, committing a league-high 162 errors. And the offense was middle-of-the-pack. The Dodgers had traded the enigmatic Dick Allen after one season because of his my-way-or-the-highway approach to life. Al Campanis chose the highway, but the team would sorely miss Allen's production. Age caught up to a few position players, including the team's key offseason acquisition, Frank Robinson. The thirty-six-year slugger hit just 19 home runs, 12 below his career average. Maury Wills's decline was even more precipitous. The veteran shortstop hit .129 in 132 at-bats with one measly stolen base. He lost his starting job, as did second baseman Jim Lefebvre, who batted a paltry .201. The Dodgers won 85 games, ten fewer than the Reds.

---

* When rosters expanded in September, Rau made his regular-season debut, tossing nine innings of one-run ball against the Cardinals. He eventually became a cog on three pennant-winning Dodgers teams, winning 81 games over the course of nine major-league seasons.

From a glass-half-full view, the first wave of players comprising the Dodgers' burgeoning youth movement made positive strides at the plate. Garvey hit .269 with nine home runs. Buckner maintained insane bat-to-ball skills, hitting .319 while striking out a mere 13 times in 383 at-bats. And Valentine and Russell each topped .270.

The infield defense left something to be desired, however. Russell, anointed to replace the struggling Wills at shortstop, committed a major-league-high 34 errors. And in 85 games at the hot corner, Garvey led all third basemen with 28 miscues. He could field the ball cleanly, but his erratic throwing created problems. Some of his troubles stemmed from the separated shoulder he sustained in college, although he later admitted that a psychological component had crept into play. If Garvey had to make a quick throw, he tended to be accurate, but if he had time to set himself, he often threw wild. Some within the organization joked that when Garvey played third, it was Ball Night at Dodger Stadium.

Alston's decision to replace Wills with Russell three weeks into the season left Valentine in limbo. Serving in a utility role, he began to wonder about his future. After the season, the former first-round pick approached Alston about competing with Russell for the shortstop job the following spring. The manager told him he could battle with Davey Lopes for second base. If he wanted to play shortstop, Alston said, it would have to be for another team. Alston's words hit Valentine like a punch to the gut. "Well, I guess I should be traded," he responded.[2]

Looking back, Valentine believed he got caught up in the middle of organizational politics. The fiery, extroverted Valentine was Lasorda's guy, and Lasorda, who had the backing of Campanis and Peter O'Malley, was gunning for Alston's job. "Bill Russell happened to be exactly what Walt Alston liked," explained Valentine. "They were from the same mold— quiet, reserved kind of guys who did their hunting and fishing. Not that it's good or bad. But Russell was so much like Alston, and I was the antithesis of Alston."[3]

On November 28, 1972, Valentine got his wish. The Dodgers pulled off a blockbuster trade, sending him to the Angels with Frank Robinson, Billy Grabarkewitz, Bill Singer, and Mike Strahler in exchange for Ken McMullen and Andy Messersmith.

. . .

Valentine won the Angels shortstop job the following spring and got off to a terrific start in '73, hitting .302, scoring 12 runs, and stealing six bases over his first 32 games. Looking back through a modern lens, he was on pace for a 6-WAR season. But then fate intervened. On May 13, Angels manager Bobby Winkles put Valentine in center field, giving Kenny Berry a day off. The struggling Angels defeated Rich "Goose" Gossage and the White Sox that day for just their second win in seven games. Winkles wrote out the same starting lineup the next day and the Halos won again. Next day, same thing. And the Angels didn't just win; their ace, Nolan Ryan, threw a no-hitter. Baseball is a game of superstition, and Winkles planned to roll out the same starting nine until the streak ended.

On May 17, the Angels, winners of four straight, hosted Oakland at the Big A. Winkles played Valentine in center for the fifth consecutive day. In the second inning, Oakland's Dick Green hit a deep fly ball to left-center field. As he raced back, Valentine gauged that the ball had home-run distance. He attempted to scale the fence, but his spike got caught in the canvas. Instead of his body absorbing the impact, Valentine's lower leg took the brunt, causing the tibia to snap in half. Angels reliever Lloyd Allen was the first to reach Valentine as he lay writhing on the warning track. He looked down and saw Valentine's bone protruding through his sock. "It was gruesome," remembered Allen.[4]

Strangely, the orthopedist who treated Valentine recommended against surgery. Instead, he wore a cast for several months, during which time his muscles atrophied. When doctors removed the cast, it became evident that the bones had not healed properly. A large calcification had formed on the shin, and the bone was bent at a seventeen-degree angle, causing one leg to be shorter than the other.

Bobby Valentine: Always a fan favorite. Courtesy Spokane Indians.

Valentine rehabbed intensely during the offseason and returned to the field in '74. He wore custom-made spikes that compensated for his leg-length discrepancy. When his teammates saw the deformed extremity, they couldn't believe he could walk, let alone run. Among them was former Hawaii Islander Winston Llenas, who had joined the big club. The two former PCL competitors, now teammates, had become good friends. "Bobby was so courageous that he tried to continue playing," recalled Llenas, "but he was not the same player. Nobody is after an injury like that."[5]

Valentine played mostly left field upon his return and performed well in spite of his limited mobility, hitting .283 through late May. But then the injury bug bit again. The latest malady resulted from a brawl with former teammate Clyde Wright. Valentine had criticized Wright on the radio after he was traded to the Brewers, so the hurler responded by buzzing Valentine's head with a fastball. He charged Wright, who body-slammed his former teammate, causing a separated shoulder. Valentine returned to the lineup two weeks later but could barely swing a bat. He hit .248 through the rest of the season as a bench player, finishing with a slash line of .261/.308/.329 for the last-place Angels. His former club thirty-five miles north, meanwhile, fared significantly better.

The '74 Series

"[The Oakland A's] were an interesting team for us to play. They had donkeys and colored balls and mustaches. But they were a veteran team, and we were still pretty young."—Steve Garvey, *They Bled Blue*

In November 1972, the Phillies filled their managerial vacancy with Dodgers third-base coach Danny Ozark. To replace Ozark, the Dodgers turned to their Triple-A manager, Tommy Lasorda. At first, Lasorda wasn't sure he wanted the promotion. He doubted whether a coaching gig would best position him to reach his ultimate goal of becoming a major-league manager. Moreover, he worried about how Walter Alston would perceive his presence. After all, it was no secret that Lasorda sought his job. Ultimately, Peter O'Malley convinced him to accept the offer. Lasorda returned to the big leagues in '73 for the first time in eighteen years, bringing his irrepressible energy and sense of humor to the Dodgers clubhouse and third-base coaching box.

By the end of the season, the Dodgers established an infield that would play together for the next eight years. The foursome consisted of Ron Cey at third, Bill Russell at shortstop, Davey Lopes at second, and Steve Garvey at first. Of the four, only Cey manned his original position. The

Dodgers had employed Branch Rickey's practice of coconut snatching with former center fielders Russell and Lopes, utilizing their athleticism to fill middle-infield vacancies. Each learned his new position in the minors and fall instructional league under the tutelage of defensive guru Monty Basgall, who joined Alston's coaching staff along with Lasorda.

Lopes had spent five full seasons in the minor leagues, including three under Lasorda in Triple-A, before winning the Dodgers second-base job in '73. The twenty-eight-year-old rookie hit .275, reached base at a .352 clip, and stole 36 bases. Because of his ability to work a walk and wreak havoc on the bases, he settled in as Alston's primary leadoff man.

Another member of the '68 draft class, Joe Ferguson, had also changed positions. Drafted as an outfielder, the rifled-armed Bay Area native converted to catcher in his second pro season. Lasorda spurred him on by telling him that Hall of Fame backstops Mickey Cochrane, Ernie Lombardi, and Gabby Hartnett had all started their careers as outfielders. "I know those guys never played the outfield," Lasorda admitted," but Ferguson didn't, and it sure sounded good to him."[1] Ferguson played two seasons for Lasorda in Triple-A before serving as the Dodgers' primary catcher in '73. The former eighth-round pick posted a robust .263/.369/.470 slash line and swatted 25 home runs, earning a handful of MVP votes. In '74, he split dish duties with Steve Yeager and saw time in right field. Ferguson would spend parts of eleven seasons with the Dodgers over the course of a fourteen-year major-league career, hitting 122 career homers while maintaining an impressive .767 OPS, mostly as a part-time player.

The Dodgers had identified certain skills and physical abilities in Russell, Lopes, and Ferguson that made them prime candidates to change defensive positions. Garvey's move across the diamond to first base, on the other hand, resulted from his inability to throw accurately with any consistency. By the spring of '73, Cey had leapfrogged him on the depth chart and would win the starting job that season. The Penguin had proven himself in the minors, hitting over .300 while averaging 26 home runs over his previous three seasons. Cey committed only 18 errors in 146 games as a rookie third baseman, a substantial upgrade over the erratic Garvey. Cey's offensive production (.245 BA, 15 HR, 80 RBI) was more than adequate and would steadily improve over each of the next four seasons. For the first time since moving to Los Angeles, the Dodgers had found stability at the hot corner.

Alston briefly tried Garvey in left field to start the '73 season, but he didn't have the arm to stick there either, leaving him relegated to pinch-hitting duties for much of the season's first half. The American League had adopted the designated hitter that year, so rumors swirled that Garvey would be better suited for an AL club. At one point, Garvey, like Bobby Valentine a year earlier, asked to be traded. But the June 15 deadline came and went, and he remained a Dodger.

Garvey performed well off the bench, but pinch-hitting grossly under-utilized his talent. In late June, Alston finally found a way to get the powerful slugger regular at-bats, moving Buckner to the outfield and installing Garvey at first base. Buckner, who had watched Garvey play a decent first base during limited action four years earlier in Albuquerque, later said he suggested the switch. Garvey wrote in his autobiography that Cyndy Garvey, his wife at the time, urged Alston to try her husband at first base. Either way, the Tampa native had finally found a defensive home. Although he was vertically challenged as a first baseman and avoided throwing on potential double plays, Garvey showed soft hands and a natural ability to scoop balls in the dirt. Just a year later, he'd win a Gold Glove Award.

The '73 Dodgers spent seventy-nine days in first place. On June 17, six days before The Infield played together for the first time, LA enjoyed an eight-and-a-half-game division lead. The team endured numerous injuries in the second half, however, and faltered down the stretch, losing 11 of 12 beginning August 31. Over a thirteen-day period, Dodgers went from four games up to five games back of Cincinnati. LA finished the season with 95 wins, three and a half games behind Sparky Anderson's Reds.

That offseason, Al Campanis traded franchise stalwarts Willie Davis and Claude Osteen to the Expos and Astros, respectively, and received rubber-armed reliever Mike Marshall and slugger Jim Wynn in return.[*] Both acquisitions proved highly productive. Marshall won the '74 NL Cy

---

[*] The Expos' trade of Marshall for Davis was a curious one. The eccentric, outspoken reliever was coming off two of the greatest seasons by a reliever in baseball history. Between 1972-73, he threw 295 innings across 157 games, accumulating 28 wins and 49 saves. Davis, on the other hand, would be turning thirty-four in early '74.

Young Award after pitching in a major-league record 106 games while Wynn led all Dodgers with 32 home runs and an .884 OPS.

Several of the Dodgers' youngsters from the '68 draft enjoyed breakout seasons in '74. Garvey produced a .312 average with 21 home runs and 111 RBI. In addition to earning Gold Glove honors, he made the NL All-Star team through a write-in campaign* and won the NL MVP Award.† Bill Buckner, the everyday left fielder, hit .314 and stole a career-high 31 bases. The leadoff man, Lopes, batted .266 and swiped 59 bags. And Cey, another All-Star, swatted 18 home runs and drove in 97. A few others from the '68 class performed well in limited duty. Tom Paciorek hit .316 as a pinch-hitter, Joe Ferguson hit 16 homers as a semi-regular catcher-outfielder, and Geoff Zahn posted a 2.03 ERA as a lefty swingman.

Like the year prior, the Dodgers started hot and built a comfortable division lead. This time, they staved off the hard-charging Reds in the second half. LA won 102 games, four more than Cincinnati. After years of leaning heavily on pitching, the Dodgers boasted the league's best offense, finishing atop the NL in runs scored, home runs, and OPS. Not to say the pitching had fallen off. The staff, led by Andy Messersmith, Don Sutton, and Marshall, led the NL in ERA and strikeouts.

The Dodgers breezed by the Pirates in the NLCS for their first pennant in eight years, earning a World Series date with the two-time defending champion Oakland Athletics. Like the Dodgers, the A's had formed a talented core of players largely through the amateur draft. Oakland's roster most prominently featured Reggie Jackson, Catfish Hunter, Rollie Fingers, Bert Campaneris, Sal Bando, Gene Tenace, Ken Holtzman, Vida Blue, and Joe Rudi. For LA, the '68 draft in particular had been instrumental building its nucleus. More than a quarter of the Dodgers World Series roster, including five of the first six hitters in Walter Alston's Game 1 lineup—Lopes, Buckner, Garvey, Ferguson, and Cey—were products of

---

* The fact that Garvey wasn't on the ballot reflects how modest expectations were of him entering the season. He joined Rico Carty as the second player in baseball history to start an All-Star game without appearing on the ballot. Garvey played the game despite having a case of the mumps and went 2-for-4 to earn the game's MVP trophy.

† Garvey edged out Lou Brock, who set a single-season record with 118 stolen bases. Two other Dodgers finished in the top five in the MVP voting. Reliever Mike Marshall finished third, and outfielder Jim Wynn, whose 151 OPS+ bested Garvey by 21 points, finished fifth.

the '68 draft. Two others from the class, Paciorek and Zahn, were part of the bench and bullpen, respectively. Yet another pair, Doyle Alexander and Bobby Valentine, had been involved in trades that either directly or indirectly helped acquire Game 1 starter Andy Messersmith.* The roster also included Bill Russell, Charlie Hough, Von Joshua, and Steve Yeager from the '66 and '67 drafts. Homegrown hurler Don Sutton started Game 2. Willie Crawford, the phenom Tommy Lasorda and Kenny Myers recruited a decade earlier, played right field.

The more experienced A's jumped to a 2-1 Series lead. Despite his team's deficit and Oakland's prior success, Buckner confidently proclaimed that the Dodgers were the better team. "The A's have only a couple of players who could play on our club," Buckner told reporters. "I think if we played them 162 times, we could beat them 100."[2]

Buckner's brash comments made him an enemy of Oakland fans and provided bulletin-board material for his opponent. "What Buckner is saying is that twenty-two of you ain't worth [expletive]," A's owner Charlie Finley told his team before Game 4.[3]

The A's won the next two to secure their third consecutive title.† During the seventh-inning stretch of the clinching game, Oakland fans pelted Buckner with debris, including a whiskey bottle that struck him on the head. An inning later, the hard-nosed competitor committed a cardinal sin on the basepaths. In the eighth inning, with his team trailing 3-2, Buckner led off with a single. He advanced to second on an error by the center fielder but then got thrown out trying for third. Of course, it would not be Buckner's last World Series blunder.

---

* Alexander was traded to Baltimore for Frank Robinson, who was then packaged to the Angels as part of the Messersmith deal.
† Tightly contested, four of the Series' five games ended in a 3-2 score.

Loyalty Pays Dividends

"That infield was tight on the field, but not anywhere else. They were all very different personalities. Bill Russell was such a mild-mannered guy. Cey was outgoing but intense. Davey was Davey—tough as nails but in your face. And then Garv, for a lack of a better term, was practiced. Totally practiced. He was the image incarnate."—Peter Schmuck, *They Bled Blue: The 1981 Los Angeles Dodgers*

Entering the 1975 season, expectations were high for a Dodgers team returning essentially the same roster that months earlier had come within three games of a World Series championship. The first fifty games went swimmingly. On June 1, LA owned a 30-20 record and a one-and-a-half-game division lead. New acquisition Burt Hooton, obtained from the Cubs in an early May trade* for Geoff Zahn and Eddie Solomon, had won three of his last four starts. Once again, a member of the Dodgers' 1968

---

* Hooton played winter ball in Venezuela during the offseason, impressing Lasorda, who recommended him to the Dodgers. Hooton, a former first-round pick in the 1971 June Amateur Draft-Secondary Phase, was coming off a disappointing 1974 season in which he recorded a 7-11 record and 4.80 ERA.

draft class—in this case, Zahn*—had been used as a trade chip to land a frontline starter. By season's end, Hooton would win 18 games, including his final 11 decisions.† But his addition was not enough to secure the NL West. Cincinnati caught fire, going 80-33 from June onward to claim another division title. Injuries to two key regulars dragged down the Dodgers, who finished in second place behind the Big Red Machine for the fourth time in six seasons.

Bill Buckner, a .296 hitter over his first four full seasons, severely sprained his left ankle sliding into second base against the Giants on April 18. He returned to the lineup four weeks later but could barely run. Determined to battle through the injury, he played in 92 games, hitting just .243 before undergoing season-ending surgery on September 1. Bill Russell, meanwhile, missed nearly the entire first half with a broken hand and a sore knee, batting a meager .206 in 84 games.

Besides weathering injuries, the '75 Dodgers also endured problems in the clubhouse, primarily centered around Steve Garvey, the team's fan-friendly, media-accessible first baseman, who had become immensely popular after his breakout '74 season. His smiling, squared-jawed face, framed by neatly trimmed sideburns, appeared in Pepsi ads and on newspaper stands across the country. On opening day, *Sports Illustrated* published a flattering cover story about Garvey titled "Born to Be a Dodger." The first paragraph of the piece stated, "If a lot of boys do not idolize him now, they are missing the truck because he smiles at everybody, gives autographs like a garage gives calendars and is known as a gentleman."[1]

The media praise heaped upon the clean-living Garvey led to feelings of resentment and jealousy amongst his less heralded teammates. Some players felt that his generosity with fans and the press served as a means of gaining endorsements. Their sentiments came to light in an eye-opening *San Bernardino Press-Telegram* article on June 15. In the piece, one anonymous source claimed Garvey had no friends on the team. In the same article, Ron Cey called Garvey a "public-relations man" and said

---

* Zahn, who had learned to throw an effective forkball from minor-league pitching instructor Roger Craig, would win 111 games in the majors, including a team-high 18 for the '82 AL West champion Angels.

† During his decade with the Dodgers, Hooton won 112 games, contributing to three pennants and a World Series title.

there were at least five other players on the team as valuable as the reigning NL MVP. Davey Lopes added, "I'd say [Garvey's] more image-conscious and public relations-minded than 99 percent of the team. That's okay for him—it's just not my bag."[2] The article resulted in some confrontations between Garvey and his teammates and a festering clubhouse tension that lingered for the remainder of the season and beyond.

STEVE GARVEY - 3rd Base

Courtesy Spokane Indians.

Although the foursome who comprised The Infield would never be best friends away from the diamond, they respected one another as baseball players and continued to produce between the white lines. Injuries slowed Russell in '75, but the other three authored strong seasons. Garvey slashed .319/.351/.476 with 18 homers and 95 RBI. Lopes led the NL with 77 stolen bases and broke a major-league record by stealing 38 consecutive bases without being caught.* Cey paced the Dodgers with 25 home runs and 101 RBI in another All-Star campaign.

NINETEEN SEVENTY-FIVE PROVED TO BE ANOTHER STRANGE YEAR FOR Bobby Valentine. The Angels cut him at the end of spring training and loaned him to the Pirates' Triple-A team in Charleston, West Virginia. A couple of months later, the Angels cleared a spot on their Triple-A roster, so Valentine reported to Salt Lake City, where he hit over .300 and earned a call-up to Anaheim in early August. Six weeks later, the Halos sent Valentine packing to the San Diego Padres—his fourth team that summer —a day after Valentine and Angels coach Jerry Adair were involved in a barroom dustup.

That winter, Valentine played in the Dominican Republic for Lasorda and sought clarity from the man he considered a second father. Lasorda, being brutally honest, saw his physical limitations and told him to start considering coaching. A few months later, at Padres camp, GM Buzzie Bavasi asked the twenty-six-year-old Valentine if he'd go to Hawaii (the Padres' Triple-A affiliate) to mentor the organization's young players and assist manager Roy Hartsfield, whose wife was battling health problems. Valentine accepted the assignment. In what would be his final season as a full-time player, he hit .304 with 13 home runs and 89 RBI as a first baseman and de facto coach. He even stole nine bases despite his damaged leg.

Valentine spent his final three seasons riding the pine with the Padres, Mets, and Mariners. He called it quits after the '79 season—his tenth in the majors. In 639 career games, Valentine hit .260 and accumulated 441 hits, 12 home runs, and 27 stolen bases.

The fact that Valentine played six seasons after his ghastly leg injury served as a testament to his competitive drive. Though his career statistics

---

* Lopes's consecutive steals streak broke Max Carey's mark of 36 set in 1922-23. Vince Coleman would later eclipse Lopes's record with 50 straight stolen bases in 1988-89.

don't accurately reflect his natural ability, in retrospect, those who competed with and against him before his injury remember his immense talent. "Bobby Valentine was destined to be a superstar," said Winston Llenas. "In my eyes, he was the best of them all. He had enthusiasm, he was aggressive, he could run, he could hit, he had power. He had all the tools to be a superstar."[3]

Post-retirement, Valentine simultaneously ventured into the restaurant business and coaching. The Mets employed him as a third-base coach beginning in 1983, a position he held until the Rangers hired him to manage during the 1985 season.

Valentine's mentor, Lasorda, had followed a similar path a decade earlier. After the '75 season, the Montreal Expos interviewed the Dodgers third-base coach and offered him a three-year managerial contract worth a total of $250,000—an enormous pay bump from his modest $17,000 coaching salary. It was a lucrative offer to fill one of twenty-four coveted managerial positions in a city he called home for nine years in the minors. How could he refuse? That's surely what Expos GM John McHale thought when he called to offer him the job. But in a remarkable display of loyalty to the Dodgers, Lasorda turned down the Expos' offer. He rolled the dice and waited for Alston's job. The Dodgers had not guaranteed Lasorda anything, yet he felt confident that Peter O'Malley would take care of him.

Lasorda returned to the Dodgers third-base coaching box in '76 for a fourth season. By then, he had befriended a number of Hollywood A-listers, including Frank Sinatra and Don Rickles. The former promised Lasorda he would sing the national anthem if and when Lasorda became manager. "He becomes a minor national celebrity, becomes a Hollywood darling, becomes a fixture in Los Angeles long before anybody should have any idea who this guy is," recalled sportswriter Mike Littwin. "I've never seen anything like this. You'd be hard-pressed to find an analogous situation. Here is this guy in one of the legendary sports franchises who had accomplished nothing ... Yet within the organization, he is already semi-legendary."[4]

The Dodgers started poorly, losing seven of eight, before rebounding to win twelve in a row from late April to early May. After Charlie Hough*

---

* Hough had his best season with the Dodgers in '76, posting a 12-8 record, 2.21 ERA, and 18 saves.

picked up a win in relief over the Giants on June 3, LA stood even with Cincinnati for first place. But as the season marched along, injuries to Reggie Smith, Dusty Baker, and Davey Lopes* caught up to Alston's club. Sparky Anderson's Reds gradually built an insurmountable lead, finishing with 102 wins. The 92-win Dodgers ended the season in second place for the sixth time in seven years. Often a bridesmaid, rarely a bride.

Throughout the season, rumors swirled that the sixty-five-year-old Alston would either retire or be pushed out at season's end. The chatter became louder as the season drew to a close. In a September *Los Angeles Times* article, an anonymous Dodgers regular was quoted as saying, "I flatly believe Walt does not deserve to be rehired. He has made too many mistakes in strategy, and he has become too stereotyped."[5] The anonymous player also recounted a clubhouse meeting in which Alston said the Reds were a better team. This type of messaging was the opposite of Lasorda's "You gotta believe!" attitude. "Our players fed off that cocky attitude," recalled Doug Rau. "But Walt had a different style. He came from a different era. It was time."[6]

Eight days after the damning *Los Angeles Times* article, Alston resigned his post with four games remaining on the schedule. A day later, Peter O'Malley offered the job to the lefty from Norristown. Lasorda's loyalty and patience had finally paid dividends.

Two-thirds of the roster Lasorda inherited had played for him in the minor leagues or winter ball, including pitchers Hough and Rau, the infield foursome of Cey, Russell, Lopes, and Garvey, and left fielder Bill Buckner. In the final four games of the season, Lasorda penciled Buckner's name on the lineup card three times. They would be the only games Buck would play for Lasorda in the major leagues.

Buckner had rebounded nicely from his injury-riddled '75 campaign, hitting .301 with seven homers, 60 RBI, and a .716 OPS. He even stole 28 bases, although his left ankle was not the same since the injury and never would be. For the next fifteen years, he endured a grueling pregame routine involving an exercise bike, ice baths, and taping just so he could he take the field.

Buckner played adequate left-field defense and led the league in putouts in 1976, but he preferred to play first base because of his gammy

---

* Lopes led the NL with 63 stolen bases despite playing in only 117 games.

ankle and wasn't shy about saying so. According to Bobby Valentine, when Campanis sent Buckner his contract for 1977, Buckner walked into Campanis's office and ripped it to pieces. He said he'd play for that salary as a first baseman but not as an outfielder.[7] The next day, Campanis jettisoned him to the Chicago Cubs, a team coming off four consecutive losing seasons. Buckner, who would play first base in the Windy City, pulled no punches in expressing his shock and disappointment to the *Los Angeles Times*: "I'm going from a contender to a non-contender, from a city I love to a city I dislike. It's a real drag. I'm very upset about it ... I feel like a piece of meat. They use you for what they can and get rid of you in the same way."[8]

Bob Buckner recalled that much of his brother's disappointment stemmed from wanting to play for the man he considered a second father. "It worked out well, and he had some good seasons in Chicago," recalled Bob, "but it was difficult because he really wanted to play for Tommy."[9]

In exchange for Buckner, the Dodgers acquired a center fielder with power in the form of Rick Monday.* It had been nearly fourteen years since Lasorda, trying to prove himself as a scout, tried desperately to sign the Santa Monica High star. Now entering his twelfth season in the majors, Monday had recently become a hero when, as a visiting player with the Cubs, he ran across the Dodger Stadium outfield and grabbed an American flag from a pair of protesters attempting to set it on fire.

In Buckner's first seven seasons as a Cub, he hit .301 and averaged 12 homers and 73 RBI. His hustle and grit made him a fan favorite on the North Side. In 1980, he won the National League batting title with a .324 average, fulfilling Ted Williams's prediction a few years late. The next year, Buckner earned his first and only All-Star nod. He always went full throttle, but he found a little extra motivation when he faced his former club. His career .348 batting average against the Dodgers was higher than any other opponent. During the '84 season, the Cubs traded Buckner to the Boston Red Sox for Mike Brumley and Dennis Eckersley.

Buckner thrived in Beantown, topping 100 RBI in each of his first two seasons as the everyday first baseman. In 1986, the Red Sox won the AL East behind the pitching of Roger Clemens. After defeating the Angels in

---

* The full trade was Buckner, Iván de Jesús, and minor leaguer Jeff Albert to the Cubs in exchange for Monday and pitcher Mike Garman.

the ALCS, Boston took a 3-2 lead over the Mets in the World Series. The Red Sox were on the precipice of breaking the franchise's sixty-eight-year championship drought. In Game 6, with the score tied at five in the bottom of the tenth, Mookie Wilson hit a ground ball that rolled through Buckner's legs, allowing the winning run to score. "I think it hit something and bounced to the right," described Buckner later. "It went above my glove, so it wasn't something that I didn't stay down on. The ball just bounced, and I missed it. It wasn't because of any stress or whatever, just a bad bounce."[10] The miscue took on even greater significance when the Mets won Game 7. Even though there were countless other mistakes, questionable managerial decisions, and turning points in the seven-game Series, Buckner's error came to define the '86 Fall Classic and would overshadow his accomplishments on the diamond. For the rest of his professional career, he endured heckling from fans and a barrage of questions from the media about the infamous play. One reporter had the audacity to call his home and ask if he had contemplated suicide.

Two weeks after the World Series, Buckner was back in California. Al Campanis called his grandson, Jim Campanis Jr., a sophomore catcher at USC, and said that Buckner would give Jim a hitting lesson. "My grandpa said, 'He's got a tee, so just bring as many baseballs as you can find,'" recalled Campanis Jr. "He gave me a great batting lesson, and I had a really good season that year using a lot of stuff he taught me hitting off a tee into a net.* That shows how great of a guy he was. He could have hidden under a rock, but instead he kept himself out there."[11]

During the winter, Buckner had surgery to remove bone spurs from his ankle. Midway through the 1987 season the Red Sox released him. He then played for the Angels and Royals before returning to Boston in 1990, making the team as a non-roster spring-training invitee. When Fenway Park public address announcer Sherm Feller introduced the Red Sox roster on opening day, Buckner received the longest and loudest ovation. Buckner played sparingly before his release on June 5. At age forty, his twenty-two-year big-league career had come to an end.

Buckner retired with a lifetime .289 batting average, 498 doubles, 174

---

* Jim Campanis Jr. set a USC record with 92 RBI as a junior in 1988. He was drafted in the third round of the 1988 June Amateur Draft by the Seattle Mariners and played six seasons of pro ball, reaching as high as Double-A.

home runs, and 183 stolen bases. As of 2025, his 2,715 career hits ranked sixty-sixth all-time—more than Ernie Banks, Reggie Jackson, and many other Hall of Famers. Buckner, who believed he would have gotten to 3,000 hits had he stayed healthy, maintained phenomenal bat-to-ball skills throughout his career. Incredibly, he never once struck out three times in a game, and his strikeout rate of one in every 20.7 at-bats ranks fourth lowest of any player in the Divisional Era behind Félix Millán, Glenn Beckert, and Tony Gwynn.* "He was the best hitter I ever played with," recalled Tom Paciorek. "You couldn't throw a fastball by him. Seaver, Gibson, Nolan Ryan, J.R. Richard, I don't care who you were. None of them could throw a fastball by him. Buck, in my opinion, should be in the Hall of Fame."[12]

Buckner, who received 2.1 percent of the vote in his only year on the Hall of Fame ballot, served as the White Sox' hitting coach 1996 and '97 and later filled the same role for the Single-A Boise Hawks. Post-retirement, he lived on a ranch in Idaho, far away from the limelight. Buckner coached his son's Little League team, owned a stake in several car dealerships, and made more money in real-estate investing than he ever did in baseball. He accepted that his infamous World Series gaffe was part of his story but refused to let it define him. "I think God does things for a reason," Buckner told the *Boston Globe* in 2003. "You got choices to make. There could be somebody in my shoes who would think that life sucks. I chose to look at it that life is great. You can make those choices. Everyone in life has things that don't go according to plan."[13]

In 2008, four years after the Red Sox exorcised The Curse of the Bambino, Buckner was invited to throw out the first pitch before Boston's home opener. The Fenway Park faithful gave him a rousing ovation. A few years later, he played himself on Larry David's HBO show *Curb Your Enthusiasm*. In the episode, Buckner consoles David after he makes an error in a rec league softball game. Later, Buckner catches a baby thrown from a burning building and is hoisted on the shoulders of onlookers and celebrated as a hero. "I saw that show in editing for weeks," David said.

---

* Millán has the lowest rate (25.0 at-bats per strikeout), followed by Beckert (24.5) and Gwynn (21.4). The Divisional Era is defined as 1969 to present. Both Millán and Beckert began their major-league careers before 1969, thus their at-bat and strikeout numbers from 1968 and prior are not reflected in the above Divisional Era statistic.

"And every time I watched it, whenever he caught that baby, I would well up."[14]

Bill Buckner died on May 27, 2019, from Lewy body dementia at the age of sixty-nine.

Lasorda at the Helm

"I'm not sure if continuity breeds success, or if success breeds continuity, but we have a lot of momentum built up in our minor-league system. We've also been a little lucky."—Bill Schweppe, Dodgers vice president of minor-league operations

Frank Sinatra kept his word to Tommy Lasorda. On 1977 Opening Day, Ol' Blue Eyes sang the "Star-Spangled Banner" at Dodger Stadium. Two hours, twenty minutes later, Don Sutton secured a complete-game, 5-1 victory over the rival Giants. From there, the Dodgers were off and running. Coming out of the gate like Seattle Slew, LA won 22 of its first 26 while building a ten-and-a-half-game division lead.

The gregarious and effervescent Lasorda became an instant hit with the press. He moved his office to a larger trainer's room, plastered the walls with photos of Sinatra and the pope, and filled the space with couches, chairs, a liquor cabinet, and a television so he could entertain sportswriters and celebrities. He traded autographed baseballs for catered meals, which he served in his office so that his players would come in and socialize. Lasorda was in extrovert heaven.

Tommy Lasorda. Courtesy Spokane Indians.

Between the white lines, the skipper focused his attention on slaying the beast known as the Big Red Machine. Lasorda wanted his players to despise the juggernaut that had won the previous two World Series and five of the last seven division titles. To fuel the rivalry, he exchanged barbs with Reds manager Sparky Anderson in the press and fined his players if he caught them wearing red.

The Dodgers came down to earth after their blistering start but still managed to reel off 98 victories by season's end. They led the NL West wire to wire, overcoming the rival Reds and winning the division by ten games. Anderson credited Lasorda with the Dodgers' success: "Their enthusiasm was their strength. And part of that was Tommy. Maybe 100 percent of that was Tommy."[1]

The Dodgers drew 2,995,087 fans, breaking their own attendance record set in Dodger Stadium's inaugural season of 1962. They also boasted MLB's lowest ERA and led the NL with 191 home runs. A decade earlier, the weak-hitting Dodgers had mustered only 82 home runs, galvanizing Al Campanis to prioritize offense in the draft. Now, the club boasted four players—Dusty Baker, Ron Cey, Steve Garvey, and Reggie Smith—with 30 or more homers, a first in baseball history. All were either products of the '68 draft or acquired using pieces from that year's crop (Tom Paciorek was part of the Baker trade, and Joe Ferguson brought Smith from the Cardinals).

In the best-of-five National League Championship Series, LA faced a talented Phillies team* that won 101 games for a second consecutive season. Manager Danny Ozark's club, led by Cy Young Award winner Steve Carlton and sluggers Mike Schmidt and Greg Luzinski, felt relieved to be playing the Dodgers as opposed to the Reds—the team that had swept them in the '76 NLCS and won eight of twelve during the regular season.

Lasorda's club ideally needed to win one of the first two game at home before the series shifted to Veterans Stadium, where the Phillies had posted .741 winning percentage during the regular season. The Dodgers offense did its part in Game 1, scoring five runs off Carlton, but a pair of costly Bill Russell errors helped Philadelphia steal a victory. Lasorda remained confident despite the deflating loss. "Tomorrow, the fruits of victory are for us," he declared.[2]

Sensing that his team needed to loosen up, Lasorda invited Don Rickles to the clubhouse before Game 2. The comedian roasted everyone in sight, starting with the manager. "Look at that stomach," said Rickles. "You think he's worried about you guys? No way. If you guys lose, he's gonna tie a cord around his neck and get work as a balloon."[3] The players roared with laughter. Lasorda's tactic worked like a charm. His team won

---

* Philadelphia's roster included former Dodgers Ted Sizemore and Tommy Hutton.

that night, 7-1, then defeated the Phillies twice more in front of raucous crowds at the Vet.

In the World Series, the Dodgers and Yankees renewed a rivalry that had been dormant for fourteen years. Each arrived by different means. Homegrown stars comprised the bulk of the Dodgers roster, whereas Yankees owner George Steinbrenner had supplemented his team with a number of high-priced free agents, including Reggie Jackson, Catfish Hunter, and Don Gullett. Team captain Thurman Munson, taken one pick ahead of Bobby Valentine in the '68 draft, was one of a handful of Yankees who had been drafted and developed by the organization. New York, piloted by Lasorda's one-time combatant Billy Martin, jumped out to a 2-1 Series lead.* In Game 4, Dodgers starter Doug Rau ran into trouble early, resulting in Lasorda's memorable mic'd-up mound visit. The Yankees prevailed that day and secured the title three days later on the shoulders of Jackson, whose Game 6 heroics earned him the moniker "Mr. October." The future Hall of Famer hit three home runs over a span of three pitches, the last coming against Charlie Hough. Aside from the disappointing ending, Lasorda's first year at the helm could not have gone better.

That offseason, the skipper's fame continued to grow. Besides his usual slew of luncheon speeches and public appearances, he guested on game shows and *The Tonight Show*, accepted honors at sportswriters' dinners across the country, and spent four days golfing with Sinatra in Palm Springs. The fifty-year-old Lasorda packed his schedule so full that he had to turn down an invitation to the White House. "Only in America could this happen to the son of an Italian immigrant," he told the *Los Angeles Times*. "I'm only trying to put something back in. I love doing it. To do your job to the best of your ability and to try to make somebody happy ... That's what life is all about isn't it?"[4]

DURING THE ENSUING SPRING TRAINING, THE DODGERS APPOINTED DAVEY

---

* In the sixth inning of Game 1, Steve Garvey was called out on a close play at home. Replays showed that Garvey beat the tag, but home-plate umpire Nestor Chylak had moved up the first-base line and didn't have a good view of the play. "[Chylak] was so far out of position that he should have been forced to buy a ticket in the loge," said Lasorda later. The blown call took on more significance when the Yankees prevailed in extra innings.

Lopes the fifth team captain in team history, following an impressive lineage of Pee Wee Reese, Duke Snider, Maury Wills, and Willie Davis. Eight years earlier, Lopes had been as quiet as a mime during his first season in Spokane. Over his next two seasons in Triple-A, he gradually came out of his shell at the urging of Lasorda, who saw leadership potential in the youngster from East Providence. "He instilled a lot of his own personality in me," Lopes said in 1978, "both in my approach to baseball and in my personal life."[5]

Once he had a few years of big-league experience under his belt, Lopes emerged as a leader on the Dodgers. When Dusty Baker missed a cutoff man shortly after joining the team in '76, Lopes approached him and said, 'We don't play that way." Baker responded, "Hey, I almost threw him out." Lopes repeated himself firmly, "We don't play that way."[6] Baker, who had never had a teammate talk to him that way, looked up and saw the whole team coming to back up the diminutive second baseman.

In his first season as captain, Lopes batted .278, slugged 17 home runs, and stole 45 bases in 49 attempts. The table-setter earned his first All-Star nod and won his only Gold Glove Award. Fellow infielders Cey and Garvey also produced All-Star campaigns. Still, right fielder Reggie Smith bested them all, slashing .295/.382/.559 with a team-high 29 homers.

Smith was arguably the Dodgers MVP. Don Sutton certainly thought so. "All you hear about on our team is Steve Garvey, the All-American boy," he told Thomas Boswell of the *Washington Post* in early September. "Well, the best player on this team for the last two years—and we all know it—is Reggie Smith ... Reggie doesn't go out and publicize himself. He doesn't smile at the right people or say the right things ... Reggie's not a façade or a Madison Avenue image. He's a real person."[7]

Garvey, popular amongst fans and the media alike, had become a spokesman for Jockey, Aqua Velva, and Chevrolet dealerships while making television appearances on *Fantasy Island* and *The Gong Show*. Meanwhile, Sutton, a thirteen-year veteran with 202 wins under his belt, resented Garvey's fame. In one breath, the hurler had complimented one teammate and disparaged another. When Garvey saw the article, he approached Lasorda at breakfast in the team hotel and asked what he would do if he were in Garvey's shoes. Lasorda, never one to back down from a fight, responded, "If it was me, and somebody said those things in the paper about me? The first time I saw him, I'd deck him."[8]

Hours later, in the visiting clubhouse at Shea Stadium, the typically mild-mannered Garvey confronted Sutton about the *Washington Post* column. After Sutton said something about Garvey's wife, the pair engaged in an eye-gouging wrestling match that would have made The Three Stooges proud. When someone came out to the field and told Lasorda that Garvey and Sutton were fighting in the clubhouse, he smiled. As Bill Plaschke later wrote, "The two players who were disliked by their teammates had beaten each other into humility ... Two problems had been fixed without Lasorda having to lift a finger."[9]

The Dodgers stood neck and neck with the Giants and Reds atop the NL West when the skirmish occurred. Both Garvey and the team caught fire afterward. The first baseman hit nearly .400 the rest of the way as the Dodgers cruised to a second consecutive division title while becoming the first team in baseball history to draw three million fans. The Dodgers postseason played out exactly as it had the year prior—a triumph over the Phillies in the NLCS* preceding a bitter World Series defeat at the hands of the Yankees.† Or rather, at the hip of the Yankees. The Dodgers won the first two games at home,‡ but the momentum swung in New York's favor following an infamous Game 4 no-call in which Jackson threw his hip into the path of Bill Russell's double-play relay. After the Yankees' Series-clinching Game 6 victory, a shellshocked Lasorda sat quietly in his office and, for perhaps the first time, shooed away reporters.

Nineteen-seventy-nine proved mostly forgettable for the Dodgers. The pitching staff sorely missed top-of-the-rotation starter Tommy John, who bolted for the Bronx in free agency. Injuries decimated an LA roster that lacked team chemistry. Anonymous name-calling in the press and near-fights behind closed doors compelled one sportswriter to describe the clubhouse as a "war zone."[10] In an effort to unify the team amidst the turmoil, Lopes relinquished his captaincy. "This way we're all equal," he explained. "I have no title. Nothing more is expected of me than from

---

* Cey, Russell, Lopes, and Garvey combined to hit .377 with six home runs and 17 RBI in the series.

† The Yankees clinched the AL East after beating the Red Sox in a one-game playoff. New York's light-hitting shortstop Bucky Dent delivered the key blow, a three-run home run over the Green Monster off Boston hurler Mike Torrez.

‡ Lopes hit a pair of homers in the Dodgers' Game 1 shellacking of the Yankees. In Game 2, Cey's three-run homer proved to be the decisive blow.

anyone else."[11] LA arrived at the All-Star break in last place with a dismal 36-57 record. Rumors swirled that Lasorda's job was in jeopardy. Then the Dodgers turned it around in the second half and wound up leading the league in home runs with 183, including 28 each by Cey, Garvey, and Lopes. But they had dug too deep of a hole. LA finished four games under .500, marking its first losing record in eleven years. On top of the team's disappointing play, Walter O'Malley died of congestive heart failure in August at the age of seventy-five.

The year wasn't a complete disaster, however. In the seventeenth round of the 1979 June Amateur Draft, the Dodgers selected Orel Hershiser, a Bowling Green State University pitcher recommended by area scout Boyd Bartley. The righty would eventually accrue 135 of his 205 career wins in Dodger blue. "When other scouts went to see Hershiser, he didn't do very well," recalled Bartley's son Dan. "But when my father went to see him, he was fantastic. He championed him at the scouts table and won the day."[12]

A month later, the Dodgers signed eighteen-year-old Mexican pitcher Fernando Valenzuela for $120,000. Scout Mike Brito had discovered the young southpaw by accident while on assignment to see a young shortstop prospect. The shortstop showed nothing to write home about, but the opposing pitcher—a rotund lefty with a high leg kick and ice in his veins—certainly did. Brito filed a glowing report on Valenzuela to his boss, Al Campanis, who eventually traveled to Mexico to see the teenager himself. By then, the Yankees were also in hot pursuit, but Campanis begrudgingly topped their offer at Brito's insistence.

Although Hershiser and Valenzuela would eventually blossom into aces, the Dodgers needed arms even sooner heading into the 1980 season. Campanis uncharacteristically looked outside of the organization to fill that need, signing starter Dave Goltz and closer Don Stanhouse to lucrative free-agent contracts. Neither signing lived up to expectations,* but others stepped up. Veteran Jerry Reuss† tied a career-high with 18 wins (including a no-hitter), Don Sutton won the NL ERA title with a 2.20

---

* In 1980, Goltz, a former 20-game winner, compiled a pedestrian 7-11 record and 4.31 ERA. Stanhouse, meanwhile, missed three months because of shoulder and low back, posting a 5.04 ERA in 21 relief appearances. The Dodgers later released Stanhouse one year into his five-year deal, eating the $1.36 million remaining on his contract.

† The Dodgers acquired Reuss from the Pirates in April 1979 in exchange for Rick Rhoden.

mark, and rookie Steve Howe took the reins of closer. In the final series of the regular season, LA swept Houston to force a one-game playoff. The next day, the Astros fought back, ending the Dodgers season with a 7-1 victory.*

By 1981, many players from the Dodgers pennant-winning teams of the '70s had moved on, including Charlie Hough, Doug Rau, and Don Sutton. Sutton, who had been the longest tenured Dodger, signed a four-year contract with Houston just weeks after the one-game playoff. Reggie Smith remained on the roster, although shoulder surgery strictly limited him to pinch-hitting.† Catchers Steve Yeager and Joe Ferguson were still in the fold but on the wrong side of thirty. Reminiscent of the '68 draft class's arrival in the early '70s, budding stars Mike Scioscia, Pedro Guerrero, and Dave Stewart emerged to take on prominent roles. Other bright prospects, including Candy Maldonado, Mike Marshall,‡ and Steve Sax, were knocking on the door. Although the infield of Cey-Russell-Lopes-Garvey remained intact for an unprecedented eighth full season, it became clear their tenure as a foursome was nearing an end. Al Campanis intimated that changes may be coming when he addressed reporters about the organization's promising minor leaguers. "If you've got the talent," said the GM, "the timing will take care of itself."[13]

Valenzuela became the biggest story in LA and across the country during the first two months of the '81 season. The young phenom won his first eight starts while registering an otherworldly 0.50 ERA. Once opposing hitters started laying off his screwball, the southpaw proved fallible, but his hot start had helped the Dodgers build an early division lead. LA stood a half-game in front of Cincinnati when a midseason players' strike interrupted the season in early June. By the time the players'

---

* With top starters Don Sutton, Jerry Reuss, and Burt Hooton unavailable, the Dodgers had to choose between free-agent bust Dave Goltz and rookie Fernando Valenzuela to start the do-or-die playoff. Valenzuela, a September call-up who had pitched 15⅔ innings of relief without allowing an earned run, threw two innings the day before. Al Campanis took the decision out of Lasorda's hands, ordering the skipper to start the veteran Goltz.
† To fill Smith's spot in the everyday lineup, Al Campanis attempted to re-acquire Bill Buckner from the Cubs. Campanis agreed to part with minor leaguer Mickey Hatcher and pitcher Joe Beckwith, but then Beckwith suffered an eye injury, so the Cubs nixed the deal.
‡ Not to be confused with the former Cy Young Award-winning pitcher of the same name. In 1981, this Mike Marshall, a first baseman/outfielder drafted in 1978, won the Triple Crown in the Pacific Coast League with .373 batting average, 34 home runs, and 137 RBI.

union and owners settled in late July, roughly one-third of the schedule had been wiped out.* After much discussion, Major League Baseball adjusted the playoff format so that the first-half winner would play the second-half winner in a best-of-five Division Series. Thus, LA wound up playing Houston, the second-half winner, in the first-ever NLDS.† The Astros won a pair of extra-inning contests at the Astrodome to start the series, but the Dodgers won the next three at Chavez Ravine. In the Game 5 clincher, Jerry Reuss outdueled Nolan Ryan, who had no-hit the Dodgers just fifteen days earlier. The Dodgers then knocked out the upstart Expos in the NLCS behind Rick Monday's game-winning, ninth-inning home run at frigid Olympic Stadium.‡ The Yankees, meanwhile, defeated the A's in a dominant ACLS sweep. The Dodgers would now have another chance at redemption against their foes from the Bronx. "Because God delays does not mean that God denies," said Lasorda, evoking the words of his father. "Well, he delayed, but he didn't deny. We got the Yankees again."[14]

Since the Dodgers and Yankees had last met in the World Series three years earlier, Steinbrenner added free agents Tommy John, Rudy May, Bob Watson,§ and Dave Winfield to his payroll, bolstering a roster that also featured 1981 AL Rookie of the Year Dave Righetti. The Yankees seemingly had the upper hand entering the Series, including home-field advantage. Sure enough, New York won the first two at Yankee Stadium despite missing Reggie Jackson, who sat out with a sore calf. To win the Series, the Dodgers would have to climb out of a two-game deficit a third time that October. Following his team's Game 2 defeat at the hands of

---

* Davey Lopes made headlines several weeks into the work stoppage when he criticized the players' union and questioned the qualifications of the union's player representatives in an interview with the *South Day Daily Breeze*. The outspoken former captain also blasted Garvey, who was receiving paychecks during the strike because of specific language in his contract. Following a players' union meeting in Los Angeles several days later, Lopes apologized and threw his full support behind the union.

† The Dodgers, having already clinched a playoff berth, ostensibly used the second half as an extended spring training. They arrived at the postseason well rested but without Ron Cey, who was recovering from a broken arm suffered from a hit-by-pitch. Houston entered the playoffs without Don Sutton, who was on the shelf with a fractured kneecap that resulted from being struck by a Jerry Reuss pitch in the final regular-season series.

‡ The gametime temperature for Game 3 was 46 degrees. Before pregame introductions, Lasorda attempted to gain a psychological advantage by having his players remove their jackets and take the field in short sleeves. "This is our weather!" he exclaimed.

§ Willie Crawford's high school teammate.

John, Lasorda held a closed-door meeting. "Seems to me," he said, "we've got them right where we want them."[15] When reporters were finally allowed in the visitors' clubhouse and mentioned the possibility of a Yankees sweep, Lasorda bristled. "Sweep?" he muttered. "My rear end, that's what they'll sweep."[16]

He was right, there would be no sweep. In Game 3, Valenzuela ran into trouble early, ceding four runs through three innings. Nevertheless, Lasorda trusted his gut, sticking with the rookie sensation in what he later called one of the most difficult managerial decisions of his career. The skipper's patience paid off. Valenzuela settled down, and the offense rallied to give LA a much-needed victory. In Game 4, Lopes, Garvey, and Cey stepped up, combining for seven hits and five RBI in the Dodgers' 8-7 triumph. After Jerry Reuss outpitched Ron Guidry a day later, the Series headed back to the Bronx with the Dodgers one win away from the franchise's first championship in sixteen years. In Game 6, with the score tied 1-1, Yankees manager Bob Lemon lifted his starter, John, for a pinch-hitter with the bases loaded in the fourth inning. The move backfired. New York failed to score, and the Dodgers offense subsequently unloaded on the Yankees bullpen, cruising to a decisive 9-2 victory. When the Dodgers recorded the final out, Lasorda sprinted out of the dugout screaming, "You gotta believe! You gotta believe!"[17]

In a baseball career that began thirty-six years earlier with the Class-D Concord Weavers, Lasorda had never been happier. "It wasn't just beating the Yankees," he later wrote. "It was doing so with Garvey and Lopes, Russell, Cey,* the people I'd been with for so long ... The thousands of groundballs I'd hit to them, the countless hours of batting practice I'd thrown, the fights we had, the sad moments we shared, this was the culmination of it all, the crowning moment."[18]

In the clubhouse, Lopes, who had just endured the worst season of his career,† popped champagne and celebrated his first championship since the Albuquerque Dukes beat the Eugene Emeralds in 1972. "They can do

---

* Garvey hit .417 in the Series, and Cey (.350 with a homer and six RBI) shared MVP honors with Guerrero and Steve Yeager.
† A first-half ankle injury and second-half groin strain limited Lopes to just 58 games in which he hit a meager .206 with five homers and 20 steals. In the World Series, he set a dubious record for second basemen by committing six errors, two more than the Yankees committed as a team.

anything with us now," he exclaimed. "I've got the ring. They can't take that away from me!"[19] His words proved prophetic. That offseason, Al Campanis created a spot for twenty-year-old Steve Sax by trading the thirty-six-year-old Lopes to Oakland for a Single-A infielder. A year later, the Dodgers traded Cey to the Cubs a pair of low-level prospects, and Garvey signed a five-year contract with San Diego after the Dodgers refused to budge on their four-year offer. With that, the last direct links to the Dodgers' famed '68 draft class were gone.

Bill Russell remained in LA until he retired after the '86 season. The pride of Pittsburg, Kansas, spent his entire eighteen-year major-league career with the Dodgers, providing Alston and then Lasorda with a reliable, unflashy presence at shortstop. His 2,181 games played for the Dodgers remains second all-time in franchise history behind Zack Wheat. The three-time All-Star retired with a career .263 batting average and 1,926 hits.

Davey Lopes also hit .263 for his career, accumulating 1,671 hits and 155 home runs over sixteen seasons in the majors despite not playing regularly until he was twenty-eight years old. He stole 557 bases at an 83 percent success rate, third-highest all-time among players with 500 or more attempts, behind only Tim Raines and Willie Wilson. Lopes holds the Dodgers record for home runs by a second baseman with 98 and made four All-Star teams. Nevertheless, the stoic captain cared little about accolades. As Jim Murray once wrote in the *Los Angeles Times*, "Lopes is not a trophy player. He's a victory player."[20] After retiring as a player, Lopes remained in baseball for another three decades, mostly as a coach, including a five-year stint as the Dodgers first-base coach. Beginning in 2000, he managed the Milwaukee Brewers until he was fired fifteen games into his third season.

Cey played seventeen seasons in the big leagues, including twelve with the Dodgers, four with the Cubs, and one with the A's. He retired with 1,868 base hits, 316 home runs, and a career slash line of .261/.354/.445. According to Baseball-Reference, Cey's career WAR of 53.7 ranks twenty-fourth all-time among third basemen. Not bad for a guy who was plan B after Garvey failed to stick at the hot corner.

Although Garvey's production began to wane as he advanced into his mid-thirties, his name recognition gave the traditionally hapless Padres instant credibility. In his second season wearing brown and yellow, San

Diego made the playoffs for the first time in franchise history. Garvey hit .400 in the NLCS and belted a Game 4 walk-off home run against the Cubs' Lee Smith, propelling the Padres to the World Series, where they lost to the Detroit Tigers in five games. In 1987, a shoulder injury forced Garvey into retirement at age thirty-eight.

Over the course of his nineteen-year big-league career, Garvey earned ten All-Star nods, won four Gold Glove Awards, and was twice named MVP of both the All-Star Game and NLCS. The .294 career hitter accumulated 2,599 hits and 272 home runs. He holds the National League record for consecutive games played with 1,207—a streak that ran from September 3, 1975, through July 29, 1983. Garvey received considerable support for the Hall of Fame from baseball writers but ultimately fell off the ballot after peaking at 43 percent of the vote. Although his best seasons came wearing Dodger blue, the Padres recognized his impact on their franchise by retiring his jersey number 6 in 1988.

During his career, Garvey contributed to a plethora of charitable causes, including serving as the National Campaign Chairman of the Multiple Sclerosis Society. In 1981, he received the Roberto Clemente Award, an honor given to the player who best exhibits strong character, community service, and philanthropy. During his playing career and into retirement, Garvey headed his own marketing and television production companies. For an individual who worked hard to create a certain public persona, his ventures into media and marketing made for a natural post-baseball transition.

Garvey's pristine image took a hit in the late '80s, however. As *Sports Illustrated's* Rick Reilly wrote in November 1989, "In the space of eight months, [Garvey] had affairs with three women at once, impregnated two and married a fourth ... He's up to his chiseled chin in debt, into the scary seven figures. Two former business associates have sued him. Other than that, it has been all apple pie and porch swings."[21]

Garvey became the butt of jokes following his highly publicized fall from grace. "I haven't seen so many gorgeous girls since I spent Father's Day with Steve Garvey," quipped comedian Bob Hope at the Academy Awards.[22] In San Diego, fans wore T-shirts emblazoned with the slogan "Garvey is not my Padre." To his credit, Garvey took accountability for what he called his midlife disaster. "I made two poor choices, but it happened," he said later. "I didn't commit a felony, and I stood there and answered every question. I took responsibility. But what I did was out of character."²³

In the same *SI* piece, Reilly wrote that Garvey's ordeal "probably has ruined his prospects for the political career he was hoping to have."²⁴ Well, he gave it a shot anyway. In 2024, Garvey ran for the U.S. Senate in California as a Republican. Campaign posters featured his image swinging a bat in a blue number 6 jersey. His bid to become the become California's first Republican elected to the Senate since 1988 ultimately fell well short.

ON APRIL 6, 1987, THE DODGERS LOST TO THE HOUSTON ASTROS IN THE season opener at the Astrodome. After the game, GM Al Campanis appeared on ABC's *Nightline* with Ted Koppel for an episode commemorating the fortieth anniversary of Jackie Robinson's groundbreaking major-league debut. The show included a taped interview with Robinson's widow, Rachel, and Koppel's live split-frame interview with Campanis and author Roger Kahn.* Producers had originally booked Don Newcombe, but he had a travel conflict, so they substituted Campanis. In Rachel Robinson's segment, which preceded the live interview, she lamented the dearth of Black managers and executives. Koppel segued into the interview with Campanis by asking if there was still prejudice in baseball. "No, I don't believe it's prejudice," he responded. "I truly believe that they may not have some of the necessities to be, let's say, a field manager or perhaps a general manager." As Koppel pushed back, Campanis dug himself a deeper hole. "Why are Black men, or Black people, not good swimmers?" he said. "Because they don't have the buoyancy."²⁵ By the end of the segment, Campanis had irreparably damaged his reputation and career. Under pressure from civil rights groups and Commissioner Peter Ueberroth, Peter O'Malley asked Campanis to resign two days later.

Years later, Koppel reflected on Campanis's fateful interview in Steve Delsohn's book *True Blue*: "I have often thought that Al Campanis got himself into terrible trouble that night in large measure because he's a man from an older generation who was still saying the kinds of things that I

---

* Kahn authored several baseball books, including *The Boys of Summer*, a brilliant nonfiction book about the 1950s Brooklyn Dodgers.

guess white ballplayers and front-office professionals were saying in locker rooms and bars and restaurants to each other back in the '50s. And back in the '50s, that wasn't considered remarkable or bigoted stuff. But in the context of the '80s, it sounded horrible."[26]

Those who knew Campanis were shocked by what unfolded on *Nightline*. His words didn't jibe with the man they knew or his actions in baseball. From Lasorda's point of view, Campanis never judged a player by his race, religion, or nationality. Newcombe, major-league baseball's first Black ace and a former teammate of Robinson, agreed: "I don't believe he has a prejudiced bone in his body. If Jackie were around today, I don't think he would appreciate what has happened to Al because Al helped him and befriended him."[27]

Campanis's son, Jim, echoed those sentiments. "In his office for twenty years, he had three pictures," recalled the younger Campanis. "He had a picture of Sandy Koufax, who is Jewish, a picture of Roberto Clemente, who is Latin, and a picture of Jackie Robinson. In a way, that summed up my dad. Only thing he cared about was if you could hit, run, field, and throw."[28]

Another of Campanis's sons, George, later explained to the *Los Angeles Times* how his father's words had been misconstrued: "When he said necessities, he was thinking experience. As for the buoyancy thing, growing up, we always used to hear about my dad's experiences in the Navy and World War II. One of his jobs was to work with the recruits when they had to make a high dive into a tank to simulate falling off an aircraft carrier. My dad would tell us how a lot of the Blacks would sink to the bottom ... My dad thought it was because they had a low fat content in their bodies and because a lot of them didn't have their own swimming pool or a place to swim growing up ... You have to remember, my dad was not a silver-tongued devil like Tommy Lasorda. If Tommy said something he regretted, he could get out of it. My dad is more the strong, silent type."[29]

Regardless of the meaning behind Campanis's poor choice of words, the ordeal highlighted the lack of minorities in leadership positions. At the time, there were no Black managers in the majors, Triple-A, or Double-A and not a single general manager of color. "He just said what a lot of people have been thinking for years," said Frank Robinson, who in 1975 had become the first Black manager in the majors. "I'm glad it's finally out in the open, so we can address it."[30]

Campanis, the architect of the greatest draft class in MLB history and an incredibly successful baseball executive, would never work in organized baseball again. He died on June 21, 1998, at the age of eighty-one.

TO REPLACE CAMPANIS, THE DODGERS PROMOTED FORMER SPORTSWRITER Fred Claire, who had first joined the front office as publicity director in 1969, just weeks after he suited up for Lasorda's Spokane club in an exhibition game on the backfields of Dodgertown. In the mid '70s, the Dodgers elevated Claire to vice president of public relations and promotions. In that capacity, he launched the famed Dodger Blue promotional campaign.

As GM in 1988, Claire oversaw a roster that won another NL West title—Lasorda's sixth in his twelve years at the helm. Staff ace Hershiser won 23 games and led the league in innings pitched, shutouts, and complete games, propelling the Dodgers to an NLCS showdown against the Mets. LA upset a New York squad that had won 100 games, advancing to the World Series to face a formidable Oakland A's team that had won 104. After a barely mobile Kirk Gibson made the impossible happen with a two-run, walk-off home run against the seemingly untouchable Dennis Eckersley in Game 1, Hershiser won Games 2 and 5, cementing the Dodgers' sixth championship.

Lasorda's Dodgers wouldn't return to the playoffs until '95, making a quick exit in the NLDS. The following June, the longtime skipper suffered a heart attack and required an angioplasty to stent a clogged coronary artery. Peter O'Malley, Claire, and Lasorda met several times over the ensuing weeks to discuss whether Lasorda would return to the dugout. Ultimately, O'Malley put the ball in Lasorda's court. "Tommy," said O'Malley, "if you want to continue to manage, you can go down to the clubhouse and put on your uniform and manage. It's up to you."[31] Lasorda felt conflicted. He thought of the sudden deaths of Don Drysdale and scout Don McMahon and wanted to avoid their fate. But baseball was his life. He maintained no hobbies or other interests. Ultimately, he made the difficult decision to step down after a heart to heart with Jo, who didn't think he should manage again. When Lasorda informed the team, O'Malley immediately gave him a front-office position as a vice president and goodwill ambassador.

Lasorda managed the Dodgers for parts of twenty-one seasons, during which he compiled 1,599 wins, 1,439 losses, seven division titles, four NL pennants, and two World Series championships. At the time of his retirement, he ranked twenty-second on the all-time wins list, and his 61 postseason games managed stood second behind Casey Stengel. As of 2025, only four other managers in baseball history—Connie Mack, John McGraw, Walter Alston, and Bobby Cox—had a longer tenure of consecutive seasons with one team.

Unquestionably, the Dodgers' success under Lasorda can in part be attributed to the team's superb scouting and development system, which remained an organizational strength relative to the rest of the league through the end of the twentieth century. Although they never came close to replicating their success in the '68 draft (nor has any other team), the Dodgers drafted five pitchers during the '70s who would pitch sixteen or more seasons in the majors—Rick Rhoden, Rick Sutcliffe, Dave Stewart, Bob Welch, and Orel Hershiser. The so-called "Me Decade" also saw LA draft three position players who would later start for the '88 championship team—catcher Mike Scioscia, right fielder Mike Marshall, and second baseman Steve Sax. And the hits kept coming. Between 1979 and 1996, the Dodgers, despite consistently picking low in the draft, boasted nine Rookies of the Year: Sutcliffe, Steve Howe, Fernando Valenzuela, Sax, Eric Karros, Mike Piazza, Raúl Mondesí, Hideo Nomo, and Todd Hollandsworth.* Valenzuela (Mexico), Mondesi (Dominican Republic), and Nomo (Japan) were products of the Dodgers' expanded international scouting efforts. During that same period, LA also signed future All-Star pitcher Chan Ho Park (South Korea) and eventual Hall of Famers Pedro Martínez and Adrian Beltré (Dominican Republic).

Lasorda's boundless enthusiasm, eternal optimism, and motivational tactics also played an important yet immeasurable role in his team's

---

* As adept as the Dodgers remained under scouting director Ben Wade, there were notable swings and misses. In 1980, Mike Brito recommended outfielder Eric Davis from Fremont High School in Los Angeles. The Dodgers ignored Brito's advice and Davis became a star with the Cincinnati Reds. Three years later, the Dodgers whiffed with the eighteenth pick of the draft, selecting pitcher Erik Sonberg over Roger Clemens, whom the Boston Red Sox chose with the very next pick.

success. Piazza and Karros, like Bobby Valentine and Bill Buckner a generation earlier, viewed Lasorda as a second father. "There wasn't a day that went by where he wasn't impacting us in some way," said Karros. "The impact that Tommy has had on those who have played for him as well as those he met outside the game is infinite. … His passion, desire to teach, his competitiveness, and most importantly, his love for his players, made him a unique and special man."[32]

The Dodgers promoted bench coach Bill Russell to replace Lasorda. The two men couldn't have been more different. Lasorda was loud and profane. Russell was quiet and unemotional. It was as if someone had changed the radio dial from heavy metal to NPR. The transition caused a palpable vibe shift within the clubhouse but did not prevent the Dodgers from securing the NL wild card, though they were summarily swept by the Braves in the NLDS.

Team brass gave Russell a two-year extension after the season. Lasorda hoped his longtime player and coach would lean on him for advice and keep him involved, but he never did. And Lasorda never forgave him for it. "Billy Russell was so worried about being undermined," Lasorda surmised, "but he had to understand that by not communicating well with the players, he was just undermining himself."[33]

In 1997, the veteran's committee elected Lasorda to the National Baseball Hall of Fame. Although the induction was a time to celebrate his illustrious career, Lasorda caused a stir with comments he made during a press conference in Cooperstown. When Tom Keegan of the *New York Post* asked what current manager Lasorda would choose if he were running a front office, Lasorda said he'd take Bobby Valentine.[34,]* Ouch. Reminiscent of Don Sutton's *Washington Post* quote about Steve Garvey and Reggie Smith, Lasorda simultaneously demonstrated his respect for Valentine and disdain for Russell.

At the time of Lasorda's controversial comment, Valentine was in his first full season as Mets manager following an eight-year stint with the

---

* Lasorda's answer angered Claire, who feared that the Dodgers could be charged with tampering. Lasorda said in the same press conference that he'd like to be a GM, leading some to speculate Lasorda was politicking to become Dodgers GM under the team's prospective new owner, Rupert Murdoch.

Rangers from 1985 until midway through '92. He went on to manage in Queens for six full seasons, piloting the Mets to the NL pennant in 2000. Three years into his Mets tenure, Valentine took a page out of his mentor's book, going incognito following an ejection in a game against the Toronto Blue Jays. The image of Valentine sitting in the dugout with a fake mustache and sunglasses remains one of the indelible images from his long managerial career. He even got a bobblehead out of the stunt—along with a $5,000 fine and two-game suspension.

Valentine also managed the Chiba Lotte Marines in Japan's Nippon Professional Baseball, first in 1995, and then again from 2004 through '09. Always putting his team's supporters first, he fostered a fan-friendly environment at the Marines' home ballpark, which is now called ZOZO Marine Stadium. The skipper invited kids on the field to run the bases and worked with the team to stage karaoke events where players would sing songs with fans before and after games. Valentine, just like his mentor, preached the power of positive thinking. His players bought in, as did the fans. When the Marines made the playoffs in 2005, thousands of spectators held signs that read, "I BELIEVE!" The Marines swept the Hanshin Tigers in the Japan Series for the team's first championship in thirty-one years. Valentine's final managerial opportunity came in 2012 with the Red Sox, a tenure that ended after one disappointing season. In parts of sixteen seasons as a major-league skipper, Valentine won 1,186 games, registering a winning percentage of .504. He won another 494 games in Japan.

In March of 1998, Peter O'Malley sold the Dodgers to Fox Group—a media company owned by Rupert Murdoch—for $311 million. In his book *My 30 Years in Dodger Blue*, Claire cited several reasons for O'Malley's decision: escalating player salaries, estate planning for the O'Malley family, residual damage from the 1994 players' strike, and the mayor's decision to drop plans for a football stadium in Chavez Ravine.

On June 22, 1998, new ownership fired Claire and Russell in tandem. Team president Bob Graziano asked Lasorda to step in as interim GM. The last threads of the frayed relationship between Russell and Lasorda were broken after Russell implied Lasorda had a hand in his dismissal. When the Dodgers hired Kevin Malone as their new GM in September 1998, Lasorda moved into a senior vice-president role, serving in the mostly ceremonial role of special advisor and goodwill ambassador. Much to his dismay, the club's new leadership shut him out of important baseball decisions.

At the 2000 Summer Olympics in Sydney, Australia, seventy-two-year-old Tommy Lasorda returned to the dugout as manager of the United States baseball team. Even before he knew the players on his roster, Lasorda boasted that the United States would beat a mighty Cuban team that had never lost in the Olympics. He displayed the same fortitude that got him to the big leagues, the same conviction that allowed him to declare that the 1970 Spokane Indians would win the PCL, and the same confidence that propelled the Dodgers to a World Series upset over the A's in 1988. The U.S. team, comprised of mostly collegiates and minor leaguers, bonded over a casino brawl in Australia. Sound familiar? Lasorda retained his desire to win at all costs. Besides arguing with umpires, he ignored pitch-count limits placed on Ben Sheets, letting the starter go the distance in the gold-medal game. Just as Lasorda predicted, the U.S. beat Cuba to bring home the gold. He considered it his greatest professional achievement.

When Frank McCourt bought the Dodgers in 2004, he welcomed Lasorda back into the fold as a special adviser. The Hall-of-Fame manager remained a fixture in the owner's box near the Dodgers' dugout after the franchise changed hands again in 2012, continuing to attend games into his nineties. In 2020, the Dodgers played the Tampa Bay Rays in the World Series. Lasorda made the trip to Arlington, Texas, a neutral site where the Series was held because of the COVID-19 pandemic. Sitting in a suite alongside Bobby Valentine, he watched the Dodgers win their first title in thirty-two years. Lasorda died just a few months later, on January 9, 2021. He spent seventy-one of his ninety-three years in the Dodgers organization.

THOSE WHO CROSSED PATHS WITH LASORDA RECALLED HIS UNIQUENESS. As former Dodgers GM Ned Colletti described, "He could make you laugh. He could motivate you. He could bring you confidence. He could question something to get you to think differently. And he could love you. And he could do all of that in about five minutes. There's only one of him. There's only one."[35]

Tom Paciorek expressed similar sentiments. Lasorda was the first person Wimpy met in professional baseball as a Rookie ball outfielder in Ogden, Utah. "I thought everybody was going to be like him," said Paciorek decades later. "Well, it's been nearly sixty years, and I still haven't come across the second coming of Lasorda. He had such a dynamic personality. He was one of a kind. Never to be duplicated."[36]

Because he had such a large personality, Lasorda naturally had his share of detractors. As one UPI scribe put it in 1988, some within baseball circles viewed him as an "overweight loudmouth who spouts baseball cliches and hogs the limelight as if it were a plate of pasta."[37] Others called him a phony and a con man. But those who knew Lasorda best discovered that his enthusiasm and competitive spirit were authentic. The expression "what you see is what you get" fit him to a tee. And to the hundreds of men who played for him—be it in Ogden, Spokane, winter ball, or the majors—he was family. If someone needed an autographed photo for charity or a speaker at a booster club fundraiser, Lasorda obliged. If a former player visited Los Angeles or ran into his former skipper on the road, Lasorda provided him with complimentary tickets and welcomed him into the Dodgers clubhouse. "Most of the opposing players hated him because he was very animated and boisterous," recalled fourteen-year major leaguer Dave LaRoche. "He was all about his guys. He was always getting on the umpires. But then I had the opportunity to play for him in winter ball, and I loved him. He was great to play for. I played with him for a month, and he never forgot me, never forgot my wife. If he saw me, he remembered my name, he'd come over and talk to me like I was his son. He made you feel great."[38]

John Werhas, a former Dodger and Hawaii Islander whose friendship with Lasorda began six decades earlier, officiated Lasorda's graveside service ten days after his death. Werhas, who became an ordained minister after his playing career, had been a struggling twenty-three-year-old minor leaguer in Greenville, South Carolina, when he first met Lasorda, a young scout at the time. "I got off to a terrible start," recalled Werhas. "And he came in to town to pump me up. He talked to me for a half-hour, telling me how great I was and how great of a career I was going to have. He became a dear friend after that."[39] Fifty-seven years after Lasorda eulogized Willie Crawford's grandfather, Crawford's former teammate, John Werhas, eulogized Lasorda.

A number of former players spoke at Lasorda's memorial services at

Dodger Stadium and Rose Hills Memorial Park, including Eric Karros, whose son, Kyle, fittingly played for the Spokane Indians in 2024. "The loyalty, the love, the passion with which he did everything was second to none," said the elder Karros. "He had a heck of a run."[40]

Second to none and a heck of a run. Just like the Dodgers' draft class of '68.

NOTES

PREFACE

1. David Schoenfield, "'68 Dodgers Still Have Greatest Draft Ever," June 6, 2011, https://www.espn.com/blog/sweetspot/post/_/id/11946/68-dodgers-still-have-greatest-draft-ever.
2. Allan Simpson, ed., *Baseball America's Ultimate Draft Book* (Durham: Baseball America, 2016), 67.
3. Jim Callis, "Here are the 10 Best Draft Hauls of All Time," July 11, 2025, https://www.mlb.com/news/the-top-10-mlb-draft-classes-of-all-time.
4. Chuck Stewart, "Sport Stew," *Spokane Chronicle*, September 8, 1970: 17.

1. LAST OF THE BONUS BABIES

1. Tommy Lasorda and David Fisher, *The Artful Dodger* (New York: Arbor House, 1985), 115.
2. Melvin Durslag, "Finley's Wonder Boy," *Warren Times Mirror*, June 26, 1964: 10.
3. Matt Kelly and Craig Muder, "Caught in the Draft," https://baseballhall.org/discover-more/stories/baseball-history/caught-in-the-draft.
4. Pat Gillick, interview with the author, January 2, 2025.
5. Durslag, "Finley's Wonder Boy."
6. Durslag, "Finley's Wonder Boy."
7. Edwin Shrake, "The Richest Bonus Baby Ever," *Sports Illustrated*, July 6, 1964, https://vault.si.com/vault/1964/07/06/the-richest-bonus-baby-ever.
8. "The Odyssey of a Bonus Baby," https://www.youtube.com/watch?v=PmGf46uGjr4&t=908s.
9. Shrake, "The Richest Bonus Baby Ever."
10. Clifford Kachline, "'Silly Season' in Big Time—Bonus Boys Rake in Chips," *The Sporting News*, June 21, 1961: 17.

2. MAJOR LEAGUE BASEBALL ADOPTS AN AMATEUR DRAFT

1. Bob Oates, "Free-Agent Draft—Death of a Salesman," *The Sporting News*, January 30, 1965: 2.
2. Bob Maisel, "The Morning After," *Baltimore Sun*, October 31, 1964: 17.
3. Russell Schneider, "LA Officials Strike Back," *Cleveland Plain Dealer*, November 21, 1964: 35.
4. Russell Schneider, "Paul Calls LA Officials 'Pied Pipers'; Deal on Fire?" *Cleveland Plain Dealer*, November 22, 1964: 52.
5. "Baseball Upset; Free Agent Draft Set," *Los Angeles Times*, December 3, 1964: 49.
6. Ernest Mehl, "Sporting Comment," *Kansas City Star*, December 11, 1964: 35.
7. Johnny Bench, interview with John Erling, "Johnny Bench: Oklahoma Baseball Player

& Legendary Catcher," *Voices of Oklahoma*, March 28, 2012, https://voicesofoklahoma.com/interviews/bench-johnny/.
8. Joe McDonald, interview with the author, August 7, 2024.
9. Milton Gross, "Baseball Draft Mixed Blessing," *Pasadena Independent*, June 8, 1965: 15.
10. Craig Dolch, "First Baseball Draft in 1965 was Riddled with Errors," *Springfield News-Sun*, June 1, 1992: 7.
11. Pat Gillick, interview with the author, January 2, 2025.
12. Colin Gunderson, *Tommy Lasorda: My Way* (Chicago: Triumph Books, 2015), 45.
13. Simpson, *Baseball America's Ultimate Draft Book*, 28.
14. Joe McDonald, interview with the author, August 7, 2024.
15. Bench, interview with Erling.
16. Bruce Weber, "Tom Seaver Dies at 75; Led Mets from Cellar to Miracle," *New York Times*, September 2, 2020: A1.
17. Simpson, *Baseball America's Ultimate Draft Book*, 31.
18. Dolch, "First Baseball Draft in 1965 was Riddled with Errors."

3. From Norristown to "The Show"

1. Bill Plaschke and Tommy Lasorda, *I Live for This: Baseball's Last True Believer* (Boston: Houghton Mifflin, 2007), 8.
2. Gunderson, *Tommy Lasorda: My Way*, 43.
3. Kevin Kerrane, *Dollar Sign on the Muscle: The World of Baseball Scouting* (CreateSpace Independent Publishing, 2013), 224.
4. Plaschke and Lasorda, *I Live for This*, 35.
5. Plaschke and Lasorda, *I Live for This*, 42.
6. Bill Shirley, "Dodgertown," *Los Angeles Times*, March 9, 1986: 43.
7. Lasorda and Fisher, *The Artful Dodger*, 26.
8. Milton Richman, "'Tommy' Climbs Dodger Ladder," *Deseret News*, December 5, 1968: 76.
9. Zack Minasian, *Lasorda University: A Recollection of My Summer with Tommy Lasorda and the Ogden Dodgers* (Self-published, 2022), 11.
10. Harold C. Burr, "Tom Lasorda Starts War in Puerto Rico," *Brooklyn Eagle*, December 24, 1954: 14.
11. Frank Vehorn, "Tommy Lasorda Would Not Quit Baseball for Batista," *Columbia Record*, July 2, 1962: 17.
12. Mike Downey, "The Stories Never Stopped, but Neither Did the Abuse," *Los Angeles Times*, June 9, 1995: 197.
13. Geroge Beahon, "The Tommy Lasorda Story: Only One Way to Play," *Rochester Democrat and Chronicle*, December 6, 1962: 51.
14. Beahon, "The Tommy Lasorda Story: Only One Way to Play."
15. Lasorda and Fisher, *The Artful Dodger*, 98.
16. Tommy Hutton, interview with the author, December 11, 2024.
17. Lasorda and Fisher, *The Artful Dodger*, 123.

4. Dodgers Draft Hough and Russell

1. Kerrane, *Dollar Sign on the Muscle*, 105.
2. Charlie Hough, interview with the author, August 11, 2024.

3. Pat Gillick, interview with the author, January 2, 2025.
4. Barney Kremenko, "'Best in Years'—That's 1966 Free-Agent Crop," *The Sporting News*, June 18, 1966: 5.
5. Joe McDonald, interview with the author, August 7, 2024.
6. Larry Hutton, interview with the author, August 1, 2024.
7. Gunderson, *Tommy Lasorda: My Way*, 76.
8. Larry Hutton, interview with the author, August 1, 2024.
9. Erik Jensen, email to the author, October 16, 2024.
10. Erik Jensen, email to the author, October 16, 2024.
11. Michael Criscione, email to the author, July 26, 2024.
12. Michael Criscione, email to the author, July 26, 2024.
13. Dick Young, "Young Ideas," *Daily News*, October 1, 1966: 30.

5. Turmoil in LA, Another Pennant in Ogden

1. Buzzie Bavasi, "The Great Holdout," *Sports Illustrated*, May 15, 1967, https://vault.si.com/vault/1967/05/15/the-great-holdout.
2. Michael Leahy, *The Last Innocents: The Collision of the Turbulent Sixties and the Los Angeles Dodgers*, (New York: Harper, 2016), 345.
3. Leahy, *The Last Innocents*, 346.
4. Steve Delsohn, *True Blue: The Dramatic History of the Los Angeles Dodgers, Told by the Men Who Live It*, (New York: Harper Collins, 2001), 86.
5. Fisher, "Pros Losing Love of Sport Says Lasorda."
6. Charles Maher, "Sandy's Fear of Permanent Injury Told," *Los Angeles Times*, November 19, 1966: 25.
7. "Induction Statistics," Selective Service System website, https://www.sss.gov/history-and-records/induction-statistics/.
8. Charlie Bevis, Draftees and Enlistments, 1965 to 1969, Bevis Baseball Research website, https://bevisbaseballresearch.wordpress.com/research-archive/vietnam-war-impact-to-professional-baseball-1964-to-1969/draftees-1965-to-1969.
9. Kara Hall, interview with the author, August 14, 2024.
10. Kara Hall, interview with the author, August 14, 2024.
11. Larry Burchart, interview with the author, October 30, 2024.
12. Minasian, *Lasorda University*, 34.
13. Larry Burchart, interview with the author, October 30, 2024.
14. Charles Maher, "Dodger Farm Deficiencies Blamed on Baseball Draft," *Los Angeles Times*, June 15, 1967: 54.
15. Maher, "Dodger Farm Deficiencies Blamed on Baseball Draft."

6. The Scouts

1. George Vecsey, "Seeds of Success from a Watermelon," *The New York Times*, May 9, 1981: 17.
2. Al Campanis, internal memo to all full-time and part-time Dodgers scouts, September 13, 1961. Obtained from the Al Campanis clipping file at the National Baseball Hall of Fame Library and Research Center.
3. Don Bryant, "Point Blank," *Lincoln Star*, January 20, 1958: 7.
4. Mike Waldner, "Campanis' Influence," *Daily Breeze*, March 25, 1966: 37.

5. Richard Goldstein, "Hugh Alexander, 83, a Scout for the Next Stars of Baseball," *The New York Times*, November 29, 2000: A33.

7. A Philosophy Shift

1. Ross Newhan, "Lopes Does His Stealing on the Base Paths," *Los Angeles Times*, July 26, 1973: 43.
2. Tim Keown, "Too Truthful for His Own Good, Davey Lopes has the Shot He Should've Gotten," https://www.espn.com/espn/magazine/archives/news/story?page=magazine-20000221-article10.
3. Newhan, "Lopes Does His Stealing on the Base Paths."
4. Todd Fertig, "Time as Ichabod Helped Shape Lopes into Big Leaguer," *Topeka Capital-Journal*, June 24, 2014, https://www.cjonline.com/story/sports/college/2014/06/25/time-ichabod-helped-shape-lopes-big-leaguer/16665017007/.
5. Bernie Bianchino, interview with the author, November 5, 2024.
6. Mark Elliott, interview with the author, November 6, 2024.
7. Fertig, "Time as Ichabod Helped Shape Lopes into Big Leaguer."
8. Mark Langill, "Draft Dodgers," *Sport*, July 1993: 49.
9. Ken Gurnick, "Dodgers Adapt to Change, Stage Best Draft of All Time," *Baseball America*, June 10, 1988: 19.
10. Gurnick, "Dodgers Adapt to Change, Stage Best Draft of All Time."
11. Bill Pennington, "Valentine Reunited with Baseball Through Luck and Loyalty," *New York Times*, February 18, 2012: D1.
12. Pennington, "Valentine Reunited with Baseball Through Luck and Loyalty."
13. Ken Borsuk, "Bobby Valentine Talks About the Importance of Luck," *Connecticut Post*, November 16, 2016, https://www.ctpost.com/local/article/Bobby-Valentine-talks-about-the-importance-of-luck-10619765.php.
14. Bobby Valentine and Peter Golenbock, *Valentine's Way: My Adventurous Life and Times* (New York: Permuted Press, 2021), 19.
15. Valentine and Golenbock, *Valentine's Way*, 23.
16. Bob Buckner, interview with the author, February 2, 2025.
17. Bob Buckner, interview with the author, February 2, 2025.
18. Bob Buckner, interview with the author, February 2, 2025.
19. Bob Hunter, "Slugger Garvey Brightest of Hot Dodger Prospects," *The Sporting News*, October 4, 1969: 10.
20. Simpson, *Baseball America's Ultimate Draft Book*, 69.
21. Ross Newhan, "Valentine Tabbed Dodger Leader of Future," *Los Angeles Times*, March 3, 1970: 43.

8. June Haul

1. "RFK was Nearly Dead on Arrival," *Minneapolis Star*, June 5, 1968: 81.
2. Simpson, *Baseball America's Ultimate Draft Book*, 70.
3. Joe McDonald, interview with the author, August 7, 2024.
4. Joseph Durso, "Snyder Drafts Pitcher for Montreal," *New York Times*, June 7, 1968: 44.
5. Steve Garvey and Skip Rozin, *Garvey* (New York: Times Books, 1986), 27.
6. Peter J. Boyer, "The Intimate Steve Garvey," *Los Angeles Times*, September 24, 1989: 392.
7. Bill Linne, interview with the author, November 3, 2024.

8. Bill Linne, interview with the author, November 3, 2024.
9. Jim Fanning, scouting report of Steve Garvey, National Baseball Hall of Fame and Museum Archives.
10. Garvey and Rozin, *Garvey*, 42.
11. Mark Heisler, "The Dodgers Test Age-Old Theory," *Los Angeles Times*, June 24, 1981: 54.
12. Gary Brenzel, interview with the author, August 16, 2024.
13. Gurnick, "Dodgers Adapt to Change, Stage Best Draft of All Time."
14. Bobby Valentine, interview with the author, September 3, 2024.
15. John Altavilla, "Valentine Didn't Miss Many Dances," *Hartford Courant*, December 21, 1999: 117.
16. Bob Buckner, interview with the author, February 2, 2025.
17. Tom Paciorek, interview with the author, September 25, 2024.
18. Tom Paciorek, interview with the author, September 25, 2024.
19. Jack Zerby, "Sandy Vance," SABR BioProject, https://sabr.org/bioproj/person/sandy-vance/.
20. Sandy Vance, email to the author, June 20, 2024.
21. Pete Scarpati, interview with the author, December 6, 2024.

9. The '68 Ogden Dodgers

1. Valentine and Golenbock, *Valentine's Way*, 26.
2. Minasian, *Lasorda University*, 85.
3. Bobby Valentine, interview with the author, September 3, 2024.
4. Minasian, *Lasorda University*, 85.
5. Gunderson, *Tommy Lasorda: My Way*, 34.
6. Minasian, *Lasorda University*, 30.
7. Gunderson, *Tommy Lasorda: My Way*, 49.
8. Tom Paciorek, interview with the author, September 25, 2024.
9. Minasian, *Lasorda University*, 98-99.
10. Minasian, *Lasorda University*, 100.
11. Tom Paciorek, interview with the author, September 25, 2024.
12. Sandy Vance, email to the author, June 20, 2024.
13. Tom Paciorek, interview with the author, September 25, 2024.
14. Minasian, *Lasorda University*, 87.
15. Tom Paciorek, interview with the author, September 25, 2024.
16. Tom Paciorek, interview with the author, September 25, 2024.
17. Charles Maher, "Dodgers in Race," *Los Angeles Times*, August 20, 1968: 36.
18. Leahy, *The Last Innocents*, 441.
19. Shlomo Sprung, "Buckner Showed Talent, Character in Minors," May 31, 2019, https://www.milb.com/news/steve-garvey-remembers-bill-buckner-s-minor-league-career-307574000.
20. Minasian, *Lasorda University*, 96.
21. Sandy Vance, email to the author, June 20, 2024.
22. Tom Paciorek, interview with the author, September 25, 2024.
23. Fred Nelson, interview with the author, July 24, 2025.
24. Minasian, *Lasorda University*, 195.
25. Minasian, *Lasorda University*, 93.
26. Sandy Vance, email to the author, June 20, 2024.

27. "Ogden Clubhouse 'Erupts' After Win," *Ogden Standard-Examiner*, August 31, 1968: 4.

10. An Organization in Transition

1. Buzzie Bavasi, "The Real Secret of Trading," *Sports Illustrated*, June 5, 1967, https://vault.si.com/vault/1967/06/05/the-real-secret-of-trading.
2. Hank Hollingworth, "Dodgers Have No Spark Left," *Long Beach Independent Press-Telegram*, August 2, 1968: 27.
3. Hollingworth, "Dodgers Have No Spark Left."
4. John Hall, "Dodger Tragedy," *Los Angeles Times*, October 4, 1968: 47.
5. Jim Campanis Jr., interview with the author, February 22, 2025.
6. Milton Richman, "'Tommy' Climbs Dodger Ladder," *Deseret News*, December 5, 1968: 76.
7. Sandy Vance, email to the author, June 20, 2024.
8. Fred Claire and Steve Springer, *Fred Claire: My 30 Years in Dodger Blue* (Sports Publishing LLC, 2004), 78.
9. Fred Claire, "Scribe Blows Chance to Wow Dodger Brass," *Long Beach Independent Press-Telegram*, March 29, 1969: 13.
10. Chuck Stewart, "Sport Stew," *Spokane Daily Chronicle*, April 17, 1969: 30.
11. Harry Missildine, "If You Can Get One, Take Two," *Spokesman-Review*, April 29, 1969: 10.
12. Lasorda and Fisher, *The Artful Dodger*, 147.
13. Zack Minasian, interview with the author, November 7, 2024.
14. Bobby Valentine, interview with the author, September 3, 2024.
15. Valentine and Golenbock, *Valentine's Way*, 41.
16. Valentine and Golenbock, *Valentine's Way*, 41.
17. Mike Lynch, "The Philosophy of Belief: Indian Guru Tom Lasorda," *Spokesman-Review*, April 20, 1969: 40.
18. Bruce Brubaker, interview with the author, December 6, 2024.
19. Harry Missildine, "Twice Over Lightly," *Spokesman-Review*, September 3, 1969: 12.
20. Bobby Valentine, interview with the author, September 3, 2024.
21. Bobby Valentine, interview with the author, September 3, 2024.
22. Bruce Brubaker, interview with the author, December 6, 2024.
23. Valentine and Golenbock, *Valentine's Way*, 46.
24. Lloyd Allen, email to the author, March 12, 2025.
25. Bob Buckner, interview with the author, February 2, 2025.
26. Lasorda and Fisher, *The Artful Dodger*, 149.
27. Bobby Valentine, interview with the author, September 3, 2024.

11. Coconut Snatching

1. Charlie Hough, interview with the author, August 11, 2024.
2. Charlie Hough, interview with the author, August 11, 2024.
3. Charlie Hough, interview with the author, August 11, 2024.
4. Gunderson, *Tommy Lasorda: My Way*, 75.
5. Steve Wulf, "Bring on the Coconut Snatchers," *Sports Illustrated*, May 30, 1983, https://vault.si.com/vault/1983/05/30/bring-on-the-coconut-snatchers.

6. Ross Newhan, "Ferguson Thinks His Way to Stardom," *The Sporting News*, June 9, 1973: 3.
7. Ross Newhan, "'Green Phantom' Strikes at Dodgertown," *Los Angeles Times*, March 28, 1970: 37.
8. Joe Moeller, interview with the author, May 23, 2025.
9. Marv Galliher, email to the author, December 9, 2024.
10. Lasorda and Fisher, *The Artful Dodger*, 149.

12. TERMITE PALACE

1. Walt Hriniak, interview with the author, February 10, 2025.
2. Darcy Fast, interview with the author, February 8, 2025.
3. Chuck Stewart, "Sport Stew," *Spokane Daily Chronicle*, April 18, 1970: 10.
4. John Werhas, interview with the author, June 28, 2024.
5. Winston Llenas, interview with the author, February 26, 2025.
6. Jeff Pentland, interview with the author, August 4, 2024.
7. John Werhas, interview with the author, June 28, 2024.
8. Harvey Shank, interview with the author, July 17, 2024.
9. Gene Rounsaville, interview with the author, July 10, 2024.
10. Al Michaels and L. Jon Wertheim, *You Can't Make This Up: Miracles, Memories, and the Perfect Marriage of Sports and Television* (New York: Harper Collins, 2014), 34.
11. Rory Costello, "Honolulu Stadium," Society for American Baseball Research, https://sabr.org/bioproj/park/honolulu-stadium/.
12. Bob O'Brien, interview with the author, June 27, 2024.
13. Pete Scarpati, interview with the author, December 6, 2024.
14. Bobby Valentine, interview with the author, September 3, 2024.
15. Bobby Valentine, interview with the author, September 3, 2024.
16. Darcy Fast, interview with the author, February 8, 2025.
17. Larry Colton, interview with the author, December 30, 2024.
18. Sandy Vance, email to the author, June 20, 2024.
19. Sandy Vance, email to the author, June 20, 2024.
20. Sandy Vance, email to the author, June 20, 2024.
21. Sandy Vance, email to the author, June 20, 2024.

13. THE OPENING HOMESTAND

1. Vincent X. Flaherty, "The Miracle Move of the Dodgers: From Flatbush to Fantasia, https://www.walteromalley.com/dodger-history/the-miracle-move-of-the-dodgers/.
2. Dick Young, "Dodgers Fly Off to L.A.? Next 6 Months to Tell," *Daily News*, February 12, 1957: 3.
3. Andy McCue, *Mover & Shaker* (Lincoln: University of Nebraska Press, 2014), 141.
4. Tom Larwin, "Elten Schiller" Society for American Baseball Research BioProject, https://sabr.org/bioproj/person/elten-schiller/.
5. Steve Sogge, email to the author, March 11, 2024.
6. Sprung, "Buckner Showed Talent, Character in Minors."
7. John Hall, "The Hex is Alive," *Los Angeles Times*, May 1, 1970: 52.
8. Charlie Hough, interview with the author, August 11, 2024.
9. Charlie Hough, interview with the author, August 11, 2024.

14. Jaw Breaker

1. Bobby Valentine, interview with the author, September 3, 2024.
2. Pete Scarpati, interview with the author, December 6, 2024.
3. Sandy Vance, email to the author, June 20, 2024.
4. Bobby Valentine, interview with the author, September 3, 2024.
5. Ken Schultz, interview with the author, June 10, 2024.
6. Bobby Valentine, interview with the author, September 3, 2024.
7. Steve Sogge, email to the author, March 11, 2024.

15. Old Jerry

1. Dorian Chastain, interview with the author, July 11, 2025.
2. Dave Vaughn, interview with the author, June 6, 2024.
3. Ken Schultz, interview with the author, June 10, 2024.
4. Charlie Hough, interview with the author, August 11, 2024.
5. Bill Nowlin, "Jerry Stephenson," Society for American Baseball Research BioProject, https://sabr.org/bioproj/person/jerry-stephenson/.
6. Frank Peters, interview with the author, June 6, 2024.
7. Ron Cey and Ken Gurnick, *Penguin Power: Dodger Blue, Hollywood Lights, and My One-in-a-Million Big League Journey* (Chicago: Triumph Books, 2023), 52.
8. Mike Wilson, "I was a Batboy to the Stars," *Rutland Daily Herald*, June 30, 1983: 21.
9. Harry Missildine, "How it Looks to Stinson," *Spokesman-Review*, May 26, 1970: 10.
10. Greg Washburn, interview with the author, June 24, 2024.
11. Frank Peters, interview with the author, June 6, 2024.

16. The Hoodlum Priest

1. Tom Paciorek, interview with the author, September 25, 2024.
2. Tom Paciorek, interview with the author, September 25, 2024.
3. Bob Buckner, interview with the author, February 2, 2025.
4. Ken Schultz, interview with the author, June 10, 2024.
5. Herb Jenkins, interview with the author, July 25, 2024.
6. Jeff Schiller, email to the author, January 17, 2024.
7. Jeff Schiller, email to the author, January 17, 2024.
8. Jim Haller, interview with the author, November 22, 2024.
9. Jim Haller, interview with the author, November 22, 2024.
10. Jim Haller, interview with the author, November 22, 2024.

17. Hutton to Operating Room, Russell to LA

1. Tom Paciorek, interview with the author, September 25, 2024.
2. Chuck Stewart, "Buckner Smiling," *Spokane Daily Chronicle*, June 9, 1970: 13.
3. Jerry Nyman, interview with the author, August 6, 2024.
4. Jeff Pentland, interview with the author, August 4, 2024.
5. Brent Checketts, "Pads Turn Tables, Beat Indians Twice," *Deseret News*, June 15, 1970: 28.

6. Bart Shirley, interview with the author, July 24, 2024.
7. Ken Schultz, interview with the author, June 10, 2024.
8. Bobby Valentine, interview with the author, September 3, 2024.

18. The Power of Motivation

1. Plaschke and Lasorda, *I Live for This*, 150.
2. Bobby Valentine, interview with the author, September 3, 2024.
3. Don Merry, "Lopes Puts on Act and Steals the Show," *Los Angeles Times*, March 16, 1977: 47.
4. Bob O'Brien, interview with the author, June 27, 2024.
5. Tim Kurkjian, "Tommy Lasorda Loved the Dodgers and Loved Being Tommy Lasorda," January 8, 2021, https://www.espn.com/mlb/story/_/id/30331870/tommy-lasorda-loved-dodgers-loved-being-tommy-lasorda.

19. Good Old Days

1. Dave Vaughn, interview with the author, June 6, 2024.
2. Dave Vaughn, interview with the author, June 6, 2024.
3. Ross Newhan, "Lopes Does His Stealing on the Base Paths," *Los Angeles Times*, July 26, 1973: 48.
4. Bruce Brown, "Buckner's Guesses Good," *Spokane Daily Chronicle*, July 24, 1970: 23.
5. Bob O'Brien, interview with the author, June 27, 2024.
6. Sandy Vance, email to the author, June 20, 2024.
7. Sandy Vance, email to the author, June 20, 2024.
8. Sandy Vance, email to the author, June 20, 2024.
9. Greg Washburn, interview with the author, June 24, 2024.
10. Chuck Stewart, "Scrapping Tribe Rests," *Spokane Daily Chronicle*, July 27, 1970: 11.
11. Jim Price, email to the author, December 16, 2024.

20. Major-League Calls and Banquet Brawls

1. Charlie Hough, interview with the author, August 11, 2024.
2. Charlie Hough, interview with the author, August 11, 2024.
3. Sandy Vance, email to the author, June 20, 2024.
4. Chuck Stewart, "Indian Keeps Vow to Fans," *Spokane Daily Chronicle*, August 19, 1970: 13.
5. Larry Colton, interview with the author, December 30, 2024.
6. Larry Colton, interview with the author, December 30, 2024.
7. Bruce Brubaker, interview with the author, December 6, 2024.

21. Dougie

1. "Tommy Lasorda and Doug Rau's mound visit from the 1977 World Series," https://www.youtube.com/watch?v=AvFMEoKI7eE&t=34s
2. "Tommy Lasorda and Doug Rau's mound visit from the 1977 World Series."
3. "Tommy Lasorda and Doug Rau's mound visit from the 1977 World Series."

4. Doug Rau, interview with the author, March 5, 2025.
5. Doug Rau, interview with the author, March 5, 2025.
6. Ken Schultz, interview with the author, June 10, 2024.
7. Ken Schultz, interview with the author, June 10, 2024.
8. Doug Rau, interview with the author, March 5, 2025.
9. Ken Schultz, interview with the author, June 10, 2024.
10. Chuck Stewart, "Results Varies for Rookie, Vet," *Spokane Daily Chronicle*, August 31, 1970: 11.
11. Doug Rau, interview with the author, March 5, 2025.

22. Re-Creating Reality

1. David Eyre, Facebook message to the author, November 23, 2024.
2. Michaels and Wertheim, *You Can't Make This Up*, 33.
3. Harry Missildine, "Stephenson-Bennett Opener Likely," *Spokesman-Review*, September 2, 1970: 11.
4. Bart Shirley, interview with the author, July 26, 2024.
5. Larry Colton, interview with the author, December 30, 2024.
6. Jeff Pentland, interview with the author, August 4, 2024.
7. Larry Colton, interview with the author, December 30, 2024.
8. Ed Honeywell, "Scorer's Pencil a Help to Tribe's Bat Cause?" *Tacoma News Tribune*, September 3, 1970: 48.
9. Michaels and Wertheim, *You Can't Make This Up*, 35.
10. Chuck Stewart, "Playoffs are Next," *Spokane Daily Chronicle*, September 3, 1970: 17.
11. Missildine, "Stephenson-Bennett Opener Likely."

23. Heavyweight Fight

1. Ken Wilson, interview with the author, January 10, 2025.
2. Ken Wilson, interview with the author, January 10, 2025.
3. Chuck Stewart, "Spokane Winner; 2nd Tilt Tonight," *Spokane Daily Chronicle*, September 5, 1970: 20.
4. Hal Wood, "Tanner: 'Series Isn't Over Yet,'" *Honolulu Star-Advertiser*, September 7, 1970: 23.
5. Jim Hackleman, "Booing was Undeserved," *Honolulu Star-Bulletin*, September 7, 1970: 31.
6. Hackleman, Booing was Undeserved."
7. Greg Washburn, interview with the author, June 24, 2024.
8. Greg Washburn, interview with the author, June 24, 2024.

24. Like Butter

1. Michaels and Wertheim, *You Can't Make This Up*, 36.
2. Chuck Stewart, "Hawaii Nine Mauled 16-2; Valentine Suffers Injury," *Spokane Daily Chronicle*, September 8, 1970: 22.
3. Stewart, "Hawaii Nine Mauled 16-2; Valentine Suffers Injury."
4. Stewart, "Hawaii Nine Mauled 16-2; Valentine Suffers Injury."
5. Stewart, "Hawaii Nine Mauled 16-2; Valentine Suffers Injury."
6. Tommy Hutton, interview with the author, December 11, 2024.

7. Ken Wilson, interview with the author, January 10, 2025.
8. Bill Kwon, "Spokane Scalps Islanders, 16-2, and Wins PCL Pennant in Four," *Honolulu Star-Bulletin*," September 8, 1970: 33.
9. Bob O'Brien, interview with the author, June 27, 2024.
10. Marv Galliher, email to the author, December 9, 2024.
11. Chuck Stewart, "Valentine Not Bitter at Injury," *Spokane Chronicle*, September 9, 1970: 35.
12. John Werhas, interview with the author, June 28, 2024.
13. Chuck Stewart, interview with the author, January 10, 2025.
14. Chuck Stewart, interview with the author, January 10, 2025.
15. Brian Stephenson, interview with the author, July 23, 2024.
16. Chuck Stewart, "Spokane's Lasorda Chosen No. 1 Manager of Minors," *The Sporting News*, December 5, 1970: 34.
17. Tom Paciorek, interview with the author, September 25, 2024.
18. Bobby Valentine, interview with the author, September 3, 2024.

25. 1971

1. Jim Murray, "A Lesson in Larceny," *Los Angeles Times*, September 1, 1974: 51.
2. Gordon Verrell, "'Unexpected' is Middle Name of Leader Lopes," *The Sporting News*, August 26, 1978: 3.
3. Garvey and Rozin, *Garvey*, 59.
4. Charlie Hough, interview with the author, August 11, 2024.
5. Charlie Hough, interview with the author, August 11, 2024.
6. Tommy Hutton, interview with the author, December 11, 2024.
7. Tom Paciorek, interview with the author, July 23, 2025.
8. Zerby, "Sandy Vance."
9. Bob O'Brien, interview with the author, June 27, 2024.
10. Bob O'Brien, interview with the author, June 27, 2024.
11. Pete Scarpati, interview with the author, December 6, 2024.
12. Tom Paciorek, interview with the author, September 25, 2024.

26. Dukes and Angels

1. Doug Rau, interview with the author, March 5, 2025.
2. Delsohn, *True Blue*, 100.
3. Delsohn, *True Blue*, 100.
4. Lloyd Allen, email to the author, March 12, 2025.
5. Winston Llenas, interview with the author, February 26, 2025.

27. The '74 Series

1. "An Infusion of Fresh Dodger-Blue Blood," *Sports Illustrated*, February 20, 2008, https://www.si.com/more-sports/2008/02/20/lasorda-flashback.
2. Ross Newhan, "Buckner's Quotes Stir Up A's; Finley Reads Them to Squad," *Los Angeles Times*, October 17, 1975: 55.
3. Newhan, "Buckner's Quotes Stir Up A's; Finley Reads Them to Squad."

28. Loyalty Pays Dividends

1. "Born to be a Dodger," *Sports Illustrated*, April 7, 1975, https://vault.si.com/vault/1975/04/07/born-to-be-a-dodger.
2. Betty Cuniberti, "Garvey: The Exception More than the Rule," *San Bernardino Press-Telegram*, June 15, 1975: E11.
3. Winston Llenas, interview with the author, February 26, 2025.
4. Delsohn, *True Blue*, 125.
5. Ross Newhan, "If Fired, I Won't Cry," *Los Angeles Times*, September 19, 1976: 49.
6. Delsohn, *True Blue*, 119.
7. Valentine and Golenbock, *Valentine's Way*, 70.
8. Ross Newhan, "Buckner on Trade: 'I Feel Like a Piece of Meat,'" *Los Angeles Times*, January 13, 1977: 35.
9. Bob Buckner, interview with the author, February 2, 2025.
10. Ben Houser, "Buckner: 'I Try to Look at it in a Positive Way,'" October 6, 2006, https://www.espn.com/mlb/news/story?id=2615471.
11. Jim Campanis Jr., interview with the author, February 22, 2025.
12. Tom Paciorek, interview with the author, July 23, 2025.
13. Stan Grossfeld, "Error Doesn't Weigh," *Boston Globe*, October 23, 2003: 61, 65.
14. Mike Lupica, "Buckner on 'Curb' Made Larry David Well Up," May 27, 2019, https://www.mlb.com/news/bill-buckner-memorable-on-curb-your-enthusiasm.

29. Lasorda at the Helm

1. Delsohn, *True Blue*, 129.
2. John Hall, "The Leader," *Los Angeles Times*, October 6, 1977: 45.
3. Michael Fallon, *Dodgerland: Decadent Los Angeles and the 1977-78 Dodgers* (Lincoln: University of Nebraska Press, 2016), 184.
4. Ross Newhan, "The Good Scout," *Los Angeles Times*, January 17, 1978: 34.
5. Ross Newhan, "Lasorda Names Lopes Captain," *Los Angeles Times*, March 2, 1978: 45.
6. Keown, "Too Truthful for His Own Good, Davey Lopes has the Shot He Should've Gotten."
7. Ron Fimrite, "Blood on the Dodgers Blue," Sports Illustrated, September 4, 1978, https://vault.si.com/vault/1978/09/04/blood-on-the-dodger-blue-division-leaders-they-might-be-but-both-the-dodgers-and-phillies-were-in-misery-especially-that-quothappy-familyquot-in-la.
8. Plaschke and Lasorda, *I Live for This*, 127.
9. Plaschke and Lasorda, *I Live for This*, 127-28.
10. Delsohn, *True Blue*, 142.
11. Gordon Verrell, "Dodgers Shape Up After Clubhouse Tempest," *The Sporting News*, August 4, 1979: 8.
12. Dan Bartley, interview with the author, September 9, 2024.
13. Mark Heisler, "The Dodgers' Future Seems to Be in a Hurry to Get Here," *Los Angeles Times*, September 15, 1981: 29.
14. Delsohn, *True Blue*, 153.
15. Lasorda and Fisher, *The Artful Dodger*, 211.
16. Mark Heisler, "It May Go Down as the Sinker That Sank the Dodgers," *Los Angeles Times*, October 22, 1981: 43.
17. Garvey and Rozin, *Garvey*, 42.

18. Lasorda and Fisher, *The Artful Dodger*, 217.
19. Mike Littwin, "The Dodgers Wins Before That Old Gang is Broken Up," *Los Angeles Times*, October 29, 1981: 62.
20. Jim Murray, "The Dodgers' .667 Hitter is a Man with a Mission," *Los Angeles Times*, October 6, 1978: III-6.
21. Rick Reilly, "America's Sweetheart," *Sports Illustrated*, November 27, 1989, https://vault.si.com/vault/1989/11/27/americas-sweetheart-life-may-seem-an-idyll-for-steve-garvey-and-his-new-wife-candace-left-but-baseballs-mr-clean-is-the-butt-of-jokes-about-his-sex-life-and-he-says-he-is-broke.
22. "Oscar Notebook," *Fort Worth Star-Telegram*, March 30, 1989: 47.
23. Bruce Schoenfield, "Steve Garvey's Public Exile," *Street & Smith's Sports Business Daily Global Journal*, March 3, 2003.
24. Reilly, "America's Sweetheart."
25. "Al Campanis Cancels Himself on National TV," https://www.youtube.com/watch?v=DFb5kEnWnKk&t=26s.
26. Delsohn, *True Blue*, 182-83.
27. Steve Springer, "The Nightline That Rocked Baseball," *Los Angeles Times*, April 6, 1997: 55.
28. Delsohn, *True Blue*, 181.
29. Springer, "The Nightline That Rocked Baseball."
30. Peter Gammons, "The Campanis Affair," *Sports Illustrated*, April 20, 1987, https://vault.si.com/vault/1987/04/20/scorecard.
31. Claire and Springer, *Fred Claire: My 30 Years in Dodger Blue*, 151.
32. Minasian, *Lasorda University*, 1.
33. Plaschke and Lasorda, *I Live for This*, 195.
34. Bill Plaschke, "To Hall and Back," *Los Angeles Times*, August 4, 1997: 27.
35. Jack Harris, Mike DiGiovanna, and Maria Torres, "They Were Bursting at Seams," *Los Angeles Times*, January 9, 2021: D6.
36. Tom Paciorek, interview with the author, September 25, 2024.
37. Fred McMane, "Lasorda Deserving of Credit," *Arizona Republic*, October 22, 1988: 106.
38. Dave LaRoche, interview with the author, January 4, 2025.
39. John Werhas, interview with the author, June 28, 2024.
40. Juan Toribio, "Dodgers Hold Memorial Service for Lasorda," January 20, 2021, https://www.mlb.com/news/dodgers-hold-tommy-lasorda-memorial-service.

Acknowledgments

A few years ago, I wrote a book about the 1946 Spokane Indians, a team involved in a tragic bus accident that killed nine players. While digging into the franchise's history, I learned about the crazy-talented '70 team, which included a laundry list of eventual big leaguers whose baseball cards I collected growing up. Seeing the names on the roster transported me back to 1986—the year I opened my first pack of baseball cards. By that time, Davey Lopes and Ron Cey (Cubs), Bill Buckner (Red Sox), Steve Garvey (Padres), Tom Paciorek and Bobby Valentine (Rangers), Doyle Alexander (Blue Jays), and Geoff Zahn (Angels) had all moved on from the Dodgers. Only much later did I learn that each of these cardboard heroes were part of the greatest draft class in baseball history.

As I contemplated writing another book, I kept coming back to the Dodgers' class of '68, a group of players that won multiple minor-league championships and then formed the nucleus of four pennant-winning Dodgers teams, including three under the bombastic Tommy Lasorda. I wondered how the Dodgers pulled off such an amazing draft and wanted to know more about the early years of the amateur draft. At the same time, I thought it would be fun to take a deep dive into the '70 PCL season. As these thoughts percolated, the book's structure began to take shape.

Having the idea for a book is one thing, but doing the necessary reporting is another. As an oncology physician assistant who writes about baseball as a side passion, I have limited contacts in professional baseball. Enter Fred Claire. I had read Fred's fantastic book, *Extra Innings*, in which he details his journey as a patient at City of Hope. On a whim, I reached out and told him about my idea for this book. He responded with great enthusiasm and connected me with a few former players, including Bobby Valentine, who could not have been more gracious. From there, I was off and running. Fourteen months and seventy interviews later, I had written 90,000 words. Next, I had to find a publisher. Thankfully, Kevin Reichard and August Publications were willing to turn my Word document into a book.

Dozens of people shared their time and memories to make this book a reality. Pat Gillick and Joe McDonald, two of the few remaining attendees of MLB's inaugural amateur draft, shared vivid recollections of that historic event. Marv Galliher, Charlie Hough, Tommy Hutton, Bob O'Brien, Tom Paciorek, Doug Rau, Pete Scarpati, Bart Shirley, Steve Sogge, Bobby Valentine, and Sandy Vance retrieved memories and told stories of playing for Tommy Lasorda in Spokane more than a half-century ago. Likewise, Dorian Chastain, Jerry Kuntz, Jeff Schiller, Kent Schultz, Frank Steidl, Robert Steidl, and Dave Vaughn eagerly provided their unique perspectives from the summer of '70. Sadly, several members of the '70 Spokane Indians are no longer with us, but their relatives—Bob Buckner, Herb Jenkins, and Brian Stephenson—helped fill in the blanks.

Dave LaRoche, Winston Llenas, Harvey Shank, Greg Washburn, John Werhas, and Ken Wilson provided fond recollections of the '70 Hawaii Islanders, a team worthy of its own book. Other players from the Pacific Coast League players whose anecdotes brought this story to life included Lloyd Allen, Bruce Brubaker, Larry Colton, Darcy Fast, Walt Hriniak, Jerry Nyman, Jeff Pentland, Frank Peters, Skip Pitlock, and Gene Rounsaville.

Fred Nelson provided valuable insights from his dual perspectives as a member of the Dodgers' 1968 draft class who later became a scout and farm director. Several other former professional players with connections to the story offered their memories, including Larry Burchart, Michael Criscione, Jim Gentile, Kara Hall, Jim Haller, Larry Hutton, Carmine Marceno, and Joe Moeller.

Rachel Wells from the National Baseball Hall of Fame Library and Research Center provided internal memos and documents from Al Campanis's tenure as a Dodgers executive. Al's grandson, Jim Campanis Jr., shared memories over the phone, in addition to the stories he wrote in his own book, *Born into Baseball*. Family members of several Dodgers scouts provided helpful information, including Dan Bartley, Gary Brenzel, Kirby Hamilton, Marlee Hanby, and Margie Myers. *Baseball America's Ultimate Draft Book*, edited by Allan Simpson, contains a wealth of information about baseball's amateur draft and proved to be an invaluable resource.

Additional recognition to Charlie Bevis, Rod Nelson, and Ed Washuta for providing research assistance and to Marshall Wright for taking the time to explain the selection criteria he and Bill Weiss used for their book, *The 100 Greatest Minor League Baseball Teams of the 20th Century*.

I'm indebted to the many journalists who diligently covered the events described within this book in real time. In particular, Chuck Stewart's game stories in the *Spokane Daily Chronicle* always seemed to contain extra nuggets of information not found elsewhere. Interviewing Chuck after reading so many of his game stories was one of the many highlights of working on this project. I'd also like to thank former sportswriter and Spokane baseball historian Jim Price for his contributions and for putting me in touch with Chuck.

Zack Minasian, who wrote a fantastic book on the 1968 Ogden Dodgers titled *Lasorda University*, kindly provided his memories over the phone and provided feedback on an early draft of the book. Many thanks to Zack for his generosity.

Viky Englund, David Eyre, Jim Gardner, Barbara Hopkins-McGee, and Erik Jensen attended games in Ogden, Honolulu, or Spokane and provided a fan's perspective.

Matt Hutchinson, Associate Athletic Director at Washburn University, connected me to Bernie Bianchino, Mark Elliott, Denis Kenney, and Gene Reardon. Each shared insights about Davey Lopes's college career. Similarly, Bill Linne provided memories of playing with Steve Garvey at Michigan State.

Robert Schweppe, the son of former Dodgers executive Bill Schweppe and an associate of Peter O'Malley, read an early draft of the book, as did fellow SABR members Andy McCue and Rick Zucker. Their feedback undoubtedly improved the manuscript.

Aaron Fischman, author of the excellent book *A Baseball Gaijin*, provided editing assistance. His suggestions were always spot-on and made me a better writer.

Kevin Reichard's revisions on the final draft I submitted to August Publications further elevated the book. He possesses a wealth of baseball knowledge and was a pleasure to work with every step of the way.

Over the last several years, I've found a supportive community of baseball writers who have provided support in many forms. My gratitude goes out to Marty Appel, Jonathan Daniel, Steve Dittmore, Doug Feldmann, Zak Ford, Eric Gray, Tim Hagerty, J. David Herman, Benjamin Hill, Will Leitch, Rob Neyer, Eric Nusbaum, and David Ostrowsky.

The Spokane Indians, now a High-A affiliate of the Colorado Rockies, are a first-class organization. Thank you to Bobby Brett, Andy Billig, Chris Duff, Otto Klein, Mike Boyle, Bud Bareither, and the rest of the staff for supporting my efforts to document the team's rich history and for providing photos. Additional photos were provided by Pacific Northwest baseball historian Dave Eskenazi.

Lastly, I'd like to thank my supportive family, friends, and coworkers. I am incredibly fortunate to have the unwavering support of my wife, Gina. Writing a book comes with sacrifice, and I can't thank her enough for giving me the latitude to pursue this project. I'm putting away my laptop for a while and looking forward to our next adventure. Of course, there's a good chance it'll involve a ballgame.

Bibliography

BOOKS, JOURNALS, AND VIDEOS

Cey, Ron and Ken Gurnick. *Penguin Power: Dodger Blue, Hollywood Lights, and My One-in-a-Million Big League Journey.* Chicago: Triumph Books, 2023.

Claire, Fred and Steve Springer. *Fred Claire: My 30 Years in Dodger Blue.* Sports Publishing LLC, 2004.

Delsohn, Steve. *True Blue: The Dramatic History of the Los Angeles Dodgers, Told by the Men Who Live It.* New York: Harper Collins, 2001.

Fallon, Michael. *Dodgerland: Decadent Los Angeles and the 1977-78 Dodgers.* Lincoln: University of Nebraska Press, 2016.

Garvey, Steve and Skip Rozin. *Garvey.* New York: Times Books, 1986.

Gunderson, Colin. *Tommy Lasorda: My Way.* Chicago: Triumph Books, 2015.

Kerrane, Kevin. *Dollar Sign on the Muscle: The World of Baseball Scouting.* CreateSpace Independent Publishing, 2013.

Lasorda, Tommy and David Fisher. *The Artful Dodger.* New York: Arbor House, 1985.

Leahy, Michaeal. *The Last Innocents: The Collision of the Turbulent Sixties and the Los Angeles Dodgers.* New York: Harper, 2016.

McCue, Andy. *Mover & Shaker.* Lincoln: University of Nebraska Press, 2014.

Michaels, Al and L. Jon Wertheim. *You Can't Make This Up: Miracles, Memories, and the Perfect Marriage of Sports and Television.* New York: Harper Collins, 2014.

Minasian, Zack. *Lasorda University: A Recollection of My Summer with Tommy Lasorda and the Ogden Dodgers.* Self-published, 2022.

Plaschke, Bill and Tommy Lasorda. *I Live for This: Baseball's Last True Believer.* Boston: Houghton Mifflin, 2007.

Simpson, Allan, ed. *Baseball America's Ultimate Draft Book.* Durham: Baseball America, 2016.

Thompson, Fresco and Cy Rice. *Inside the Dodgers.* Los Angeles: Holloway House Publishing Company, 1966.

Turbow, Jason. *They Bled Blue: The 1981 Los Angeles Dodgers.* Boston: Houghton Mifflin-Harcourt, 2019.

Valentine, Bobby and Peter Golenbock. *Valentine's Way: My Adventurous Life and Times.* New York: Permuted Press, 2021.

ARCHIVAL NEWSPAPERS AND MAGAZINES

Arizona Republic
Baltimore Sun
Baseball America
Boston Globe
Brooklyn Eagle
Cleveland Plain Dealer
Columbia (SC) *Record*
Connecticut Post
Daily Breeze (Torrance, CA)

Daily News (New York, NY)
Daily Oklahoman
Deseret News (Salt Lake City, UT)
Fort Worth Star-Telegram
Hartford Courant
Honolulu Star-Advertiser
Honolulu Star-Bulletin
Kansas City Star
Lincoln (NE) *Star*
Long Beach Independent Press-Telegram
Los Angeles Evening Citizen News
Los Angeles Times
Manhattan (KS) *Mercury*
Minneapolis Star
Montreal Star
New York Times
Ogden Standard-Examiner
Orlando Sentinel
Pasadena Independent
Rochester Democrat and Chronicle
Rutland (VT) *Daily Herald*
San Bernardino Press-Telegram
Spokane Daily Chronicle
Spokesman-Review (Spokane, WA)
Sport
Sports Illustrated
Springfield (OH) *News-Sun*
Street & Smith's Sports Business Daily Global Journal
Tacoma News Tribune
The Sporting News
Topeka Capital-Journal
Warren (PA) *Times Mirror*

WEBSITES
ancestry.com
baseball-reference.com
baseballhall.org
bevisbaseballresearch.wordpress.com
espn.com
milb.com
mlb.com
newspapers.com
sabr.org
sss.gov
youtube.com
vault.si.com
voicesofoklahoma.com
walteromalley.com

Index

The pages referenced in this index refer to the page numbers in the print edition. If you are accessing this index on an eBook reader, please use your device's search function.

2000 Summer Olympics, 280

AABC World Series, 88
Aaron, Hank, *232n*
Adams, Dwight "Red," 62, 68, 206
Adair, Jerry, 255
Adlesh, Dave, 196-197
Albert, Jeff, 258*n*
Albury, Vic, 21
Albuquerque Dodgers, 48*n*, 107-108, 111, 123, 125-126, 155*n*, 170, 226*n*
Albuquerque Dukes, xii*n*, 150, 187*n*, 235, 239, 241-242, 271-272
Alexander, Cliff, 44
Alexander, Doyle, x, 82-83, 93, 117-118, 170, 172-173, 186, 187, 219, 233, 237, 238, 241, 251
    traded to Baltimore Orioles, 237
    drafted by Los Angeles Dodgers, 83
    promoted to Spokane Indians, 170
    traded for John Smoltz, 238
Alexander, Hugh, 9, 64-66, 91, 108, 182
    accident, 64-65
    passing on Mickey Mantle, 66
    playing career, 64
    scouting career, 65-66
Allen, Bob, 181, 218
Allen, Dick, 232, 234, 242
Allen, Lloyd, 81, 82, 116, 244
    facing Bill Buckner, 116
Almendares Scorpios, 33
Alou, Jesús, 208
Alston, Walter, 22, 30, 31-32, 48, 51, 52, 85, 106, 118, 124, 125, 154, 200, 202, 231-232, 233, 237, 239-240, 243, 247, 248, 249, 250-251, 272, 277
    named Brooklyn Dodgers manager, 31-32
    retirement, 256
Amateur Draft (MLB) ix, x, 5, 11, 12-22, 38, 42, 53, 54-55, 57, 68, 72-73, 74, 77*n*, 84, 86, 91, 93, 106*n*, 109, 112, 122, 126, 127, 133, 169, 175-177, 220, 247, 250, 252*n*, 259*n*, 268
    1965 draft, 17
    1967 draft, 53, 55, 220
    1968 draft, 81-84, 91, 93, 109, 122, 133, 247, 250-251, 252, 282

1969 draft, 126, 180
1970 draft, 175-177
1971 draft, 252
1979 draft, 268
American Legion draft, 15
and military draft, 54-55
and Vietnam War, 54, 88
Amsterdam Rug Makers, 27
Anderson, Sparky, 249, 256, 263
Arizona State University, 18, 43, 91, 92, 100, 101, 137, 231-232
Armstrong, Dick, 125, 165, 196
Atlanta/Milwaukee Braves x, 16, 63, 84, 90, 219n, 234, 236, 238, 278L
Autry, Gene, 9

Bailey, Bob, 6, 99
Baker, Dusty, 53, 236, 256, 264, 266
Bakersfield Dodgers, 89, 100, 103, 107, 108-109, 111, 113, 117, 207, 226n
Baldschun, Jack, 133, 180
Baltimore Orioles, 13, 14, 51, 77, 207, 237-238
1966 World Series, 51
Bando, Sal, x, 21, 250
Banks, Ernie, 220n, 260
Barber, Red, 84
Barbieri, Jim, 111
Barnes, Frank, 35
Barry, Rich, 183
Barry, Rick, 135
Bartley, Boyd, 66-68, 268
college career, 66
signed by Brooklyn Dodgers, 67
military career, 67
demoted to Montreal Royals, 67
transition to scouting, 67-68
Bartley, Dan, 268
Baseball America, xi-xii, 21n
Basgall, Monty, 62, 63, 64, 101, 122, 233
signed by Brooklyn Dodgers, 63
Batista, Fulgencio, 33
Bauer, Hank, 35, 51
Bavasi, Emil "Buzzie," 13, 14-15, 17, 23-24, 34, 35, 39, 49-50, 52, 53, 57, 82, 103, 104, 105, 106, 255
Bavasi, Peter, 151
Baylor, Don, 53
Beckert, Glenn, 260
Beckwith, Joe, 269n
Beltré, Adrian, 277
Bench, Johnny, 15-16, 19, 21, 175-176
Bender, Chief, 21

INDEX 305

Bennett, Dennis, 135, 141, 219
Berry, Kenny, 244
Berra, Yogi, 9, 218
Bevacqua, Kurt, 185*n*
Bevis, Charlie, 55
Billingham, Jack, 41*n*-42*n*, 62
Black, Joe, 30
Blue, Vida, x, 53, 250
Boise Hawks, 260
Bonds, Bobby, 163
Bonus Rule ("bonus babies") 6
Borunda, Eli, 180
Boston Red Sox, 6, 9, 18, 63, 157, 165, 165-167, 238-239, 257-258, 260, 267*n*, 277*n*
    Fenway Park, 260, 267*n*
Boswell, Thomas, 266
Boudreau, Lou, 34-35
Bove, Harmon, 54
Bowa, Larry, 21
Boyer, Ken, 105
Bradley, Tom, 135-136, 181, 217
Branca, Ralph, 30
Brandon, Darrell, 186
Brayton, Chuck, 88
Brenzel, Bill, 68, 88-89, 90
Brenzel, Gary, 88-89
Brett, Ken, 43
Brito, Mike, 268, 277*n*
Broberg, Pete, 81-82
Brock, Lou, 250*n*
Brooklyn Dodgers *see Los Angeles Dodgers*
Brubaker, Bruce, 111, 114, 115, 116, 161, 167-168, 169, 203
    evaluation of Tommy Lasorda as Spokane manager, 115
Brumley, Mike, 258
Bryant, Clay, 29, 35
Buckner, Bill, x, 62, 74-79, 81, 82, 89-90, 93, 96, 98, 99, 100, 102, 108-109, 110-111, 116-117, 118, 124, 133, 142-143, 153, 154-155, 156, 159-161, 169, 174, 175, 179, 180, 187, 193, 193-194, 196, 197, 198, 202-203, 214-215, 216, 218, 219, 224, 225, 226, 232, 233, 240, 241, 243, 249, 250, 251, 252, 256-261, 269*n*, 277-278
    1980 NL batting title, 258
    1980 All-Star, 258
    assigned to Albuquerque Dodgers, 111
    traded to Boston Red Sox, 258
    traded to Chicago Cubs, 258
    negotiating first contract, 89-90
    drafted by Los Angeles Dodgers, 82
    family life, 78
    broken jaw, 159-160
    with Ogden Dodgers, 96

306 INDEX

    demoted to Spokane Indians, 154
    promoted to Spokane Indians, 116
    committing to USC, 79
    World Series error, 259
    in youth baseball, 78
Buckner, Bob, 77-78, 90, 118, 172, 258
Buckner, Jim, 77
Buckner, Marie, 90
Bunning, Jim, 119
Burbrink, Nelson, 81
Burchart, Larry, 55, 56
    drafted by Los Angeles Dodgers, 55
Burke, Michael "Mike," 76
Burke, Pat, 101-102
Burks, Ellis, x*n*

Cabrera, Chiquitín, 33
Caldwell Cubs, 48*n*
California League, 117, 207
Callis, Jim, x
Calvert, Dick, 68, 88
Cambria, Joe, 68
Campaneris, Bert, 250
Campani (Campanis), Alessandro, 58-59
Campani, Tulla, 58
Campanis, Al, x, xii, xiii, 5, 8, 9, 17, 18, 23, 35-37, 38, 40, 42, 58-62, 63, 68, 73, 74, 79, 80, 89, 90, 92, 103, 106-108, 112-113, 122-123, 137-138, 154, 207, 232, 235, 236, 242, 243, 249-250, 258, 259, 264, 268, 269, 272, 274-276
    college, 59
    The Dodger Way, 60
    promoted to Dodgers GM, 106-107
    hiring Tommy Lasorda as Spokane manager, 107-108
    developing draft strategy with Al LoCasale, 73-74
    managerial career, 59
    military service, 59
    Nightline interview, 274-276
    numerical grading system, 60, 74
    resignation as Los Angeles Dodgers GM, 275
    scouting for Brooklyn Dodgers, 60
    scouting Roberto Clemente, 60
    scouting Tommy Davis, 60-61
    signed with Brooklyn Dodgers, 59
Campanis, George, 275
Campanis, Jim, 275
Campanis Jr., Jim, 60*n*, 61*n*, 106, 259
Campanella, Roy, 32, 85, 123
Canseco, José, 238
Capps, Billy, 15-16, 19

INDEX 307

Carey, John, 37, 68, 126
Carey, Max, 255*n*
Casey, Hugh, 63
Carty, Rico, 250*n*
Cey, Ron, x, xii, 62, 88-89, 90, 93, 111, 117, 124, 133, 167, 185*n*, 233, 239-240, 241, 247-
    248, 250, 252, 253-254, 255, 256, 264, 266, 267, 268, 269, 270*n*, 271, 272
        assigned to Albuquerque Dodgers, 111
        drafted by Los Angeles Dodgers, 88
        drafted by New York Mets, 88
        traded to Chicago Cubs, 272
Chambers, Al, ix
Chambers, Udell, 54
Chambliss, Chris, 205
Chance, Dean, 220
Charleston Charlies, 255
Chase, Charles, 54
Chastain, Dorian, 164
Cheney Studs, 88
        and Ben Cheney, 88*n*
        see also Tacoma Cubs
Chiba Lotte Marines, 279
Chicago Cubs, 15, 16, 18, 19, 43, 54, 68, 143, 146, 165, 175*n*, 193-194, 201-202, 212, 220*n*,
    239, 258, 272, 273
        Wrigley Field, 201-202
Chicago White Sox, 9, 133, 165, 175*n*, 196*n*, 217, 220, 233, 234, 236, 237, 260
Chilcott, Steve ix, 43
Cincinnati Reds, 13, 16, 19, 133, 200, 226, 242, 249, 250, 252, 256, 263-264, 267, 269, 277*n*
Claire, Fred, 109-110, 276, 278*n*, 279
        Named Los Angeles Dodgers GM, 276
Clemens, Roger, x*n*, 258, 277*n*
Clemente, Roberto, 5-6, 32*n*, 60
        signed by Brooklyn Dodgers, 60
        Rule 5 draftee, 60
Cleveland Indians, 12, 13, 16, 20, 21, 53*i*, 55, 64, 82, 88, 90, 176
Coates, Jim, 135, 141, 196
Cochrane, Mickey, 248
Colavito, Rocky, 105
Colborn, Jim, 143
Coleman, Choo-Choo, 41*n*-42*n*
Coleman, Joe, 18
Coleman, Vince, 255*n*
College World Series, 76, 84, 89, 91, 159
Colletti, Ned, 280
Collins, Jocko, 25-26
Colton, Larry, 143, 203, 212, 213
Cott, Marty, 82
        drafted by Houston Astros, 82
Cox, Bobby, 277

Craig, Roger, 107, 253*n*
Crandall, Del, 123
Crawford, Clara, 3, 4, 8
Crawford, Willie, 3, 4-6, 7-9, 11, 15, 38, 48*n*, 105, 232, 251, 270*n*, 281
Criscione, Mike, 47-48
Christopher, Loyd, 90
Crosby, Bing, 172
Crosby, Ed x*n*, 73
    drafted by Los Angeles Dodgers, 73
Cuellar, Mike, 237*n*
Curtis, John, 43, 87*n*

David, Larry, 260-261
Davis, Brock, 198
Davis, Eric, 277*n*
Davis, Tommy, 5-6, 13, 51, 53, 60, 61
    signed by Brooklyn Dodgers, 60
    traded to New York Mets, 53
Davis, Willie, 13, 37, 51, 57, 62, 99, 108, 111, 149, 200, 214, 232, 249-250, 266
    traded to Montreal Expos, 249-250
Daytona Beach Dodgers, 117, 126
de Jesús, Iván, 258*n*
Dean, Tommy, 9, 11, 108
Decker, Joe, 143
Dedeaux, Rod, 76-77, 79, 89, 95
Delgado, Félix, 136
Delsohn, Steve, 274-275
Dent, Bucky, 267*n*
Dempsey, Rick, 53
Denbow, Donny, 53
    drafted by Los Angeles Dodgers, 53
Detroit Tigers, 6, 13, 16, 54, 238
Devine, Bing, 9, 18
DiMaggio, Joe, 139
Dodgertown, 27-28
Dobson, Chuck, 11*n*
Dobson, Pat, 237*n*
Downing, Al, 232
Dressen, Charlie, 31-32
Drysdale, Don, 13, 22, 49-52, 54*n*, 63, 80, 106, 109, 111, 195, 276
    holdout with Sandy Koufax, 49-52
Dunning, Steve, 176
Durocher, Leo, 59

Eckersley, Dennis, 258, 276
El Paso Sun Kings, 136
Ellingsen, Bruce, 53
Ellis, Dock, 191*n*

Elliott, Larry, 72
Elliott, Mark, 72
Encerti, Gary, 78
Englund, Viky, 174
Erskine, Carl, 30
ESPN.com, x
Eugene Emeralds, 131, 170, 172, 173, 175, 179, 188, 191, 198, 202, 242, 271-272

Fairey, Jim, 41n-42n
Fairly, Ron, 13, 51, 57, 62, 99, 105, 119, 149
Fast, Darcy, 48n, 132, 143
Federoff, Al, 161
Feller, Bob, 20
Ferguson, Joe, x, 82-83, 93, 123, 233, 241, 248, 250, 264, 269
Fingers, Rollie, 250
Finley, Charlie, 7, 8, 10-11, 15, 43, 81-82, 251
Fisk, Carlton, 72, 264
Florida Marlins, 120, 234, 235
Foli, Tim, 81
    drafted by New York Mets, 81
Foote, Barry, 176
Fosse, Ray, 18, 21
Foster, George, 73n, 153, 189
Foster, Alan, 19, 111
Fox, Charlie, 144, 152
Foxx, Jimmie, 25
Franco, John, 68n
Freese, Gene, 32
Freese, George, 32
Frick, Ford, ix, x, 11, 13, 17

Gabrielson, Len, 104, 105, 135
Gallagher, Bob, 82-83, 233, 239-240
Galliher, Marv, x, 72n, 127, 149, 188n, 224-225, 233
    drafted by Los Angeles Dodgers, 72n
Gamble, John, 44
Garber, Gene, 20-21
Garman, Mike, 258n
Garvey, Cyndy, 249, 267
Garvey, Joe, 83-85, 91-92
Garvey, Millie, 91-92
Garvey, Steve, x, xii, 62, 84-87, 89, 91-92, 93, 95, 96, 98, 99, 100, 102, 108-109, 110-111, 117, 118, 124, 133, 145, 153-154, 155-156, 160-161, 169, 173, 174, 175, 179, 180, 187-188, 198, 202-203, 213, 215, 216, 218, 224, 225, 226, 232, 233-234, 240, 241, 243, 247-248, 249, 250, 252, 253-255, 256, 264, 265n, 266, 267, 268, 269, 270n, 271, 272-274, 278
    assigned to Albuquerque Dodgers, 111
    drafted by Los Angeles Dodgers, 84

310 INDEX

    negotiating first Los Angeles Dodgers contract, 91-92
    first All-Star Game, 250
    first Gold Glove, 249
    shift to first base, 249
    drafted by Minnesota Twins, 86
    growing up in Tampa, 84
    high school career, 85-86
    Michigan State career, 86-87
    MVP award, 250
    with Ogden Dodgers, 95, 96, 98, 99, 100, 102
    personal problems, 273-274
    winning Roberto Clemente Award, 273
    San Diego Padres honors/records, 273
    signed free agent contract with San Diego Padres, 272
    scouting report, 87
    demoted to Spokane Indians, 154, 198
    problems with Don Sutton, 266-267
    U.S. Senate run, 274
    Vitalis Hair Tonic commercial, 153
Gehrig, Lou, 25, 139, 187
Gentile, Jim, 88-89, 149
Gibson, Bob, 106, 183, 260
Gibson, Kirk, 276
Gilhousen, Rosey, 38
Gilliam, Jim, 13
Gillick, Pat, 7, 17, 42
Gleason, Roy, 6, 110, 119*n*
Glinnen, Eddie, 54
Goggin, Chuck, 119
Goltz, Dave, 268
Gooden, Dwight, x
Goodson, Ed, 236
Gordon, Joe, 79
Gossage, Goose, 175*n*, 244
Grabarkewitz, Billy, 44, 108, 111, 112
    traded to California Angels, 243
    drafted by Los Angeles Dodgers, 44
Grant, Jim "Mudcat," 104
Graziano, Bob, 279
Green, Dick, 244
Grich, Bobby, 53
Griffey Jr., Ken, ix
Griffin, Doug, 135-136, 141, 183, 214, 218, 225
Guerrero, Pedro, 53*i*, 269
Guidry, Ron, 271
Gullett, Don, 265
Gwynn, Tony, 260

Haak, Howie, 38
Hackleman, Jim, 221
Hall, Kara, 55
    drafted by Los Angeles Dodgers, 55
Haller, Jim, 176
Haller, Tom, 104
Hamilton, Leon, 40-42, 64, 66, 83, 119n
    with Binghamton Triplets, 41
    childhood, 40
    with House of David, 41
    with Kinston Eagles, 40-41
    scouting transition, 41
    players signed by Hamilton, 41n-42n
Harper, Bryce, ix
Harrelson, Ken, 237
Hart, Jim Ray, 153
Hartnett, Gabby, 248
Hartsfield, Roy, 33, 106, 115, 255
Hashem, Tufie, 136
Hatcher, Mickey, 269n
Hawaii Islanders, xii, 116-117, 131, 134-143, 165, 168-169, 181, 183, 193-198, 202-203, 212-213, 214, 215, 216-221, 222-225, 239-240, 245, 255
    Honolulu Stadium (Termite Palace), 138-139, 140-141, 181, 219, 222
    Pacific Coast League playoffs, 216-221
Hebner, Richie, 43
Hendrick, George, 73n
Herron, Frank, 213
Hershiser, Orel, 68n, 72n, 120, 268, 276, 277
Hicks, Jim, 181, 225
Hibbs, Jim, 72n
    drafted by Los Angeles Dodgers, 72n
Hickman, Jim, 53
Hisle, Larry, 235n, 241
Ho, Chinn, 134, 140
Hodges, Gil, 85
Hollandsworth, Todd, 277
Hollywood Stars, 63, 149
    Gilmore Field, 149
Holt, Goldie, 62, 120-122
Holtzman, Ken, 54, 250
Hooten, Burt, 252-253, 269n
    traded to Los Angeles Dodgers, 252
Hope, Bob, 273
Hopkins-McGee, Barbara, 174
Hough, Charlie, x, 39, 42, 46-47, 111, 120-122, 124, 125, 133-134, 141, 152, 153, 155, 161, 165, 168-169, 175, 175n, 181, 187, 192, 194, 196, 198-199, 200-201, 213, 217, 218, 232, 234-235, 236-237, 241, 251, 256-257, 265, 269
    assigned to Albuquerque Dodgers, 111

        called up to Los Angeles Dodgers, 200-201
        drafted by Los Angeles Dodgers, 46
        knuckleball, mastering, 121-122
        post-Dodgers career, 234-235
Houk, Ralph, 35
House of David, 41, 66
Houston Colt .45s/Astros, 7, 16-17, 18, 42, 82, 182-183, 219n, 269, 270, 274
        Astrodome, 270, 274
Howard, Frank, 8, 13, 57, 62, 149
Howe, Steve, 269, 277
Hriniak, Walt, 132
Hunt, Ron, 53, 104
Hunter, Herb, 209-210
        radio game re-creations, 209-210
Hunter, Jim "Catfish," 11n, 250, 265
Hunter, Willard, 35
Hutton, Larry, 43-44, 46
        drafted by Los Angeles Dodgers, 44
Hutton, Tommy, x, 38, 111, 113, 116, 125, 126, 140-141, 142-143, 149-150, 153, 155, 169, 173, 178, 179-180, 183, 191, 198, 215, 216, 218, 224, 225, 232, 235, 264n
        injured, 179-180
        traded to Philadelphia Phillies, 235

Iba, Hank, 65
Idaho Falls Angels, 39, 101
Indianapolis Indians, 62
Ivie, Mike, 175-176

Jackson, Reggie, x, 43, 205, 250, 260, 265, 267, 270
James, Cleo, 111
Jenkins, Jack, 100, 125, 141, 174, 187, 196-197, 208, 233
Jestadt, Garry, 198
Jobe, Dr. Frank, 176, 220
John, Tommy, x, 176, 184, 267, 270, 271
Johnson, Bart, 87n
Johnson, Lou, 51, 104
Johnston, Johnny, 82
Jones, Chipper, ix
Joshua, Von, 111, 124, 126, 155, 241, 251

Kahn, Roger, 274
Kamzic, Nick, 220
Kansas City Athletics, x, 7, 8, 10, 11, 15, 16, 17, 18, 20, 21, 43, 136
        see also Oakland Athletics
Kansas City Monarchs, 59
Kansas City Royals, 133
Karros, Eric, 68n, 277-278, 282
Karros, Kyle, 282

Kawano, Nobe, 124-125
Kealey, Steve, 135-136, 181
Keegan, Tom, 278
Keenan, John, 46, 58, 64, 72
Kendall, Fred, 165
Kennedy, Robert, 80-81
Keynerd, Tom, 3-4
King, Clyde, 30
King, Larry, 55
Kingman, Dave, 185n
Kittle, Ron, 72n
Kline, Ron, 181, 218
Koenig, Fred, 39
Koppel, Ted, 274-275
Kosco, Andy, 111, 232
Koufax, Sandy, 13, 20, 22, 34, 49-52, 54n, 60, 63, 106, 183, 191, 195, 201-202, 238
    1966 season, 50-51
    holdout with Don Drysdale, 49-52
    retirement, 52
Kranepool, Ed, 81
Kritchell, Paul, 41n
Kroll, Gary, 195-196
Kubek, Tony, 35
Kuntz. Jerry, 163, 219

Lacy, Lee, 236
    traded to Atlanta Braves, 236
Lamarr, Hedy, 212n
Lamb, Ray, 44
Lamoriello, Lou, 74-75
LaRoche, Dave, 135-136, 139, 181, 217, 281
Lasorda, Carmella, 24
Lasorda, Joan "Jo" (Miller), 30, 37, 134, 159, 276-277
Lasorda, Tommy, ix, xii, 3-4, 5, 7-9, 15, 17-18, 19-20, 22, 23-39, 44-45, 46, 47-48, 49, 52, 55-56, 68, 72n, 76-77, 92, 93, 94-103, 107-108, 109-110, 111-115, 119, 120, 121, 122, 123, 124-125, 126-127, 132, 133, 134, 137, 140-141, 143, 144, 146, 149, 154, 155, 157-158, 159, 163, 164, 165, 167, 168, 171, 172, 174, 175, 179, 180, 184-186, 187n, 188, 189-190, 191, 194, 196-197, 201, 202-203, 205-206, 207-208, 211-212, 213, 215, 217, 218, 219, 220, 222-223, 225, 226-227, 232-233, 235-236, 238, 239, 240, 241-242, 243, 247, 248, 251, 255, 256-257, 258, 262-282
    1996 heart attack, 276
    1977 World Series, 265
    with Almendares Scorpios, 33
    Army years, 27
    love of betting, 171
    Batista, Fulgencio, meeting, 33
    and boxing, 25
    Cabrera, Chiquitin, fighting with, 33

sudden celebrity, 265
children, 37
teaching Roberto Clemente English, 32*n*
with Concord Weavers, 25-26, 271
recruiting Willie Crawford, 3-5, 7-8
with Denver Bears, 35
named Los Angeles Dodgers interim GM, 279
named Los Angeles Dodgers manager, 256
record as Los Angeles Dodgers manager, 277
retirement as Los Angeles Dodgers manager, 276
managing Dodger Rookies, 37
recruited as Brooklyn Dodgers scout, 36-37
traded to Brooklyn Dodgers, 35
family background, 24
with Greenville Spinners, 29
inspirational speaking, 47-48
sold to Kansas City Athletics, 34-35
speaking at Tom Keynerd funeral, 3-4
cut from Brooklyn Dodgers for Sandy Koufax, 34
letters sent to major leaguers, 99
with Los Angeles Angels, 35
and Billy Martin, 35
with Mayaguez Indians, 32
joining Montreal Expos staff, 107
Montreal Royals, playing with, 29, 30, 31, 32, 35
elected to National Baseball Hall of Fame, 278
brawling with New York Yankees, 34-35
traded to New York Yankees, 35
growing up in Norristown, Pennsylvania, 24-25
managing Ogden Dodgers, 44-45, 46, 47-48, 55-56, 93-103
first managerial job with Pocatello Chiefs, 23-24, 38-39
motivational speaking, 184-186
passing away, 280
pranks on, 124-125
first pro contract, 25
responding to proselytizing, 47
joining San Diego Padres staff, 103, 107
playing in Schenectady, 27
scouted as high schooler, 25-26
hired as Spokane manager, 107-108
spring training 1949, 27-29
sold to St. Louis Browns, 30
named *The Sporting News* Minor League Manager of the Year, 227
managing U.S. Olympic baseball team, 280
committing to Bobby Valentine in Spokane, 113-114
recruiting Bobby Valentine, 76-77
Waxahachie Swap, 196-197
Lasorda, Sabatino, 24-25

Lavelle, Gary, 53
Lawing, Gene, 16
Lazzeri, Tony, 187*n*
Lefebvre, Jim, 51, 62, 105, 112, 125, 154, 232, 242
Lehman, John "Pappy," 25-26
Leigh, Vivian, 10
Lembo, Steve, 84
Lemon, Bob, 163, 271
Liberatore, Ed, 68
Linne, Bill, 86-87
Lis, Joe, 175*n*
Litwhiler, Danny, 86
Llenas, Winston, 135-136, 141, 168, 194, 197, 209, 211, 212, 213-214, 218, 219, 224, 225, 245, 256
LoCasale, Al, 73-74
    football background, 73
    ranking system for players, 74
Lockman, Whitey, 143, 202-203, 211-212, 213-214
Lockwood, Skip, 11*n*
Loes, Billy, 30
Lolich, Mickey, 54
Lombardi, Ernie, 248
Lopes, Davey, x, xii, 62, 69-73, 101, 117, 124, 126-127, 153, 155, 156, 159, 174, 183, 188, 189, 193, 197, 215, 218, 232-233, 240, 241, 243, 247-248, 250, 254, 255, 256, 265-266, 267-268, 269, 270*n*, 271-272
    named All-Star, 266
    college career, 70-72
    named Los Angeles Dodgers captain, 266
    winning Gold Glove, 266
    growing up in East Providence, 69-70
    drafted by Los Angeles Dodgers, 72-73
    drafted by San Francisco Giants, 72
    traded to Oakland Athletics, 272
Los Angeles Angels (MiLB), 68, 146-147, 148
    move to Spokane, 148-149
    Wrigley Field, 146-147
Los Angeles/California Angels (MLB), 7, 9, 10-11, 12, 72*n*, 79, 82, 116, 134-135, 136, 181, 191*n*, 220, 243-246, 255, 259
Los Angeles/Brooklyn Dodgers, ix, x, xii, 3, 4, 5, 6, 7, 8, 13, 14-15, 17, 19, 21-22, 23, 24, 27-29, 30, 31-32, 33, 34, 35, 36-37, 38-39, 41, 43-44, 46, 48, 49-52, 53, 55, 56-57, 59, 60-63, 64, 66, 67, 68, 72-74, 76-77, 79, 80, 82, 83, 84, 85, 86, 87-88, 89, 90, 91, 92, 93, 94, 95, 101, 103, 104-114, 118-119, 120-123, 124, 127, 132, 135, 137-138, 142-143, 146-149, 153-154, 167, 175, 176-177, 182-183, 185*n*, 187-188, 191, 198, 200-202, 205, 216-217, 221, 222, 226-227, 231-237, 238-240, 241-243, 247-251, 252-255, 262-282
    1949 spring training, 27-29
    1966 World Series, 51
    1966 Japan tour, 51-52
    1967 draft, 72-73

1968 draft, x-xi, 81-84, 93, 109, 122, 133, 247, 250-251, 252, 269, 272, 277, 282
1970 draft, 176-177
1974 World Series, 250-251
1975 season, 252-255
1977 playoffs, 264-265
1977 World Series, 265
1978 playoffs, 267
1978 season, 267
1978 World Series, 267
1979 draft, 268
1981 playoffs, 270
2020 World Series, 280
coconut snatching, 120, 122-123, 248
Dodger Stadium, 5, 24, 38, 55, 80, 105n, 112, 127, 137, 144, 153, 168, 191, 203, 226, 232, 243, 262, 264, 270, 279, 281-282
The Dodger Way, 60
developing draft strategy with Al LoCasale, 73-74
sale to Fox Group, 279
sale to Frank McCourt, 280
Operation Bounce Back, 104-114
ranking system for players, 74
scouting structure, 62
Lott, George, 111, 126, 133, 171, 180, 187, 188, 196
Lung, John, 213
Luzinski, Greg, 79, 82, 264
drafted by Philadelphia Phillies, 82
Lynch, Mike, 115

Mack, Connie, 277
MacPhail, Larry, 7
MacPhail, Lee, 14
Maddox, Garry, 73n
Magic Valley (Twin Falls) Cowboys, 99-100, 101-102
Maglie, Sal, 191
Mahoney, Neil, 165
Major League Baseball, ix, x, 5, 12, 14, 17-18, 21, 38, 175-176, 196n, 270, 274
lack of Black managers, 275
See also amateur draft
Maldonado, Candy, 269
Malone, Kevin, 279
Maltz, Maxwell, 114-115
Mantle, Mickey, 34-35, 76
Marceno, Carmine, 56
Marichal, Juan, 112, 144
Marshall, Mike (1B/OF), 269, 277
Marshall, Mike (pitcher), 249-250
traded to Los Angeles Dodgers, 249-250
Martin, Billy, 35, 108, 163, 265

Martínez, Pedro, 277
Marvin, Lee, 10
Matthews, Gary, 82
May, Carlos, 43
May, Rudy, 270
Mayaguez Indians, 32
Mayberry, John, 53
Maynard, Buster, 29, 96-97
Mays, Willie, 6, 32, 105, 144
McCarthy, Joe, 54
McCourt, Frank, 280
McCovey, Willie, 144
McCue, Andy, 147
McDonald, Joe, 16, 18, 21, 43, 81
McDowell, Roger x
McGraw, John, 277
McGrew, Harry "Ted," 62-63
McGwire, Mark, 238
McHale, John, 11, 256
McKechnie, Bill, 212, 214
McKnight, Jim, 153
McLaughlin, Dick, 111, 114, 127, 178, 180, 186, 195, 226
McLaughlin, Jim, 16
McMahon, Don, 276
McMullen, Ken, 243
    traded to Los Angeles Dodgers, 243
McNally, Dave, 237*n*
Messersmith, Andy, 43, 243, 250, 251
    traded to Los Angeles Dodgers, 243
Metzger, Roger, 198
Miami Dolphins, 90-91
Michael, Gene, 53, 104
Michaels, Al, 137-138, 210-211, 214, 222, 223-224
Michigan State University, 84, 86, 87, 91
Mikkelsen, Pete, 111, 200
Millan, Félix, 260
Miller, Bob, 22, 51, 104
Miller, Marvin, 237-238
Milwaukee Brewers, 11, 91*n*, 176, 235*n*, 272
Minasian, Eddie, 222-223
Minasian, Perry, 56*n*
Minasian, Rudy, 56*n*
Minasian, Zack (Giants GM), 56*n*
Minasian, Zack (elder), 30, 55-56, 96, 97, 101, 112-113, 140
    family tree, 56
    with Ogden Dodgers, 55-56, 96
Minneapolis/Los Angeles Lakers, 135
Minneapolis Millers, 147-148

Metropolitan Stadium, 148
Minnesota Twins, 22, 43, 86, 105, 235n
Mitchell, Ron, 119
MLB.com, x
Moeller, Joe, 51, 125, 239-240
Monday, Rick, 17-18, 21, 57, 185n, 257, 270
Mondesi, Raúl, 277
Money, Don, 21
Montañez, Willie, 175n
Montreal Expos, 81, 105, 107, 119, 123, 133, 144, 176, 235, 256, 270
    Olympic Stadium, 270
Montreal Royals, xii$n$, 29, 30, 31, 32, 35, 59, 60, 67
Moon, Wally, 33
Moses, Robert, 147
Mota, Manny, 119
Mulcahy, Tom "Hoodlum Priest," 171-172
Mulleavy, Greg, 68
Munson, Thurman, 76, 82, 265
    drafted by New York Yankees, 82
Mungo, Van Lingle, 25
Murdoch, Rupert, 278n, 279
Murff, Red, 18, 20
Murray, Jim, 272
Musial, Stan, 33-34
Myers, Kenny, 4, 7, 8-9, 15, 37, 68, 251

National Baseball Congress, 63
National Football League (NFL), 12-13
draft as model for MLB draft, 12-13
Nee, Johnny, 41n
Nelson, Fred, 92-93, 100-101
    drafted by Los Angeles Dodgers, 92-93
Nettles, Graig, 206
Newcombe, Don, 30, 33, 274, 275
New York Mets, x, 16-17, 18, 20-21, 43, 53, 81, 88, 116, 144, 200, 234, 255, 256, 258-259, 278-279
    Shea Stadim, 267
New York Yankees, 7, 9, 34-35, 41, 76, 82, 84, 135, 165, 187, 205-206, 219n, 242, 265, 267, 268, 270-271
    1977 World Series, 265
    1978 World Series, 267
    1981 World Series, 270-271
    Yankee Stadium, 270
Neyer, Rob, 196n
Niekro, Joe, 43
Nolan, Gary, 43
Nomo, Hideo, 277
Norman, Fred, 111, 114

Northwest League, 93, 213*n*, 241*n*
Nyman, Jerry, 133, 179, 180, 193

Oakland Athletics, 11*n*, 81, 219*n*, 238, 250, 251, 270, 272, 276, 280
    see also Kansas City Athletics
O'Brien, Bob, 125, 126, 139, 149, 170, 175, 186-187, 188, 189-190, 194, 223, 224, 225, 232, 237-238
    traded to Baltimore Orioles, 237
Odom, John "Blue Moon," 11*n*
Ogden Dodgers, 39, 44-45, 46-47, 55-56, 93-103, 107, 176, 281
    1968 season, 94-103
    Affleck Park, 46-47, 98
    playing conditions, 46-47
Oliver, Al, 201
Oliver, Nate, 41*n*-42*n*
O'Malley, Peter, 50, 107-108, 243, 247, 256, 274, 276-277, 279
O'Malley, Walter, 13, 14-15, 28, 31-32, 49, 50, 51, 52, 53, 62, 76, 105, 106-107, 125, 146-147, 148, 268
    replacing Ebbets Field, 147
    obtaining rights to Los Angeles market, 146-147
Omaha Cardinals, 35, 150
Ortega, Phil, 135
Osteen, Claude, 22, 51, 63, 111, 144, 242, 249-250
    traded to Montreal Expos, 249-250
Ozark, Danny, 247, 264

Pacific Coast League (PCL), xii, 36, 63, 68, 88*n*, 107, 111, 112, 113*n*, 119, 131, 133, 136, 140, 142, 143, 147, 148, 149, 159*n*, 163, 169, 170, 175*n*, 178, 183, 189*n*, 193, 194, 201, 202, 207, 208, 209, 211, 212, 215, 217, 219, 225, 226, 232, 235, 239, 241, 242, 245, 280
    1970 playoffs, 216-221
Paciorek, Jim, 91*n*
Paciorek, John, 91*n*
Paciorek, Tom, x, 82-83, 89, 90-91, 93, 94-95, 96-97, 98-99, 100, 108-109, 117, 126, 133, 141, 155, 158, 160-161, 169, 172, 174, 178-179, 180, 186, 187*n*, 195, 202-203, 208, 212, 213-214, 215, 218, 219, 222, 224, 225, 226, 227, 232, 235-237, 241, 250, 251, 260, 264, 280-281
    named All-Star, 236
    traded to Atlanta Braves, 236
    with Bakersfield Dodgers, 100, 117
    baseball vs. football, 90-91
    with Ogden Dodgers, 94-95, 96
    signed by Los Angeles Dodgers, 91
Palmer, Jim, 237*n*
Park, Chan Ho, 277
Parker, Dave, 175*n*, 233
Parker, Wes, 51, 99, 105, 116, 124, 125, 142-143, 200, 232
Patterson, Arthur "Red," 104
Paul, Gabe, 12, 13, 14-15

Pazik, Mike x*n*
Peña, Alejandro, 72*n*
Peña, Jose, 218
Pentland, Jeff, 132, 136, 180, 213, 221
Perez, Marty, 135-136, 181, 218
Perranoski, Ron, 22, 51, 104
Perry, Gaylord, 118
Philadelphia Phillies, 9, 25-26, 63, 82, 106, 133, 135, 191, 235, 247, 264-265
    Veterans Stadium, 264, 265
Phoenix Giants, 131, 151-153, 158-159, 187, 188-189, 215
    Phoenix Municipal Stadium, 158, 188
Piche, Ron, 143
Pignatano, Joe, 81
Pitlock, Skip, 158-159
Peters, Frank, 169
Peters, Hank, 18
Piazza, Mike, ix, 68*n*, 277-278
Piniella, Lou, 205
Pittsburgh Pirates, xii, 6, 13, 16, 20, 32, 53, 60, 63, 80, 88, 119, 175*n*, 191*n*, 200, 201, 250, 255
    Three Rivers Stadium, 200, 201
Pizzaro, Juan, 168, 181, 193-194, 212, 217
Plaschke, Bill, 32, 185, 267
Pocatello Chiefs, 23, 107
Podres, Johnny, 13
Popovich, Paul, 104, 119
Porter, Darrell, 176
Portland Beavers, 131, 161, 169-171, 186-188, 197, 198-199, 202-203, 208, 242
    Civic Stadium, 161*n*
Powell, Boog, 51
Price, Jim, 198
Pujols, Albert ix
Purdin, John, 125, 133, 165, 174, 189, 193-194, 217-218, 224
    sold to Hawaii Islanders, 193-194
Puente, Miguel, 189

Quad Cities Angels, 136
Queen's Hospital, 223-224
Quinn, Jack, 135, 137, 168, 181, 193-194

Raines, Tim, 272
Randall, Bobby, x*n*
Randle, Lenny, 92*n*
Ranew, Merritt, 181, 218
Rau, Doug, 168*n*, 176-177, 203, 205-208, 241, 242, 256, 265, 269
    winter ball, 206
Rautzhan, Lance, 176-177
Rhoden, Rick, 206, 241, 268*n*, 277

Redmond, Wayne, 181, 183
Reese, Pee Wee, 32, 63, 85, 123, 266
Regan, Phil, 51
Reichardt, Rick, 9-11, 12, 17, 220
Reilly, Rick, 273-274
Reiser, Pete, 63
Renko, Steve, 21
Reuss, Jerry, 53, 268, 269*n*, 270, 271
Reynolds, Allie, 65-66
Reynolds, Archie, 193-194, 218
Richard, J.R., 260
Richards, Paul, 17, 43, 196*n*
Richert, Pete, 62, 237
Rickey, Branch, xiii, 13, 27-28, 59-60, 83, 105, 106-107, 122-123, 248
Rickles, Don, 256, 264-265
Righetti, Dave, 270
Robello, Tony, 16
Robinson, Bill, 213*n*
Robinson, Brooks, 51
Robinson, Eddie, 17
Robinson, Frank, 51, 237, 242, 243, 251, 275-276
    traded to California Angels, 243
Robinson, Jackie, 32, 59, 60, 61, 85, 138, 238, 274, 275
Robinson, Rachel, 274
Robles, Sergio, 237
    traded to Baltimore Orioles, 237
Robustelli, Andy, 89-90
Roe, Preacher, 30
Rohr, Les, 18
Rose, Pete, 153
Roseboro, John, 13, 51, 104, 123
Ross, Gary, 193
Roundtree, Marge, 112
Rounsaville, Gene, 137, 188*n*
Royster, Jerry, 236
    traded to Atlanta Braves, 236
Rudi, Joe, 11*n*, 250
Rudolph, Ken, 19
Rufer, Rudolph "Rudy," 68, 84, 90
Ruth, Babe, 139, 187
Russell, Bill, x, xii, 39, 44, 45-46, 47, 101, 111, 122, 124, 126, 141, 155-156, 169, 173, 175, 179-180, 183, 187-188, 200, 232, 241, 243, 247-248, 251, 252, 253, 255, 256, 264, 267, 271, 272, 278, 279
    called up to Los Angeles Dodgers for good, 183
    drafted by Los Angeles Dodgers, 44
    named Los Angeles Dodgers manger, 278
    in high school, 45-46
    playing for Ogden Dodgers, 45, 47

Ryan, Nolan, 20, 144, 244, 260, 270

Saccomanno, Frank and Katy, 148-149
Salt Lake City Giants, 56
Salt Lake Padres, 131-133, 162, 164-165, 175-176, 179-180, 211, 212-213, 214, 255
    Derks Field, 133
San Diego Padres, 103, 105, 106, 107, 108, 131, 133, 143, 154, 171, 180, 255, 272-274
San Francisco/New York Giants, xii, 15, 21-22, 72, 82, 88, 106, 112, 143, 144, 147-148, 151, 165, 239, 252, 256, 262, 267
    replacing Polo Grounds, 147
Sandberg, Ryne, ix
Santo, Ron, 220*n*
Sax, Steve, 68*n*, 72*n*, 269, 272, 277
Scarpati, Pete, 83-84, 93, 125, 126, 140, 141, 158, 165, 239
    drafted by Los Angeles Dodgers, 84
    signed by Los Angeles Dodgers, 93
Schaffer, Jimmie, 111
Schiller, Elten, 115, 150-151, 174, 179, 192, 227
Schiller, Jeff, 174-175
Schmidt, Mike, 163, 242, 264
Schmuck, Peter, 252
Schoenfield, David, x
Schultz, Kent, 160, 162-164, 172, 183, 207
Schweppe, Bill, 17, 93, 108-109, 262
Scioscia, Mike, 68*n*, 269, 277
Scully, Vin, 28, 98, 137-138
Seattle Mariners, 236, 255
Seattle Pilots, 133, 167-168
    see also Milwaukee Brewers
Seattle Rainiers, 63, 149
Seaver, Tom, 19-20, 144, 260
Seinsoth, Bill x, 89
    drafted by Los Angeles Dodgers, 89
Shanahan, Greg, 176-177
Shank, Harvey, 137, 218
Sheldon, Bob, x*n*, 82*n*
Sheets, Ben, 280
Shirley, Bart, 6, 111, 126, 133, 149, 153, 157, 169, 181, 182-183, 188, 196, 211-212, 218, 218, 223, 225, 233
    called up to Los Angeles Dodgers, 182-183
    signed by Los Angeles Dodgers, 182
Signoret, Simone, 10
Silverio, Tomás, 135-136, 181, 194, 196
Simmons, Ted, 53
Sinatra, Frank, 256, 262, 265
Singer, Bill, 106, 111, 143, 187, 191, 201, 243
    traded to California Angels, 243
Singleton, Ken, 72

INDEX   323

Sizemore, Ted, 44, 108, 111, 122, 183, 200, 232, 264*n*
    drafted by Los Angeles Dodgers, 44
Slapnicka, Cy, 64, 65-66
Smith, Charley, 41*n*-42*n*, 149
Smith, Reggie, 256, 264, 266, 278
Smoltz, John, ix, 238
Snider, Duke, 32, 62, 85, 106, 183, 266
Soderholm, Eric, 73*n*
Sogge, Steve, 76, 110, 126-127, 133, 153, 161, 168, 178, 196, 198-199, 202*n*, 218, 224, 233
Solomon, Eddie, 252
Sonberg, Erik, 277*n*
Spahn, Warren, 163
Spokane Indians, x-xi, xii, 57, 103, 106, 107-108, 109, 111-112, 113-114, 115, 117, 119, 125-126, 127, 132, 133, 140, 141, 142, 144-145, 148-149, 150-156, 157, 165, 167, 168, 169, 170, 171, 172, 173, 174, 175, 177, 179-181, 182, 183, 186-187, 188-189, 191-192, 191-198, 201, 202-203, 206-208, 209, 210, 211, 212, 213-215, 216-221, 222-227, 222, 223-227, 232-237, 232-239, 241, 242, 266, 280, 281, 282
    Fairgrounds (Avista Stadium), 148-149, 163, 174, 175, 191-194, 197, 209, 217
    Pacific Coast League playoffs, 216-221
Sposito, Gustavo "Gus," 127, 149, 178-179, 180, 188*n*, 196
Spring, Jack, 111, 114
St. Louis Browns, 63
St. Louis Cardinals, 9, 15, 21, 59, 106, 111, 165, 202, 219*n*, 242, 264
St. Paul Saints, 150
Staab, Larry, 111, 125, 141
Stanhouse, Don, 268
Stargell, Willie, 201
Staub, Rusty, 81
Steidl, Frank and Robert, 149-150
Stengel, Casey, 79, 277
Stephenson, Brian, 226-227, 239
Stephenson, Jerry, 6, 125, 141, 162, 165-168, 169-170, 178, 189, 194, 196, 202-203, 211, 218, 226-227, 233, 238-239
    called up to the Dodgers, 226-227
Stephenson, Joe, 38, 162, 165, 167, 168
Stephenson, John, 112
Stewart, Chuck, 111, 196, 208, 225-226
Stewart, Dave, 68*n*, 269, 277
Stillman, Royle, 237
    traded to Baltimore Orioles, 237
Stinson, Bob, x, 43, 111, 123, 126, 141, 153, 158, 168-169, 196, 218, 226, 232
Stoneham, Horace, 147-148
Strahler, Mike, 111, 125, 141, 150, 152, 155, 161, 168, 170, 187, 196, 218-219, 226, 243
    traded to California Angels, 243
Strickland, Jim, 38
Stubing, Moose, 136
Suarez, Ken, 11*n*
Sudakis, Bill, 123, 187-188

Sutcliffe, Rick, 68*n*, 168*n*, 277
Sutter, Bruce, 175*n*
Sutton, Don, 41*n*-42*n*, 51, 64, 106, 111, 125, 242, 250, 251, 262, 266, 268-269, 270*n*, 278
    signing with Los Angeles Dodgers, 64
    problems with Steve Garvey, 266-267

Tacoma Cubs, 131, 143-145, 173-174, 198-199, 202-203, 211-213
    Cheney Stadium, 143, 199, 202
Tampa Bay Rays, 280
Tanner, Chuck, xi, 136, 137, 163, 193, 195-196, 209, 213, 216, 217, 219, 220, 224
Tatum, Jarvis, 181
Taylor, Brien, ix
Taylor, Kerry, 54
Thompson, Fresco, 3, 13, 17, 23, 29, 82, 105, 106
    death, 106
Thompson, Rick, 47 161
Thurman, Bob, 16
Texas League, 136, 241*n*
Texas Rangers, 234, 236-237, 256
Tidwell, Donny, 54
    drafted by Los Angeles Dodgers, 54*n*
Tiefenauer, Bobby, 143
Tenace, Gene, x, 20-21, 250
Tolan, Bobby, 4
Torborg, Jeff, 200
Toronto Blue Jays, 235
Tri-City Atoms, 93, 172
Trois-Rivières Royals, 27
Tucson Toros, 131, 155, 186, 188*n*, 233
    Hi Corbett Field, 188*n*
Tulsa Oilers, 215*n*

Ueberroth, Peter, 274
Unser, Del, 43
UCLA, 89
USC, xi, 19, 73, 76, 77, 79, 81*n*, 89, 90, 94, 95, 108, 112, 124, 126-127, 135, 155, 179, 231, 233, 259,

Vail, Mike, 176-177
Valentine, Bobby, x, 62, 74-77, 79, 81, 82, 89-90, 93, 94-95, 96, 98, 100, 101, 102, 108, 110-111, 112-114, 115-116, 117, 118, 119, 122, 123-124, 126, 133, 140, 141, 146, 155-156, 158, 159, 160-161, 169, 171, 173, 174, 175, 176, 181, 186, 187, 188, 189, 195, 196, 198, 202-203, 208, 210, 211, 212, 214, 218, 219-220, 221, 222-227, 231-232, 235, 236-237, 239-240, 241, 243-246, 249, 251, 255-256, 257, 265, 277-279, 280
    broken leg injury, 244
    and Cape Cod League, 75-76
    managing Chiba Lotte Marines, 279
    childhood, 74-75

facial injury, 222-227
high-school career, 75-76
knee injury, 231-232
evaluation of Tommy Lasorda as manager, 115-116
recruited by Tommy Lasorda, 76-77
released by California Angels, 255
traded to California Angels, 243
drafted by Los Angeles Dodgers, 82
managing New York Mets, 279
with Ogden Dodgers, 94-95, 96
rookie MLB season, 239-240
traded to San Diego Padres, 255
shifted to shortstop, 108
assigned to Spokane Indians, 113
managing Texas Rangers, 278-279
committing to USC, 76-77

Valenzuela, Fernando, 268, 271, 277
Vance, Gene, 92
Vance, Sandy, x, 87-88, 92, 93, 97-98, 99-100, 102-103, 109, 111, 125, 141, 143-144, 154, 158, 187, 194-195, 198, 201-202, 217, 232, 237
drafted by Los Angeles Angels, 88
drafted by Los Angeles Dodgers, 87
negotiating Los Angeles Dodgers contract, 92
Vancouver Mounties, 167
Varona, Corito, 68
Vaughn, Dave, 151, 163-164, 192-193
Veeck, Bill, 30
Vermeil, Dick, 79
Versalles, Zoilo, 104, 105, 108
Vike, Herb, 222-223, 226
Vinson, Charlie, 141, 181, 183, 225
Virdon, Bill, 33
Vukovich, John, 175*n*

Wade, Ben, 37, 38, 68, 277*n*
Wakefield, Dick, 6
Washburn, Greg, 135-136, 169, 194, 220, 221, 222, 224, 232
Washington Senators, 43, 63, 124, 175*n*, 219*n*
See also Texas Rangers
Watson, Bob, 4, 270
Waxahachie Swap, 196-197
Weaver, Earl, 238
Weaver, Michael, 82
drafted by Cleveland Indians, 82
Weiss, Bill, x-xi*n*
Weiss, George, 16
Welch, Bob, 68*n*, 277
Wells, Bert, 63, 64, 67, 87

Wellman, Guy, 67-68, 87, 91-92
Werhas, John, 135, 137, 141, 150, 168, 224, 225, 281
    officiating at Lasorda graveside service, 281
    signed by Los Angeles Dodgers, 135
Wheat, Zack, 272
Whitaker, Steve, 189
Wiggins, Alan, 72n
Wilhelm, Hoyt 234-235
Williams, Bernie, 189
Williams, Billy, 220n
Williams, Ted, 124, 257
Wills, Maury, 13, 50, 51, 52, 53, 108, 119, 123-124, 149, 153, 200, 232, 234, 242, 243, 266
    traded to Pittsburgh Pirates, 53
Wilson, Ken, 138, 209, 210-211, 217, 223-224
Wilson, Mike, 163-164, 168
Wilson, Mookie, 259
Wilson, Willie, 272
Winfield, Dave, 176, 270
Winston-Salem Red Sox, 165
Winkles, Bobby, 92n, 100, 244
Wood, Kerry, 15n
World Series, 205-206
Wright, Clyde, 191n, 245
Wright, Marshall, x-xi$n$
Wrigley, Philip, 146-147, 147
Wyatt, John, 18-19, 39
Wyatt, Whit, 63
Wynn, Jim, 236, 249-250
    traded to Atlanta Braves, 236
        traded to Los Angeles Dodgers, 249-250

Yawkey, Tom, 165
Yeager, Steve, 53, 241, 248, 251, 269
Young, Ray, 79

Zahn, Geoff, x, 73, 111, 117-118, 124, 149, 189, 192-193, 194, 196-197, 241, 250, 251, 252
    assigned to Albuquerque Dodgers, 111
    traded to Chicago Cubs, 252
    jaw injury, 192-193
Zimmer, Don, 131-133, 164-165, 180, 211
    golfing with Tommy Lasorda, 164

About the Author

Eric Vickrey is a baseball historian and author of two books, *Runnin' Redbirds: The World Champion 1982 St. Louis Cardinals* and *Season of Shattered Dreams: Postwar Baseball, the Spokane Indians, and a Tragic Bus Crash That Changed Everything*. The latter was a finalist for the 2024 CASEY Award for Best Baseball Book of the Year. He has also contributed to several books and written dozens of online articles as a member of the Society for American Baseball Research and is co-editing a forthcoming book on the 2001 Seattle Mariners. Originally from Illinois, he now lives in Washington state with his wife, Gina, and their two cats, Edgar and Ralphie.

Also from August Publications

Jim Gilliam: The Forgotten Dodger
The Complete Guide to Spring Training 2026 / Florida
The Complete Guide to Spring Training 2026 / Arizona
My 1961
Baseball Like It Ought Be: How a Shoe Salesman's Madison Mallards and His Renegade Staff Ignited a Summer Collegiate Baseball Revolution
The Right Thing to Do: The True Pioneers of College Football Integration
Home Runs: Tales of Tonks, Taters, Contests and Derbies
The Baseball Thesaurus, 3e
The Football Thesaurus, 2e
Cradle of the Game: North Carolina Baseball Past and Present
Raye of Light: Jimmy Raye, Duffy Daugherty, The Integration of College Football, and the 1965-1966 Michigan State Spartans
Goodfellows: The Champions of St. Ambrose

Available from Amazon, Ingram, and *augustpublications.com*!

www.ingramcontent.com/pod-product-compliance
Lightning Source LLC
Chambersburg PA
CBHW070127080526
44586CB00015B/1582